THE
COLONEL'S
TABLE

Recipes & Tales

THE COLONEL'S TABLE

Recipes & Tales

By
Henry Stanhope
Tank Nash
with food by Brian Jones

BRASSEY'S
LONDON·WASHINGTON

First English edition 1994

UK editorial offices: Brassey's, 33 John Street, London WC1N 2AT

UK orders: Marston Book Services, PO Box 87, Oxford OX2 0DT

USA orders: Order Department, Macmillan Publishing Company, 201 West 103rd Street, Indianapolis, IN 46290

Distributed in North America to booksellers and wholesalers by the Macmillan Publishing Company, NY 10022

Henry Stanhope, Tank Nash and Brian Jones have asserted their moral rights to be identified as authors of this work.

Library of Congress Cataloging in Publication Data

available

British Library Cataloging in Publication Data

A catalogue record for this book is available from the British Library

Hardcover 1-85753-006-3

Designed and typeset by Fathom Graphics

Printed in Great Britain by The Bath Press

CONTENTS

Acknowledgements

'The Pig' and 'We will have coffee now' were first published in the British Army Review, and are reproduced here by kind permission of the Editor. Cover design by Jefferson Godwin.

Introduction

The aim of this book is to do for cooking what Clausewitz did for war, eating and drinking being the continuation of diplomacy by other means. Primitive man ate to live, while nowadays the reverse is almost true. We entreat, do business, flirt, mourn, celebrate, plight our troth, give thanks and occasionally join battle at the table. Few items of furniture, including our beds, see so much action.

It follows that one should approach the subject with due care, whatever the level of ambition or culinary skill. She who seeks to seduce her intended with shepherd's pie should ensure at least that the shepherd is well cooked. He who wishes to cement a business deal would do well first to check that the cement is at room temperature. A poor cook or a careless connoisseur of wine betrays an indifference, a misunderstanding of priorities, which could well reflect a fundamental weakness. Should a young girl throw away the best years of her life on a lover who knows not his Riojas from his Rhônes?

Earlier generations had Mrs Beeton to guide them. 'A being, well-fed and warmed, is naturally on better terms with himself and his surroundings than one whose mind and body are being taxed by the discomfort and annoyance of badly cooked or insufficient food', she roundly declared in her corpulent volume on household management.

In her sermon on the 'monotony of breakfast', for example, she offered this helpful advice to the young housewife:

> Notwithstanding the plea for something new, there are 200 ways of dressing eggs, to say nothing of grilled chops, steaks, cutlets, kidneys, fish and mushrooms, anchovy and sardine toast, sausage rolls, sausages grilled, boiled or fried, meat pâtés, rissoles, croquettes and croutes, fish omelette, fish cakes, fish soused and kedgereed, pressed beef, galantine

of beef, potato chips, potatoes fried in a variety of ways and a host of other inexpensive and easily prepared dishes.

Now we are carrying on where she left off.

There are right ways and wrong ways to entertain, and none understands this better than does the Army. The organisation which has a drill for all procedures, developed through hard experience the world over, here reveals its most cherished secrets for the first time. We have moreover tried to present these as the Army would – by numbers, in an orderly progression.

The Army has always taken its cooking seriously – even when, some years ago, nobody else did – and has kept an eye on soldiers' victual statistics. It once reasoned that troops fought best when lean and hungry, so fed them after each battle and not before (which had the added advantage that there were usually fewer of them). Those who scaled the Heights of Abraham in Quebec during the Seven Years War were not inspired by the thought of winning Canada, still less of pleasing that crazy redhead General Wolfe. They knew it was the only way to get their breakfast.

The strategy changed in 1963 – not only the year of Christine Keeler and the Great Train Robbery, but that in which the last conscript left the Army. Faced with the problem of tempting volunteers to join, the General Staff switched to an 'epicurean response'. Instead of keeping its soldiers lean and hungry, it aimed to turn them into an Army of fat cats.

The result was a military kitchen revolution. *Boeuf bourgignon* took the place of cookhouse stew, *filets de plie meunière* that of battered cod. Chocolate gâteau replaced rock-cakes on the tea table, Bourbon fingers took over from 'biscuits, standard plain'. This led to a call for stronger tank chassis and new engines, while military tailoring underwent a sudden expansion. But the Army has thereby escaped recruiting crises, and has fortunately not had to fight much after lunch.

None of this has affected the Colonel all that much since the 'lean and hungry' look did not apply to him. This was why, throughout the Napoleonic Wars, when Bonaparte fed 'chicken marengo' to his marshals, the British were able to reply with 'beef Wellington' – an early example of the epicurean response. Such traditions have since been kept alive by Sandhurst, whose directing staff have managed to ensure that no young British officer passes out without at least knowing which way to pass the port.

Even during those dismal days of National Service, when the cold war cast its damp chill over the Mess, the Colonel maintained the standards of his regiment. On manoeuvres over the bleak north German plain, beneath the branches of trees and sparkling stars, he would nightly join his brother officers at a trestle table glittering with Mess silver. As they sipped their claret, maintained carefully at tent temperature, the Colonel would rise by the flickering light of candles and, raising his glass to the moon, solemnly declare: 'Gentlemen, the Queen.' Ah, how such British sangfroid warms the blood!

Few chefs can cook as diversely and as well as those whose talents are reflected in this book. They have cooked for the Colonel outdoors as well as in, for big dinners or small parties, standing up or sitting down, for government ministers, the Household Cavalry, bombardiers' wives and Challenger tank crews ... in Chelsea, the Gulf, Port Stanley and Hong Kong. Their range of expertise is quite unequalled.

Fewer still can match the genius of Brian Jones, who has trained a generation of young chefs and can stand beside the very best in Britain. In this, the first manual of five-star Army cooking, he takes the lid off a selection of his best dishes.

Wheresoever a host or hostess is at work, from the lobster belt in SW1 to the windswept grouse moors in the north or sunlit cricket grounds, from breakfasts with smoky kedgeree and warm brioches to lunches of spiced curries and crisp pappadoms ... we reveal how things are done, the Colonel's way.

Henry Stanhope

REVEILLE

Reveille

Two early mornings linger in the memory – though one of them I would cheerfully erase, given the chance. Both happened during Army National Service.

One of these was my first morning in the Army. I had long held a preconceived vision of reveille: of tents emerging through the morning mist, the first rays of sun warming the canvas and drying the dew which dampened the cropped grass; the scent of wood-smoke hanging over the fires, beside which the dozing sentries gently stirred; the songs of larks high in the clearing sky and, on the still air, a distant bugle-call...

At Park Hall camp, Oswestry, Shropshire, it wasn't like that. There they favoured the sharp shock alternative to dawn. A bombardier stormed through our slumbering barrack room, banging the iron bedsteads with his stick and screaming abuse at those who were still sleeping. The effect was psychologically disturbing, and some of our lot required counselling to get over it.

I have always since thought that the Army had it wrong. One's natural reaction to being bugled by a madman is to hide beneath the sheets until he's gone. It is certainly not an inducement to getting up. After all, when a ferret is shoved into a warren the rabbits don't usually queue up to be slaughtered: they burrow further into Watership Down. Our rodent had to make several darting runs before his flopsy bunnies showed their scuts.

Had a nubile young barely-clad lady been hired instead to skip through our recumbent barrack room at 6.30 the squad would all have showered and shaved by 6.31 – and been outside in three ranks waiting for breakfast. The scent and sizzle of frying bacon and eggs, the aroma of warm toast and fresh ground coffee, if piped round the camp, would have been an added encouragement, were one needed. Our commanding officer simply lacked imagination.

This brings me to that other early morning some 10 months later, one hot

August day in the middle of rural Saxony. Our mortar locating battery was on exercises – a 'scheme', as these were inappropriately known. We always went on exercise in conditions of extreme cold or intense heat, so that one either caught frostbite while shaving or was paralysed with sunburn and ant-bites. This had something to do with our imperial past.

Our unit had put me in charge of an LP, with a combined force of two under my command: the driver of our one-ton truck, called Wigmore, and a signaller from the Scottish Highlands known as Worpleden. Wigmore was a big, strong, uncomplicated Yorkshireman; Worpleden by contrast had the sobriquet 'Wee Willie' – to which he did not seem to take offence. He had never been south of Inverness before and found England, let along Germany, strange and alien.

I think that 'LP' stood for listening post, though I soon discovered that nobody was too sure. The Army operated according to the rules of 'need to know' and we rarely needed to know what initials stood for.

Our function, I think, was to listen for enemy mortars – though what we did on hearing them I forget. The enemy must have spent their time listening to Wigmore's portable which seemed to be permanently tuned to Elvis Presley. At least it worked, which was more than could be said for Worpleden's radio. This, like most of our wireless sets, had broken down. They all worked quite efficiently in camp but consistently packed up once they were moved. Like some German *tafelweins*, they didn't travel well.

Worpleden kept swearing at it in broad Gaelic – or perhaps it was English with a Ross-and-Cromarty accent – while Wigmore and I would take turns at talking to it. This consisted of repeating in a monotone: 'Hullo four five, hullo four five, how d'you hear me? Over.' Who or what 'four five' was I don't know. But it seemed to work – or not, as the case may be – and it made a change from sunbathing or playing pontoon for Woodbines.

In the daytime we lived in a slit trench, under camouflage netting strewn with branches chopped down by Wigmore's machete – these being the days before the environment was invented; and one night we moved into our tent, similarly accoutred, which we had sited in the shade of an old barn. In between talking to, or tinkering with, his wireless, Worpleden cooked our meals on a primus stove. One of the few benefits of our schemes was that we lived off 'compo' ration tins, whose contents were better than the food we had in camp.

Anyway, there we were fighting the Russians, under canvas, our tent-flap open to encourage what breeze there was as we dreamed of demobilisation and

Diana Dors – or even demobilising Diana Dors. Of the three spreadeagled sleeping-bags mine was the nearest the entrance to the tent (the other two, fearful of bats, had bagged the inside berths), so I was the first to be conscious of an intruder.

Opening my eyes and blinking in the sunlight (we didn't get up too early while on location), I saw someone's legs silhouetted in the aperture. Stranger still, the legs were clad in honey nylons and tapered off into shoes which were less than sensible. Squinting up towards the apex of the tent-flap, I saw looking at me, tolerant and amused, a face that was unambiguously female.

Contrary to the German dream, her hair was black – and gathered in a silk square tied behind her neck. She wore a white shirt-blouse and flared navy skirt, with a crimson leather belt and large brass buckle. With her ever-so-slightly slanted deep brown eyes, she could have passed for an Eastern European. Aged about 40, she looked experienced and cool – like the *femme fatale* whom every young man dreams of from the age of 12.

'*Guten tag*,' I said, and she laughed at my English-German before speaking in no less accented German-English.

'Good morning,' she said. 'You are English soldiers, yes?'

Denying it was pointless. I nodded, wondering whether propriety demanded that I remained lying down or risked standing in my blue-and-white striped military pyjamas.

'I wish to borrow a strong young man,' she said.

Casting aside the old Army maxim that one should never volunteer for anything, I forgot all previous doubts about propriety and was halfway out of my sleeping-bag when she stopped me.

'I think perhaps I need to borrow him,' she said, pointing with a long, painted fingernail into the interior.

How she could have seen Wigmore so clearly from outside is something I have never understood. I experimented out of interest later that day, but could make out nothing more than dark shadow.

Nonetheless he undoubtedly fitted her criteria. Disappointed, I reached back and shook Wigmore none too vigorously by the shoulder. I hoped that he wouldn't wake up; but he snored for the last time, grunted and stared at me. 'You're wanted,' I said, 'for allied exercises.'

'*Ja, ja*. Do you think you could help me?' called our temptress.

Wigmore did. He was out of his bag like a child on Christmas morning, which proves my original point. For a big man he could move very quickly when he wished to, and in no time at all he was stumbling over Worpleden and myself towards his client. He was about to start shaving in his mess-tin when our lady friend stopped him.

'Come, you can at my house', she said impatiently, immediately setting off across the fields to our left, with Wigmore loping along clumsily beside her, towering above her like a gorilla on a lead.

'He, d'you reckon she...?' said Worpleden, now fully awake, breathless and round-eyed.

I nodded glumly.

'Bluidy hell!' said Worpleden, swallowing hard as Wigmore disappeared on the horizon.

'He'll be crowing about it at breakfast,' I said bitterly.

But Wigmore wasn't, because he wasn't back for breakfast. We opened a tin of bacon bits and dried egg and ate it from our mess-tins in total silence.

'Wonder what they're doing now,' said Worpleden wistfully. 'D'you reckon they're...?'

'I reckon so,' I said.

'Aye, I do too. Bluidy hell.'

We tried saying 'Hullo four five' to Worpleden's radio. But our hearts were not in it somehow – and pontoon for two was never very much fun. Moreover, Wigmore wasn't back for lunch (Irish stew followed by stewed rhubarb) or when our battery adjutant paid a call.

Our adjutant had a reputation as an intellectual, a term which the Army always used somewhat loosely. He looked with disdain at our *art nouveau* home from home.

'Where's Wigmore?' he demanded, suddenly remembering that somebody was missing.

'He's gone to spend a penny, sir,' said Worpleden with unusual delicacy.

'Well, tell him when he comes back to move his truck. He's parked it in full view of the enemy,' complained the adjutant, sharply slapping the sides of our tent with his stick. 'At the double.'

But Wigmore hadn't doubled back by teatime and was still missing when the adjutant returned.

'I thought I told Wigmore to move that one-tonner,' he snapped. 'Where's he gone now?'

'He's spending another penny, sir,' said Worpleden.

'Good God, has he been drinking or something?' said the adjutant. 'I suppose he's got the blasted keys along with him... WIGMORE!'

He cupped his hands and bawled over the fields. Not even an echo came back in reply.

'He hasn't gone looking for a public convenience, has he?'

'Yes, I think that must be it, sir,' said Worpleden, grasping at straws. 'He's probably had to walk a little way.'

'A little way! More like 90 miles back to camp!' snapped back the adjutant. 'Kick his backside for me when he gets back. And we're moving to a new RV tomorrow morning. I'll come round with the coordinates before breakfast since all our radio sets are out of action.'

Night fell without sign of the missing driver. We turned in under the stars full of foreboding.

'Perhaps she's a Russian,' I said, recalling those sloe-black Slavonic eyes. 'P'raps she's slowly extracting the secrets of the motor pool!'

'Lucky bugger!' said Worpleden with feeling.

But we agreed to set my alarm clock for 5.30, and that if by that time Wigmore was still absent without leave, Worpleden would set off in pursuit of him. As Wigmore's sleeping-bag was still empty when we woke, he duly set out across the sunlit fields. Two hours later he had gone missing with Wigmore.

The adjutant called at eight. He was almost speechless with fury – but not quite.

'Don't tell me he's powdering his nose again,' he yelled. 'And where the hell's Worpleden now?'

'He's gone with Wigmore,' I said.

There was a pause while he tried to control his strained emotions. Sandhurst had not prepared him for this moment.

'Have you lot caught some infection?' he snarled. 'If you're not at this RV by 1200 hours, I'll have you court-martialled. The lot of you!'

He stalked off back to his jeep, slamming the door, and after he was safely out of sight I set off after Worpleden, grimly determined. I crossed two fields, negotiated a small copse ... and there on the other side, below a slope, lay a large house. It was long, low and white, with a clock tower and a terrace beyond which stretched formal gardens. It looked like a farmhouse which had, in modern parlance, been gentrified.

(Clockwise from the bottom) **Compôte of Fresh Fruits** (page 18), **Orange Marmalade with Whisky** (page 24), **Croissants** (page 21), **Brioches** (page 22), **Kedgeree** (page 19), **Quails' Eggs Monte Carlo** (page 20)

Steak, Oyster and Brown Beer Pie (page 34)

Descending the slope, I walked warily round to the terrace and peered in through a set of tall French windows. There, sitting at the head of a long polished table, sat our temptress, with Wigmore and Worpleden plonked on either side. An elderly *frau* in an apron was pouring coffee. I was stretching out to rap sharply and angrily on the glass when she saw me and gave me a wave and a smile of such enchantment that my hand remained suspended in mid-air.

She moved lightly across the thick carpet to unbolt the window.

'Ah, the Third Man,' she said gaily as if her happiness was now complete, and led me by the hand towards the table.

There lay a basket full of those oval-shaped crusty rolls without which breakfast is not *frühstück* in Germany; and a platter of smoked ham, salami and sliced Gouda. The rolls smelt warm and bready, straight from the oven, and the coffee was hot and strong and served *mit sahne*...

Every man has his price ... and what was it that Mrs Beeton said: 'The moral and physical welfare of mankind depends largely on its breakfast.'?

We set back across the fields at half-past nine, fortified by a perfumed embrace from our hostess, though Wigmore's I felt lasted rather longer and was discernibly more affectionate. He (Wigmore) was also suspiciously reticent on the walk back.

'Hey, did she ... you know...?' asked Worpleden as soon as we were securely out of earshot.

'I've been workin' bloody hard,' said Wigmore stoically. 'Her 'usband was killed in the war, see? He were a U-boat captain or somethin'. She needed someone to 'elp dig the garden and chop down some trees. Then I had to take up a carpet and carry some coal... There's only Lisette and Frau Worner to help her, see...'

'Go on. Where were you last night, then? I bet she gave you the old ... you know...' persisted Worpleden.

'You're a dirty-minded little bugger, Worpleden,' said Wigmore virtuously. 'I'll tell you what though, she gave me this before I left.'

He took out a small locket and, snapping it open with big clumsy fingers, revealed a photograph of his lady of the night, together with a short strand of rich black hair. She looked as if she could hear our every word.

'Bluidy hell!' said Worpleden, licking his lips. But Wigmore dourly refused to tell us more.

I was reprimanded when we got back to camp, which was further proof of life's basic unfairness. Wigmore was sent to the doctor for a check-up, though I don't think he ever knew the reason why. Many years later I tried to locate Frau Lisette's house – but without success. In that sense she was indeed the German dream.

Anyway, it shows what I mean about reveille. A breakfast carrot is always superior to the stick.

⚔

And talking of breakfasts, here are a few of the Colonel's favourite early-morning dishes.

H.S

COMPÔTE OF FRESH FRUITS

Serves: 4

Preparation: 20 minutes

Cooking: 10-15 minutes

Ingredients

450g (1lb) apricots, gooseberries, figs, cherries, raspberries, strawberries, greengages, cumquats or plums (or a mix)
Stock syrup
350g (12oz) caster sugar
1 litre (1¾pts) water
1in cinnamon stick
zest and juice of 1 lemon and 1 orange

Drill

1. Make the stock syrup by first placing the sugar in the water. Add the cinnamon, zest and lemon and orange juice. Bring to the boil and simmer for 3-4 minutes. Allow to cool.

2. Wash and, if necessary, halve and stone the fruit. Place in an ovenproof dish and pour the syrup over it. Cover with a sheet of greaseproof paper and poach in the oven until tender.

3. Remove from the oven and allow to cool. Carefully lift out the fruit and place in a serving dish. Cover with the syrup and chill well before serving.

Note: When possible, allow the cooked fruits to stand in the syrup for 24 hours before serving.

KEDGEREE

📖

Serves: 6-8

Preparation: 10 minutes

Cooking: 25 minutes

Ingredients

300ml (½pt) fish stock
450g (1lb) salmon, turbot, Finnan haddock (preferably a mix)
20ml (2tsp) olive oil
50g (2oz) onion, finely chopped
225g (8oz) basmati rice
1tsp chopped parsley and coriander
½" cinnamon stick
8 quails' eggs (medium boiled and peeled)
300ml (½pt) light curry sauce (*see* basic recipes)

Drill

To cook the fish

1. Place prepared fish ie skinned and filleted into a shallow baking dish that has been lightly buttered, season with pepper, and add fish stock until it just covers the top of the fish. Cover with buttered paper and bring to boiling point on top of the stove, then place in a medium oven until just cooked. Leave to cool in the stock. When cool, remove from the stock.

To cook the rice

2. Heat the olive oil in a pan and add the cinnamon stick. Add the chopped onion and cook until soft. Stir in the rice and cook, stirring until the rice looks transparent. Add the stock that the fish was cooked in and bring to the simmer. Cover and cook in the oven for about 15-16 minutes or until the rice is just tender and has absorbed the stock. Once cooked add a knob of butter.

To make the kedgeree

3. Remove all skin and bone from the fish and flake gently. Add the rice and place in a serving dish. Garnish with the quails' eggs and some coriander leaves. Serve with the curry sauce.

QUAILS' EGGS MONTE CARLO

Serves: 4

Preparation: 10 minutes

Cooking: 20 minutes

Ingredients

350g (12oz) Finnan haddock

parsley and chervil stalks

225g (8oz) smoked salmon

12 ovals of toast or toasted brioche

12 quails' eggs (cooked soft and shelled)

50g (2oz) salmon caviar

For the sauce:

15g (½oz) butter

¼tsp chopped dill

¼tsp chopped tarragon

¼tsp chopped chives

¼tsp chopped chervil

¼tsp chopped parsley

300ml (½pt) fish stock

¼ bottle dry white wine

450ml (¾pt) double cream

6tbs whipped cream

3 egg yolks

Drill

1. Cook the haddock in a little water, flavoured with stalks from the parsley and chervil. Do not use salt. Leave to go cold, then flake the fish, discarding the skin and any bones.

2. Dice the smoked salmon and mix with the haddock.

3. Make the sauce by melting the butter in a small pan. Add the herbs and sweat until soft. Add the fish stock and reduce. Add the white wine and reduce to a light syrup consistency.

4. Add the double cream and reduce by a third. Season to taste, remembering the sauce will dilute with the addition of the whipped cream and egg yolks. Pass the sauce through a fine strainer. Mix about a third of it with the fish so that it just holds its shape when spread on toast. Keep the rest at blood temperature.

To serve

5. Add the whipped cream and egg yolks to the sauce. Spoon the fish mix on the toast and place three on each plate. Top with the quails' eggs. Spoon the sauce over them and glaze under a hot grill. Garnish with the salmon caviar and serve.

Note: This dish could also serve as a first course for dinner.

CROISSANTS

Makes: 16

Preparation: 2 hours

Resting: 8 hours

Cooking: 20 minutes

Ingredients

40g (1½oz) sugar

1½tsp salt

320ml (11fl oz) cold water

15g (½oz) fresh yeast

25g (1oz) milk powder

500g (1lb 2oz) strong flour

300g (10oz) butter

1 egg yolk (beaten with 1tbs milk to glaze)

Drill

1. Dissolve the sugar and salt in a third of the cold water.

2. In a separate bowl, beat the yeast into the remaining water and add the milk powder.

3. Place the flour in the bowl of an electric mixer and, while operating the dough-making attachment at slow speed, add the sugar and salt mix, then the yeast mix. Beat until all the ingredients are well blended and the dough comes away from the side of the bowl, but take care not to overwork the dough.

4. Cover with a tea-towel and leave to rise in a warm place for about 30 minutes. The dough should double in size.

5. Knock back the dough to its original size, cover with a polythene bag and place in a refrigerator for 6-8 hours

6. After it has risen, take it out and put it on a lightly floured work surface. Roll out the ball of dough from the corners; it should look like four large ears around a small head.

7. Put the butter in the centre. It must be firm but not rock hard. Fold the ears over the butter, completely enclosing it.

8. Roll out the dough into a rectangle about 40 x 70cm (16 x 27in). Brush off excess flour and fold into three layers by bringing one end towards the middle, then covering it with the other end – as if folding a long sheet of paper for an envelope. Wrap in polythene and refrigerate for at least 20 minutes.

9. Repeat this process twice more. Roll in the opposite direction each time, allowing it to rest for 20 minutes in between.

10. After resting it for a further 20 minutes, roll out the dough into a rectangle 40 x 76cm (16 x 30in). Trim the edges with a large knife, then cut lengthways into two equal strips.

11. Cut each strip into triangles (8 or 9 from each strip).

12. Dampen each one with water and, starting from the base of each triangle, roll up as firmly as possible. Place on a baking tray, cover with a tea towel and allow to rest until they are 50 per cent bigger. Brush with egg wash.

13. Bend each one into a crescent shape and leave to rest again until double the original size. Re-egg wash and bake in a hot oven at 220°C (425°F, Gas Mk 8) until crisp and golden-brown – about 20 minutes. Serve hot with butter.

Note: Croissants freeze well after they have been cooked. Simply reheat in a medium oven when required.

Brioches

📖

Makes: one 8-inch bread tin or 6-8 individuals

Preparation: 1 hour

Resting: 4 hours

Cooking: 40-45 minutes

Ingredients

25g (1oz) fresh yeast
30ml (1fl oz) warm milk
7g (¼oz) salt
270g (9oz) strong flour
2 medium eggs
75g (2½oz) butter
25g (1oz) sugar

Drill

1. Place the yeast and warm milk in a mixing bowl and beat lightly with a wire whisk. Then add the salt, flour and eggs and knead the dough until it is smooth and elastic. This will take about 10 minutes.

2. Beat the butter and sugar together, then add this to the dough a little at a time, making sure that it is completely amalgamated each time. Continue to mix for about 5 minutes or until the dough is perfectly smooth; it should be glossy and fairly elastic. Cover with a cloth and leave in a warm place for about 2 hours, until the dough has doubled in bulk.

3. Knock back the dough to its original size, cover with the cloth and refrigerate for several hours. Then knock back the dough again on a lightly floured work surface.

4. Lightly butter and flour individual brioche or other suitable moulds. Divide the dough into 30g (1oz) pieces and mould into round dumb-bell shapes, like small cottage loaves. Place in the moulds. (If using a loaf tin, put all the shaped pieces in the tin, side by side).

5. Egg wash the top, leave to rise in a warm place until the dough has almost doubled in bulk (about 20 minutes for small brioches or 1½ hours for the large ones).

6. Bake in a pre-heated oven at 230°C (450°F, Gas Mk 8) for 10 minutes for the small brioches and 40-45 minutes for the large ones, or until golden brown. De-mould immediately and leave to cool on a wire rack.

ORANGE MARMALADE WITH WHISKY

Makes: 6-8 jars

Preparation: 10 minutes

Cooking: 2¾ hours

Ingredients

1kg (2lb) Seville oranges
3 litres (5¼pts) water
1 lemon or ½tsp citric acid
2kg (4lb) sugar
150ml (¼pt) whisky

Drill

1. Rinse the fruit and wipe dry. Cut and de-pip the oranges and lemon (if used). Tie the pips in a muslin bag.

2. Cut the fruit into slices and place in a preserving pan with the water. Add the citric acid (if used) and the bag of pips, which will help the marmalade set. Stand overnight.

3. Next day, bring the fruit and water to the boil and simmer slowly for about 1 hour or until the rind is tender. Remove the bag of pips and add the sugar, stirring until dissolved. Boil briskly for about 1-1½ hours or until the marmalade is on the point of setting. (Test by placing a spoonful of the hot marmalade on a cold plate. It will set after a few minutes if cooked to the correct degree).

4. Add the whisky. Re-boil for 15 minutes and repeat the test. The mix should set when cold. Pot and cover immediately.

LUNCHEON

'We will have coffee now'

What, you may ask, induces a normal rational individual, anxious though he may be to serve his Queen, to involve himself in operations hazardous to his mental health?

In comparison parachuting is routine, cliff-assault leading is undemanding and bomb disposal banal. True, for some these pursuits have an attraction, and although one might suffer the odd contusion whilst engaged in them it's difficult to ruin a career between beach and cliff-top unless one is just an old butter-fingers.

Should you have nerves of steel and the constitution of the Jolly Green Giant, and if you're prepared to risk all on a single throw of the dice, then catering is the sport for you.

A grateful government (no really, don't snigger) has provided the Army with well-appointed facilities. Superb kitchens serve functional dining-rooms. It is, however, a fact that the military caterer spends a significant proportion of Service life feeding his customers in tents, aircraft hangars, ploughed fields, church halls, gymnasia, bashas, sangars, forests, barns, and pouring rain. In every case constraints that would have caused Escoffier to erupt, Egon Ronay to run a mile and Sir Charles Forte and Clement Freud to fume, are imposed upon the Friendly Formation Caterer Adviser and, what's more – he thinks he enjoys it.

A simple tale to illustrate my theory: some years ago I was invited by a member of the Army Board of the day to make the arrangements for a modest luncheon he proposed to hold in a conference room high up in the Ministry of Defence.

I 'recced' the site and, as conference rooms go, it was fine. In fact, as conference rooms go, it was superb. However, without overstating the case, it wasn't much good for anything else. From a catering point of view, it could only have been more inconvenient if, for example, the General had asked some chums to join him for lunch on the top of Nelson's Column.

The member of the Army Board (let us call him MAB) was charming. I let him talk me into taking on the job, but fear I confused him when I said that the gentlemen's lavatory adjacent to the conference room would have to be 'out of order' on that day.

The day duly dawned, and by 1205 hours the MAB and a multitude of his influential friends were chewing on a little Tio Pepe served by a Colour Sergeant and twelve guardsmen from Chelsea Barracks.

The atmosphere in the conference/dining-room was one of sophisticated calm, in sharp contrast to the activity in the lavatory next door where, in each of four cubicles, a soldier cook was preparing his contribution to my gastronomic *tour de force* over a four-burner camping-gas stove resting upon the lid of the loo, his knives laid out with surgical precision on a pristine white cloth upon the cistern.

Centred on a pair of six-foot tables, propped on the wash-hand basins, a myriad of culinary activities were being orchestrated by my Warrant Officer, the redoubtable Mr Etherington, who from time to time would encourage the troops by advising them that, 'If you can't take a joke you shouldn't have joined.'

The Colour Sergeant entered the lavatory and I held a quick 'O' group. At its conclusion the Colour Sergeant said, 'Sir,' in that manner peculiar to the Household Division, and strode off to advise one of the professional heads of the Army that the men locked in the lavatory were now ready to serve his lunch.

The party sat and, even if I say so myself, the '*Crêpe de Fruits de Mer*' was good enough to eat. The mussels, the prawns, the oysters, the scallops all got into bed together, pulled Mr Etherington's exquisite sauce about their ears, wrapped themselves in the blanket of the crêpe and offered themselves to the guests.

The plates were cleared from the table with a flourish by the Colour Sergeant and his guardsmen, borne from the dining-room and placed in a box located under the roller towel in the 'comfort station' (to use a coy American expression). I nodded to Mr Etherington, he nodded back and I sauntered through my command post to a telephone in the lobby adjacent to the lifts. I dialled a number and got an immediate response from Wellington Barracks only one thousand yards away (sadly, with inflation, it's now almost a kilometre).

'Household Cavalry Regiment, Soldiers' Mess, Corporal Ramsbotham, Sir,' said a voice.

'Ah, Corporal Ramsbotham, we'll have the coffee now if you please,' I intoned smoothly.

'Sir,' said the voice, and the telephone died peacefully in my hands.

In the 'rest room' (another American euphemism) Mr Etherington had busied himself and when I returned it was in time to see him inspect, in turn, each silver salver of his unbelievably good 'Poulet sauté Alexandra'. He wiped away a minute speck of sauce that had sullied the gleaming edge of one salver, adjusted the angle of three sticks of asparagus on another. Then he looked up.

'That,' he pronounced, 'is not at all bad.'

The guardsmen went over the start line in good order on their next sortie.

'I've called for the coffee,' I advised Mr Etherington. We indulged in a few moments of mutual congratulations on having reached the decision not to make the coffee on site, and agreed that producing it in a military kitchen fairly close to hand and then calling it forward was a catering master-stroke. A vehicle was standing by and we should, within minutes, be serving our Chief with Brazil's finest and freshest.

The Colour Sergeant joined us, a stack of dirty plates in his hand. 'The General says that time's a bit short and he'd like coffee just as soon as possible after the pud, sir.' Nodding acquiescence, I walked to the window and opened it. I had to because, despite the fact we were umpteen stories up and not overlooked, the glass was of the frosted variety. I leaned out, more, more yet, a strong hand grasped the waistband of my trousers and, as we had established during the 'recce', it was now just possible to see the length of Whitehall. It is a stimulating experience to be dangled by your trousers high above the London traffic, and it concentrates the mind wonderfully.

Those contemplating a career as a military caterer are advised to choose their tailor with some care, because it's at moments like this that a great deal depends upon a chap's braces buttons.

A pigeon, en route to Trafalgar Square, made a sharp stall turn and inspected me closely. A clerk in the office on the other side of Whitehall, who saw me through her window, rushed to the 'phone and advised the constabulary that a man was hanging from a window opposite. A correspondent from a top people's newspaper, who had observed me from the street below, returned to his office and wrote a stern leader for the following day's edition with the headline, 'Defence suicide rate up in Ministry of Defence.'

Blissfully unaware, I heard the confection of fresh blackcurrants, cream and impossibly delicate pastry being despatched to the diners by Mr Etherington when, from around the corner from Parliament Square into Whitehall, there appeared a beautiful sight. It was a standard olive-green Bedford British Army 3-ton truck – alas, inflation has now made them 4-tonners.

'Coffee's on its way,' I said over my shoulder. 'Let's get it in there in double-quick time.'

I watched the truck's progress up Whitehall to the musical accompaniment of the clatter of cups as the coffee service was made ready. The truck stopped at the Cenotaph. Why? Silence from behind me, then...

'Wasaform, sir?' questioned one of my soldiers.

'The truck has stopped,' I yelped.

There was a corporate sucking of teeth behind me.

'The driver's getting out of his cab,' I added in a shriek.

'What a silly billy' – or similar words – adjudged Mr Etherington.

'We'll have coffee now,' interjected the Colour Sergeant as he strode in through the door.

There are moments in every man's life when he has good and valid reason to panic. This was such a moment, but I thought better of it because, if the situation deteriorated further, I would do better to wait and really indulge myself later.

'My compliments to the General,' I snapped. 'The coffee is being brewed and will be served with the utmost despatch.'

Stark disbelief was writ large upon the Colour Sergeant's face. 'Sir,' he said briskly and marched off to deliver the message of hope.

I clambered back into the building and Etherington, who had replaced me at the window, leaned right forward and said in the sort of voice used by a hanging judge, 'He's opened the bonnet.'

'We're all doomed,' intoned a cheerful voice.

'The driver has closed the bonnet,' announced the Warrant Officer.

'Ah!' came the response from a dozen throats.

'He's kicking the bumper,' added Etherington.

'Oh!' came the chorus.

'Someone's got problems, we've got the fire brigade and the police down there,' speculated our observer.

The sounds of the sirens wafted up from Whitehall far below and drifted in through the open window.

'He's sitting on the kerb with his head in his hands – I think he's crying,' came from Etherington.

'Gawd!' said someone succinctly.

I flew to the telephone. Now from that building it would have been a mere bagatelle to call the Monarch, the Prime Minister, the Archbishop of Canterbury or, for that matter, any other luminary in town. The Transport Control Officer of 20 Squadron Royal Corps of Transport was a different matter – he wasn't listed on the various pieces of multicolored paper that decorated the surfaces around the telephone, but a flash of inspiration and I remembered.

A cool, unflustered voice answered the insistent ring of the 'phone somewhere in Regent's Park Barracks.

'TCO,' it said.

I took a deep breath – never easy with a mouthful of fingernails – and said, 'This is a national crisis. Pay attention and do exactly as I say. There is a 3-ton vehicle broken down by the Cenotaph in Whitehall...'

'OK,' said the cool, unflustered voice as I finished and the line was disconnected.

I fled back to the window, my arrival coinciding with that of a red-faced, very aggressive fireman, who appeared outside atop one of those rather splendid extending ladders. He addressed me thus: 'Are you the bleeder what was going to jump?'

'Er, no ... well no ... ah ... I did think about it perhaps but...'

I stopped in mid-stream as I saw, at the far end of Whitehall, a Ford Zephyr staff car. The car's lights suddenly flicked on and it accelerated through the traffic like a little boy through currant buns. It braked to a halt alongside the truck, to the dismay of the motoring public, and the driver leapt out. There was a hurried conversation between the two soldiers but within seconds the staff car was heading our way, the boot-lid banging rhythmically on the tops of the urns. The truck driver was left standing on the pavement scratching his head. I saw him aim a final kick at his mount.

'You must excuse me,' I apologised. 'It's the coffee, you know.'

'Now just a minnit,' said the fireman, and to my dismay he clambered through the aperture into the toilet-cum-kitchen and pursued me into the far corner.

'You can't just go 'anging around outside like that, it's not bleedin' on,' he complained.

The door flicked open and the imaginative Ministry of Defence poster that enjoins you to 'Now wash your hands' was caught in the same stray shaft of sunlight that was illumining 'Notes for Food Handlers' pinned thoughtfully on the back of the door by Mr Etherington. The Colour Sergeant appeared not a little harassed.

'The General says we must have coffee now, at once, this minute or better still immediately ... and this copper want to arrest someone,' he added as an afterthought.

A policeman stood at the Colour Sergeant's elbow, his notebook at the 'standing alert' position. He flexed his knees and I got the distinct impression that he was about to say, 'Hello, hello, hello.'

But he didn't get the chance because he was struck in the back, first by the door and then by an urn carried by two of my soldiers.

'Here they are, here they are,' I rejoiced.

'Let's get it in, get it in, d'you hear?' Etherington barked.

Less than a minute later, coffee-pots and milk jugs were filled and an excellent cup of coffee was being served.

Everyone started to speak at once. The policeman finally got round to it and uttered the immortal words, 'Hello, hello, hello, what's goin' on 'ere?'

Etherington said, 'The Supremes were really not too bad.'

The fireman said, 'Is any bleeder jumpin' today or not?'

I said, 'Let me explain.'

The Colour Sergeant reappeared and said in sepulchral tones, 'The General would like to see you, sir – at once,' he added gratuitously.

The MAB was in the lobby outside; his erstwhile and replete dining companions were dispersing around him and disappearing down what the press chooses to call 'the corridors of power'. The MAB had two companions with him – both had dark uniforms, silver buttons and peaked caps. One, an awe-inspiringly senior policeman, was saying something about, 'Sinister implications, deserves fullest investigation.'

The other dark-suited bod was every schoolboy's idea of a senior fireman. He'd have chopped down CGS's door and doused his ashtray in foam without a second thought. He was clearly frustrated, clearly *very* frustrated.

'It's all very well,' he complained. 'Here I am with thirty men down there holding a net and no one jumping, but,' he finished brightly, 'you never know, it might encourage people who'd not given it a thought.'

'My goodness,' said the MAB, 'is that the time? I must fly,' and so saying he did.

It took effort, a great deal of patience, and most of the afternoon and an incredibly detailed explanation before the dark-suited pair made their departure, their two underlings in hot pursuit. The policeman, who still bore the imprint of the urn on his back, said darkly over his shoulder, 'You'll hear more of this.'

I returned to my command post in time to hear one of the soldier chefs indicate that he wished to make use of one of the WCs.

'Not in my kitchen you don't,' roared Etherington. 'What do you think this is?'

'Now, sir,' he added in a kinder, warmer tone, and having moved a gas-stove, 'you sit down here and I'll get you a nice cup of coffee.'

✤

Some of the Colonel's recipes for lunch in more conventional settings follow.

T.N.

Feuilleté de Poussin (page 36)

Lime Soufflé (page 40)

DUBLIN BAY CHOWDER

This comparatively simple dish makes a nourishing light lunch for four or an extremely satisfying one for two. The Colonel's Lady is of the opinion that frozen prawns are if anything more suitable than cooked fresh ones, provided that they are added while still frozen.

Serves: 4

Preparation: 15 minutes

Cooking: 30 minutes

Ingredients

25g (1oz) butter
3 rashers bacon, chopped
1 large onion, chopped
1 clove garlic, crushed
450g (1lb) potatoes
300ml (½pt) fish or chicken stock
600ml (1pt) milk
salt and freshly ground black pepper
225g (8oz) cooked prawns (fresh or frozen)
450ml (¾pt) single cream
1-2tbs chopped parsley

Drill

1. Melt the butter in a large saucepan. Add the chopped bacon and fry gently until cooked. Add the chopped onion and the garlic and continue to fry until the onion is soft but not brown.

2. Peel the potatoes and cut into rough cubes about 1½cm (½in) across. Add to the pan and toss until well coated.

3. Add the stock and the milk, season to taste and bring to the boil. Cover and simmer until potatoes are quite soft.

4. Add the prawns and cook until they are heated through. Add the cream and re-heat without boiling. Add the parsley, reserving a little to garnish each bowl after serving. Try garlic bread as an accompaniment.

Recommended drink: Dry or medium-dry white wine.

STEAK, OYSTER AND BROWN BEER PIE

This rich and filling pie combines the flavours of beef and brown beer with the succulence of fresh oysters, a combination long used in English cookery and, of course, extensively by Chinese chefs with the help of oyster sauce. The pie can be topped with either puff pastry or suet pastry (both are included in the basic recipes section).

Serves: 4

Preparation: 30 minutes

Cooking: 2¾ hours

Ingredients

675g (1½lb) lean rump steak

oil

150g (5oz) diced onion

100ml (4fl oz) beef stock

300ml (½pt) brown beer or stout

½tsp mixed herbs

25g (1oz) sugar

450g (1lb) puff or suet pastry

8-12 fresh oysters

1 egg yolk for brushing

1 litre (1¾pt) pie-dish

Drill

To cook the pie filling

1. Cut the meat into 2.5cm (1in) cubes, trimming away all fat etc.

2. Heat some oil in a thick-bottomed pan and brown the meat. Do this in several batches to retain the heat in the pan.

3. Remove the meat and glaze the diced onion in the pan for a few minutes. Return the meat to the pan and add the stock and the beer or stout.

4. Bring to the boil and add the herbs. Simmer for 1½-2 hours until the meat is tender.

5. Bring the sugar to the boil with a little water and stir into the meat. Reduce to a nice sauce consistency, take off the heat and leave to cool.

To make the pie

6. Roll out the pastry to a thickness of 3-4mm (¼in). Cut a strip about 1.5cm (¾in) wide and place around the lip of the pie dish.

7. Add the oysters to the meat and fill the pie-dish. Brush the pastry rim with egg yolk and top with the pastry. Trim the excess pastry and use to decorate the top of the pie. Brush with a mixture of egg yolk, a pinch of salt and a little water. Make an opening in the top to let the steam escape.

8. Bake in a hot oven at 220°C (425°F, Gas Mk 7) for about 25 minutes.

Recommended drink: Full-bodied red wine like a Burgundy.

FEUILLETÉ DE POUSSIN

This light and tasty dish is ideal for lunch or as a light dinner in summertime. The pastry cases can be made well in advance and stored ready for use. A spot of cream may be added to enrich the sauce.

📖

Serves: 4

Preparation: 45 minutes

Cooking: 45 minutes

Ingredients

2 poussins or small chickens
2 shallots roughly chopped
75g (3oz) chicken livers
175g (6oz) mushrooms (preferably wild)
225ml (8fl oz) madeira
sprig of thyme
225g (8oz) puff pastry
100ml (4fl oz) vegetable stock
225ml (8fl oz) chicken stock
20ml (1tbs) olive oil
25g (1oz) butter cut into cubes
lemon juice to taste
sprig of chervil for garnish
asparagus to garnish

Drill

To prepare the meat

1. Separate the supremes (breasts) from the carcass and remove the skin and bones. Make a slit in the back of the supremes to form a small pocket. Trim and bone the leg meat.

2. Fry the shallots in a little oil and then add the leg meat and the chicken livers. Add the mushrooms, then the madeira, and flavour with the sprig of thyme.

3. Cook and reduce the liquid. Cool and purée in a food processor. Fill the cavity in the breasts with the purée and refrigerate.

To prepare the pastry case

4. Roll out the pastry on a lightly floured surface to a thickness of about 5cm (¼in), then cut into 4 rectangular cases, 10 x 4cm (4 x 1½in).

5. Place them on a baking tray which has been lightly greased and sprinkled with water. Brush the tops with egg wash and bake in a preheated oven at 200°C (400°F, Gas Mk 6) for 20 minutes or until golden-brown. Keep the cases warm until required.

To make the sauce

6. Combine the vegetable and chicken stocks in a saucepan and bring them to the boil. Boil rapidly to reduce them by about one quarter.

7. Whisk in the olive oil and butter and season with the lemon juice and a little salt and pepper. The sauce should be light and have a slight bite to it.

To cook the supremes

8. Season the supremes, wrap them in clingfilm and steam or poach until just firm. Keep them warm until required.

To serve

9. Cut a lid off the top of each pastry case. Spoon out a little of the soft dough from the middle of the pastry to make a cavity. Fill each one with the remaining mushroom and chicken-liver mix used for stuffing the supremes.

10. Place a pastry case in the middle of each of the four warmed plates. Slice the cooked supremes and arrange on the top of each one. Top each with a lid.

11. Sauce the plates and garnish with the chervil and with small asparagus heads that have been lightly cooked in salt water until just tender.

Recommended drink: A good Riesling or perhaps a light claret.

ORIENTAL PORK

The Colonel developed a taste for sweet and sour dishes while serving in far-flung corners of the empire. He knows of no better example of the genre than this easy, quick and delicious blend of flavours. If preferred, chicken can be substituted for the pork.

Serves: 4

Preparation: 20 minutes

Cooking: 1 hour

Ingredients

4 pork steaks
salt and freshly ground pepper
1-2tbs oil
25g (1oz) butter
1 green pepper, deseeded and chopped
2 medium/large onions, chopped
1 clove garlic, crushed
4tbs tomato ketchup
2tbs red wine vinegar
1tbs Worcester sauce
1tsp Dijon or English mustard
1 rounded tbs brown sugar

Drill

1. Pre-heat the oven to 200°C (400°F, Gas Mk 6). Heat the oil in a roasting pan, then lightly season the pork steaks and place in the pan and cook for about 30 minutes, turning occasionally.

2. Meanwhile, melt the butter in a large saucepan. Add the chopped green pepper and onions and fry gently with the garlic until soft but not brown.

3. Add the tomato ketchup, the wine vinegar, the Worcester sauce, mustard and brown sugar to the pan and stir into the vegetables. Keep warm.

4. Remove the pan from the oven, drain away all fat and cut the pork into neat cubes, approximately 1½cm (½in) across. Return these to the pan and pour the vegetable sauce over the top.

5. Lower the heat to 175°C (350°F, Gas Mk 4) and cook for a further 30-45 minutes or until the pork is cooked through and tender. Add seasoning to taste and serve with rice and a green salad.

Recommended drink: Medium white or well-chilled rosé wine, or cold lager.

SALISBURY LAMB

Get a friendly gunner to target a lamb on Salisbury Plain. Failing that, ask your butcher to advise on the best cuts. The Colonel's village tradesman specialises in diced leg, which is wonderful, but neck or shoulder cuts are also suitable.

Ingredients

2 large onions
675g (1½lb) braising lamb, diced
freshly ground pepper and salt
50g (2oz) butter
15g (½oz) plain flour
1 clove garlic, crushed
1tsp tomato purée
750ml (1¼pts) stock
1 bouquet garni
1 tsp sugar
1 parsnip, sliced
2 carrots, sliced
12 small new potatoes

Drill

1. Slice one of the two onions and season the lamb with the salt and freshly milled pepper. Heat half of the butter in a large saucepan, add the meat and sliced onion and fry quickly to brown.

2. Sprinkle with the flour and continue to cook for a few minutes. Add the crushed garlic, the tomato purée and the stock. Bring to boil, stirring continually, then add the bouquet garni. Cover and simmer gently for 1 hour.

3. Meanwhile, heat the rest of the butter in a separate pan. Add the sugar and the sliced parsnip and carrots. Fry them to brown, then place them in a dish and keep warm.

4. Lift out the meat, strain the sauce into a bowl and skim off any fat lying on the surface.

5. Return the meat to the pan and add the sauce, the new potatoes, the browned vegetables and the remaining onion – cut into quarters.

6. Cover and simmer for a further 30 minutes, or until the meat and all the vegetables are tender, removing any more fat which might accumulate.

7. Remove the meat and vegetables when cooked and place in a serving dish. Reduce the sauce, if necessary, to a thick, rich consistency and spoon over.

Recommended drink: A good claret.

LIME SOUFFLÉ

Much mystery surrounds the making of a soufflé, whether it be of the sweet or savoury variety. By breaking down the method into three parts, however, one can make this a less nerve-shattering experience. The awful question, 'will it rise or collapse in ruins?' can be eliminated for those who follow these guidelines.

Serves: 6

Preparation: 45 minutes

Cooking: 40 minutes

Ingredients

butter for greasing

caster sugar for dusting the moulds

50g (2oz) butter

50g (2oz) flour

225ml (8fl oz) milk

grated rind from the limes

3tbs lime juice

5 egg whites

4 egg yolks

75g (3oz) caster sugar

icing sugar for dusting the soufflés

Drill

To prepare the soufflé dish

1. The dish must be lightly and evenly greased with melted butter. Dust the inside with caster sugar and turn and tilt it until the base and sides are thoroughly coated. Tip out any excess. Take your time with this, as a poorly prepared mould will stop the soufflé from rising.

To make the soufflé

2. Blend the butter and flour together to form a paste. This is known as a *beurre-manie*.

3. Boil the milk and add the *beurre-manie*, a little at a time, whisking continuously until you have a sauce of a smooth, thick and even consistency.

4. Take off the heat and add the lime rind and juice. Add one egg white to the mix (this acts as an additional stabiliser) and beat until evenly distributed. Tip the mixture into a bowl and allow to cool.

5. Add the egg yolks, one at a time, beating the mixture until smooth and creamy.

To prepare the egg whites

6. Place the remaining egg whites in a mixing bowl and add the caster sugar. Beat until firm and the mixture stands up in peaks (if using an electric mixer, begin at a slow speed and increase the tempo as the 'snow' thickens).

7. Mix this snow into the sauce, adding about a quarter to start with, then carefully fold in the rest. Be careful not to over-mix.

To cook the soufflé

8. Pour the mixture into the moulds; fill to about 1cm (½ inch) below the rim of the dish. Stand the mould in a water bath of a temperature of about 80°C, 190°F. The water must reach at least halfway up the sides of the dish.

9. Cook in a moderately hot oven at 200°C (400°F, Gas Mk 6) for about 40 minutes if using a large mould or 20 minutes for individual ones.

To serve

10. Dust the top with icing sugar and either serve the soufflé in the mould accompanied by a suitable sauce or de-mould and serve as shown in the photograph.

CURRY
LUNCH

Currying on

In the days when I was serving Queen and country, the distinction between officers and men was most marked by their treatment of India's cuisine. Curry in the cookhouse always ended the food chain. Sunday's roast beef became Monday's cold cuts, was transmogrified into Tuesday's cottage pie and then ended up as Wednesday's chicken madras (the meat being fairly indistinguishable by this stage).

In the Officers' Mess it was almost the reverse. Had the Russians wished to overpower this country they should have tried out their luck around 3 p.m. one Sunday. Not only was the War Office deserted, apart from some duty clerk dozing over his sandwiches, but the Army was immobilised by curry lunch.

Curry lunch was the lasting legacy of the Raj. It consisted of a variegated buffet at which one helped oneself to rice and meat, then piled on top not only mango chutney but chopped fresh fruit from a regiment of side dishes. Apple, banana, coconut and sliced onion, tomato, orange segments, raisins, peanuts, the contents of a passing ashtray and so on ... made one's plate look like a church font at harvest festival. Bending under the weight of this unaccustomed load, slightly woozy from pre-prandial gin and tonic, the flower of English chivalry weaved their way back through an obstacle course of chattering wives and children, to render themselves unfit for duty until next day. In its bases throughout the world that afternoon, the British Army was incapable of resistance.

This exemplifies not only the caste system but the versatility of Indian cuisine. It can either be used to disguise what has been put into it – contraband, classified information etc.; or itself can be neutralised by what goes on top. In between these extremes there lies a band, however, in which a chef can achieve near-perfection, when the delicate blend of aromatic spices, of cumin, turmeric and coriander, of ginger, cinnamon, peppers and soft, ripe cloves...can coax and seduce the flavour of fresh lamb into an unforgettable relationship. Such perfection, fortunately, remains uncommon – otherwise the occasions would not be unforgettable. Delhi-catessen resembles life itself: one remembers the good bits and happily not the rest.

There are, however, exceptions to this rule. I am now about to tell two cautionary tales because they carry a moral for mankind: if at first you don't succeed, give up.

It is frequently said that the best curry in the world is eaten in Britain. This is not because all India's chefs have come here, but because the quality of the meat or fish is better than that available in the sub-continent. This may be true. Football, invented in Britain, is played with greater panache everywhere else; the Japanese now make the best cameras and TVs; and the finest Mozart is not always played in Salzburg. Imitations are not necessarily second-best.

One night, while staying at a Singapore hotel where they specialised, strangely enough, in Scottish food, I felt a taste for curry coming on. Those of us who are addicted need regular intakes, or we become fidgety and difficult to control. So I put on a tie and set out for a well-known restaurant down town where they specialised (presumably still do) in Indian cooking. In the hotel lobby, however, I foolishly made known my intentions to the reception desk where I was overheard by an American fellow guest.

'You don't wanna go there,' he said. 'That's too commercialised. You wanna go where the real Indians eat' – and he gave me directions to find the Indian quarter. I instinctively knew that I should disregard him, but then I was new to the island so acquiesced.

The street lamps grew fewer, the neon dimmer as I walked through the tropical night, down the lone street where I had been dropped by my taxi. I walked past grubby restaurants and small shops, the only Occidental for some miles. At last, desperate for food and sore of foot, I entered a caff which was indisputably uncommercialised. Could this be where the real Indian people ate?

That some of them did so was beyond all question. It was equally clear, however, that no one else did. Several pairs of dark brown eyes swivelled towards me as I sat down at a greasy plastic table and picked up the plastic-coated *table d'hôte*. If the restaurant was anything to write home about, I was almost certainly guaranteed an exclusive.

The dishes were listed authentically in Hindi. The waiter, excitingly enough, spoke nothing else. Nor, it seemed, did his other customers that night.

For religious reasons, it seemed, they were unlicensed.

In the end he brought me, I think, his *plat du jour*. This turned out to be an arthritic leg of chicken which I suspect had died from natural causes, malnutrition having hastened the onset of old age. It now lay in peace, in a pool of tepid sauce, atop a funeral pyre of damp rice. The other diners watched with interest as I ate, absorbed by this eccentric British tourist.

It was indeed where the real Indians ate. But they clearly did not do so out of choice. Given the Singapore dollars in my wallet, they would have hoofed it to the ritzy joint in town. If something has been commercialised, go for it; it usually means it has something people want.

⚔

My second tale concerns the Rev. Basil Bluett, who had entered the Church after failing to win a place at Sandhurst. It was either the Church or the dustcart, said his father, a colonel in the Royal Regiment of Artillery, and although the latter paid marginally more, it did not offer a free house or car expenses.

That he did not come to regret this choice of calling was due almost entirely to his marriage. Barbara Bluett was a perfect vicar's wife. Not only was she attractive to behold but she brimmed over with other female strengths and virtues. She was lively, intelligent, industrious and kind, loyal, supportive, thrifty and warm-hearted. Her blue eyes sparkled with energy and good humour. Yet her tactfulness in dealing with parishioners, her wise counsel and intuitive understanding, her efficiency, smartness, literacy and style made her one of the true treasures of the Church. She dressed well, sewed well, spoke well when required – yet never stole the limelight from her husband. Moreover, she had borne him two fine children, on whom she lavished a mother's love and care. Basil, his friends agreed, had been thrice blessed.

Barbara Bluett, however, had one flaw. However hard she tried, she couldn't cook. Though she spent hours of practice trying to correct this, she bungled every dish she tried her hand at. Her pastry emerged as hard and heavy as lead; her cakes sank without trace – or obvious cause. Roast meat was either charred or underdone, milk puddings swan in a sea of boiled milk. As for her scrambled egg and home-made jam... When the parish held its annual Summer Fête, the sandwich and rock cakes given by the vicarage were discreetly fed to the birds by the churchwardens. It was not that Mrs Bluett did not try. Like Robert the Bruce, she tried and tried again. Her Bannockburn, however, proved elusive.

This flaw, for most of the time, could be bypassed. Her husband developed a taste for concrete scones and for eggs boiled as hard as cricket balls. The children assumed that all sausages were burnt. And when the bishop or some other dignitary came to visit, the Bluetts arranged with the local pub's landlady for some of her home-made steak and kidney pie. The Church had learned to live with her misfortunes.

A crisis arose, however, when the suffragan Bishop of Madrutha came to the parish. The local bishop had been on a freebee to southern India and was now repaying the courtesy to his ex-host on one of those 'Anglican communion' exchange visits. While arranging an interesting schedule for his guest, his thoughts turned to that nice young couple, the Bluetts.

'I thought perhaps ... an ecumenical service?' he suggested. 'The chapels and the RCs to be invited... And preceded by a luncheon at the vicarage? I imagine some form of curry would be appropriate and I thought immediately of your dear lady wife, whose quite mouth-watering steak and kidney pie is something I remember with great pleasure.'

Now while it was true that the local pub's landlady could prepare an excellent steak and kidney pie, a lamb vindaloo or chicken biryani lay well outside her culinary experience. Nor was it part of the rural cooking repertoire of any other household in the village, most of whose residents had only just come to terms with scampi. At an emergency family meeting in the vicarage, the Bluetts came to one inescapable conclusion: 'I'm very much afraid, my darling wife,' summed up the vicar, 'that you'll have to turn a hand to it yourself.'

Being of an understanding disposition he promised her all the help that he could think of, which largely consisted of driving into town and buying her several books on Indian cookery, together with a dazzling range of spices.

'There you are,' he said as he generously unpacked them. 'All you need to make a genuine Indian feast.' Then he went off for a quiet snooze in his study, dreaming of his imminent advancement in the Church.

Now Barbara Bluett was game for anything and as the daughter-in-law of an officer and gentleman, she had a highly developed sense of duty. The night before the great coming of the clergy, she was up until the early hours of the morning – reading, practising, preparing for the feast which, she hoped, would be a stepping-stone to glory. Three chapel ministers had accepted the invitation and so had the local Roman Catholic priest. The weather forecast promised warm spring sunshine. What could possibly now go wrong to cloud the day?

But alas...

Two sets of circumstances were against her, one beyond her control and the other, sadly, within it. For instance, she could not possibly have known that the suffragan bishop of Madrutha detested curry. Orphaned soon after birth, he had been reared on a hill station in the north of the sub-continent by Anglican nuns belonging to some deeply obscure order which was not only well endowed but rather worldly. As all the sisters had come from western Europe he had been brought up on saddle of lamb and Chateaubriand and Sister Hermione's steak and kidney pie – all accompanied by fine clarets and Moselweins. Moreover, he had usually managed to serve God at some distance from the country of his birth: whether at college, on special missions or long freebees. A cross he had always had to bear, however, was that wherever he went he was fed hot curry – badly cooked at that. He was therefore hoping that on a visit to rural England, he would surely at last have steak and kidney pie.

The other misfortune lying in wait for Barbara Bluett was that on the morning of the great day she lost her reading glasses. The circumstance was not all that unusual and her husband and children, with God's guidance, always found them. But the children were away, staying with their grandmother, while her husband was out showing the two bishops round his church – and preparing for the service that afternoon.

She held the cookery book four feet away from her. She squinted through a magnifying glass and made out the blurred instructions as best she could, as she measured out the numerous ingredients in the dish – one described as most popular in Madrutha.

Unfortunately when she came to 'chilli powder' she read the abbreviation 'tsp' as 'tbs'. The recipe book, moreover, failed to specify whether the spoonfuls should be rounded, level or heaped. Not wishing to short-change her special guest, she plumped for 'heaped'. Accordingly, instead of using two level teaspoonfuls, Mrs Bluett threw in two towering tablespoonfuls – and then added a third for good measure. The dish, coming from southern India, was a hot one. Barbara Bluett had made it positively explosive.

The suffragan bishop had so convinced himself beforehand that for once he would be served steak and kidney pie that he returned to the vicarage after a fairly tedious morning, anticipating the scent of onions and rich gravy. His heart sank when the bishop said on entering: 'Now, we have a real treat for you

(Clockwise from the bottom) **Lamb Kebabs** (page 54), **Naan Bread** (page 55),
Chapatis (page 56), **Kashmiri Rogan Josh** (page 50), **Indian Spiced Vegetables** (page 53),
Prawns in Curry Sauce (page 52)

Roast Stuffed Suckling Pig (page 68)

today, eh, Mrs Bluett?' How often had he heard those words before...

He was, however, a kind and generous man who did not wish to return to India all that quickly. So he did not react with more than an inward shudder as his hostess helped him to a giant-sized portion.

He dug his fork into the rich aromatic dish and spoke with enforced good humour as he lifted it to his mouth. 'Something to warm the cockles of my haaaaaaaagh!' he began in a brave attempt at jocularity. They were the last words he spoke throughout the lunch.

One by one the bishop and Basil Bluett, the ministers and the Roman Catholic priest followed their guest into the fiery furnace. One by one, tears streaming down his cheeks, each guest blindly groped for the glass of iced water placed before him. But as any *aficionado* will appreciate, taking in water after a mouthful of hot curry is like pouring it on a pan of blazing oil.

Only Barbara Bluett was unaffected. Not wanting to risk running out of her *chef d'oeuvre*, she had ordered herself a small steak and kidney pie – using the excuse that she was feeling 'slightly tummyish'. She was therefore quite oblivious to the silence which had settled on the table. She took this to be a sign of their enjoyment as they concentrated on the feast in front of them.

'Do *please* have some more,' she insisted and heaped another large portion on to the suffragan bishop's steaming plate. By now he was quite incapable of protest and his feebly waving arms were taken by the kindly Mrs Bluett to signify his eager acquiescence. 'More! More!' he seemed to be pleading to his hostess. Meanwhile the other ministers of religion, not wishing to offend their brother in Christ by appearing to turn aside his national dish, looked on in perspiring, horrified dismay as she heaped second helpings on to their plates as well.

Not even the fresh fruit salad and hot black coffee could revive the damaged sinews of the Church. After incoherently mumbling their thanks they staggered down the winding vicarage drive towards the eagerly waiting congregation.

Each had eaten, however, a great volume of hot curry, washed down by a gallon of water, a large bowl of fresh fruit salad and black coffee...

And so it came to pass that the service to celebrate man's unity before God was taken by the churchwarden, a local farmer, who was summoned from the hay harvest to help out, while the vicar, the bishop, the three nonconformist ministers and the RC priest, not to mention the suffragan Bishop of Madrutha, lay trembling and ashen-faced in the church vestry as they queued for the tiny offices outside.

I don't think Barbara Bluett cooked again, except that is for her husband and two children. She had learned the motto which should decorate every kitchen: who dares does not invariably win.

✂

However, no such problems will envelop the host or hostess who follows the Colonel's Curry Lunch suggested here. *H.S.*

KASHMIRI ROGAN JOSH

The popularity of rogan josh has grown in recent years. Its chief characteristic is the deep red colour imparted by the paprika and/or red chilli. The heat of a curry dish is largely determined by the amount of chilli used. Those of a nervous disposition might prefer to opt instead for cayenne pepper, which is slightly less intimidating than chilli.

📖

Serves: 5

Preparation: 15 minutes

Cooking: 1½ hours

Ingredients

6 cloves garlic, peeled and chopped
100g (4oz) fresh ginger, peeled and chopped
300ml (½pt) water
675g (1½lb) lean diced lamb
150ml (¼pt) vegetable oil
10 whole cardamon pods
1 bay leaf
6 whole cloves
10 black peppercorns
1in cinnamon stick
225g (8oz) finely chopped onions
2tsp ground coriander
4tsp ground cumin
3tsp bright red paprika
1tsp chilli powder or cayenne pepper

1tsp salt
150ml (¼pt) natural yoghurt
½tsp garam masala
fresh coriander for garnish

Drill

1. Purée the garlic and ginger in a blender or food processor with just enough of the water to make a fine paste.

2. Brown the meat in the hot oil. Remove with a perforated spoon and keep warm.

3. Add to the hot oil the cardamon, bay leaf, cloves, peppercorns and cinnamon stick. Stir, then add the onions and cook until soft.

4. Add the garlic and ginger paste, then the coriander, cumin, paprika, chilli/cayenne and salt. Stir-fry for 1 minute.

5. Return the browned meat to the pan and slowly add the yoghurt, blending it in as you do so. Top up with the remaining water, bring to the boil, then lower the heat, cover and simmer for 1 hour, stirring frequently.

6. Remove the cover and, if necessary, boil away any excess liquid. Any fat that collects on the surface can be skimmed off. Add the garam masala for seasoning and mix well.

7. Place in a hot dish, garnished with fresh coriander. Serve with pilau rice and/or naan bread or chapatis.

Recommended drink: Lager.

PRAWNS IN CURRY SAUCE

Serves: 4

Preparation and cooking: 45 minutes

Ingredients

75g (3oz) onions, coarsely chopped
5 cloves garlic, peeled
75-100g (3-4oz) fresh ginger, peeled and chopped
3tbs water
4tbs vegetable oil
1in cinnamon stick
6 whole cardamon pods
2 bay leaves
2tsp ground cumin
1tsp ground coriander
175g (6oz) tomatoes, peeled and finely chopped
5tbs plain yoghurt
½tsp ground turmeric
½tsp cayenne pepper
300ml (½pt) water
pinch salt
350g (12oz) good quality prawns
¼tsp garam masala
chopped fresh coriander

Drill

1. Place the onions, garlic, ginger and the 3tbs water in the bowl of an electric blender and blend to a paste.

2. Heat the oil in a pan (8-9in diameter) on a high flame. Put in the cinnamon, cardamon pods and bay leaves. Stir, then add the paste from the blender and cook for about 5 minutes until coloured light brown.

3. Add the cumin and ground coriander and stir-fry for about 30 seconds. Add the tomatoes. Add the yoghurt, a little at a time, until well blended in. Add the turmeric, cayenne pepper and the ½ pint of water. Season with salt.

4. Add the peeled prawns, bring to the boil and cook for about 5 minutes until the sauce is quite thick. Sprinkle with the garam masala and served garnished with the fresh coriander.

Note: Take care not to overcook the prawns or they will become tough and rubbery.

Recommended drink: Lager (or a traditional hock/mosel if desperate for wine).

INDIAN SPICED VEGETABLES

Serves: 6

Preparation: 20 minutes

Cooking: 25 minutes

Ingredients

1in cube fresh ginger, peeled and coarsely chopped

6 cloves garlic, finely chopped

7tbs water

5tbs vegetable oil

225g (8oz) aubergines, cut into small wedges

225g (8oz) carrots, cut into batons

225g (8oz) cauliflower florets

225g (8oz) green beans, trimmed and cut into one-inch strips

225g (8oz) onions, peeled and coarsely chopped

1tsp ground cumin

1tsp ground coriander seeds

175g (6oz) tomatoes, peeled and finely chopped

½tsp ground turmeric

½tsp cayenne pepper

salt

1tbs lemon juice

¼tsp garam masala

Drill

1. Place the ginger and garlic in the bowl of a food processor or electric blender. Add the water and blend to a smooth paste.

2. Heat some oil in a frying pan and fry the cut aubergines until brown. Remove from the fat and drain.

3. Blanch the carrots, cauliflower and green beans until tender.

4. Heat some oil in a frying pan over a medium heat, add the onion and stir-fry for a few minutes. Add the cumin and coriander, cook for a few minutes; then add the ginger and garlic mix and the chopped tomatoes. Finally add the turmeric, cayenne pepper, salt and lemon juice. Cook to reduce until the mixture is quite thick.

5. In a fresh frying pan, stir-fry the cauliflower, carrots and beans. Add the sauce mixture and continue for a few minutes, until the vegetables are just cooked (you may need to add a little water if the sauce becomes too thick).

6. Add the cooked aubergines and heat through. Sprinkle with garam masala and serve very hot.

Recommended drink: Lager (or just possibly a hock/mosel type).

LAMB KEBABS

📖

Serves: 4

Preparation: 25 minutes

Cooking: 15 minutes

Ingredients

450g (1lb) diced lamb

1tbs fresh coriander leaves

1tbs garam masala

1tbs ground cumin

1tbs paprika

2 cloves garlic, crushed

½tsp ground ginger

½tsp cinnamon

½tsp ground star anise

1-3tsp (according to taste) chilli powder

75ml (3fl oz) fresh natural yoghurt

Drill

1. Remove all unwanted fat and gristle from the lamb.

2. Place the lamb and all the other ingredients in a food processor (alternatively use a mincer, but the texture will be different). Pulse the processor, then run it for a short while, trying to obtain a well-ground effect.

3. Remove and ensure that everything is well mixed. Divide the mix into four and mould into sausage shapes.

4. Pre-heat the oven to 190°C (375°F, Gas Mk 5). Place the kebabs on an oven tray and bake for 15 minutes.

5. They are best eaten fresh, but can also be frozen and reheated later. Serve with a yoghurt.

Note: An alternative method of cooking is to mould the mix around skewers and cook on a barbecue.

🍷

Recommended drink: Lager (or perhaps a well-chilled hock).

NAAN BREAD

Serves: 8-10

Preparation and Resting: 1½ hours

Cooking: 5-6 minutes

Ingredients

150ml (¼pt) hand-hot milk

2tsp caster sugar

2tsp dried yeast

450g (1lb) plain flour

½tsp salt

1tsp baking powder

2tbs vegetable oil

150ml (5fl oz) plain yoghurt, lightly beaten

1 large egg, lightly beaten

Drill

1. Place the milk in a bowl, add 1 teaspoonful of the sugar and yeast. Stir to mix and then set aside for 15-20 minutes – until the yeast has dissolved.

2. Sift the flour, salt and baking powder into a large bowl. Add the remaining teaspoon of sugar, the yeast mixture, the vegetable oil, yoghurt and beaten egg.

3. Mix together to form a ball of dough. Knead well until smooth. Brush with oil, cover with a piece of clingfilm and set aside in a warm place for 1 hour – or until the dough has doubled in bulk.

4. Pre-heat the oven to the highest temperature and place in it your heaviest baking tray. Pre-heat the grill.

5. Punch down the dough and knead it again. Divide it into 6 even balls. Keep five covered while you work with the sixth. Roll this ball into a tear-shaped naan about 25cm (10in) long and 13cm (5in) at its widest.

6. Place on the pre-heated baking tray and cook in the oven for 3 minutes. It should puff up.

7. Now place the baking tray and the naan under the grill for about 30 seconds or until the naan browns. Complete all the naans in this way. Serve hot.

CHAPATIS

Indian breads like chapatis are eaten in northern India instead of rice. Gluttonous Westerners tend to eat them as well as rice, as an additional means of counter-balancing the richness of hot curries. Unlike poppadoms, chapatis – the floppy discs of Indian cuisine – are not commonly mass-produced, but are worth persevering with in one's kitchen to give one's curries the authentic Indian flavour.

Serves: 8-10

Preparation and Cooking: 30 minutes

Ingredients

270g (9oz) sieved wholemeal flour
150ml (¼pt) water

Drill

1. Put the flour in a bowl and slowly add the water, gathering the flour together as you do so until a soft dough has formed.

2. Knead the dough for 6-8 minutes or until it is smooth. Put it in a bowl, cover with a damp cloth and leave to stand for 15 minutes.

3. Knead the dough again and divide roughly into 15 parts. It will be quite sticky, so rub your hands with a little flour to make the handling easier.

4. Form each portion into a ball. Flour the work surface well and roll each ball in the flour, pressing down on it to make a patty. Roll this out, dusting frequently with flour, to a size of 14cm (5-6in) in diameter.

5. Heat a frying pan, preferably cast-iron, until very hot, then turn down the heat to low. Shake off the excess flour on the chapatis and cook in the hot pan, turning once. Serve hot.

PILAU RICE

The preparation of pilau rice takes a little more time and trouble than it does simply to boil the appropriate quantity in a saucepan. But the effort is worth it because the result has a huge impact on the flavour of an Indian meal.

Serves: 4-5

Preparation: 5 minutes

Cooking: 30 minutes

Ingredients

60g (2½ oz) vegetable oil or ghee
½ onion, chopped
2 cloves garlic, crushed
1tsp fresh ginger, grated
½tsp ground turmeric
1tsp garam masala
1tsp ground cardamon
350g (12oz) basmati rice
450ml (¾pt) lamb or chicken stock

Drill

1. Heat the oil or ghee in a pan and fry the onion until soft.

2. Add the garlic, ginger and the remaining spices and stir. Add the rice and stir well to ensure that all the grains are well coated with the mixture.

3. Pour in the stock. Bring to the boil, cover with a tightly fitting lid and cook in a medium oven for 20 minutes.

4. At the end of the cooking time, remove the lid and gently fork over the rice (this will stop the cooking). Allow it to steam for a few minutes, then serve it very hot.

Note: Cooking times and the amount of liquid needed are bound to vary, so one should follow the manufacturer's instructions when provided.

SUMMER
DAYS

Shall we eat out?

The British Army is the organisation internationally recognised as being that most given to alfresco dining, picnicking, eating out, tail-gating or whatever other expression you favour.

For upwards of 300 years the Army has fought its battles at night, uphill, in the rain, and at the junction of four maps. It has made it a practice to stop for a snack during the process and thus, those charged with the duty of feeding the Army need to have excellent night vision, strong navigational skills and a degree of luck if they are to bring their food and their customers into meaningful contact.

It's a well-known military maxim that a cup of cocoa before you cross the 'start line' is worth cod, chips and mushy peas in another setting. The positive morale factor of hot food in a cold place cannot be overstated. Your scribe recalls that the most memorable breakfast of his life was served at about 0800 hours one bitterly cold, dark January morning, high in the Brecon Beacons.

My platoon had 'stood to' half an hour before first light as is the normal practice. Eyes gritty from a sleepless, agonisingly cold night, stubble on our chins and with boots packed with cold lifeless feet, we checked our weapons and communications, peered into the grey of the approaching dawn and tried not to be irritated by our Platoon Sergeant as he scrambled from weapon pit to weapon pit, dispensing his own brand of bonhomie and bullshit.

The attack at first light did not materialise and thirty minutes later we 'stood down' and trickled to the rear towards the wonderful aroma of bacon and eggs cooking. It was irresistible and it blended with that of the coffee, a beverage usually reserved for the officers.

As we got closer to the field kitchen our taste-buds jumped through hoops, morale lifted and it all augured well for the new day, even though there were now flurries of snow on a wind fresh in from Canada.

The promise of a hot meal was one thing, the chance of hot shaving water was another; and in combination quite stunning. One by one we filtered back and there, by the light of a well-shielded Tilley lamp, we found Corporal McCall. Bent double over a device known as the 'No.1 Burner', he plied his trade as countless other members of his Corps had done before. His cooking device, this No.1 Burner, was little more than a crude flame-thrower and it first came into service in 1937. Today, as the millenium approaches, it remains the weapon of choice to many members of the former Army Catering Corps. It operates on a flame fuelled by petrol under pressure, and is not much more than a sort of bomb on a short leash.

WO2 (SOMS) Hawks ACC used his at the Battle of the Hook in Korea and, it is alleged, pumped up his machine past the danger point, lit it and hurled it at the advancing Chinese. It went off with a bang and did nothing to help Anglo-Sino relations. The Chinese were very cross with Mr Hawkes and locked him up with the other survivor of 1st Battalion, the Gloucestershire Regiment, whose gallant Colonel Carne won a V.C. that day.

McCall rose from his crouched position and, on a 6ft table, he placed the product of his labours: eggs, bacon, fried bread, baked beans and tomatoes. Frozen aluminium mess tin in hand, we shuffled down the line towards the repast. But, before we got there, we plunged our tins into a container of boiling water, shook them vigorously and presented, at the least, a warm receptacle for breakfast.

Bliss.

Yummy.

The tea was hot and sweet, slabs of bread and jam (don't bother with the butter, it's too hard and breaks the bread and Real Men don't eat marmalade so enjoy the plum and apple).

Smashing! 'Thanks, Corp.'

Back to the hole in the ground with a tin of hot water for a shave. Suddenly all was right with the world, despite the now drifting snow.

There is an image of eating out in God's great outdoors. You know the scene; basking in summer sunshine whilst sitting on the terrace of the Mess, gazing out over manicured lawns and watching the swans glide over the lake below. A tall gin and tonic, a pretty girl and half a pint of Beluga complete the picture.

But it's never really like that.

A decision to eat or drink outside is serious stuff. The factors must be carefully weighed. A decision to go ahead has to be taken secretly and silently because, by some means, every fly, midge, beetle and wasp for ten miles around will hear that there is a party and will pole up and gatecrash. What is more they bring along most of their friends and relations. If they don't care for the food that is on offer, they have no hesitation in dining off the diners.

An elegant summer supper party around the pool loses something when the guests devote a deal of their energy to the slapping of their exposed areas and restrict their conversation to 'insects I have known', or the rather vulgar comparison of midge bites.

Similarly, the alfresco meal is more than a little dependent upon the weather. Sod, that well-known philosopher, gave it thought and produced several laws that are germane here.

Sod's 4th Law states: 'In England it usually rains at picnics.'

His 5th Law opines that: 'In Scotland and Wales it always rains at picnics.'

You will note here that no reference has been made to Ireland. That is simply because no one from that green and lovely isle ever eats out. They are all down the pub giving the Guinness a bashing. Anyway, what ingredient do you suppose makes their grass so lush and green?

Drinks outside can be abandoned in the face of multiple midge attacks, snow squalls or tempest fairly easily. It's less easy when food is involved and a decision to lay tables with crystal, silver and napery is on a par with that made by Hitler to invade Russia. The losses can be frightful and the human suffering out of proportion to the anticipated gain.

Hitler, and Napoleon before him, learned the hard way that the elements take no prisoners. There is nothing so rigorous or inclement as an English summer day, and a cricket tea with strawberries and cream should never be contemplated unless there is readily to hand an ample supply of thigh-length boots, sou'westers, stormcoats and thermal underwear. Incidentally, it's useful to note here that the stormcoat goes on top of the thermal underwear. To dress otherwise would be to appear ridiculous as one stands in teeming rain eating one's strawberries. On to technical matters – and do be sure not to serve either shortcake or a *'Langue du Chat'* when eating out, because experience shows that the rain makes them soggy and rather unattractive.

I once served under a Colonel who was an eating-out enthusiast; he was heavily into Pimms on the lawn and barbecue suppers. We were in Singapore at the time and so it was, if nothing else, always warm. However, the tropics breed particularly vicious bugs, one has to cope with wall-to-wall snakes underfoot, and when it rains it monsoons. The eating-out bit, therefore, was adapted to meet local conditions and thus the 'basha' came into its own.

A basha is an open-sided shelter with a roof made of palm fronds, all very Gauguin or Somerset Maugham. The warm, tropical breeze can pass through unhindered and in the event of rain, there is ample overhead cover.

A signal arrived to say that the Secretary of State for Defence would visit the Brigade as part of his Far Eastern Tour, and that he intended to take luncheon with our unit. The Colonel was unimpressed. Secretaries of State are far too far up the ladder to have any immediate effect upon a serviceman's life. The Brigadier, on the other hand, now he *really* was important. The Brigadier said that he was 'confident that we'd lay on a good lunch'. What's more, he'd be accompanying the Minister.

The Colonel decided that we'd eat in the basha and appropriate arrangements had been made when the Great Man arrived. He turned out to be quite a nice chap and, against my better judgement, I found I rather liked him. The Brigadier was in fine form and the pre-luncheon drinks were relaxed and great fun.

We sat promptly at 1300 hours and, in due course, the *'Tournedos Gabrielle'* were presented by the Steward. This dish, as the reader will instantly recall, is your bog standard fillet steak, cooked in butter, dressed upon a flat chicken croquette mixed with chopped truffles. The top of the tournedos is garnished with slices of truffle alternately with slices of marrow fat and the whole is surrounded by croquette potatoes and stuffed, braised lettuce. What other sauce than a Madeira demi-glace? 'Tis a charming little number that any half-decent chef can chuck together at the drop of a haddock. Sergeant Bannerman, the Mess Chef was half-decent at his job.

At one side of the basha was a hot-plate fuelled by methylated spirit and on the hot-plate were the extra potatoes, vegetables and sauces.

It is normal to string a fillet of beef before cutting into tournedos, and the string remains on the steak whilst it is cooked to keep it in shape. In most establishments seeking to make a profit and encourage return business, the string is removed prior to serving because research has indicated that no matter how well cooked butcher's string is, it is always indigestible and, not to put too fine a point on it, 'stringy'.

Sergeant Bannerman had, in time-honoured fashion and like countless others before him, reminded his staff to 'count the strings'.

They did.

They miscounted.

One Tournedos Gabrielle was not de-stringed. It was sent to the table.

There was an embarrassed silence as first one and then another member of the luncheon party noticed that the Minister of Defence, a man who could quell the House of Commons by a curl of a patrician lip, was in deep trouble with the string around his steak. His knife would not cut it and he embarked upon an interesting manoeuvre, never seen before, to slide the string up and off the meat. The Minister's plate rocked and the sauce swilled from side to side. The Brigadier, with a face like thunder, snapped at the steward, 'A sharp knife now, d'you hear?'

The steward, a Chinese gentleman called Mr Tan, leapt into action and fled for the kitchen and as he did so his hip knocked the service table that bore the hot-plate and, in so doing, caused some of the flaming methylated spirit to splash on to the crisp white tablecloth.

All eyes were on the Minister. Profuse apologies were being proffered. The Colonel, not used to dramas at his table, was sending out very negative vibrations. The other diners put down their knives and forks as it didn't appear seemly to eat whilst the Minister of Defence had the best of three falls, a knock-out or a submission with 7½oz of prime Angus.

The food on the table started to cool despite the heat of the day, but we really should not have worried because by now the tablecloth on the service table was gloriously, deliriously alight. Flames were running down the table leg, but one more adventurous flame licked upwards and caressed a wisp of palm frond which, from the heat of the Singaporean sun, was explosively dry. In seconds the flame had reached the roof and the basha was a beacon that could be seen for miles.

Mr Tan arrived with a knife.

The Brigadier thought about throwing himself on it.

The Colonel did his appreciation and uttered the immortal words, 'Abandon the basha'. Like a Captain in the Royal Navy he stayed on the bridge until all souls were safe and then, with great dignity and soot on his nose, he stepped on to the lawn into the opening salvo of water directed by the fire brigade that threw him on to his back under a watching palm tree. 'Goodness

Potage Babbacombe Bay (page 81)

(Foreground left) **Plate of Cold Meats**, *(foreground right)* **Slice of Salmon and Turbot Strudel**
(page 83), *(background)* **Strawberry Shortbread** (page 71)

me, golly gosh, oh dear,' he said, or similar words. He was not best pleased: I could tell by the way he kicked the palm tree. A fruit from the palm dislodged by the vibration of the kick fell with a thud and landed on the polished toecap of his shoe. He let out an anguished yell and repeated the 'Golly gosh' speech, only this time with feeling.

As an eating-out experience it was different, exciting in parts, but not very sustaining. The fire brigade, having turned up, nearly drowned our Colonel and caused him to suffer a broken toe, now made a dog and pony show of it as they hosed down the smoking embers of our basha. In the bar the survivors ate sandwiches and started on the post-mortem. Singed, soaking wet, limping badly and having lost his basha, some Mess silver and crystal, the Colonel was upset. A state of mind not helped when commanded by the Brigadier to 'hold a regimental enquiry'. The Brigadier and the Minister swept off.

The findings of the inquiry, when published, laid the blame for the loss of the basha, regimental property and the humiliation of the Colonel and his unit firmly at the door of Sergeant Bannerman. 'Strings' Bannerman left the Army soon after and has since made a million running a company specialising in event catering at races, auctions, regattas and the like. The Minister lost his seat at the General Election a couple of months later and the Brigadier hinted darkly that Bannerman had a part to play here too. The Colonel was never really the same again. He took to 'bar snacks' at lunchtime, a particularly low-grade form of catering. But, as he remarked when questioned, 'At least it's safe.' He, for one, never ate outside again – and what's good enough for my Colonel is good enough for me.

✄

If you feel you must, however, the recipes that follow will certainly help.

T.N.

SHANNON PÂTÉ

Serves: 4

Preparation: 15 minutes

Ingredients

1tbs olive oil
50g (2oz) butter
225g (8oz) smoked salmon
1-2tbs lemon juice
4tbs double cream
freshly ground black pepper

Drill

1. Blend the oil and butter thoroughly in a basin. Mince the salmon and add it, whisking to achieve a creamy paste.

2. Add the lemon juice, cream and freshly milled pepper and beat well into the mixture.

3. Decant into a serving dish and refrigerate overnight. Try eating with crusty French bread and Irish butter.

SALADE NIÇOISE

📖

Serves: 6

Preparation: 15 minutes

Ingredients

450g (1lb) tomatoes
1 small cucumber, sliced
1tbs freshly chopped basil, thyme and parsley
squeeze lemon juice
salt and freshly ground black pepper
75g (3oz) black olives, sliced
225g (8oz) cooked French beans
vinaigrette dressing (see Salad Dressing in basic recipes)
10 anchovy fillets

Drill

1. Peel and slice the tomatoes. Arrange them with the sliced cucumber in a fireproof dish. Sprinkle with chopped herbs, the lemon juice, the salt and freshly ground pepper.

2. Spread the sliced olives and the beans over the surface, add more seasoning and then pour over the dressing. Finally, arrange the anchovy fillets in a decorative fashion on the top.

3. Serve with brown bread and butter. Salade Niçoise makes an excellent accompaniment to a picnic or alternatively can be served as a first course at dinner.

ROAST STUFFED SUCKLING-PIG

A suckling-pig cooked whole makes a spectacular dish, either for a cold buffet or as a spit roaster for an open-air meal. In this recipe the pig has been boned and stuffed, which helps when serving as well as making it easier and tastier to eat.

Serves: 12-14

Preparation: 30 minutes

Cooking: 3-3½ hours

Ingredients

1 small pig, weighing about 12kg (27lbs)
salt and pepper
oil
150ml (¼pt) white wine
150ml (¼pt) veal stock
stuffing (see below)

For the stuffing

handful of fresh rosemary, roughly chopped
handful of fresh fennel leaves, roughly chopped
1 head of garlic, peeled and crushed
liver and heart of the pig, finely chopped
salt and ground black pepper

Drill

1. Ask your butcher to bone out the rib-cage from the pig. Season the inside, mix the ingredients for the stuffing and then stuff the carcass in the usual way.

2. Sew up the pig, liberally season the outside and place on an oiled roasting tray or spit.

3. Cook in an oven for about three hours at 190°C (375°F, Gas Mk 5), or for 3½-4 hours if using an open spit.

GENERAL'S RELISH

Serves: 4-6

Preparation: 15 minutes

Ingredients

450g (1lb) red peppers
1-2 red chillies
3 ripe tomatoes
1tbs caraway seeds
2-3 garlic cloves, crushed
2-3tbs olive oil

Drill

1. Cut the peppers and chillies in half and place in a lightly oiled ovenproof dish. Bake in a hot oven for about 30 minutes or until well browned and the skins are starting to crack.

2. Leave them to cool for 10 minutes, then peel, de-seed and place in a blender or food processor. Slice and add the tomatoes, caraway seeds, garlic and olive oil. Blend well and serve with cold meat, slices of the Colonel's Game Pie or Double Gloucester cheese.

ALPINE QUICHE

Serves: 4

Preparation: 15 minutes

Cooking: 45 minutes

Ingredients

8 eggs

225g (8oz) pie-crust pastry (see basic recipes)

25g (1oz) butter

200g (7oz) smoked bacon

oil

175g (6oz) Gruyère cheese

500ml (¾pt) double cream

salt and freshly ground black pepper

pinch nutmeg

Drill

1. Beat one of the eggs. Lightly butter the base and sides of a pie tin. Roll out the pastry. Line the tin with the pastry and brush with the beaten egg.

2. Chop the bacon and fry it in a little oil, taking care not to overcook it. Chop the cheese and sprinkle it with the cooked bacon over the pastry.

3. Beat the remaining eggs into the cream, add a little seasoning and the nutmeg and pour over the cheese and bacon in the pie tin, leaving enough room for the contents to rise during cooking.

4. Pre-heat the oven at 240°C (475°F, Gas Mk 9) and bake the quiche for 20 minutes, before reducing to about 190°C (375°F, Gas Mk 5) for a further 25 minutes. Serve hot or refrigerate for a picnic.

Recommended drink: dry or medium-dry white wine.

STRAWBERRY SHORTBREAD

Serves: 6

Preparation: 15 minutes

Resting: 1 hour

Assembly: 15 minutes

Ingredients

270g (9oz) flour
200g (7oz) unsalted butter
100g (4oz) icing sugar
pinch of salt
2 egg yolks
1 drop vanilla or lemon essence
800g (1lb 12oz) fresh strawberries
For the sauce
450g (1lb) fresh strawberries
110ml (4fl oz) sorbet syrup at 30 deg. density (see basic recipes)

Drill

To make the shortbread rounds

1. Sift the flour on to a work surface and make a well in the centre. Dice the butter, place in the well and work until soft.

2. Sift the icing sugar into the butter, add a pinch of salt and work together. Add the yolks and mix well. Gradually draw in the flour and mix until completely amalgamated. Add the vanilla or lemon essence and rub into the dough.

3. Place in a refrigerator to rest for at least 1 hour (it can be made up to a week in advance if wrapped in clingfilm and refrigerated).

To cook

4. Pre-heat the oven to 200°C (400°F, Gas Mk 6). Roll out the dough on a floured surface to a thickness of 2mm ($^1/_8$in).

5. Cut out 18 circles with a 10cm (4in) cutter and arrange on the baking sheet. Bake in the pre-heated oven for 6-9 minutes until lightly coloured. Leave to cool, transferring after a while to a cooling rack.

To make the sauce

6. Wash, drain and hull the fruit. Place in a food processor or liquidiser with the lemon juice and sorbet syrup and then purée them all together. Pass through a sieve and reserve in the refrigerator until required.

To assemble the dish

7. Wash the remaining strawberries, reserving half-a-dozen for garnish. Hull them, cut them in half and mix with a little of the sauce.

8. Place one of the shortbread rounds on the serving plate and cover with strawberries. Place another round on the top and add another layer of strawberries, topped with the last shortbread round. Dust with icing sugar. Then garnish with a strawberry dipped in the sauce. Serve with some of the sauce spooned round the plate.

Note: To make the dish richer, pipe cream on to each layer of strawberries.

FISH DAYS

Fish on fry-days

I don't know who discovered that fish were edible, but it must have been a very long time ago. In the history of the development of man's palate, their pedigree must rival that of apples:

Harry Nean d'Erthal: 'Hey, you know those funny scaly things that get in the way when you're having a bath? Well, guess what?'

Cyril (next cave): 'What?'

Harry: 'Well, I was down by the river the other day, doing my ablutions like, when this brute leapt right out of the water on to the bank!'

Cyril: 'Get away.'

Harry: 'No, it didn't get away, see. Straight up, I took it back to the wife, who banged on about messing up the cave. You know what women are like.'

Cyril: 'Yeah.'

Harry: 'Then she chucked it on the fire, see? "Not having that great thing staring at me", she says. Sizzled like heck it did, being a bit damp like, but after a bit I said: "Hey, that don't smell too bad, what you think?"'

Cyril: 'Blimey, don't tell me you went and ate it?'

Harry: 'Well, we tarted it up of course, added a sprig of origanum, couple of bay leaves, some crushed garlic and black peppercorns, and had it with a lemon wedge and some of those funny things that keep coming up on the lawn. And I tell you what, it were a bit of all right.'

Cyril: 'Stone the pterodactyls! What d'you reckon on calling it then?'

Harry: 'Well, the wife wanted to call it "Saumon grillé aux herbes avec champignons sauvages". But I reckon that a bit fancy like, so I've named it "Fish" 'cos that's what it sounds like when you're cooking it. 'Course, what would really go nicely with it would be a plate of French fries and a bottle of Chablis... But you can't have everything can you – not for a few more millenia anyway. And it makes one hell of a change from frozen McMammothburgers...

And so a new cuisine was born. By the time the Romans had got as far as Britain their taste-buds were so into eating seafood that Colchester oysters were ferried as far as Hadrian's wall to liven up regimental suppers for the legions ... and no doubt causing the odd bout of legionnaires' disease.

The Brits have always been less adventurous in their eating habits. 'Cow's udder and turnips was good enough for my mother and it's good enough for me' seems to sum up the attitude of the Middle Ages. When Henry I died in 1135 from a surfeit of lampreys, it only confirmed their suspicions about eating fish.

This was always seen as a kind of self-sacrifice – as indeed it literally was in Henry's case. By the 13th century there were 200 'fast days' in Britain, on which not only red meat but milk and eggs were off the menu. People were forced to eat fish as a form of penance. The French actually called their fish days *jours maigres* – lean days – which suggests that Henry I, who made his assault on the lamprey-eating record while on a cross-Channel away-day, was merely trying to fill up.

Even so, by the 16th century so few people were eating seafood that Elizabeth I was worried about the fishing fleets, on whose sailors the kingdom depended in wartime. Moreover, they were gobbling so much meat that farmers were giving over all their land to animals. In 1564 she brought in an act which turned Wednesdays as well as Fridays into 'fish days' to force people into eating more *sole meunière*. It said: 'It shall not be lawful ... to eat any flesh upon any days now usually observed as fish dayes, or upon any Wednesday now newly limited to be observed as fish dayes.'

Not until the 17th century were fish days done away with. Even then the Catholic Church, obliged to try doing without something every Friday, chose not to eat meat – which usually meant eating fish. This lasted until 1967, when it was tossed aside by an impetuous papal bull.

It should therefore come as no surprise to learn that the British come well down the world's league of fish-eaters. Each man, woman and child here ate the equivalent of 19 kilograms every year at the last count (as did the Greeks) compared with the Icelanders 88, the Japanese 74, the Norwegians 46, the Portuguese, Spanish and Finns 74, the Swedes and Russians 30, the French 25 and the Danes, Belgians, Luxembourgers and Canadians 24kg. Only the Americans and Poles with 17, the Italians and Irish (15), the Germans (12) and the Dutch (11) ate less.

Consumption in Britain, moreover, has halved since the Second World War, either because of rising prices or because the national fish-'n'-chip eating habit has given way to the tandoori chicken and Chinese takeaway. Englishmen usually prefer catching fish to eating them. The total of those who keep trying to is 4,000,000, though most catch only a cold or the bus home – and some of them not even that.

In my case I was caught by Maurice Bardelow, who was 6ft long in his socks and weighed 180lbs, dressed for winter in his Viyella woollen shirts and hacking jacket...

Maurice Bardelow was a self-professed fishing snob. He held in open contempt most of those other 3,999,999 anglers – that is to say those who spend their Sunday mornings crouched over some urban gravel pit in the rain, dangling morsels of damp dough or wriggling worm in the grey water, in the hope of ensnaring some inedible creature from the depths. He did not even recognise anglers on holiday who trail silver paper behind some chugging mackerel boat, within sight of the windswept pier and peeling bandstand. That did not, in Maurice's eyes, constitute 'fishin'. Perhaps he was right – I don't know.

The reason he invited me to join him on my one and only angling expedition was that he was really trying to hook a girl. She was the sister of some friend of his from schooldays, who was blessed with the memorable name of Esmerelda (she was that is, not her brother). I suspect that the chief reason why Maurice fancied her was that she was a distant cousin of some baronet. It was a fairly obscure British baronetcy, or would have been had not the present incumbent's mating habits earned him regular coverage in the Sunday newspapers. But this was not a deterrent to Maurice Bardelow who was a snob in his other pursuits as well as fishing. A degenerate squire was good enough for him.

Perhaps he was hoping that her noble cousin's libido had been passed, like the family plate, to Esmerelda, because he had persuaded her to accompany him on a visit to one of Britain's more famous trout streams. She had countered by asking if she could bring a friend and Maurice had reluctantly agreed, inviting me to complete a fishing foursome.

The idea was that Maurice and I would do the fishing, displaying the predatory instincts of the male, while the girls would fill the traditional woman's role – making sandwiches, pouring tea and picking wild flowers. I should explain that this was shortly before women's liberation turned such a division of labour into an indictable offence.

Anyway, there we were down by this river on what Englishmen think of as a perfect day. The water foamed and tumbled over stones or drifted in translucent, sunlit pools. A faint breeze stirred the branches of an alder tree while a kingfisher darted between the shelving banks. Maurice had somehow engineered permission to fish there through a business 'contact' of his in the City. He worked as a PR consultant – whatever that means – and shamelessly exploited his acquaintanceships. For all I know we were poaching, but I don't think so.

Esmerelda had turned out to be overtly nubile, but within a fetlock or two of sounding horsey. Plump and determined, sired by some cavalry colonel, she was trained one day to lead the Mothers' Union and open the occasional village fête. Her friend, by contrast, was quiet and self-absorbed and kept her long nose buried in a book. Nonetheless, both sat obediently on the river bank while Maurice and I proceeded to do our stuff.

Now those who have ever tried their hand at fly fishing will know that it's much more difficult than it looks – a characteristic it shares with downhill skiing and snooker. For one thing one's line gets mysteriously tangled, tying knots which Baden-Powell could not have dreamed of. For another ... well, one need not go into that because I never really surmounted the first hurdle. After two or three inexpert casts across the stream my line resembled a skein of wool which a family of cats had commandeered. After wrestling with the knots for half an hour, I recognised that my brief fishing career was over.

Maurice more than made up for my inadequacy however. Motivated by the presence of his intended, he laid on the kind of sporting demonstration worth a chapter in any manual of courtship. In his floppy tweed hat, to which clung a collection of fairly repellent flies, and with a briar pipe firmly clenched between his teeth, he looked like a television advertisement for tobacco.

Maurice saw himself in the role of big game hunter, calling on his reserves of guile to bag his prey. He selected his flies, frowning with concentration, in the manner of a housewife buying lipstick and, having tied the unpleasant creature to his line, flicked his rod with admirable skill across the stream. The fly flew temptingly above the water, skimming then briefly settling on the surface. Could any brown trout resist such a con?

Not that Maurice was at all times clearly visible. Fish, he argued, were hypersensitive to intruders. It followed that one should seek total concealment. He would hide behind a tree surveying the water, his grim expression defying one to speak, until he saw or heard a sign of movement. A soft splash in the water to his left ... an unexplained ripple on the surface to his right ... would then alert him and, bent almost double, he would sneak up behind a screen of reeds and nettles and, with a deft movement of his wrist, despatch his lure, unseen and unheard.

There was however one fly in the ointment, so to speak. This was that he failed to ensnare any fish. In at least one respect Maurice was right: the fish were not as stupid as people thought. Indeed they were even brighter than he reckoned – more intelligent, no doubt, than he was. Perhaps they caught the aroma of his pipe ... though Maurice scornfully dismissed this suggestion.

To encourage him, when his back was turned I would lob an occasional stone into the water, creating a healthy 'plop' on the far side. 'Aha,' Maurice would mutter in excitement and creep forward once more to stalk his elusive prey. But alas... For reasons which he could not understand, the trout firmly resisted all temptation. At first Maurice expressed his mild surprise. However, this changed to acute disappointment and, after two hours, to profound irritation. In planning the day he had not allowed for failure.

'I think we've struck unlucky', he kept saying. 'They probably heard us arriving on the bank and have gone orf to some quieter feeding grounds.' Then, leaning towards me with a conspiratorial whisper, he would add: 'It's the gels, you know. The fish can hear them chattering. Ah, well...'

This was in fact rather an unfair slur on womanhood because the girls had kept remarkably docile. Esmerelda, who had a country girl's healthy appetite, had already transferred her attention to her lunch and was halfway through a Melton Mowbray pie, while her more literary friend, whose name was Jane, was still lost in the latest Barbara Cartland.

Brushing away the pieces of pie-crust from her lap, Esmerelda suddenly rose authoritatively.

'Tell you what, let us have a go', she said, in a voice which brooked no denial. 'Come on, Jane' – and Jane obediently laid down Madam Cartland.

Maurice was curiously relieved by the suggestion. Those who can, do; those who can't, teach. As he seemed incapable of catching trout himself, he could at least restore his male authority by showing the young ladies how to do it.

'Splendid idea', he exclaimed – and spent the next 10 minutes or so bending over the buxom figure of Esmerelda, adjusting the rod, positioning her hands and generally testing the patience of his pupil. Eventually pushing him firmly to one side and without any pretence or subterfuge or cunning, she bawled: 'Mind your flies!' and flicked back the rod over her shoulder.

It was soon clear that she needed no help from Maurice Bardelow. The line hissed as the brightly coloured fly buzzed through the air to touch the surface of the stream as softly as a mother's kiss upon her baby. There was a flurry of movement in the water ... and then, as Esmerelda jerked the rod, a wriggling trout rose, dripping from the river.

'Good God!' said Maurice as she reeled it in. He looked hopefully along the bank to Jane, who had untangled my fishing line in 30 seconds and was discarding my bait in favour of another. She was in no more need of help than Esmerelda. He tried vainly to regain some glory as their tutor. Could it be that his expert advice ... coupled of course with a beginner's good fortune...? But by the time he had reviewed this range of options Esmerelda had captured her third while Jane was calmly unhooking her first catch.

'Maurice! Why don't you make up the sandwiches?' Esmerelda commanded, rubbing salt into a deepening open wound.

He vanished behind the trees after a while. I supposed he was answering the call of nature or was sulking in some solitary confinement. Whatever the reason, the girls seemed unaware of it. Each stood, happily chatting to the other as they steadily divested the river of its fish. For the first time they seemed to be relishing their day out.

Esmerelda was concentrating on the far bank where, in a pool beneath a protective overhanging branch, she suspected a large specimen to be lurking.

'I'll get you, you bugger!' she was murmuring to herself as she took an unusually generous measure of backswing.

As she swept the rod forward there came an agonised shriek. Clinging to it was a small circle of black velvet – which fell into the stream and disappeared. It was followed by a distressed Maurice Bardelow, stumbling blindly after the fishing line with arms outstretched.

'My contact lenses!' he cried. 'My contact lenses!'

He teetered for a second, uncertainly, on the brink – then desperately plunged into the stream. But his pursuit was far too late and badly timed.

'Oh, no, I've lost it now,' wailed Esmerelda as Maurice floundered in the muddying current. She glared unsympathetically at her host – or at what part of his corduroys was visible. His dive was indeed quite clearly in vain...

Jane skilfully drove us home in the Land Rover while Maurice sat wrapped in a car rug in the back.

'Well, I didn't know you were cleaning your beastly specs', complained Esmerelda as she counted the day's tally of brown trout. She insisted on sharing them out, saying that this was only right and proper. In happier circumstances Maurice might have interpreted the gesture as a splendid example of *noblesse oblige*.

As it was, it could not repair their romance. Some years later I asked him about Esmerelda.

'Esmerelda? Esmerelda? Esmerelda?' He puckered his brow in a great effort of recall. 'Could you just remind me, old boy...?' He remains the only fisherman I know who prefers to forget the one that got away.

✂

The Colonel, however, has never got away from his liking for eating fish, and some of his best dishes are presented below. *H.S.*

Ragoût de Poisson St Omer (page 84)

Crêpes de Fruits de Mer (page 85)

POTAGE BABBACOMBE BAY

Though mussels are among the most common varieties of shellfish, they should not be overlooked when planning a formal dinner menu. Most mussels sold in the fishmongers are now cultivated in the sea on wooden hurdles – which produce plump and tender, delicately flavoured fish. When buying mussels you should check that the shells are tightly closed and that there are not too many barnacles clinging to them.

Serves: 4

Preparation: 40 minutes

Cooking: 25 minutes

Ingredients

450g (1lb) fresh mussels
50ml (2fl oz) dry white wine
600ml (1pt) fish stock
pinches of dill, parsley and fennel
2 sticks celery, roughly chopped
½ onion, roughly chopped
50g (2oz) leeks, roughly chopped
3 cloves garlic, crushed
pinch of saffron
1tbs tomato purée
50ml (2fl oz) double cream
100g (4oz) unsalted butter
good pinch salt
sprigs of dill for garnish

Drill

1. Wash and scrape the mussels in plenty of cold water, discarding any that have open shells (cultivated mussels will have less sand and grit than those gathered from the rocks).

2. Put them in a large saucepan with a splash of white wine. Cover the saucepan and shake over a high heat. As soon as they open, remove from the heat and drain through a colander, retaining the liquid in a bowl.

3. Pass the liquid through a fine sieve into a saucepan and add the fish stock, herbs and chopped vegetables, the crushed garlic and remaining white wine. Add the saffron and the tomato purée, bring to the boil and simmer for 30 minutes.

4. Meanwhile, remove from the mussels the beards (wire-like threads found in the centre of the shellfish) and discard the shells.

5. Strain the bouillon and return to the heat. Add the double cream and butter and reduce a little by rapid boiling.

6. Remove from the heat and add the mussels (leaving behind some whole ones for garnishing). Then liquidise the mussels and bouillon in a food processor.

7. Bring the soup back to the boil and add seasoning. Garnish each soup plate with the remaining whole mussels. Pour the soup and garnish with some sprigs of dill.

Note: As an alternative method of presentation, the cream can be whipped and spooned into the soup before serving.

Recommended drink: Chilled dry sherry or dry white wine.

Salmon and Turbot Strudel

📖

Serves: 4-6

Preparation: 45 minutes

Cooking: 45 minutes

Ingredients

175g (6oz) melted butter

6 sheets filo paste

450g (1lb) salmon fillets, cut into small slices

450g (1lb) turbot fillets, cut into small slices

salt and pepper

lemon juice

3tbs olive oil

1 mix mushrooms duxelles (see basic recipes)

225g (8oz) cooked long grain rice

3 hard-boiled eggs, chopped

15g (½oz) finely chopped parsley

15g (½oz) finely chopped chervil

Drill

To prepare

1. Brush the bottom of a suitable oven-proof dish with melted butter. Lay in it one full sheet of filo paste and brush this too with butter. Repeat until you have 4 layers. Do not trim the overhang at this stage. Cover with a cloth.

To cook the fish

2. Season the fish with salt and pepper and a squeeze of lemon juice. Dribble some olive oil over the fish and leave for a few minutes.

3. Heat the rest of the oil in a thick-bottomed pan and cook the fish on both sides until set. Remove and allow to cool.

To make the strudel

4. Have all the ingredients at hand before you start to fill the dish. Begin by putting in the turbot, then a layer of Mushroom Duxelle. Add the rice, followed by the chopped egg, and sprinkle with the chopped herbs. Finish with the layer of salmon.

5. Draw up the filo overhang, brush with butter and top with 2 layers of filo paste. Brush the top with butter again and bake in a pre-heated oven at 180°C (350°F, Gas Mk 4) for about 45 minutes. Cover with foil if it colours too quickly.

🍷

Recommended drink: A chilled dry-ish white wine. The Colonel goes for Sancerre.

RAGOÛT DE POISSON ST OMER

This dish can be served as a fish or main course and can be made with almost any kind of fresh fish and shellfish. To make it lighter, leave out the pasta and garnish with fine strips of vegetables.

📖

Serves: 4

Preparation: 45 minutes

Cooking: 15 minutes

Ingredients

4 large scallops with coral

100g (4oz) each of salmon, turbot and John Dory

4 large uncooked prawns

100g (4oz) cooked lobster

6 shelled cooked mussels

30g (1¼oz) leeks, carrot and celeriac, cut into fine strips, or 75g (3oz) mixed cooked noodles

20ml (4tsp) olive oil

25ml (1fl oz) Noilly Prat

50ml (2fl oz) dry white wine

200ml (7fl oz) fish stock (see basic recipes)

50ml (2fl oz) double cream

salt and cayenne pepper

100g (4oz) diced tomato flesh

Drill

To prepare the fish

1. Open the scallops with the tip of a strong knife. Remove the scallop and coral and wash them quickly (it is best if you get your fishmonger to open them for you).

2. Cut the salmon, turbot and John Dory into small slices. Shell the prawns and slice the lobster flesh. Clean the mussels.

To cook

3. Sweat the vegetables (i.e. soften them without browning) in the olive oil for about one minute. Add the turbot, John Dory and raw prawns. Sauté for another minute, then add the scallops and salmon and cook till the flesh is just stiff. Add the Noilly Prat and dry white wine and bring to the boil.

4. Remove all the fish and vegetables with a perforated spoon and keep warm. Strain the stock into a clean pan and reduce by boiling until almost nothing is left.

5. Add the cream and boil down until it coats the back of a spoon. Return the seafood and vegetables to the liquid. Add the lobster and mussels, heat through and test for seasoning.

To serve

6. Arrange the fish and shellfish on deep plates. Spoon the cream sauce over and garnish with noodles rolled on a fork.

Recommended drink: A dry-ish white wine. The Colonel buys Chablis.

CRÊPES DE FRUITS DE MER

These sea-food pancakes could either be served as a main dish at lunchtime or made smaller and used as a starter or fish course.

Serves: 4

Preparation: 35 minutes

Cooking: 30 minutes

Ingredients

tomato coulis (*see* basic recipes)
fish cream sauce (*see* basic recipes)
4 cooked crêpes (*see* basic recipes)
100g (4oz) cooked lobster meat
225g (8oz) scallops
225g (8oz) cooked prawns
25g (1oz) butter
pepper
1tsp chopped dill
1tsp fresh basil
2 eggs
150ml (¼pt) white wine
100g (4oz) Parmesan cheese

Drill

1. Have ready the tomato coulis, fish cream sauce and the cooked crêpes. Cut the lobster and scallops into small slices, reserving a nice piece of lobster meat for decoration. Shell the prawns.

2. Heat the butter in a suitable saucepan and add the shellfish. Season with pepper and add the dill and basil. To this add about a third of the cream sauce and heat through. Keep warm. (Do not overcook or the shellfish will become rubbery.)

To finish the cream sauce

4. Mix the egg yolks with the wine and cook over a low heat or in a water bath, whisking all the time; this is called a *sabayon*. When cooked it should be the consistency of lightly whipped cream.

5. Heat the remaining cream sauce and add to the *sabayon*. Strain, cover and keep warm.

To assemble the dish

6. Mix a little of the sauce with the shellfish and divide the filling between the crêpes. Place the filling in the centre of each crêpe and fold into a small parcel.

7. Place in a serving dish, coat with the remaining fish cream sauce and dust with Parmesan cheese. Spoon the tomato sauce round the crêpes and glaze under the grill. Garnish with the remaining lobster and serve very hot.

Recommended drink: Medium white wine.

TIMBALE DE SAUMON FUMÉ AU MOUSSE DE CRABE

This dinner starter combines the flavour of smoked salmon with the richness of crab mousse. Added to this is the surprise of cutting into the soft-boiled quail's egg. The dish can be lightened by serving with an olive oil vinaigrette in place of the asparagus sauce.

Serves: 2

Preparation: 45 minutes

Ingredients

4 slices smoked salmon
225g (8oz) fresh white and dark crabmeat
fish cream sauce (see below)
2 quails' eggs, soft boiled
25g (1oz) caviar (preferably salmon)
few drops lemon juice
dill (for garnish)
asparagus sauce (see basic recipes)

For the fish cream sauce:
1 leaf gelatine
5g (¼oz) butter
1 medium-sized shallot
450ml (¾pt) fish stock
half a bay leaf
50ml (2fl oz) Noilly Prat
300ml (½pt) double cream
salt and pepper
8 peppercorns

Drill

To prepare the moulds

1. Line 2 small ramekins with the smoked salmon, allowing the edges to hang over the side of each dish. Store in the refrigerator until wanted.

To make the base sauce for the mousse

2. Soak the leaf gelatine in cold water until soft.

3. Melt the butter in a pan and add the chopped shallot. Cook until soft but without browning.

4. Add the fish stock and bay leaf and then reduce by three-quarters. Add the Noilly Prat and reduce by the same amount again. Add the double cream and reduce to the consistency of a thin sauce.

5. Add the leaf gelatine and stir until dissolved. Pass the sauce through a fine strainer. Do not let this get too cold or the sauce will set before it has been mixed with the crab meat.

6. Mix the sauce and crab flesh together, season with salt and pepper and flavour with lemon juice.

7. Cook the quail eggs to the degree you like them, cool in iced water and remove the shells.

To assemble the mousse

8. Half fill the salmon-lined moulds. Put the quails' eggs into the moulds and press down lightly. Top up with the rest of the mousse and fold over the flaps of salmon to form a neat parcel. Chill for 1½ hours.

To serve

9. Turn out the moulds on to a chilled plate. Brush the top with olive oil and decorate with salmon caviar and dill. Serve with asparagus sauce or vinaigrette dressing.

Recommended drink: A medium white wine such as a Riesling.

LOBSTER SOUFFLÉ

📖

Serves: 4

Preparation: 40 minutes

Cooking: 25 minutes

Ingredients

For the soufflé
1 cooked lobster

150ml (¼pt) white wine

300ml (½pt) fish stock

15g (½oz) butter

50g (2oz) butter

50g (2oz) flour

4 egg yolks

150ml (¼pt) single cream

Parmesan cheese to dust

cayenne pepper and salt to taste

For the sauce:
300ml (½pt) fish stock

250ml (¼ bottle) dry white wine

450ml (¾pt) double cream

3 egg yolks

6tbs whipping cream

Drill

1. Take all the meat from the lobster by first detaching the tail from the head. Make a cut down the middle of the underside of the tail and then, by pulling open the two sides of the shell, the meat can be lifted out easily. Make a shallow cut down the top of the tail meat and remove the gut (a small tube that will probably be full of sand).

2. Remove the claws and extract the meat from these by tapping the shell with the back of a large knife. Split the head down the middle and reserve the liver (a small grey-green paste) which can be added to the soufflé mix to improve the flavour.

3. Remove the stomach sac, found directly behind the eyes, and discard. Reserve some of the head shell and legs for decoration. Chop the remainder of the shell into small pieces.

4. Slice the meat into medium slices. Any trimmings can be finely diced and added to the soufflé.

5. Add the shell and white wine to the fish stock and cook for 5-10 minutes to extract the flavour. Strain and rectify the amount to ½pt, using water.

6. Butter and flour 4 individual soufflé moulds, making sure that they are well covered (or the soufflés will not rise).

To make the soufflé

7. Melt the butter in a pan. Add the flour and cook for a few minutes. Add the fish stock, a little at a time to form a thick sauce. Cook for 3-4 minutes. Remove from the heat and allow to cool a little.

8. Add the egg yolks, beating well, and the single cream. Season and add any lobster trimmings at this stage. Set aside on a cool part of the stove.

To make the sauce

9. Reduce the fish stock and white wine to the consistency of a light syrup. Add the double cream and reduce again by a third. Season to taste. Add the egg yolks and whipped cream to the sauce and keep at blood heat.

10. Whip the egg whites to a stiff snow and add half to the base soufflé mix. Fold in well. Add the other half, mixing very lightly with a large spoon.

11. Pour the mix into the moulds to just below the rim. Dust with Parmesan cheese and place in a very hot oven at 204°C (400°F, Gas Mk 7). They will take about 20 minutes to cook.

To serve

12. Heat the lobster meat in a pan with a small knob of butter. Arrange a little in the centre of each plate.

13. When the soufflés are cooked, de-mould and place a soufflé on the top of the lobster meat. Spoon the sauce over all and glaze under a hot grill. Arrange the shell as decoration.

Note: You must work at speed from the time that the soufflés are put on the plate or they will lose their height. Fresh herbs may be used in the sauce and on the shell to enhance the appearance of the dish.

Recommended drink: Medium-dry white wine.

THE
SHOOTING
PARTY

The shooting party

No shooting party is complete without the Colonel, but this is not because he is an especially good shot. The only people in the Army who can shoot straight are its cooks, which is why those who run the Service, like the Royal Greenjackets, keep them safely out of range behind their hotplates. The Catering Corps is the army's secret weapon.

No, the Colonel is there in an ex-officio role. Like oak trees, Ann Hathaway's cottage and the vicar, he belongs to that job lot known as rural Britain. In Harris tweed and thornproof hat, he stands in the saloon bar of the pub, saying things like 'absolutely grand' and 'capital'. He calls the landlord 'John', 'Sam' or 'Bert' and the landlord calls him 'Colonel' in return. No parochial church council or village fête could take place while the Colonel is on holiday. He belongs to a world reassuringly arcane, preserved from Panda cars and fast food takeaways. He may no longer know how things are done, but he understands better than anyone how they should be. A shooting party without the Colonel and his Holland and Holland would be like rhubarb crumble without cream.

He was missing from the shoot that I went on – the first and almost certainly the last. I like to think that his absence was to blame for the sequence of events which came to pass. Without a pillar of the Establishment to lean on, a host enters unknown territory at his peril.

It was at a dinner party some few years ago that a friend – well, more of an acquaintance really – casually asked me if I shot and, if so, would I care to join a shooting party? I think he asked me only because he had drunk half a bottle of Margaux; and I said 'Yes' because I had had the other half. It is usually more prudent to say 'perhaps' – then wait till dawn.

The nearest thing to a shooting party I had been on had been organised by the Royal Regiment of Artillery, who had taken my participation somewhat for granted. It had happened one Winter's day during National Service when, as a change from burnishing boots and boxing socks, we had been allowed out from out hutted camp in Shropshire to fire our 25-pounders among the sheep-sprinkled hills of North-West Wales.

This particular shoot could have ended in disaster because there was a misfire on our gun (things always seemed to happen on our gun). We had been taught a simple drill for such occasions, which was just to sit tight and call for help. It was the one drill that I not only remembered but fully endorsed. At the controls that day, however, was a Welshman called Jones who, evidently thinking he could handle things himself, pulled the reject lever instead. Thereupon the breech flew open and the live shell with its charge shot out backwards, to land with a dull thud upon the heather. This was followed by an awful lot of shouting, most of it by our sergeant who, having survived the battle of El Alamein in the Western Desert, felt unprepared to meet the Great Reaper in West Wales.

It was hardly a shoot in the classic sense of the word. But I have always looked back on the drama with some pleasure, as the only one during two years in the Army for which I was not held entirely to blame. Our sergeant was as surprised by this as anyone. He kept looking at me warily ever afterwards, unwilling to believe it was not somehow my fault.

I had, however, a preconceived vision of the real thing, following a lifetime of thumbing through *The Field* in dentists' waiting rooms. The opening scene in this featured a great house (either in Scotland or East Anglia) whose towering escarpments overshadowed the shooting brake in the forecourt. From this spilled tweedy girls in cashmere scarves, husky men (called 'Clive) in caps and springer spaniels. There were picnic hampers from Fortnums and gleaming shotguns, their double barrels poking out from the bottles of Highland malt. Of such ads in the Sunday supplements are dreams made of.

The house to which I repaired that Autumn day was neither in Scotland nor in Norfolk but in Wales. It turned out to be one of those isolated farms which farmers desert because they can't get BBC2 or running water, and which are bought by TV producers and their live-ins. It was a long, low ramshackle dwelling built round a yard, with cowsheds now housing my friend's Volvo, a rusting trailer and several bikes.

I was late arriving, thanks partly to British Rail and partly to the station being 30 miles away. Our host, whose name was Helmwood, was pacing impatiently up and down the yard, waiting for everyone else to finish breakfast. An aroma of burnt toast and coffee hung in the air, and by the time we broke camp and departed for the shoot, it was already nearly time for lunch.

The party consisted of Helmwood, who was going through a phase of playing the country squire – a symptom of the male menopause in West Hampstead; his wife, who was sensibly waiting for him to get over it; my host's solicitor, whom he was trying to impress, with a girl-friend called Sue; an Indian doctor; and a neighbouring farmer who was cast in the part of local guide. There was no sight of tweedy birds or barking blokes, no team of faithful beaters and no Colonel. The nearest thing Helmwood had to an old retainer was a cleaning lady who came round on Tuesdays and Fridays to do the floors and had gone off that day on a trip to Marks and Spencer. We had to lock up the house ourselves before leaving.

The farmer led the way in an old Vauxhall, accompanied by the solicitor and Sue and a smelly sheepdog with one blue eye and one brown, which was playing the demanding role of faithful gun-dog. I travelled in the back of the Volvo with the Indian doctor – whose name, confusingly enough, was not Patel. We turned off along a bumpy track and after plunging and swaying up and down, at one point crossing a turbulent little stream, climbed steadily for several miles on to the moors. After a while the farmer ahead of us began making elaborate hand signals, like someone on his third or fourth driving test, and pulled off the track beneath a belt of trees. We parked our car beside his and climbed out.

It was at that point that somebody spotted that I had no gun. I suppose most people know that to take part in any shoot one needs a gun. To turn up without one is like going to work without one's trousers. Even Sue and the Indian doctor, who was called Mr Veera-something, each had guns. Mr Veera-something had even brought two of them, each of which looked expensive and unfashionably new. But then the Army had previously supplied mine.

'I thought you said you shot,' said Helmwood somewhat testily.

'I'm terribly sorry,' I said, 'but I forgot it.'

The others looked at me gravely, as if having unmasked a member of the Travellers' Club who had never been farther than Brighton.

In the end Mr Veera-something lent me one of his, after patiently showing me how to load it. I have always regretted the passing of the muzzle-loader, which left one in little doubt about such matters.

And so, to the butts: stumbling along for a few hundred yards just below a ridge – the kind of position Wellington favoured for his infantry – before our host began stationing each of us at our firing points. I was given a spot between Mr Veera-something and friend Helmwood, though fortunately just out of sight of either of them. I say 'fortunately' because this is how it seemed to me at the time: with hindsight, a clearer view of them might have helped.

I swivelled my gun experimentally round wild Wales. I was just beginning to realise that I had no idea of what we were supposed to be shooting. On this point Helmwood had been imprecise, and the moment to ask had surely passed by.

After a while I heard some distant hollering by the farmer in the manner of one who was either trying to flush out game or had shot himself rather painfully in the foot. This was followed by a ragged volley of small-arms fire. But what they were aiming at remained a mystery. A curlew wheeled and fluted overhead, apparently unaware of any threat. A lark rose from the grass some 50 yards away – a tempting target in Italy perhaps, but hardly worthy of the term 'country pursuit'.

It was at that point that I heard Helmwood bawl out my name, followed by the time-honoured call to arms: 'Your bird!'

Perplexed, I scanned the horizon in vain. Alas, of a target there was no obvious sign. Not even a rabbit scuttled over the purple moor. Moreover, my arms were beginning to ache from the weight of bearing arms for half-an-hour or so.

Suddenly there flew into my line of vision a rook, which flapped noisily towards a nearby tree, cawing like crazy. So that was it, it dawned upon me – rooks! Relieved at having the problem solved at last, I levelled the gun, shut one eye and squeezed the trigger. The recoil and deafening report were followed several milliseconds later by a sound which was less identifiable but infinitely more alarming: a crash indicative of some collateral damage. There was then an uneasy calm and ominous silence, during which the rook, its feathers and its temperament unruffled, reached the relative security of its tree.

'What was that?' I heard someone call to my right.

'No idea', someone responded to my left.

Then, 'Good God!' cried Helmwood. 'He's shot my bloody car!'

Amid the confusion which followed, one thing was clarified. I had been facing in the opposite direction to 'the shoot'. It was not much consolation, but it was something. So was the fact that had I been aiming for the Volvo it would have been a very fine shot indeed. The windscreen had been very absolutely middled.

Helmwood spoke little to me after that. He would, I suspect, have said more, had he not discovered that his wife had forgotten to bring the picnic hamper. The wind had increased by now and a fine rain was sweeping the moor, accompanied by a sharp drop in the temperature. Still clinging to his theme of gracious living, Helmwood called for a generous slug of cherry brandy. It was then that his wife's misdemeanour came to light. Breakfast suddenly seemed an awfully long time ago and the discovery that we had no food or drink created a temporary, not unwelcome diversion. The journey back to the farm was long and cold, with the pure Welsh air and rain whipping in through the damaged windscreen of the car.

I offered to pay for the damage of course – and of course he refused to accept. I have not seen him since. I believe he got rid of the farm-house shortly afterwards: it got caught up in the long divorce proceedings. It had been only a phase of Helmwood's middle life. Still, I wished I had found out what targets I had missed. The Army had, at least, always made this clear.

Had the Colonel been there, of course, it would all have been so different. In Isabel Colegate's book *The Shooting Party* they shot pheasant and later wild duck and ate lobster vol-au-vents and chicken mayonnaise, washed down by chilled champagne (or lemon squash). Even the loaders and beaters had rabbit stew.

It is therefore with the benefit of experience that I commend these following pages to the reader. In case he or she stops a Volvo in its tracks, a little care with the victuals is advisable. Ask the Colonel.   *H.S.*

Timbale de Saumon Fumé au Mousse de Crabe (page 87)

Lobster Soufflé (page 89)

POACHER'S POT

📖

Serves: 4

Preparation: 15 minutes

Cooking: 15 minutes

Ingredients

25g (1oz) butter
1 large onion, sliced
175g (6oz) cooked game (pheasant, partridge, grouse or hare)
1tbs mixed herbs
25g (1oz) flour
900ml (1½pts) stock
1 glass sherry
1tsp redcurrant jelly
1tsp lemon juice
salt and pepper
croûtons for accompaniment

Drill

1. Melt the butter in a large saucepan, add the sliced onion and sauté gently until soft but not brown.

2. Mince the cooked game and add to the pan, stirring into the onion. Add the mixed herbs, then sprinkle on the flour and mix well.

3. Gradually add the stock and bring to the boil, then pass the soup through an electric blender or rub through a fine sieve.

4. Return to the stove and bring back to the boil. Simmer for several minutes, then add the sherry, redcurrant jelly and lemon juice. Stir into the soup.

5. Skim off any fat on the surface, then season to taste and serve with fried bread croûtons.

HIGHLAND PÂTÉ

Serves: 6

Preparation: 30 minutes

Cooking: 3 hours

Ingredients

450g (1lb) veal
1-2tbs Armagnac
2tbs red wine
1 pheasant
25g (1oz) butter
450g (1lb) pork fat
1 egg
pinch mixed herbs
1tbs chopped parsley

Drill

1. Pre-heat the oven to 200°C (400°F, Gas Mk 6). Slice the veal, place in a basin and add the Armagnac and red wine. Leave to marinade for 1 hour.

2. Season the pheasant, put it in a roasting tin with a little butter and cook it in the oven for up to 20 minutes.

3. Take out the pheasant and, after it has cooled, cut away the meat from the carcass.

4. Mince the pheasant meat, veal and about half of the pork fat together. Add the mixed herbs, parsley and the liquid from the marinade, season well and beat in the egg.

5. Butter the sides of a dish and fill it with the pâté, spreading sliced of pork fat on the top. Cover with tinfoil.

6. Pre-heat the oven to 110°C (225°F, Gas Mk¼). Stand the pâté dish in a baking pan with a little water around it to keep it moist and cook very slowly for about 2-2½ hours. Remove and refrigerate overnight before serving.

SADDLE OF HARE WITH BEETROOT SAUCE

The flavour of hare has been appreciated in the countryside for generations, but only of late has it become popular on restaurant menus in the cities. The saddle of the hare is the only part suitable for the dish, the rest being reserved for the game pie recipe or for pâtés and terrines.

📖

Serves: 4

Preparation: 20 minutes

Cooking: 30 minutes

Ingredients

2 loins of hare cut from the saddle
salt and freshly ground pepper
25g (1oz) butter
225g (8oz) fresh noodles
2 small cooked beetroot

For the sauce:

1 shallot, finely chopped
1 heaped tbs redcurrant jelly
50ml (2fl oz) raspberry vinegar
100ml (4fl oz) port
150ml (6fl oz) red wine
150ml (6fl oz) veal stock
150ml (6fl oz) game stock

For the marinade:

150ml (6fl oz) red wine
100ml (4fl oz) port
small amount crushed garlic to taste
4tbs oil

Drill

1. Ask your butcher to prepare the hare. Trim all the sinews from the two loins and marinade overnight in red wine, port, crushed garlic and oil.

2. Remove the hare from the marinade and pat dry. Season with salt and pepper, then pan-fry in a little butter and oil until pink. Remove from the pan, pour the juice over the meat and keep warm.

To prepare the beetroot and cook the noodles

3. Cook the noodles in plenty of water. Strain and twist with a fork into four portions. Keep warm.

4. Cut the beetroot into short strips, reserving the trimmings for the sauce.

To make the sauce

5. Add the chopped shallots to the same pan and sweat until soft. Add the redcurrant jelly and slightly caramelise. Add the vinegar and the port and reduce until a syrup forms. Add the red wine, game and veal stock and the beetroot trimmings. Reduce until the liquid coats the back of a spoon.

To serve

6. Slice the hare by carving at an angle, and arrange on four plates.

7. Reheat the sauce and strain. Return the sauce to the heat and shake in the butter, a knob at a time. Do not re-boil. Adjust the seasoning and spoon the sauce around the meat. Garnish with the noodles and beetroot.

Recommended drink: Full-bodied Burgundy-type red wine.

THE COLONEL'S GAME PIE

Cold game pie is a traditional British dish which can be made with any combination of game that is in season. To give the pie more flavour, the game can be marinated in port or red wine for 24 hours before making the pie. The back fat used to line the inside of the pie can be replaced with rashers of bacon if preferred.

📖

Serves: 6-8

Preparation: 1½-2 hours

Cooking: 2½ hours

Ingredients

1kg (2¼lbs) pie pastry (see basic recipes)
350g (12oz) bacon back fat
675g (1½lbs) hare or pheasant or partridge or grouse or a mixture of all
225g (8oz) lean pork
225g (8oz) fat pork
1 glass madeira
½ glass brandy
½ glass port
salt and pepper
pinch mixed spice
100g (4oz) pistachio nuts
1 bay leaf
1 egg
600ml (1pt) Game jelly (see basic recipes)

Drill

1. Prepare the pie pastry according to the basic recipe and place to rest for 20 minutes. Grease a raised pie mould (or high-sided cake or bread tin) and line it with two-thirds of the paste, leaving an overhang at the top. Then line the pastry, bottom and sides, with the thin slices of the bacon back fat.

To make the filling

2. Bone the game and remove the fillets. Roll some of the fillets in back fat to form a decoration. Remove all sinews from the rest of the game and place in a food processor with the lean and fat pork. Process to the texture of a fine paste, add the madeira, brandy and port, season well and add the pistachio nuts.

To fill the pie

3. Place half the mixture in the prepared mould and arrange the fillets all facing the same way; cover with the rest of the mixture. Do not over-fill as the mixture will expand during cooking.

4. Cover with the rest of the back fat and place a small bay leaf on top, then cover with the rest of the pastry. Trim the excess pastry and use to make decorations for the top. Make a hole in the centre to allow the steam to escape during cooking. Brush with beaten egg and rest the pie in a cool place for one hour.

To cook the pie

5. Brush the pie once more with the egg and bake in a medium oven at 375°F (190°C, Gas Mk 5) for 2½ hours. To test if it is cooked, insert a thin skewer into the middle.

6. Remove from the oven and rest the pie for 20 minutes, leaving it in the mould. Fill the pie with Game jelly through the hole. You may need to top up with the jelly several times. Leave to cool overnight before removing the mould and slicing.

Recommended drink: Claret or, if eaten with salad, an unabashed fruity white wine.

ROAST GROUSE WITH LENTILS AND WALNUT SAUCE

First shoot your grouse, preferably during the season: August 12th (the 'Glorious Twelfth') to December 10th. Alternatively your poulterer should oblige. If he too finds grouse elusive, other game birds like pheasant or partridge might deputise. Few *aprés*-shoot dishes we know make a tough day on the moors seem so worthwhile.

📖

Serves: 2

Preparation: 35 minutes

Cooking: 30 minutes

Ingredients

2 grouse

30ml (2tbs) clarified butter (see basic recipes)

salt and freshly milled pepper

4 rashers bacon

For the lentils:

225g (8oz) green lentils

1 sprig thyme

½ bay leaf

1 clove garlic

15g (½oz) butter

1tsp each of finely diced carrot, celery and shallot

For the walnut sauce:

3tbs walnut oil

8 shallots, finely chopped

1tbs finely chopped walnuts

1 clove garlic

½tbs cognac

1tbs wine vinegar

100ml (4fl oz) dry white wine

450ml (¾pt) Madeira

450ml (¾pt) chicken stock

1 sprig thyme

salt and pepper

knob of butter

Drill

For the grouse and lentils

1. Take out the wishbone from the grouse (this will help when later removing the breast from the carcass), brush all over with clarified butter and sprinkle with salt and pepper.

2. Cover with the bacon and place in the centre of a medium oven at 180°C (350°F, Gas Mk 4) for 20-30 minutes.

3. Meanwhile put the lentils, thyme, bay leaf and garlic into a pan. Add just enough cold water to cover, bring to boil and simmer for 25 minutes.

4. Take out the grouse from oven at the end of their cooking time and rest in a warm place for 15 minutes.

5. Drain the lentils when ready, remove the herbs and leave to cool.

6. Remove the breasts from the grouse at the end of the 15 minutes resting period and keep warm.

7. Place the butter for the lentils in a frying pan and heat over a moderate flame until foaming. Add the *brunoise* of finely diced carrot, shallot and celery and cook until soft. Add the lentils and heat gently to warm through.

For the sauce

8. Chop up the legs and carcass of the grouse.

9. Heat the walnut oil in a heavy pan, add the shallots and cook until soft.

10. Add the chopped-up carcass, the chopped walnuts and the garlic. Increase the heat, add the cognac and flame.

11. Add the vinegar and reduce, then add the wine and Madeira and reduce by two-thirds. Add all the stock and reduce by two-thirds again. Flavour with the thyme and season with salt and pepper.

12. When the sauce is rich and will cover the back of a spoon, strain through a fine strainer and keep hot.

To serve

13. Arrange the lentils in the middle of a warm serving dish, slice the breast of grouse and arrange on top.

14. Shake the butter into the sauce (this is called 'mounting' the sauce and will give it richness and shine). Pour over the grouse and garnish the dish with skinned walnuts and grapes.

Recommended drink: Full-bodied red wine.

STALKER'S SUPPER

Venison has grown in popularity in recent years. Lean and richly flavoured, it provides a welcome diversion from other red meats. The Colonel's Lady finds this casserole an easy way of keeping her own stag happy.

Serves: 4

Preparation: 10 minutes

Cooking: 2¾ hours

Ingredients

675g (1½lb) lean venison (boned haunch)
75g (3oz) butter
good pinch cinnamon
good pinch nutmeg
salt and pepper
100g (4oz) diced bacon
1 large onion, sliced
75g (3oz) flour
25g (1oz) tomato purée
300ml (½pt) red wine or port
175g (6oz) mushrooms
1 small tin cranberries

Drill

1. Dice the venison and sauté in the butter until lightly coloured.

2. Add the spices, seasoning, bacon and onions and sauté a further 2 minutes.

3. Add the flour, and mix in well with the other ingredients.

4. Add the tomato purée, wine or port and bring to the boil; correct the consistency with stock or extra wine if necessary.

5. Add the mushrooms and cranberries, check the seasoning.

6. Cover and simmer for 2-2½ hours in a slow oven at 150°C (300°F, Gas Mk 2), until the meat is tender.

7. Serve with hot noodles.

Recommended drink: Full-bodied red wine.

AFTERNOON TEA

'... There's nothing quite like a nice cup of tea'

Lieutenant Colonel George Clarence Clarence had just been appointed to command and was already bored with explaining why his long-dead father had, in a whimsical moment, given him the second Christian name 'Clarence'. It was a turgid exercise and one that the Colonel had had to endure for the entire 20 years he had been in the Service. To his irritation, he was known throughout the Army as 'Clarrie' Clarence and only his wife called him George. On a brighter note, however, he had noticed that the family parrot was also giving 'George' a go.

Clarrie Clarence took command on the Friday and let it be known that during the following week he intended to 'visit all departments'. There was to be 'no fuss' and his visits were to be 'informal'. He also let it be known that he was a 'stickler for excellence' and an 'upholder of high standards'.

Colonel Clarence, now referred to joyously by his soldiers as 'C²', decided to visit the catering department on Tuesday, a sound base for his subsequent forays to the Warrant Officers' and Sergeants' Mess and the Officers' Mess.

It is against the setting of Colonel Clarence's arrival in his Regiment that you, gentle reader, should be aware that there are many areas of human endeavour in which the British Army excels. It has found fame in all corners of the globe by its skill at arms and its gallantry. Similarly, it is public knowledge from Calcutta to Catterick, and from Tobruk to Tidworth, that the British Army is incapable of making a half decent cup of tea.

Tea remains the staple drink of the British soldier, although coffee is now making its presence felt; indeed Colonel Clarence had just had a cup of coffee that brisk October morning and he felt replete as he strode out on one of the first of his visits to what he was pleased to call 'the cookhouse'.

Staff Quartermaster-Sergeant Durrington, the Master Chef, was a man known throughout the Regiment as hard to please and on no account to be upset. He was large, fierce, red-haired, tattooed and very, very good at his job. What's more, he knew it. He didn't actually need anyone, but everyone at all levels in the Regiment needed him and his goodwill. Warrant Officer Durrington knew that too.

Lt. Col. Clarence Clarence and WO2 (SQMS) Durrington met at 'the cookhouse' door. The military rituals were observed and Durrington's arm almost caused a sonic boom as it snapped to his side after his salute. Following a few pleasantries, Durrington ushered his Colonel into his office, sat him down and, in a bellow that might have given the local environmental group cause to complain about noise pollution, howled 'Arkwright – get in 'ere now.'

There was a sound of frantic activity outside the office and suddenly a young soldier chef catapulted into the office. 'Salute, you 'orrible idle man,' snarled Durrington and Private Arkwright, still off balance from his precipitate entry into the office, banged his elbow painfully on a filing cabinet as he sought to pay compliments to his Colonel.

Durrington eyed Arkwright as a stoat would eye a rabbit and then commanded 'a mug of my special tea for the Colonel and another one for me'. He paused and added, rather unnecessarily, 'Now.' Arkwright saluted, banged his damaged elbow on the ill-named funny bone, and went about his master's bidding. 'There's nothing quite like a nice cup of tea,' philosophised Durrington, and George Clarence nodded, absently, in agreement.

Seconds only passed and Arkwright returned bearing two pint china mugs, from each of which a plume of steam rose to the nicotine-stained ceiling above. A fly passing through the vapour did a complete barrel roll and hit the window with a soft thud. It fell to the window-ledge, jerked spasmodically and then, its limbs rigid, lay still.

Colonel Clarence viewed his mug of tea with stark disbelief.

It was deepest mahogany in colour.

It had an oily scum upon the surface.

It smelled highly unattractive and it looked a deal worse.

The Master Chef's 'tea' was, it seems, the stuff of which legends are made. The early shift chef who paraded for duty at 0500 hours was charged, each morning, with making a bucket of strong tea – the Army being provisioned by a thoughtful and caring government with a piece of equipment called to this day a 'bucket tea stainless steel 3 gall'.

At about 0510 hours each morning this bucket of tea had added to it several tins of condensed milk, and the resulting mixture was placed on a corner of the stove to brew, simmer, infuse, mature, fester, suppurate or whatever other verb takes your fancy. Within the hour this 'tea' had developed a thick crust that broke from time to time as the boiling action of the liquid created pressure and fractured the surface. It was not a pretty sight.

The Master Chef usually got to his office at 0730, having first inspected breakfast in the Warrant Officers' and Sergeants' Mess and then in the Officers' Mess. It was thus at 0733 that he sent for his first mug of 'tea' and, during the course of the day, he drank the entire bucketful. He was wont to favour a few special friends with a share of his bucket. Lesser people were offered coffee or nothing, and the pecking order was well-known within the Regiment.

Very new Second Lieutenants were given 'tea' on first joining but rarely afterwards, as they were creatures of no possible consequence in the life of the SQMS, but he felt the need to be welcoming.

The Commanding Officer was clearly a person of consequence and his invitation to take tea with the SQMS a tangible product of his seniority.

C^2 raised the mug to his lips, anxious not to give offence to his host, but now only too aware of the significance of the Regimental Sergeant Major's remark, 'You'll enjoy a cup of tea and a yarn with old Durrington, sir.' The mug hovered below Clarence Clarence's nose and the bitter odour of long boiled tea combined with the sickly properties of condensed milk assailed his nostrils.

He took a tentative sip.

The tea was ghastly.

The flavour was something far beyond the experience of his taste buds.

The liquid coated his teeth and they shrieked in protest.

Colonel Clarence Clarence realised that this was ridiculous. He was, after all, the Commanding Officer and he did not have to do any damned thing he didn't want to do. He had just resolved to reject the tea when Durrington murmured, 'Drink up, sir, not everyone gets a wet from my special bucket, only you and the RSM.' C^2 wavered, the choices not being great: drink the tea and probably die in excruciating pain from some frightful malady, or reject the tea firmly and offend a very senior Warrant Officer and a key member of the Regiment.

Command is a lonely state, a fact which countless officers will confirm. It requires a man to appreciate a situation, make a judgement and implement a course of action. Lt. Col. Clarence knew the theory and now he was faced with the practice. He had only the two options: he did the decent, gentlemanly and officer-like thing.

C^2 raised the mug to his lips and quaffed deeply of the contents. He closed his mind to the anguish of his tortured taste buds and his nostrils to the pungent, bitter smell of the noxious fluid.

It was hell but, as someone once said, 'Life's a bitch.'

He quaffed again.

He took a third deep draught.

His stomach said, 'Now hang on a minute.'

A surreptitious glance into the deeply stained mug revealed that half of the contents remained. With a sigh of resignation the Colonel launched himself again. Three vast swallows later, he banged the now empty mug down upon the desk. His stomach had had enough, rebelled and gave early warning that it was going to pop up and visit its good friend throat.

The wave of nausea passed and, given firm assurances by its owner that the abuse was at an end, C^2's stomach returned home grumbling.

Colonel Clarence Clarence, by his body language, sent signals tht he was about to leave. Durrington appeared not to notice, nodding at the empty mug, 'Enjoy that, Colonel?' he enquired. C^2 made a non-committal movement of his shoulders and prepared to make a statement on his position vis-à-vis tea. He didn't get the chance because Durrington with a beam on his face summoned Arkwright with an ear-blistering bellow: 'Arkwright, bring me two more mugs of my special tea,' and then, in an aside to his Colonel, he said apologetically, 'I almost forgot.' Raising his voice to its previous volume, he added, 'and bring in the cucumber sandwiches from the fridge.'

⚔

There follow suggestions for an altogether more delectable afternoon tea.

T.N.

FRUIT AND WALNUT CAKE

Serves: 8-10

Preparation: 30 minutes

Cooking: 2½ hours

Ingredients

225g (8oz) butter
225g (8oz) soft brown sugar
4 eggs, separated
3tbs brandy, rum or sherry
225g (8oz) plain flour
pinch salt
½tsp mixed spice
½tsp nutmeg
100g (4oz) currants
100g (4oz) raisins
100g (4oz) sultanas
100g (4oz) chopped walnuts
To decorate:
100g (4oz) whole walnuts

Drill

1. Set the oven to 160°C (325°F, Gas Mk 3). Line an 8in cake tin with a double thickness of greaseproof paper.

2. Soften the butter in a bowl, using a wooden spoon. Add the sugar and beat thoroughly until soft and light. Then beat the egg yolks into the butter with the sherry (or spirit).

3. Sift the flour with the salt and spices and divide it into three portions. Very lightly fold one portion into the butter and egg mixture and mix the second portion with the prepared fruit and walnuts.

4. Whisk the egg whites until stiff, add the fruit and nuts to the butter mixture, then fold in the remaining portion of the flour and egg whites.

5. Turn the mixture into the prepared tin and decorate the top with whole walnuts. bake in the pre-heated oven for about 2½ hours. Test if the cake is cooked by piercing with a trussing needle or fine skewer (which should come away clean). Turn cake out of tin to cool.

Saddle of Hare with Beetroot Sauce (page 99)

The Colonel's Game Pie (page 101)

CREAM SCONES

📖

Serves: 4-6

Preparation: 30 minutes

Cooking: 15 minutes

Ingredients

225g (8oz) flour
pinch salt
15g (½oz) baking powder
60g (2½ oz) butter
50g (2oz) caster sugar
150ml (¼pt) sour cream
egg wash

Drill

1. Sift the flour, salt and baking powder into a bowl and rub in the butter, achieving a rich, fine sandy texture.

2. Make a well in the centre, add the sugar and sour cream and gradually mix in the flour to create a soft dough (beware of toughening it by over-mixing).

3. Roll out the dough to a thickness of ½-¾ inch and, using either a plain or fancy cutter, divide it into scones about 2-2½ inches in diameter.

4. Place these on a baking sheet and brush with milk or egg wash. Allow to stand for about 15 minutes in a warm part of the kitchen before cooking in a fairly hot oven at 380°F (190°C, Gas Mk 5) for about 12-15 minutes.

5. After taking them out, allow to cool and then split them and serve with cream and jam.

Note: 3oz sultanas can be added to the above mix at the same time as the flour.

FARMHOUSE CAKE

Serves: 6-8

Preparation: 35 minutes

Cooking: 2 hours

Ingredients

450g (1lb) self-raising flour
pinch salt
225g (8oz) butter
225g (8oz) demerara sugar
225g (8oz) raisins
225g (8oz) sultanas
225g (8oz) currants
100g (4oz) mixed peel
pinch ground nutmeg
3 eggs
110ml (4fl oz) milk
granulated sugar for the top

Drill

1. Line a 9in tin with greaseproof paper. Sift the flour and salt into a bowl and rub in the butter until the mixture becomes fine and crumbly. Add the sugar and mix well. Then add the fruit which has been mixed with the nutmeg.

2. Beat the eggs and add to the flour and butter mix, using enough milk to make the mixture just drop from the spoon. Put the mix into a prepared tin and lightly sprinkle with granulated sugar.

3. Bake in a moderate oven at 150°C (300°F, Gas Mk 3) for 2 hours.

Date and Honey Cake

Serves: 6-8

Preparation: 30 minutes

Cooking: 1 hour

Ingredients

350g (12oz) flour
15g (½oz) milk powder
1½tsp baking powder
200g (7oz) caster sugar
50g (2oz) honey
150g (5oz) butter
2 large eggs
125ml (4½fl oz) water
1tsp glycerine
100g (4oz) dates, chopped
50g (2oz) sultanas
nib sugar for the top

Drill

1. Sieve the flour, milk powder, baking powder and sugar, then mix with the honey and butter until a crumbly consistency is achieved.

2. Mix the eggs, water and glycerine into the above mixture and beat until smooth. Add the chopped dates and the sultanas, taking care not to over-mix at this stage. Allow to rest for 15 minutes.

3. Place the mixture in a 9 x 3in loaf tin which has been greased with margarine and lined with greaseproof paper. Sprinkle the top with nib sugar.

4. Bake in a pre-heated oven at 185°C (360°F, Gas Mk 4) for about 1 hour.

CORNISH FRUIT BREAD

📖

Serves: 6

Preparation: 10 minutes

Resting: 2 hours

Cooking: 30 minutes

Ingredients

550g (1¼lb) strong flour
1tsp salt
15g (½oz) fresh yeast
300ml (½pt) lukewarm milk
100g (4oz) butter
75g (3oz) caster sugar
3 eggs
grated rind of one lemon
pinch saffron powder
75g (3oz) currants
100g (4oz) raisins
12 glacé cherries

Drill

1. Sift the flour and salt into a bowl and make a well in the centre. Stir the yeast into the lukewarm milk and pour this mixture into the well. Cover with a cloth and leave for 15 minutes.

2. Melt the butter and add the sugar, eggs and rind of lemon. Pour this mixture into the well with the saffron powder and knead all the ingredients to make a smooth dough.

3. Cover with oiled clingfilm and leave to rise for 1-1½ hours – or until doubled in size.

4. Knead in the currants, raisins and cherries. Divide the dough in two and put into two small bread tins. Brush the top with egg yolk. Cut a line down the middle of each one and leave to rise for 15 minutes.

5. Bake in a hot oven at 220°C (425°F, Gas Mk 7) for the first 5 minutes, then reduce to 190°C (375°F, Gas Mk 5) for 25-39 minutes or until cooked.

DUNDEE CAKE

Serves: 8-10

Preparation: 20 minutes

Cooking: 2 hours

Ingredients

200g (7oz) plain flour
1 orange (zest and juice)
175g (6oz) butter
175g (6oz) brown sugar
3 eggs
25g (1oz) ground almonds
100g (4oz) sultanas
25g (1oz) mixed peel
caramel colouring (if desired)
split almonds to decorate the top

Drill

1. Prepare a 10in cake tin with butter and line with greaseproof paper.

2. Sieve the flour and prepare the zest and juice of the orange. Cream the butter and sugar thoroughly together until light in colour; this can be done by hand or machine.

3. Add the eggs, a little at a time, beating well between each addition. When all the eggs have been added and the mix is smooth and shiny, add the zest of orange and juice. Fold in the flour, ground almonds and the fruit (a little caramel colouring can be added at this stage to give a darker colour to the cake).

4. Place the mixture in the cake tin, smooth the top very lightly and dust with caster sugar (this will give the cake a nice shine when baked). Then neatly arrange the split almonds on the surface and bake in a moderate oven 180°C (350°F, Gas Mk 4) for about 2 hours.

STANDING
AT EASE

'Who the hell enjoys cocktail parties?'

Who in their right mind would stand for two hours in a noisy, crowded, smoke-filled room sipping tepid gin and tonic, brushing curried prawn off his suit whilst making social chit-chat to a twit with a serious hang-up on Etruscan pottery?

Is there anyone out there who likes meatballs in piquant sauce? Who knows anyone able to eat a creamed chicken bouchée without getting (a) goo on their tie, (b) grease on the carpet, and (c) pastry flakes in their companion's drink?

In a nutshell, who the hell enjoys cocktail parties?

Actually, I do.

I know it's irrational, but I can't help it. My wife despairs and always says, 'Let's rush home for a nice cup of cocoa and "Coronation Street".' The reality is that we never do.

We leave at 9 p.m. and I feel no pain. My wife, on the other hand, does feel pain. She is 5ft 0½in and will have spent the last couple of hours bending her neck backwards in order to achieve a degree of eye contact with a chap of 6ft 4in, recently returned from Upper Volta, or British West Hartlepool, and anxious to discuss with her 'Urban sewage disposal for the 21st century' or 'The Meaning of Life' or both.

I, on the other hand, have had a smashing time. I have been happy chatting to a variety of nubile ladies whilst taking a little of the grape and probably some of the grain.

Cocktail parties, their composition, style and success are a reflection of the host, be that host a corporation, an individual or, for the purpose of this exercise, a British Officers' Mess.

The party that is the most fun is that which is 'in-house'. All people you know, no tedious guests, and the chance to shout at long-standing friends across the 2ft gap between you, and to catch up with all the regimental news and gossip shouted back in deepest confidence. It's all very relaxed and usually ends with a buffet supper (and for those who need to know the drill on buffet suppers, see *The Pig* on page 166).

There are times, however, when duty calls and usually the President of the Mess Committee (PMC) will make an announcement to the assembled officers at a mess meeting. He will say something along the lines of 'It's high time that we returned some of the hospitality that we have had from nearby units and the local community. The Colonel and I have decided that we will have a cocktail party on...'

An audible groan wafts to the ceiling at this statement and the scene is set for what can be a less than riveting, but nevertheless an expensive, evening. Let's face it, someone has to pay and, contrary to popular belief, the Army does not eat and drink for free.

The guests have first to be identified, but with the best of intentions and with their partners, they will outnumber the hosts by a significant margin. All manner of local luminaries figure on the list: the Mayor and his lady, the Lord Lieutenant (rarely a lord and never a lieutenant), the Bishop and various of his saintly colleagues. The Police Superintendent is an absolute must because, sadly, he may have had dealings with some members of the unit. His only professional contact with the officers will be by way of the Adjutant who, like the Superintendent, is 'into' crime.

The editor of the local rag serving the garrison area must not be missed. No effort should be spared in ensuring that this man of letters has a very positive attitude towards the unit and all its works. The editor can do the unit a deal of good; he can also, by damning it with faint praise, cause a few eyebrows to be raised and questions to be asked. The effect would be to cause irrevocable damage to the career of the Commanding Officer. He wouldn't damn the Regiment, of course ... but then ... you never know.

The Matron of the local hospital, be it military or civilian, will be invited. She and her staff will have patched up innumerable soldiers injured in training accidents and damaged in sporting contest. What's more, she leads a team of charming nursing sisters and, if encouraged to bring a slack handful with her, she will add immeasurably to the success of the party. The invitation to the nursing sisters will be warmly applauded by the bachelor subalterns but the fact is that, come the night, it will be the married majors who will seek to dominate their company until dragged home to hot chocolate by their protesting wives.

The range of civilian guests will be matched by a salmagundi of military from adjacent units. Old friends of individual officers appear – but, more important, officers who are in a position to assist the Regiment in its day-to-day activities. The Major at District Headquarters who allocates ranges and training areas is a person of great influence. He is at the top of the list, together with an officer who works just down the corridor, charged with allocating funds for the maintenance of the barracks. These two worthies, predictably, see a great deal of each other as they are invited to every unit cocktail party.

The Senior Catering Officer is invited, really as a means of goading the Regiment's Master Chef into producing excellent food at little cost. The Senior Transport Officer is invited because there are never enough vehicles to go round at the best of times, and now the Colonel's staff car is starting to go on the blink it might be a good move

The list of military guests grows and grows, but it is not complete without the Brigadier and his wife. The Brigadier it is who holds all of the officers' futures in his podgy little hand. He initiates a document, called a 'confidential report', upon the Commanding Officer each year, and that report ultimately determines the Colonel's future career. The Brigadier also has, as they say, 'input' into the report on each of the other officers. His presence is vital if he is to note and record the efficient organisation and high standards in the Mess and the social graces and abstinence of all the officers complemented, in turn, by the charm of their wives.

The guest list will be subject to innumerable amendments before it can be finalised, and when that point is reached there arises the deeply vexing matter of hosting.

Hosting is hell.

It does not follow that, because someone has an interesting job he is an interesting chap, not does it follow that his wife is interesting either. It's a problem, and that's what makes hosting hell.

Against the name of each of the guests are appended the names of the hosts. Some of the decisions are easy. The second in command is a natural to look after 'Ranges and Training Areas' because training is his affair. The Quartermaster looks after the finance wizard, the Adjutant takes on the Superintendent, the PMC, Major Calthorpe, with an eye to the main chance, announces that he will 'look after the Brigadier and his wife because we know them so well ... they are old friends, you know'. For the rest of the officers it's 'pot luck' on who they get. The evening dawns ... can that be right? Probably not, but anyway, on the evening of the event Lieutenant Tiddlypush was found hovering near the door of the Mess, close enough to hear the Mess Sergeant announce the guests to Major Calthorpe, but not so close as to be trampled underfoot as the guests stampede toward the booze, *les pointes d'asperge*, *saumon fumé*, *filet de boeuf en brochette*, *crevettes en croûte*, knocking over the peanuts, twiglets and crisps on the way.

The Mess Sergeant announced in ringing tones: 'Councillor Albert Thistlethwaite, Justice of the Peace, His Worship the Mayor of Little Barnton and Mrs Thistlethwaite.'

Tiddlypush fielded the pair as they left the PMC's side and said 'Good evening, Sir. Good evening, Mrs Thistlethwaite – I'm Rodney Tiddlypush, can I get you both a drink?'

Tiddlypush beckoned to a passing soldier waiter burdened under a heavy tray that was covered in drinks of all shapes, sizes and colour, most of them clinking with ice and adorned with a wide miscellany of vegetables and assorted undergrowth.

'Well, yung mon, myself and Mrs Thistlethwaite don't hold with drink. We've been temperance these 45 years and proud of it,' His Worship replied with a note of triumph in his voice. 'Ah yes, jolly good, quite right, sooper,' agreed Tiddlypush, taking a stiff gin from the tray before dismissing the waiter to more productive work.

'Well, how about a nice glass of chilled orange juice? Grapefruit juice? Malvern water?'. At each question the Mayor shook his head, lips pursed. The Lady Mayoress underlined the rejection by saying 'No' decisively. 'Cola? Barley Water? Ginger Beer? Lemonade?' Tiddlypush ran out of ideas and paused. Councillor Thistlethwaite said helpfully, 'What ah'd like is a tomato juice, Angostura bitters, ice and lemon, and sprinkled with a level dessertspoon of bran. Mrs Thistlethwaite would like a nice cup of tea, not too strong, with a rich tea biscuit.'

Tiddlypush gulped, and gulped again. 'Absolutely,' he enthused, 'right away, but in the meantime how about some of these pieces of lamb's kidney wrapped in bacon?'

The guests looked even more po-faced. 'Ah think you should know that the Mayor and I are total vegetarians and we don't hold with the killing of animals for any purpose whatsoever,' advised Mrs Thistlethwaite, her crocodile handbag threatening to clear the tray of a passing waiter.

'Right ... yes ... OK ... yes ... I'll be back,' said Tiddlypush. He made his way behind the scenes in the Mess to find two waiters busily pouring water into a gin bottle: by their side they had two lemonade bottles filled with clear fluid. 'Hello, chaps, where the hell is the Mess Sergeant?' 'In the kitchen,' replied one of the waiters rather indistinctly through a mouthful of smoked salmon.

'C'mon, Sir, you're pulling my leg,' ejaculated the Mess Sergeant. 'You give bran to horses and, in dire circumstances, people who are constipated have it for breakfast. I've certainly never yet served it in a drink,' he ended with a note of finality in his voice. 'Anyway, we haven't got any, all we've got is Weetabix.'

Tiddlypush was only too aware that his guests were unattended and realised he had to get back to them. 'Tea OK?' he questioned. Grudgingly the Mess Sergeant agreed that a pot of tea could be produced.

Elsewhere in the room a small social disaster had engulfed Second Lieutenant George Fanshaw who had joined the Mess from Sandhurst only a matter of three weeks before. He was dreadfully anxious to please and prone to blush. As is the form on these occasions, he had been introduced to the wife of the Lord Lieutenant, a formidable lady. Fanshaw, striving for conversational gambits, had just reached down to a coffee table and his hand encountered some form of sweetmeat that he transferred swiftly to his mouth.

He found the contents of his mouth resistant, stony and indigestible, and he wondered what it was that he was eating. He dragged his eyes from the well-worn face of the guest and looked down.

There were two dishes side by side on the table. One dish was piled with olives and the other dish was filled with the stones.

The realisation dawned upon him that, not only was he in the process of chewing second-hand olive stones, but he had now to get them from his mouth – and quickly. He hoped that the formidable lady had not noticed.

But she had. She watched in fascination as she saw Fanshaw's face change colour from white to crimson to green at a speed that would have done credit to a chameleon. He was revolted, but didn't know what to do. 'Tell me,' interrogated the guest, 'do you like olives?'

It was about ten minutes later that the Brigadier, accompanied by Major Calthorpe, had just shaken off the Lord Lieutenant. 'Bloody man,' he snarled at the PMC. 'Never did like him, man's a fool.' Calthorpe was torn; he didn't go a bundle on the Lord Lieutenant himself, but he was a close acquaintance of the Commanding Officer and was, tonight, the Colonel's principal guest; on the other hand, he didn't want to disagree with the Brigadier and certainly not when the great man was clearly working up a liver. Calthorpe compromised; he cleared his throat in a sort of affirmative noise, but not a noise that could ever be quoted.

The Brigadier gazed out over the throng, conscious that his haemorrhoids hurt, and grated, 'Who is that officer holding a packet of Weetabix behind his back and why?'

'Tiddlypush, and I don't know, sir,' whined Calthorpe, very aware that the evening wasn't turning out the way it had been planned. 'Perhaps he's having a late breakfast,' he offered lamely.

'It's 1915 hours.' The Brigadier sounded as if he had a mouthful of broken glass.

'Ah... well, yes. It must be an early breakfast then,' Calthorpe riposted brightly.

'Idiot,' judged the Brigadier, and Calthorpe had the horrid realisation that perhaps the judgement was of him and not of Rodney Tiddlypush. Calthorpe's resolve not to drink alcohol all evening in order to keep a clear head went out of the window. He took a large whisky soda and resolved, instead, that he would maim Tiddlypush on the morrow. The idea appealed to him and he smiled. The Brigadier saw the smile and growled under his breath, 'Simpering idiot.'

Elsewhere in the room snippets of conversation could be heard.

'Three down and four to play, so on the 15th tee I took a 2 iron and...'

'I tell you, as God is my witness, 50 miles to the gallon at a steady 85 miles per hour.'

'The cheque is actually in the post.'

'But where is my rich tea biscuit?'

'He said he'd never seen me with all my clothes on before, and you can imagine the trouble I had convincing George that the man was only the lifeguard at the pool.'

The activity in the public rooms of the Mess was matched by the alternative party being enjoyed by the Staff. Not all the crayfish tails reached the official guests. Private Arnold, drafted in from 'B' Company to act as a temporary waiter for the evening, had liberated a trayful and found them most agreeable. The sparkling Saumur with which he was washing them down was not really his tipple, but when it's free a chap can't be too choosy.

The PMC wandered among his guests, noted that the Colonel had an empty glass and despatched a waiter through the mob. The noise volume was at the top end of the scale and the PMC imagined people in Krakatoa looking nervously at their mountain. Consulting his watch, he saw it was 2000 hours. He caught the Mess Sergeant's eye, just in time, as it seemed to be about to fall inside the cleavage of a well-endowed young lady talking to the Padre. Calthorpe made a sign and within moments the Mess Sergeant had turned off the tap.

There is a moment of realisation at every cocktail party that there really is no more booze – bags of peanuts, twiglets and crisps, but no more booze. A charming and attentive host who says, 'Let me get you one for the road' will find that in the interests (a) of economy and (b) of getting the Mess cleaned before midnight, there really is no more booze.

The room that had filled so quickly emptied just as quickly.

'Lovely to see you again, we'll be in touch.'

'I'll let you have the recipe.'

'Give me a ring and we'll knock a ball around a few holes at my Club.'

'I'll put the cheque in the post.'

'Yes, the Mess does need redecorating, but then money is so very tight.'

'I am not tight.'

'You are.'

'We must meet for lunch sometime.'

Suddenly the room was empty, the only noise the snapping of twiglets underfoot as the waiters started to clear the storm damage. Calthorpe replayed the evening in his mind and despaired. The bill would be much higher than anticipated, the carpet would never be the same again, his wife had taken severe 'um' over a chance remark made by Major Swindon's wife. The Brigadier did not enjoy himself, probably because the Lord Lieutenant obviously did.

The Colonel swept into the room. 'Thank you, chaps,' he boomed expansively to the waiters and, putting his arm around Calthorpe's shoulder, he said, 'Crashing success, well done, Charles. First class. Enormous fun. Full marks to all the boys.' Calthorpe brightened, thinking that perhaps life wasn't totally bad after all.

'Let's start planning now and have another cocktail party in a couple of months' time,' added the Colonel.

Calthorpe considered his position and then he said, through firmly clenched teeth, 'Who in their right mind wants to stand for two hours in a noisy, crowded, smoke-filled room, sipping tepid gin and tonic, brushing curried prawn off their suit, whilst making social chit-chat to a twit with a serious hang-up on Etruscan pottery?'

✄

But if you do, the following pages are essential reading.   *T.N.*

SMOKED SALMON AND ASPARAGUS CANAPÉS

📖

Serves: 4-6

Preparation: 20 minutes

Ingredients

3 slices brown wholemeal bread
50g (2oz) butter
50g (2oz) sour cream
225g (8oz) sliced smoked salmon
9 asparagus tips

Drill

1. Slice the bread very thinly and spread half with butter and half with sour cream – reserving some of the cream.

2. Sandwich with the smoked salmon to make three layers.

3. Spread the top with sour cream and smooth. Garnish with asparagus tips and cut into portions.

Note: Before cutting, it is best to wrap the slices in clingfilm and chill well. This will make cutting easier.

SMOKED DUCK CANAPÉS

Serves: 4-6

Preparation: 10 minutes

Ingredients

1 brioche loaf
350g (12oz) duck pâté
1 smoked duck breast

Drill

1. Slice the brioche to a thickness of about a ¼ inch. Toast on both sides and cut into rounds (or ovals) using a pastry cutter.

2. Spread with the duck pâté and arrange thin slices of smoked duck breast on top.

CAVIAR BLINIS

Serves: 4-6

Preparation: 30 minutes

Resting: 3 hours

Cooking: 10 minutes

Ingredients

For the fermentation:
250ml (9fl oz) lukewarm milk
15g (½oz) fresh yeast
25g (1oz) wholemeal flour
Main recipe:
100g (4oz) wholemeal flour
2 eggs, separated
pinch salt
300g (10oz) caviar, lumpfish or salmon roe

Drill

Fermentation

1. Whisk together the lukewarm milk and the yeast in a bowl and add 25g (1oz) of wholemeal flour. Cover the bowl with a plate and leave at room temperature (24°C, 75°F) for two hours.

Roast Grouse with Lentils and Walnut Sauce (page 103)

(Clockwise from the bottom) **Battenburg Slice** (page 161), **Cream Scones** (page 113), **Dundee Cake** (page 117), *(on silver platter)* **Fruit and Walnut Cake** (page 112), **Farmhouse Cake** (page 114), **Date and Honey Cake** (page 115), **Cornish Fruit Bread** (page 116)

Making the batter

2. Add the flour and egg yolks to the fermentation and mix with a spatula. Cover with a plate and leave at room temperature for 1 hour.

3. Place the egg whites in a clean bowl and beat well; add a pinch of salt and beat until stiff. Fold the egg whites carefully into the batter. The mix is now ready for use.

To cook

4. Brush a heavy-bottomed frying pan with a little clarified butter. Leaving plenty of space between them, spoon in 6-8 good teaspoonfuls of the batter.

5. Cook the blinis for 30 seconds on each side, turning with a palette knife. Drain on kitchen paper. Cook the remaining blinis in batches.

To serve

6. Spoon a teaspoonful of caviar on to each one and serve.

CHEESE PUFFS

Serves: 4-6

Preparation: 20 minutes

Cooking: 25 minutes

Ingredients

Basic choux mix (see basic recipes)
50g (2oz) Parmesan cheese
salt and cayenne pepper
25g (1oz) almonds, chopped
225g (8oz) cream cheese
25g (1oz) chives
1 clove garlic, crushed.

Drill

1. Make the choux paste according to the basic recipe, adding the Parmesan cheese, salt and cayenne pepper.

2. Lightly grease a baking sheet and, using a ½in tube and piping bag, squeeze out the choux paste mixture into little rounds (about 1in in diameter and 1in high).

3. Dust with Parmesan cheese, chopped almonds and cayenne pepper, then bake in a hot oven at 220°C (425°F, Gas Mk 7) for 20 to 25 minutes or until golden brown.

4. Remove from the oven and leave to cool. When cold, make a slit in the side.

To fill

5. Mix the cream cheese until light. Add the chives and the crushed garlic; season and spoon into the cold choux puffs.

CHOUX PUFFS

Serves: 4-6

Preparation: 15 minutes

Cooking: 20 minutes

Ingredients

50g (2oz) basic Choux paste mix (*see* basic recipes)
50g (2oz) Parmesan cheese
salt and cayenne pepper
oil

Drill

1. Make the choux paste using the recipe in the basic recipes section. Add the Parmesan cheese, salt and cayenne pepper.

2. Cut small strips of greaseproof paper and lightly oil. Using a piping bag fitted with a ½in piping tube, pipe out the mixture onto the greaseproof paper to the size of small walnuts.

3. Heat the oil in a deep fryer. By holding the corner of each strip of paper carefully, place into a deep fryer withdrawing the paper. The choux mix will release from the paper as they hit the hot oil. Fry until golden and well puffed. Drain and lightly dust with Parmesan cheese and cayenne pepper. Serve hot.

DINNER

Staying above the salt

There is nothing that so divides the British nation as the time of day at which they choose to dine. The upper classes do so in the dark; those below the salt eat 'dinner' at mid-day. Those who get it wrong may occasionally be seen wandering friendless through the foothills of society, pariahs in the land where they were born.

As with mixing up *le* and *la* when speaking French, there is no possibility of compromise. He who enters the Savoy Grill at noon and orders 'dinner' has immediately wiped out all other assets: his Daimler, Savile Row suit and smouldering bimbo. It is like buying a shirt, hand-made from wild silk, then spilling tomato ketchup down the front, or standing at the bar of the Travellers' in Pall Mall and extolling the virtues of Morecambe in the season. There are certain things which, in England, are not done.

The distinction is not as clear-cut as it used to be, thanks to the influence of the business lunch. This made eating big meals at mid-day *de rigeur* again; it had the advantage that someone else was paying the bill, and made a pleasant interlude during work.

In fact, working was an unpleasant prelude to having lunch. The businessman entered his office at 9.30 and then, two-and-a-half hours (plus a coffee break) later, left it. He had to leave early to ensure a clear approach run, because everyone else was doing the same thing. The roads to restaurant-land at mid-day were constipated.

Three sherries, half a bottle of Mosel, an avocado filled with crabmeat in pink sauce, *escalope de veau cordon bleu*, strawberry gâteau, assorted cheeses, two cups of coffee and a double Rèmy Martin later, he stumbled back to his sanctum feeling terrible. His secretary then took over till going-home time. It is not Britain's industrialists but their secretaries who are to blame for the decline in the economy.

The present situation is more confused than ever because the business lunch has fallen out of fashion. In the green and unpleasant land of Yuppie England, steak pie and claret lunches are on the slide again. The thrusting young executive today favours sandwiches from the automat and Perrier water. At cocktail parties in the boss's office, he shuns the Bloody Marys and martinis. The wretched man turns up late (delayed by a crucial phone call from Kyoto) and asks for a straight tonic, ice and lemon wedge. The tray of double gins goes unattended.

The good news is that dinner after dark is once more becoming the high point of the day. No longer need the housewife slave away over meals which her slumbering husband cannot eat. She still slaves away all day, but he now eats them – no longer pie-eyed and porcine after lunch.

A similar revolution is taking place in France, that temple of European *haute cuisine*. There was a time when their *déjeuner* was a real occasion – a semi-colon punctuating the long sentence of the day. The quality of the *tables d'hôte* in Paris testified to the Gallic enthusiasm for lunch. Now the fast food restaurants in the Champs Elysées show that *plus ça change, plus ça n'est pas le même chose*. In the hectic round of life in the late 20th century, most Frenchmen save up their appetite for the evening.

There is everything to be said for dining after dark. The very word 'dine' rolls slowly and luxuriously off the tongue, suggesting *boeuf bourgignon* and rich red Beaune. To take one's place at the table in midwinter, at the end of a day fraught with mischief and business strain ... to watch the candlelight winking in the glasses and apprehend the aroma of good food, is surely an experience to savour. The word 'dine' implies good fellowship and long dresses, mutual indulgence and 'laughter learnt of friends'.

But the British are out of practice, while even the French are showing signs of being demoralised by fast food. This is why the West now needs the Colonel's guidance in finding its way back to culinary rectitude. Listen to this...

We were driving back to Britain not so long ago after spending a holiday in the French Alps, and had laid up at a hotel in rural Burgundy – that rich vein of food and wine flowing with goodness. It was one of those hot and dusty summer days on which nature seems in need of air-conditioning. The image of crisp white tablecloths and striped awnings hung before one like a mirage on the autoroute.

We reached the hostelry in time for dinner and, after a shower, a change of clothes and a sit-down, made our way to the large cool dining-room overlooking the still sunlit square of the small town. The tablecloths were indeed crisp and fresh, and had they been served up for dinner might have proved delicious. Opting for a more conventional diet, however, we spent some time poring over the large menu, in anticipation of superlative cuisine.

But alas... The steaks braised in wine and served with truffles were generously laced with fat and gristle, the *poisson* an anaemic mish-mash fit for invalids. An omelette, the *pièce de résistance* of French housewives, would have made an effective weapon for casual mugging. As we chewed away, more slowly with each morsel, the equally unpalatable truth was all too obvious: the French had finally learnt how to cook badly.

Now the British are not given to complaining, and I had been an outstanding model of national phlegm. Saddle-sore schnitzels in Bonn, middle-aged mullet in Muscat or bottles of Chablis *chambré* in Torquay ... had been accepted and downed without demur. No hostess need have trembled in her tights on hearing Stanhope's cab purr to a halt. I was the very paragon of politeness.

This called, however, for an epicurean response. With the feeling of one about to tell his best friend that he had halitosis, I solemnly beckoned the waiter towards our table...

The waiter listened in silence to my French (all credit to him) and, in reply, summoned the *maître d'hôtel* – more to act as an interpreter, I suspect. The *maître d'hôtel* called the under-manager from the foyer, the under-manager brought in the manager himself. By this time a silence had settled on the dining-room as people at neighbouring tables lowered their cutlery. For an Englishman to eat in France was a privilege. For him then to complain was tantamount to perfidy. One could have heard a toothpick clattering to the floor.

The manager was very patient with me. He made it clear that my French could be improved upon, occasionally correcting my use of the imperfect. He had never thought it necessary to learn English. He then explained with an air of injured dignity and pride that of course I must have been mistaken. He had personally supervised the cooking of the omelette since dawn, while the sea bass had been caught that very morning in the stream beside the mill of his aunt in Mâcon. As for the steak, it had won the Arc de Triomphe three years before. Although I could not follow all he said, that was, I think, the gist of his remarks. Like Henry V, when the Dauphin sent him tennis balls, he made it clear that he had taken it pretty badly.

Of course, I said I was sorry for being so gauche. I had acted without regard for the proprieties. No, I had not known that he had once been mentioned, if only in passing, by the Michelin Rouge. Had he told me before, I would have treated the *hors-d'oeuvres* with more respect. In return he seemed willing to forget my indiscretion, so we added a generous tip to the large bill and left as early as possible the next day. The manager kindly showed us out through the back door, to avoid the embarrassment of meeting the other guests.

But I think I might send him a copy of this book.

Despite my customary reticence at the table, this was not the first time I had been driven to complain. Indeed the other occasion was in the Army. The casus belly, as it might be called, was thus.

We were all sitting in the cookhouse having supper. In my day the officers had dinner and the other ranks supper – another interesting comment on Britain's social mores. More accurately we were preparing to have high tea, which meant separating the rice pudding with cherry jam from the grilled kipper.

In those days soldiers ate off large tin trays, divided into a number of indentations into which the cooks deposited the food. Airlines deploy a similar kind of platter, but whereas they put one course into each space, our cooks used to empty them all into the same one. Either this cut down on the washing-up or, being attached to the Royal Horse Artillery, they regarded the serving of lunch as target practice. They adjusted their range and bearing as the first few hungry gunners filed past, then dropped everything on the same spot with deadly accuracy. The Regiment once shelled a German village with equal skill, though as the war had been over for 10 years by this time, admiration for their expertise was muted.

In time one became quite accustomed to the taste of, say, roast beef and vanilla blancmange, or baked beans on a bed of bread and butter pudding. A whole generation was introduced to sweet 'n' sour by the Army, at a time when for most people Eastern cuisine meant eating fish and chips on Folkestone pier. I remember becoming personally addicted to salmon and shrimp fish-paste on Dundee cake.

However, even the most sophisticated palate needed a modicum of preparatory spadework before tucking into his pot-pourri of food, and it was during this preliminary canter that the orderly officer entered on his rounds.

Swagger-stick under his arm, a lugubrious Cook-Sergeant in attendance, he strode slowly forward between the busy tables, inviting, 'Any complaints?' with the optimism of one selling shoelaces in a Khatmandhu bazaar. As he drew level with my table I complained.

Now, complaining was practically a court martial offence, second only to losing one's greatcoat or catching 'flu. The orderly officer was a young Second Lieutenant who had managed to persuade the Officers' Selection Board that he could get a platoon of men across a gorge with the help of a barrel, two knitting needles and a matchbox. Nothing, however, had prepared him for this moment. When in Meerut in 1857 the sepoys declined to use cartridges smeared with pig-fat, their officers must have felt very much the same.

Moreover, we had been given centre-stage. Those soldiers round about us who had been discussing such military affairs as the size of the girls' breasts in the Church of Scotland canteen, shut up like clams. Those whose hunger had finally got the better of them, quietly stopped eating, forkfuls of rissole and mandarin slices in mid-air – like crane grabs after the drivers have gone home. A regiment of eyes was drilled upon us.

'It's the rice pudding, sir,' I said, pointing to it beneath its layer of Naafi jam. 'It's like a paddyfield in Vietnam.'

'Well,' said the Second Lieutenant, recoiling slightly, 'I'm sure it's jolly good for you, you know. We have a lot of it in the Officers' Mess.' He turned to survey the others at my table. 'Any other complaints about today's rice pudding?'

'No, sir,' they all cried loyally in response, which shows that their is no honour among allies.

'Take his name, Sergeant,' said the Second Lieutenant, moving on.

'Yes, sir,' said the Cook-Sergeant, licking his pencil, as I gave him the name of our Lance-Bombardier.

Though it is commonly supposed that the great turn-round in military cuisine was occasioned by the end of National Service, which meant that the Army lost its captive diners, I like to think I played a minor role in it. Whether it had any immediate effect is hard to say. Revolutionaries are not always well rewarded. Look what happened to Danton, Robespierre and Trotsky. In my case it always seemed to me thereafter that our cooks paid more attention than was customary in spreading my porridge with scrambled egg and marmalade.

We have tried to avoid including such exotica on the grounds that the

Colonel's guests might not be ready for it. Spaghetti bolognese with syrup pudding would come under the heading, I think, of advanced eating. Another time perhaps... Meanwhile, on the polished oak tables of old England we hope that the following listings by the Colonel will recapture the standards of the past.

H.S.

RUSHMOOR PÂTÉ

Serves: 6

Preparation: 30 minutes

Cooking: 2 hours

Ingredients

1 onion
350g (12oz) bacon
450g (1lb) calves' liver
1 clove garlic
pinch mixed herbs
1tsp salt and freshly ground pepper
50g (2oz) butter
1tbs flour
300ml (½pt) milk

Drill

1. Chop the onion and put through a mincer, together with half the bacon, the liver, the garlic and mixed herbs. Add the salt and freshly milled pepper.

2. Melt half the butter in a saucepan, add the flour and slowly stir in the milk. Bring to the boil, then blend with the minced meats in a basin.

3. Line a large loaf tin or ovenproof dish with the rest of the bacon and pour in the pâté mixture. Melt the remaining butter and pour over the surface. Cover with tinfoil.

4. Pre-heat the oven to 170°C (325°F, Gas Mk 3). Place the pâté dish in a roasting tin with a layer of water in the bottom and bake for 1½-2 hours.

5. Remove from the oven and refrigerate overnight before serving.

GÂTEAU OF SMOKED POULTRY WITH ORANGE OIL DRESSING

📖

Serves: 4

Preparation: 30 minutes

Cooking: nil

Ingredients

350g (12oz) smoked chicken or a selection of both chicken, duck and guinea fowl

walnuts chopped, leave 4 whole for decoration

25g (1oz) green peppercorns, chopped

150ml (¼pt) mayonnaise

150ml (¼pt) double cream

1tsp curry paste

150ml (¼pt) olive oil

25g (1oz) sugar

3tsp orange juice

15g (½oz) orange zest

2tsp white wine vinegar

25g (1oz) toasted pine kernels

paprika

mixed salad leaves for garnish: radicchio, frissée, lollo rosso

Equipment: small plastic rings or a pastry cutter 1½" high x 2" diameter

Drill

1. Trim smoked poultry into small strips. Add chopped walnuts and peppercorns. Mix with a little of the orange zest and moisten with olive oil.

2. Wash and trim salad leaves.

3. Make the dressing by mixing the white wine vinegar with the sugar and orange juice. Add the olive oil and mix well. Season to taste with salt and ground black pepper.

4. To make the topping mix the mayonnaise with the double cream and blend with the curry paste.

5. To assemble the dish place the plastic ring or pastry cutter on a cold serving plate and fill with the smoked meat mix till just below the top of the ring. Top-up the ring with the cream/mayonnaise mix and smooth the surface. Decorate with half walnut and dust with paprika. Arrange the salad leaves on the plate and garnish with the toasted pine kernels. Spoon the dressing over and serve.

MEDALLIONS OF BEEF WITH A CHICKEN AND SWEETBREAD STUFFING

This dish has been very popular as a main course on regimental supper nights. It needs care and attention in both the preparation and cooking of the meat. The sauce should be light and not too strong or it will kill the delicate flavour of the sweetbreads. The shallot 'marmalade' gives a nice piquancy to the dish.

Serves: 4

Preparation: 40 minutes

Cooking: 1 hour

Ingredients

4 beef medallions cut from the fillet
1 veal sweetbread
225g (8oz) crepinette (caul of pig fat)
225g (8oz) chicken mousse (see basic recipe section)
8 tarragon leaves (for decoration)
2tbs chopped tarragon
salt and freshly ground pepper
For the shallot 'marmalade':
6 shallots (shredded)
¼ bottle red wine
100g (4oz) sugar
1tbs oil
1tbs balsamic vinegar
salt and ground pepper
For the sauce:
900ml (1½pts) veal stock
900ml (1½pts) chicken stock
225ml (8fl oz) dry white wine
1 clove garlic
1tsp (heaped) tomato purée

Drill

1. Ask your butcher to cut four nice medallions (about 115g (4oz) each from the beef fillet.

2. Soak the veal sweetbread in cold running water for 2 hours. It should look clean and white by the end of this time. Trim away skin and blood clots before cooking.

3. Poach the sweetbread in chicken stock for 7-8 minutes and leave to cool in the cooking liquor. When cool, cut into 8 slices approximately 6mm (¼in) thick.

4. Mix the chicken mousse with the tarragon and add any sweetbread trimmings. Cut into small dice.

5. Spread a little of this mixture on each of the medallions and top with two slices of sweetbread. Decorate with whole tarragon leaves, season and wrap each one in some of the caul fat. Twist the caul fat under each medallion to seal, then trim off any excess. Refrigerate until required.

Making the shallot 'marmalade'

6. Heat the oil in a small thick-bottomed pan. Add the shredded shallots and cook until soft but not coloured. Add the sugar and cook until it just starts to caramelise. Add the vinegar and reduce. Season, cover with a lid and set to one side of the stove to cook until the liquid has formed a nice shiny coating. (It should look like cooked red cabbage.) Keep it hot.

To cook the meat and make the sauce

7. Heat a little oil in a thick-bottomed frying pan. Add the medallions and cook according to taste (the Colonel likes them very pink in the middle).

8. When cooked, keep them hot in the oven until you are ready to serve.

9. Add to the hot pan the crushed garlic and then the wine. Reduce and add the veal and chicken stocks and the tomato purée and reduce by two-thirds. Season.

To serve

10. Spoon a portion of the shallot marmalade on to each warmed plate and set the medallions on top.

11. Strain the sauce and spoon around the plate. Serve with a vegetable and potato dish of your choice.

Recommended drink: Medium-bodied red.

CHICKEN MARENGO

This was said to be Napoleon's favourite dish, which might (or might not) explain why it bears the same name as his horse. The Colonel took to it in the hope that some of Bonaparte's genius might rub off on him. Fortunately for Western Europe this did not happen, but at least he now shares the emperor's taste in food.

📖

Serves: 3-4

Preparation: 20 minutes

Cooking: 1 hour

Ingredients

1 chicken portioned into 8
salt and freshly ground pepper
1tbs oil
1tbs clarified butter
300ml (½pt) chicken stock
10 button onions, peeled
225g (8oz) tomatoes, peeled and chopped
1½tbs tomato purée
2 cloves garlic, crushed
1 bouquet garni
100g (4oz) button mushrooms, quartered
1 glass white wine
4 fried croûtons
chopped parsley

Drill

1. Rub the chicken well with salt and pepper. Dip into flour and then sauté to brown in the oil and butter.

2. Add the chicken stock, onions and tomatoes, tomato purée, garlic and bouquet garni.

3. Cover and simmer for 50 minutes or until chicken is tender.

4. Sauté the mushrooms in a little butter, add the white wine and pour this into the chicken mixture. Cook for a further 5 minutes.

5. Remove the chicken with a slotted spoon and keep warm in a serving dish. Discard the bouquet garni.

6. Reduce the sauce according to taste and pour over the chicken. Garnish with the croûtons and chopped parsley.

Note: Classically, this dish should be served with French fried eggs (egg fried in deep oil), and cooked crayfish.

🍷

Recommended drink: Medium-dry white wine.

ROYAL WELCH LAMB

Serves: 4

Preparation: 30 minutes

Cooking: 2 hours

Ingredients

900g (2lb) boned loin of lamb
2-3tbs oil
For the stuffing:
25g (1oz) butter
1 leek, chopped
5tbs white breadcrumbs
2tbs chopped mixed herbs
1 lemon
salt, pepper and seasoned flour
1 egg, beaten
browned breadcrumbs
For the sauce:
1 onion, sliced
1-2tsp flour
300ml (½pt) stock
1-2tbs redcurrant jelly

Drill

1. Melt the butter in a saucepan and fry the chopped leek until soft but not brown.

2. Place the leek in a basin, together with the white breadcrumbs, the herbs, the rind of the lemon, a teaspoonful of the lemon juice and seasoning. Mix well and add a little beaten egg to bind.

3. Spread the stuffing over the inside of the lamb. Roll the meat round it and secure with string. Season the outside of the lamb, brush with beaten egg and coat with the browned crumbs.

4. Pre-heat the oven to 175°C (350°F, Gas Mk 4), heat the oil in a baking tin and roast the lamb for 1½-2 hours. When cooked, remove the string and keep warm while preparing the sauce.

Making the sauce

5. Pour off excess fat from the roasting tin, leaving about 1tbs in the bottom, together with the sediment. Add the sliced onion and cook to brown. Sprinkle with the flour, gradually blend in the stock and redcurrant jelly and bring to the boil, on top of the stove. Check the seasoning, add a little lemon juice if required to sharpen the flavour and strain.

6. Carve the lamb in thick slices and arrange in a serving dish. Serve with the sauce.

Recommended drink: Claret or other lightish red wine.

BEEF WELLINGTON

As Napoleon is remembered for brandy and cigars, so is his opponent at Waterloo for large rubber boots and Beef Wellington. This makes frequent appearances at Mess dinners – and justifiably so.

Serves: 4-5

Preparation: 20 minutes

Cooking: about 1½ hours

Ingredients

675g (1½lb) beef fillet
350g (12oz) Mushroom duxelles (see basic section)
225g (8oz) Puff pastry (see basic section)
1tbs Napoleon brandy
1 egg
1tbs sherry or Madeira
1tbs clarified butter
salt and freshly ground pepper

Drill

1. Pre-heat the oven to 190°C (375°F, Gas Mk 5) and heat the butter in a roasting tray. Season the meat with salt and pepper, brush with the brandy and cook for 30-40 minutes, turning occasionally. Remove from the oven and cool, reserving the juices and any sediment in the pan.

2. Raise temperature of oven to 230°C (450°F, Gas Mk 8).

3. Roll out the pastry into a rectangle about 35 x 25cm (14 x 10in), spread about half of the duxelles in the middle of the pastry, place the fillet on top, cover with the rest of the duxelles and then fold the pastry over the top and seal the sides, using a little water to stick the pastry together. Decorate the top with pastry trimmings.

4. Brush with beaten egg, place on a lightly greased baking tray and rest for 15 minutes. Then bake in the oven for about 30 minutes.

5. Meanwhile, pour away any excess fat from the roasting pan and make a gravy in the usual way with stock and the sherry or Madeira. Slice the Beef Wellington thickly and serve with the gravy.

Recommended drink: Full-bodied red wine.

CHOCOLATE AND COFFEE CREAM PROFITEROLES

📖

Serves: 6

Preparation and Cooking: 45 minutes

Ingredients

1 mix of Choux paste (*see basic recipes*)
350ml (12fl oz) whipping cream
50g (2oz) icing sugar
1tsp coffee powder

Drill

1. Using a ½in plain nozzle and piping bag, squeeze choux paste mixture on to a greased baking sheet, shaped into little mounds about 1in in diameter and 1in high. Leave about 2in between each one.

2. Bake in a hot oven at 220°C (425°F, gas mark 8) for 20-25 minutes. Remove from oven and make a split in the sides with a sharp knife. Leave to cool.

To make the filling

3. Whip the cream until stiff. Stir in the icing sugar and coffee powder.

4. Pipe or spoon the filling into the puffs through the slits, and dust with icing sugar. Serve with a light chocolate sauce.

WHITE CHOCOLATE AND CHEESE MOUSSE

📖

Serves: 6

Preparation: 45 minutes

Ingredients

175g (6oz) white chocolate
2 egg yolks
50ml (2fl oz) water
1 sheet leaf gelatine
100ml (4fl oz) double cream
100g (4oz) cream cheese (mascarpone)
4 egg whites
25g (1oz) caster sugar

(Left to right) **Caviar Blinis** (page 128), *(behind)* **Choux Puffs** (page 130),
Cheese Puffs (page 129), **Smoked Salmon and Asparagus Canapés** (page 127),
Smoked Duck Canapés (page 128)

Medallions of Beef with a Chicken and Sweetbread Stuffing (page 139)

6 bunches fresh redcurrants
150ml (¼pt) redcurrant sauce (see basic recipes)

Drill

1. Melt the chocolate. Add the egg yolks and mix well. Add the water.

2. Soak the leaf gelatine in cold water until soft. Add this to the warm chocolate, mix well and leave to cool.

3. Whip the cream until it peaks. Add to the cream cheese and mix well.

4. Whip the egg whites until stiff. Add the sugar and beat until smooth. Fold this into the chocolate mix.

5. Fill into sundae glasses or round moulds. Leave to chill for half an hour. Serve garnished with redcurrants and pour redcurrant sauce round the plate.

CHOCOLATE TRUFFLE SLICE

Serves: 6

Preparation: 45 minutes

Ingredients

1 sheet of chocolate sponge (see basic recipes)
1 tot Grand Marnier
225g (8oz) white chocolate
225g (8oz) dark chocolate
600ml (1pt) double cream
50g (2oz) dark chocolate, grated
icing sugar (for dusting)
Dark chocolate sauce (see basic recipes)

Drill

1. Line the bottom and sides of a suitable mould with the chocolate sponge and brush with the Grand Marnier.

2. Melt the white and dark chocolate and whip the cream until stiff. Mix half the cream with the dark chocolate and the other half with the white, then blend both light and dark mixes to create a marbled effect.

3. Fill the mould and top with a layer of sponge. Place in the refrigerator to set.

4. De-mould, thinly coat with cream and roll in the grated chocolate. Dust with icing sugar and slice. Serve with dark chocolate sauce.

CHOCOLATE NOODLES WITH WHITE CHOCOLATE SAUCE

Serves: 6

Preparation: 15 minutes

Cooking: 2-3 minutes

Ingredients

450g (1lb) unbleached flour or plain strong flour

¼tsp salt

3tbs cocoa powder

5 extra-large eggs

1tbs olive or vegetable oil

1tbs icing sugar

Chocolate sauce (see basic recipes)

Drill

To make the pasta

1. Measure the dry ingredients and place directly on to a work surface. Make a well in the centre and pour the wet ingredients (eggs and oil) into it.

2. Using a fork, beat the egg mixture and gradually draw in the dry mix to form a soft dough. Work the dough until smooth. The kneading of the dough is important as this will make rolling and cutting easier.

3. Roll out a portion of the dough to about $^{1}/_{16}$in. It can now be cut by hand into fine strips or passed through a pasta machine, using a fine cutter.

To cook

4. Bring plenty of water to the boil in a large pan. Add the noodles, bring back to the boil and cook for about 5 seconds.

5. Drain the pasta immediately and serve hot with Chocolate sauce. Alternatively, leave to cool, dust with icing sugar and serve with white, milk or dark chocolate sauce.

Note: Pasta can be left to dry until required, or can be frozen. If dried, it will take a little longer to cook.

CHILDREN'S PARTIES

Coming to the aid of the party

Most children's parties are best viewed from a safe distance, like volcanoes, the Loch Ness monster and black mambas. This is especially so when the children are one's own. One has seen fathers unavoidably called abroad, grow misty-eyed at the poolside in Singapore on reading the latest faxed message from their wives on the time they were all having back at home. Absence generally makes the heart grow fonder, and sadly the reverse is also true.

There are, however, exceptions to this rule, and among these was the tale of Kenneth Bolingbroke. In case the name evokes schoolday memories of Richard II, not to mention Henry IV (parts 1 and 2), I should add that in his case the Bolingbroke lineage was a short one.

Kenneth's father, a commercial traveller called Ballsbrook, had married the daughter of the under-manager (sales), a lady with a taste for light historical romances. Ballsbrook senior, on her insistence, underwent a name change – though, having been known throughout schooldays by his first syllable, Mr Ballsbrook (hereinafter Bolingbroke) needed little persuading.

The dowager Mrs Bolingbroke always claimed that it was due to his new up-market identity that her son Kenneth had become an Army dentist. The high point of Colonel Bolingbroke's career came when he once carried out a check-up on a military cousin, twice removed, of the royal family. He had moreover 'married money', so it was said, his wife being the heiress of a scrap merchant in Sheffield.

Together they had produced a pair of twins. If Belinda and Berenice Bolingbroke were not identical, they were as near as dammit to most people. Their mother swore she could always tell one from t'other, though even she, to make sure, tied Belinda's hair with pink ribbon and that of her twin sister with primrose.

Other mothers looked at the Bolingbroke girls with envy. Each was healthy, disturbingly beautiful and blonde. Each angelic face was framed with golden hair which, like that of every princess in a fairy tale, hung in long silken tresses to the shoulders. Not only that, but they were impeccably behaved. While their contemporaries tore their frocks on blackberry bushes or publicly campaigned for sweets and ice-cream, Belinda and Berenice sat quietly reading, like candidates for the title of Miss Pears.

'Why can't you behave like the Bolingbroke girls?' wailed other mothers as their own offspring played them up while shopping in Tesco's.

Alas, appearances were – as is often the case – deceptive. Behind the damask cheeks and wide blue eyes, the demure countenances and young innocence, there lay a depth of talent for mischief-making which would have shocked and grieved their proxy aunts. Beside the Bolingbroke heiresses, Lucrezia Borgia was as Mother Theresa to the daughters of Count Dracula. All that distinguished them from such notorious forebears was their enviable aptitude for total concealment. The Bolingbroke girls were wholly beyond reproach.

There had been the Nativity Play at the garrison church in Germany, when some unseen hand (or hands?) had locked the Three Wise Men inside their dressing-room.

'Lo, I see men riding out of the East,' said Joseph, shading his eyes and gazing into the middle distance from the stable. He repeated it more loudly ... then once more. But the only response was a distant muffled banging and voices crying 'Hullo' from below the stage. Though the padré, traumatised by the experience, had held an official inquiry the next day, the culprit (or culprits?) were never found.

Nor had anyone ever discovered who ordered a lurid copy of *Men Only* to be delivered, without plain covers, to their school's geography master in mid-class.

Those children who had their suspicions lacked clear evidence – and were firmly rebuked by their elders when they voiced them. They were lectured on the virtues of George Washington and on the vices of jealousy, mendacity and spite. To accuse the Misses Bolingbroke of such crimes was like querying the chastity of the vestal virgins.

This explains why the Bolingbrokes senior had few qualms about being away from home on the day of the twins' birthday party. The decision was not one that they made lightly, but the invitation from Kenneth's Major-General was not something that they could easily ignore.

'I'll ask Captain Clayton-Whalley to keep an eye on them,' suggested Kenneth. 'She's very good at looking after children.'

The suggestion was greeted by Frances Clayton-Whalley with mixed feelings. As the only Women's Royal Army Corps officer in the Mess, she was not short of similar invitations. The principal military objective of her career had been to find a rich husband p.d.q. – then leave the country's defences to those who cared. As it was, she found herself spending her spare hours minding the babies of those who had already achieved victory.

Still, the Bolingbrokes were then living in a large house, the produce of Sheffield's discarded pots and pans, which lay in a picturesque village in rural Surrey. And as everyone knew, their daughters were enchanting and no test for Clayton-Whalley's powers of leadership. Moreover, she was cleverly ambushed by the request before she had time to think of an excuse.

So it was that on the Saturday in question she drove to the Bolingbroke's house in her third-hand Mini. The sun shone, the birds sang, the hedgerows blossomed and she even smiled indulgently at a long hippie convoy whose battered vehicles, apparently held together with bits of string, obstructed her progress through the lanes of rural England. She swung up the Bolingbroke's drive in sparkling mood and was humming to herself as she crunched to a halt on the gravel alongside the front steps.

Mother Bolingbroke had compensated for her absence by preparing a cornucopia of good things. The table in the large, cool family dining-room bloomed with trifles, jellies, cream cakes and chocolate biscuits. Not one but two birthday cakes (one for each twin) sported the appropriate number of candles; a cracker adorned each place, with a parting present for each guest; a pitcher of orange juice stood in the 'fridge. There were prizes for games (for all winners and runners-up) and chocolates, a bowl of fresh fruit and bags of crisps for those who could not hold out until teatime. It resembled not so much a dentist's diet chart as the offerings of an indulgent, doting parent.

Yet, what impressed Captain Clayton-Whalley most of all was that neither Belinda nor Berenice Bolingbroke had helped herself to even a stray peanut. They sat side by side, like models for Laura Ashley, in quiet, demure repose on the chintz sofa. As they politely shook 'Aunt Frances's' proffered hand, the captain's maternal heart went out to them.

She warned the Bolingbrokes to avoid the hippie convoy, then stood on the steps to bid them au revoir, before letting out the girls to play quietly in the garden and sitting down herself to start organising some games. She had brought along the whistle she used for refereeing netball and a pair of navy blue shorts she wore in the gym.

The young guests started to arrive an hour later. A procession of Jaguars purred up the long drive to deposit little girls in party frocks, each bearing birthday-wrapped gifts – one for each twin. Frances Clayton-Whalley, as surrogate mother, felt she was already entering into the spirit of the thing.

Her whistle in one hand, millboard in the other, she summoned the party to rounders on the back lawn. After half-an-hour – when the children were growing bored – she imaginatively switched to a treasure hunt, then blind man's buff... The summer air was full of childish laughter. With the scent of newly mown grass and rambler roses, it made an intoxicating cocktail before tea.

It was halfway through the treasure hunt that she noticed it: a curious, rumbling noise of cars and voices. She assumed it was traffic passing along the road – or perhaps the Bolingbrokes' neighbours were having a party too. Anyway, her attention was distracted by delighted shrieks as the treasure trove was discovered beneath a cherry tree in the orchard beyond the shrubbery.

During the blind man's buff though she heard the noise again, accompanied this time by a most peculiar and less than pleasant ambient smell. She frowned, wrinkled her nose and shrugged her shoulders. Perhaps someone nearby was burning rubbish.

They were halfway through the last game before tea, according to Captain Clayton-Whalley's organised programme, when she was conscious of an uninvited guest. Turning round, she saw a young man (or was it a man?) walking in through the Bolingbrokes' open kitchen door.

'Excuse me,' she called sharply. 'May I help you?'

'Thank you, lady,' said the man, handing her a battered, old-fashioned kettle. 'Fill this up for us, would you?' he asked.

Captain Clayton-Whalley recognised that peculiar smell again as, somewhat taken aback, she took the kettle inside the kitchen and filled it for him. He had not washed, she decided, for several days if not weeks. Long frizzy hair hung down his back, which was covered by a formerly white shirt and holed Fairisle pullover.

''Ere, do you reckon we could bring the vans round 'ere?' he asked suddenly. 'Well, some of them, anyway,' he added helpfully, as he caught sight of Captain Clayton-Whalley's expression.

'Some ... of ... the vans...' she repeated faintly. Then, recovering her wits, she added more crisply: 'I think I had better investigate what's going on.'

She marched round to the front of the house and then stopped, aghast. Along the whole length of the Bolingbrokes' gravelled drive were parked the entire hippie convoy. At least, that was her immediate impression. On closer examination it was clear that by no means all of it was yet there. Those vehicles still arriving, on finding the drive full, were already driving over the flower-beds on to the lawn.

Some of the cars and lorries were pulling caravans, and all seemed to be equipped with children and mongrel dogs. A young girl who was even dirtier than the man – but with shorter hair – stamped out a cigarette on the front steps and stared at Frances without evident embarrassment. The air was full of exhaust fumes and ... that smell again. Heavy rock from ghetto-blasters drowned the bird-song and the drone of bumble-bees...

''Ere, Pete, we're running out of room 'ere,' said the girl.

'S'orl right. She says we can put some round the back,' said the young man.

'I said nothing of the kind!' snapped back Captain Clayton-Whalley, drawing on her reserves of leadership potential. But her voice was being drowned by the roar of diesel engines as the first few rusting trucks shook themselves into life. She gave a frantic blast upon her whistle, but Radio One passed by, giving no quarter. The gallant Captain leapt in front of the first lorry, but smartly jumped back as it showed no sign of stopping. Indeed, its ability to do so looked in question. Shaken, she leaned for support against one stationary mudguard, which promptly fell off on to a bed of white carnations. More and more vehicles were still queuing up at the front entrance.

Suddenly remembering her charges she dashed back, dodging between the swaying, groaning vans. She found the children excitedly leaping up and down while one or two were already clambering over the trucks.

'Belinda, Berenice! I mean ... Berenice, Belinda! Come down at once!' she screamed wildly. But her voice, so effective in the gym and on the barrack square at Guildford, made little impression on the situation now developing.

'I'll phone the police,' she said loudly, then to herself, 'That's it,' she muttered, 'the police ... the police...'

She ran through the open back door, nearly colliding with a mangy-looking greyhound with a wall eye who grasped in his jaws the remains of Belinda's birthday cake – or could it have been Berenice's?

'Give me that, you disgusting brute!' she screamed with fury and grabbed somewhat imprudently at a candle. The hound dropped the cake but lunged at her with a snarl of such wild-eyed venom that she hastily handed it back and said, 'Good dog.'

The hippie children obscured the rest of the tea-table. Those who weren't actually eating were unwrapping the presents and pulling crackers. Half-sobbing, Frances dialled 999.

'Fire, police or ambulance?' asked the operator calmly.

Through the window Frances saw the smoke of wood-fires as the hippies established their camps on the Bolingbrokes' lawn.

'The lot!' she screamed distractedly down the line.

An hour later the fire, police and ambulancemen arrived on foot, having had to abandon their vehicles half a mile away.

'You'll have to get more of these trucks inside,' said the police sergeant. 'You can't leave them blocking the road, you know. What's your name, madam?'

He reached for his notebook and unsheathed his ballpoint.

'For God's sake, I'm trying to get rid of them!' yelled poor Frances.

The police sergeant looked at her stonily. 'But you invited them in lady,' he said.

'I did nothing of the kind!' she shouted back at him.

Crooking a finger, he beckoned her to follow him down the drive, stepping over recumbent hippies and wood-fires. Outside on the road, he pointed up at a large sign; thereon it said, in large black spray-can capitals: 'HIPPIE CAMP SITE. ALL HIPPIES WELCOME HERE.'

Frances Clayton-Whalley stared at the invitation open-mouthed.

'I didn't put that up,' she protested loudly.

'I see. And this is your house, madam, is it?' asked the police sergeant.

'Well, no, not exactly,' she stammered.

'I see, madam,' he said impassively. 'Well, no doubt the genuine owners put it there. I think you'd better give me your name after all, miss ... if you don't mind.'

Out of the corner of her eye Frances saw one of his colleagues realigning trucks on the front lawn while another was guiding more in over the flower-beds. A muddy track had by now been carved between the roses...

The police left when the main road had been cleared and all the hippie vehicles packed into the garden. The fireman and ambulancemen had gone, not before promising to report her for misuse of the emergency services.

'You want to get this place cleaned up,' said an ambulanceman disgustedly, surveying the garden.

The Bolingbrokes senior arrived home shortly afterwards.

'Yer can't come in here, mate,' said one of the hippies as their Rover stopped abruptly at the entrance. He was indeed speaking no more than the truth.

Silently, half-dazed, they walked up the long drive, past the lines of washing and belching caravan smokestacks, stumbling over spare tyres and piles of rubbish.

They found their daughters and their friends in the back garden, singing peacenik songs with Pete, his three common-law wives and seven children. They had swapped their Laura Ashley dresses with Pete's children and were wearing torn jeans and grubby jumpers.

'Where's Captain Clayton-Whalley?' asked Kenneth faintly. But the twins said they had not seen her for hours and hours.

After picking their way through the ruins of afternoon tea and negotiating their passage upstairs with two rotweilers, they found the Captain giggling hysterically in a bedroom.

It took the Bolingbrokes over two weeks to get rid of their guests and several months to redecorate the house. Even then that peculiar smell still lingered on, while the flower-beds and lawns were never quite the same.

Nor indeed was Captain Frances Clayton-Whalley who, after a long rest abroad, left the Army by mutual consent.

'Who would have thought it, a nice girl like that?' said Mrs Bolingbroke, shaking her head. 'And such a good family, too. It shows that appearances can be deceptive, doesn't it? I'm afraid that she simply fell into bad company. But when I think of the dangers our poor gels were exposed to...!'

I don't know what became of the Bolingbroke twins, but I am sure it included nothing untoward.

The moral of this tale is that those who are tempted to leave town till the party's over should think again. Just have faith in our Colonel's advice and trust in God.

✄

You can also have faith that the young guests will greatly enjoy the Colonel's treats.   *H.S.*

ETON MESS

This is a traditional dish from Eton College, the Colonel's old school, and consists of fresh strawberries, crushed with a fork and mixed with equal quantities of whipped cream. We have given two versions, to help separate the men from the boys.

📖

Serves: 6

Preparation: 15 minutes

Ingredients

For boys
450 (1lb) fresh strawberries, hulled
25g (1oz) icing sugar
325ml (12fl oz) fresh whipped cream

Drill

1. Crush two-thirds of the strawberries with a fork or cut into small pieces. Mix the icing sugar with the cream, then add the crushed strawberries.

2. Place in a suitable bowl or individual dishes and decorate with the remaining strawberries.

Ingredients

For the Old Boys
450g (1lb) fresh strawberries, hulled
325ml (12fl oz) fresh whipped cream
75ml (3fl oz) kirsch
6 small meringues, crushed
6 ratafias (small almond biscuits), crushed

Drill

1. Reserve a few strawberries for decoration, then chop the remainder and place in a bowl. Sprinkle with the kirsch. Cover and chill for 2-3 hours.

2. Whip the cream until it is stiff and holds its shape. Then gently fold in the strawberries and their juice. Add the crushed meringues and ratafias. Serve in a chilled dish, decorated with the reserved fruit.

CLOWNS' HATS WITH ICE CREAM

This ice cream sundae can be made with any combination of ice cream, fruit sauce, nuts, cream, whipped cream and biscuits. Although ready-made ice cream can be used, the home-made produce is better and the variety of flavours almost infinite. The recipes we give are the Colonel's favourites and can be made either in an ice-cream machine or by using a food mixed and home freezer.

Serves: 15-20

Preparation: 10 minutes

Resting: 1 hour

Cooking: 5-10 minutes

Ingredients

75g (3oz) sugar
25g (1oz) almond paste, cut into small dice
pinch of cinnamon
1 large egg
65g (2½oz) plain flour
pinch of salt
1½tbs single cream

Drill

1. In a bowl, cream together the sugar, almond paste, cinnamon and egg. Let this stand for a few minutes.

2. Sift the flour and salt, then add this to the egg and sugar mix. Blend in well to ensure that there are no lumps and the mix is smooth. Cover, and let it rest for at least 1 hour in a refrigerator.

3. Stir in the cream (*this must be done just before baking*).

4. Lightly grease a baking sheet and dust with flour. Using a cutter, mark the rings, about 4in in diameter, or make a stencil from a card about 2mm thick. Spread the mixture thinly and evenly.

5. Bake in a medium oven for 3-4 mins or until the edge of the biscuit has a nice golden colour.

6. Lift the biscuits from the baking sheet one at a time and shape round a cream horn mould to form a cone.

7. When cold, pipe three chocolate buttons on each hat.

To make the ice cream sundae

8. Fill chilled sundae glasses with a mixture of ice creams.from the recipes on the following pages. Then decorate with raspberry or chocolate sauces (see Basic recipe section). Top with Clowns' Hat Biscuits.

RICH CHOCOLATE ICE CREAM

Serves: 6-8

Preparation: 25 minutes

Freezing: 1½-2 hours

Ingredients

225g (8oz) good quality plain chocolate, chopped
2 eggs
50g (2oz) caster sugar
150ml (¼pt) double cream
65ml (2½fl oz) single cream
1tsp Grand Marnier (optional)

Drill

1. Melt the chocolate in a bowl over a pan of boiling water.

2. Put the eggs and sugar into a bowl and whisk together until very light and fluffy. Then quickly but lightly fold in the chocolate.

3. In another bowl, lightly whip the cream and Grand Marnier (if used) together, and fold into the chocolate mixture.

4. Pour the mixture into a container and cover. Freeze until firm, beating well after 1½ hours.

5. About 15 minutes before serving, transfer the ice cream to the refrigerator.

STRAWBERRY ICE CREAM

Serves: 6-8

Preparation: 10 minutes

Freezing: 1½-2 hours

Ingredients

675g (1½lbs) strawberries, hulled
juice of ½ orange
175g (6oz) caster sugar
450ml (¾pt) double cream, whipped

Drill

1. Purée the strawberries with the orange juice. Add the sugar and strain through a fine sieve.

2. Fold the whipped cream into the purée.

3. Pour the mixture into a container. Cover and freeze until firm, beating twice at hourly intervals.

4. About 30 minutes before serving, transfer the ice cream to a refrigerator.

HAZLENUT ICE CREAM

📖

Serves: 6-8

Preparation: 30 minutes

Freezing: 1½-2 hours

Ingredients

100ml (4fl oz) water

175g (6oz) sugar

5 egg yolks

450ml (¾pt) fresh whipped cream

75g (3oz) hazelnuts, lightly toasted and finely chopped

Drill

1. Place the water and sugar in a small saucepan and cook until the sugar has caramelised. To stop it cooking, take off the heat and add a few drops of water. Be careful, as it will spit and froth at first. Keep it warm.

2. Whisk the egg yolks in the bowl until very thick and pale in colour. Pour in the caramel in a slow steady stream, whisking continuously until the mixture is cool.

3. Fold in the cream, vanilla essence and hazelnuts. Pour the mixture into a container. Cover and freeze until firm.

4. Transfer to the refrigerator 30 minutes before serving.

SORBETS

Both ice creams and sorbets have been around for a long time. Historians have found records of the Chinese first discovering the art of making iced puddings. Good quality ice cream and sorbets can be bought ready-made, but with a little time and imagination an infinite variety can be made at home. Domestic ice cream/sorbet machines now available are ideal, because they mix and freeze at the same time. A food processor used in combination with your ordinary freezer makes an equally good product, but the process takes a little longer. The estimated timings and serving numbers given below apply to all three of our sorbet recipes. A mix of all three makes an attractive presentation.

📖

Serves: 6-8

Preparation: 15 minutes

Freezing: 1½-2 hours

Drill

Redcurrant Sorbet

450g (1lb) redcurrants
2 egg whites
100g (4oz) sugar
150ml (¼pt) Sauternes

1. Purée the redcurrants and add the wine. Sieve through a fine strainer.

2. Whip the egg whites to a snow, slowly adding the sugar as you whisk.

3. Fold the redcurrant purée into the egg white.

4. Freeze in the ice-cream machine or use the food processor and freezer in combination. Serve piped, or scoop into chilled glasses. Decorate with redcurrants or lemon balm leaves and serve with a biscuit.

Strawberry Sorbet

450g (1lb) strawberries
2 egg whites
100g (4oz) sugar
scant 150ml (¼pt) water
juice of ½ lemon
strawberries for decoration

1. Purée the strawberries and add the water and lemon juice. Sieve through a fine strainer or muslin.

2. Whip the egg whites to a stiff snow, adding the sugar a little at a time.

3. Fold in the strawberry purée and freeze as above.

Orange Sorbet

175g (6oz) sugar
150ml (¼pt) water
rind of an orange
225ml (8fl oz) freshly squeezed orange juice
juice of 1 lime
225ml (8fl oz) white wine

1. Bring the sugar and water to the boil. Add the orange rind and cook for 3-5 minutes.

2. Allow to cool and strain on to the orange juice. Add the lime juice and white wine.

3. Whip the egg white until it is half stiff and fold it into the mixture with a balloon whisk.

4. Freeze to a smooth consistency in an ice-cream machine, or use the food processor and mixer method.

5. Serve in chilled glasses with a biscuit.

TRIFLE

Serves: 6

Preparation: 45 minutes

Ingredients

1 small Swiss roll, cut into slices
150ml (¼pt) raspberry sauce
150ml (¼pt) sweet sherry
25g (1oz) almonds, blanched and flaked
18 ratafias
300ml (½pt) double or whipping cream to decorate

For the custard:
2 eggs
3 egg yolks
300ml (½pt) milk
450ml (¾pt) single cream
50g (2oz) caster sugar
1 vanilla pod

Drill

1. Blend the eggs and egg yolks with the milk, cream and sugar. Pour into the top of a double saucepan or a heatproof bowl standing over a pan of boiling water.

2. Add the vanilla pod and allow the water to simmer gently. Stir until the custard coats the back of a spoon. Remove the vanilla pod.

3. Meanwhile, arrange the slices of Swiss roll around a glass serving dish.

(Bottom left) **Chocolate Noodles with White Chocolate Sauce** (page 146), *(bottom right)*
White Chocolate and Cheese Mousse (page 144), *(centre)* **Chocolate and Coffee Cream
Profiteroles** (page 144), *(behind)* **Chocolate Truffle Slice** (page 145)

(Clockwise from the bottom) **Sorbets** (page 159), **Clowns' Hats with Ice Cream** (page 156), **Trifle** (page 160), **Eton Mess** (page 155)

4. Mix the sherry with the raspberry sauce and pour over the Swiss roll. Add the flaked almonds and half of the ratafias.

5. Pour the warm custard over the Swiss roll and nuts. Place a plate over the bowl to prevent a skin forming as the custard cools.

6. Whip the cream until it just holds its shape, and spread or pipe over the custard base.

7. Decorate with the remaining ratafias or with maraschino cherries, toasted almonds or shaped chocolate. Serve well chilled.

Variations:

Some fresh raspberries, strawberries, or slices of peach or bananas can be added before covering with the custard. White wine or brandy can be substituted for the sherry.

For young children, omit the sherry and double the amount of raspberry sauce.

BATTENBURG SLICE

Serves: 6

Preparation: 25 minutes

Ingredients

Sponge, half white, half pink (see basic recipes)
Apricot glaze (see basic recipes)
675g (1½lb) white almond paste

Drill

1. Prepare the base sponge according to the basic recipe, making half vanilla flavour (white) and half raspberry (pink).

2. When cold, remove the skin from the top and bottom with a sharp knife. Sandwich the two pieces together with apricot glaze and cut into strips about ¾in wide.

3. Join the strips together with apricot glaze, alternating the colours.

4. Roll out the almond paste (using caster sugar to dust) to just over 6in wide and the length of the strips of sponge. Spread the almond paste with apricot glaze and roll around the sponge strips, trimming any surplus. Cut into slices and serve for afternoon tea.

ON THE BOTTLE-FIELD

On the bottlefield

What the Colonel drinks with his meals depends partly on a set of old conventions and partly on Julie, who serves in his local supermarket. The former guide him towards the wines he *should* buy; the latter smartly tells him those he *can*.

In this age of colour supplements, however, he is starting to have ideas of his own. This is why he sometimes appears mildly confused.

He often sighs for the simplicity of the old days. The English then drank Graves with fish and chicken, and Beaujolais with everything else. Beyond a 20-mile radius of London, there were indeed few alternatives open to them.

Then came Liebfraumilch, Mateus rosé and Chianti, whose picturesque labels and bulbous flasks not only looked desperately chic when bathed in candlelight, but could also be turned into table-lamps when empty. Anyway, as long as one kept to the simple rules – red plonk with red meat, white plonk with white, and rosé for those who wanted to match the curtains – those with reasonable eyesight couldn't go wrong.

Those were the days when men were men etc. etc., when all London buses were scarlet and the Sunday papers could still be lifted manually. Only Ministers of the Crown crossed the Atlantic, while Lambrusco was thought to be a type of foreign car.

Alas, as he now reviews the regiment of bottles lined up in close order on the shelves, how the Colonel regrets the passing of those years.

Not only is the choice itself bewildering, but the French (ah, them again) have recently tried to destroy the simple faith of men like him by contradicting the basic tenets of religion. From Beaujolais to Bordeaux, from Lyon to the Loire, they are not only drinking white wine with *le bifsteak* but copious quantities of red with *sole colbert*. Those who did to French cooking with *nouvelle cuisine* what architects have done to London's skyline, are now vandalising the foundations of wine drinking.

The principle is sensible enough. One should drink whatever one likes and when one likes – while keeping a wary eye on the Great Reaper. She who fancies a tall, slender bottle of Hock to accompany our Steak, Oysters and Brown Beer Pie should indulge her natural taste-buds and enjoy it – though whether her judgement should be swayed by the crenellated schloss on the label is more doubtful.

The cost of a bottle of wine, assuming that it is bought in a reliable wine-shop, is usually as good a guide as any to its quality. Buy the best one can afford, then sit back and think of France, is sensible advice for the wine virgin.

One need not be shy of one's guests. The assumption that they know all about wines is almost invariably false. In case they do, however, it might be a sensible precaution to murmur as one pours from one's bottle of Egyptian Riesling: 'I'd be interested to hear your opinion of this *parvenu*. An unusual marriage, I'm sure you'll agree, but I think it should work.'

On the other hand, there are some marriages which are clearly made in Heaven and others which are destined for divorce. Unless and until one knows form, it is wiser to follow the old broadly-based conventions. One might not break new gastronomic ground, but one's reputation should survive unsullied. 'Play safe' is the Colonel's strategy at the table.

Serve chilled dry sherry (either fino or manzanilla) with the soup, and afterwards play it according to the rules. Fish is usually best accompanied by dry whites like Muscadet, Soave, Chablis or Sancerre. Should the fish dish incorporate a creamy rich sauce, however, the Colonel favours a more winsome blonde like Vouvray or a bustling, fruity fraulein from the Rhineland. Hocks and Mosels are usually safe with chicken dishes, though turkey tastes equally well with a good claret.

Drink claret (red Bordeaux) with your roast lamb and the more robust, full-bodied Burgundies with beef and game. Spanish Rioja and traditional Rhone wines (e.g. Chateauneuf du Pape) make reliable escorts for a wide range of meat entrées, and Chianti is naturally safe with any pasta.

If one can afford to serve special wines with the dessert, stay with the sweet wines like Barsac or Sauternes, and revert to claret or Burgundy with the cheese. For those rich enough to drink champagne throughout the meal, one's worries are virtually over – though socialites rather than gourmets will be impressed. By no means everyone agrees that this is the ideal solution. The same money might be better spent on an interesting variety of plonks, each wedded to an individual course.

The few samples cited above represent only some of the more familiar illustrations of an ever-increasing variety of wines. Elegant New Zealand whites and hearty, rumbustious Australian reds, bottles of California sunshine and golden, svelte young temptresses from South Africa now compete successfully with those from France, Germany, Italy and Spain – not to mention Yugoslavia, Bulgaria, Hungary and Greece. Even sun-starved Britain has a growing number of vineyards, though the cost of their products is rarely very competitive.

To sift one's way through the brightest and the best one needs a constantly updated guide to wines and/or to follow the wine columns in the press. That is why it is generally safer for the Colonel to follow his primitive drill: the more strongly flavoured the food, the bolder the wine which accompanies it – and vice versa.

Many dishes now in the multi-cultural British Isles are hard to team with any well-known wine. Vinegary dressings and sauces and oriental flavours like sweet and sour are notoriously difficult to match. Hot curries are virtually impossible – though some people persevere valiantly with Hock-types. A typical Rhine wine might go tolerably well with the prawn curry in this book, but most Indian food is best accompanied by beer.

If you have any doubts after that, do what the Colonel does and just ask Julie...   *H.S.*

The Pig

The exercise was not without merit. There was only one fatality – but then war is hell. Napier turned a profit for the benefit of the soldiers' messing account.

And Mrs Middleditch was never the same again.

The list of functions that the Regiment planned to hold during the Christmas period was daunting in the extreme. They ran the full range from the Rugger Club dance, through the Corporals' Mess 'Smoker' and the Warrant

Officers' and Sergeants' Mess Draw to the Officers' Mess Ball. The 'All Ranks' Dance was to be held in the gymnasium, the Saddle Club Buffet Supper in the YMCA and the Civilian Staff Party was planned for the Garrison Study Centre. Wherever there was room for two or three to gather together, a party was to be held.

Lieutenant Napier was responsible for catering for them all.

Napier considered the list of functions on the sheet before him and patted his pockets for a cigarette. Not finding one he looked up hopefully at his Master Chef who, avoiding Napier's eye, slid his own cigarettes and lighter across the desk and out of Napier's reach.

'Christmas starts on 1 December and ends in about mid-March next year,' pronounced Napier gloomily: not having a cigarette to console him, he worried a fingernail.

SQMS Horsefall, the Master Chef, examined the offending list and, nodding his head, said, 'Not only is there one hell of a lot of extra work here, but the frustration is that a great deal of it is repetitious. For instance, the Sergeants' Mess want a cold buffet, so do the Saddle Club, so do the Guild of St Helena and the Townswomen's Guild and the Officers' Mess and so on. I'm going to have to produce game pies for them all. They will all want centre-pieces, and it's those that take up so much time.'

Napier nodded in agreement.

The Warrant Officer continued, 'Now the game pies, for example, have got to be fresh, otherwise they won't be at their best. The same is true of all the other buffet items like the salmon and venison. But the centre-pieces are a different matter. We don't expect them to be eaten...'

Napier nodded quickly and interrupted. 'OK, why not make up several centre-pieces that we can use throughout the Christmas period? We can ring the changes and no one will be any the wiser. We can...' he added slowly '...bill them all for everything, thereby keeping the old account in good nick.'

Both heads were nodding metronomically as they considered the task in more depth. Napier worried his nail. Horsefall wanted a cigarette, but he was damned if he'd offer the seventh of that day to his officer – knowing that it would not only be accepted but would not be reciprocated.

'What we want is a pig,' judged the SQMS.

'Pig?'

'Pig!'

'What sort of pig?'

'A suckling-pig.'

Thus the stage was set for the ghastly events that followed.

At a local farm several days later, the suckling pig – an endearing little fellow – was selected whilst still on the pap. The piglet was a dirty pink colour and covered in a fine silky down, of the quality normally found only upon chins of Second Lieutenants. He squeaked and squealed as he gambolled innocently in his sty.

'He won't make as much noise as that with an apple in his mouth,' remarked the SQMS, leaning on the side of the sty in an appropriately bucolic manner.

'We'll take him,' said Napier.

The next time the Catering Officer saw the pig he was dressed – the pig, that is – in a smart overcoat of honey-coloured aspic jelly. His eyebrows, ears and the line of his snout were all accentuated by carefully cut pieces of truffle and egg-white arranged in mosaic pattern. He looked quite beautiful in death, albeit a little uncomfortable with a Cox's Orange Pippin jammed between his bicuspids. His tail curled at a jaunty angle and in this the SQMS took a modest pride because, as he explained to his young soldiers, roasting a suckling-pig is not easy, and he who can cook it correctly but at the same time prevent the tail burning in the process scores maximum points, passes 'go' and collects £200.

The suckling-pig was magnificent.

The Corporals' Club, first on Lieutenant Napier's list, was delighted with its buffet upon which the suckling-pig took pride of place. Suggestions that the pig should be cut were met by the chefs behind the buffet with cold humourless stares. Corporal Carstairs poured scorn upon a fellow member of the Corporals' Club who had asked for 'just a slice' by saying: 'This pig's for lookin' at, not for eatin'.'

It was rather a shame that the Commanding Officer's Lady did not hear the exchange, because she might then have been more accommodating later. Lieutenant Colonel Middleditch was a charming old chap who was invited to all the Regiment's Christmas functions and indeed most of the Garrison functions. To the dismay of all, however, he invariably brought his Lady. She breathed fire and brimstone and there was not a man – nor for that matter a wife – in the Regiment who did not scan the horizon each day hoping to see St

George riding into town.

The evening after the Corporals' Mess Smoker, the suckling-pig paraded at the Guild of St Helena and the Women's Institute Combined Christmas Social.

It sounds awful, doesn't it?

It was.

But the suckling-pig was the centre of admiration and Mrs Middleditch made enquiries about his availability.

'Well, madam, I will carve it if you *really* insist,' offered Corporal Rix helpfully, making no attempt to do anything of the sort and making it pretty evident that he never heard such an absurd idea in his life. Predictably, Mrs Middleditch agreed that it would be a shame to disturb the pig and so it soldiered on, gazing unblinkingly at the bored-looking lobster artistically displayed to his front.

The Guild of St Helena and the Women's Institute were billed for a suckling-pig.

They paid.

The pig was refrigerated, and later that week he reappeared at the Rugby Club Dance. 'Twas a riotous assembly and Colonel Middleditch, President of the Club, had a splendid evening. Mrs Middleditch was not 'into' rugby club dances and so gave the buffet her particular attention. She noted the suckling-pig, asked for a portion, and was told that it was to be carved 'later'.

The Rugby Club was billed for a pig.

It paid.

Mrs Middleditch next encountered the pig at the Garrison Hunt Club Ball, a pretentious affair to which 'everyone' had been invited save the hounds. When supper was announced in ringing tones by the toastmaster, she made a beeline for Corporal George Arbuthnot Pike who was engaged in steeling a knife behind the buffet counter.

'Aha!' she neighed.

George Arbuthnot Pike continued to steel his knife and thought how much his feet ached. He had an arrangement with one of the waiters, and knew that a pint of foaming ale was his for the drinking just as soon as he could leave his post.

'I want some suckling-pig,' demanded Mrs Middleditch.

'Of course, madam. A particularly wise choice, if I may make so bold. I played a personal part in its production only this afternoon and it really is bleeding good. Oh! I'm sorry, ma'am, excellent, ...'

'Now!'

As George Arbuthnot Pike looked round for help, the snowy figure of the SQMS hove into sight. With a yelp and muttered apology Pike legged it to the side of his leader and sought sanctuary in the all-enveloping presence of SQMS Horsefall.

'She wants some pig,' he hissed.

'No!' pronounced the SQMS in a voice last used at Taunton by Judge Jeffreys in response to an appeal from the dock.

'Then what the hell do I say?' pleaded Pike.

Horsefall leant forward and whispered in Pike's receptive ear and the latter then doubled back to his post, almost transfixing a horsey-looking gent who was approaching the buffet at full gallop from the opposite direction as if it were a five-barred gate.

'Madam, as I was saying before the SQMS sent for me, this suckling-pig will be a delight and will do the sort of things to your taste buds that you only read about in books.'

At this point Pike looked quickly over each shoulder in turn and gave a convincing demonstration of a man wrestling with his conscience. 'But...' he lowered his voice and his demeanour became more conspiratorial. 'But pork is, well ... pork, and if you fill up your plate with plain old roast pork you will not have room for the 'Coquilles de foie gras en gelée' nor for the 'Dodine de Canard Charles Vaucher', both especially created for this evening by Mr Horsefall.'

By an inclination of his head, Pike indicated the Warrant Officer. The great man was patrolling the limits of the buffet, acknowledging the plaudits of the horse-fancying public. Suddenly, he wheeled and swooped down on Pike and Mrs Middleditch. With a gesture of dismissal he dispatched Pike and turned his considerable personality to bear with singular concentration upon Mrs Middl-editch.

'Mrs Middleditch, how thoroughly nice to see you with us tonight, and thank you for coming to the buffet so early. It's a constant joy to Mr Napier, myself and our soldiers that this Regiment has one or two people who really appreciate good food. Now, I last produced this for the King of Tonga when His Majesty visited Sandhurst in 1968.'

As Horsefall was speaking, he had taken the plate from Mrs Middleditch's unresisting fingers and was applying to it, with great panache, a prodigious portion of what, in more prosaic parlance, would have been described as stuffed duck. It looked good, it smelled delicious.

'But...' brayed Mrs Middleditch.

Horsefall affected not to hear and, moving swiftly to one side, he paused for only a moment to add three slices of rare roast fillet of beef before addressing a dish of goose livers. He covered with the goose livers the last area of exposed china upon the plate's surface and then, avoiding her gaze, thrust the plate at Mrs Middleditch and greeted the Master of the Garrison Hunt.

'General, how thoroughly nice to see you here this evening...'

Mrs Middleditch, thoroughly ungruntled – or is it disgruntled – left the buffet and made her way back to her table. Over her retreating back, Horsefall and Pike exchanged a smile. Napier mopped his brow.

The following morning a post mortem was held upon the evening's events and it was decided that the pig needed to be re-dressed. His shining coat had lost its glaze and in several places it had split and had a crazed effect. He would have made an excellent spinner's wicket, looking as he did.

Private Palmer was invited to try his hand at redecorating the pig and he was delighted to have the opportunity. Bubbling with enthusiasm, he submitted his design to the SQMS. Horsefall made one or two minor suggestions and then let Palmer loose. Napier and Horsefall were in earnest conversation when, some forty minutes later, Palmer appeared at the office door.

'Yes, Palmer?' said Napier.

'He stinks!' stated Palmer flatly.

'Who does?' interrogated Horsefall.

'The Pig.'

'My sainted Aunt,' croaked Napier.

'I hope not, sir, but she would if she'd died a violent death, been covered in aspic jelly and left lying around in smoke-filled rooms for the last ten days or so, taking time out to spend her nights in a refrigerator with a miscellany of corned beef and left-over baked beans', contributed Horsefall crisply, adding 'Palmer, here is what you do...'

The following evening the suckling-pig, despite now being well into middle age, was in sparkling form. Palmer had done a splendid job on him and he was the star of the All Ranks' Dance held, inevitably, in the Gymnasium.

Mrs Middleditch, looking utterly repellent in an evening dress of deep burgundy that accentuated her florid complexion and toned with the 'Tomatoes Neapolitan Style', surveyed the buffet.

'I've seen him before.'

'Yes, dear,' replied the Colonel.

Mrs Middleditch pointed dramatically in the direction of the buffet, and the Colonel looked along the line of her finger.

'Oh, Palmer... Yes, jolly good chap, frightfully good pistol shot, I'm told ... excellent cook.'

'No, No, No, No! ... not Palmer ... the pig!' brimstoned Mrs Middleditch.

'Well, dear, you've seen one pig you've seen them all, you know, and I wouldn't like to try to tell two of them apart ... now really, would you?'

Mrs Middleditch agreed with striking lack of enthusiasm, but muttered under her breath, 'It's the tail, the bend in the tail.'

The Paymaster, who had joined the party halfway through the conversation, remarked to his wife in bed that night, 'That Mrs Middleditch is a strange woman, don't you think?'

During the festive season Mrs Middleditch made several further attempts to induce someone, anyone, to serve her with a slice of suckling-pig, but all the Chefs had strict instructions that on no account was the pig, now a popular member of the catering troop, to be touched. It called for some very fancy footwork from time to time but, when the Officers' Mess Ball took place, the pig was ... complete.

The Officers' Mess Ball was the last major function in the regimental calendar and a multitude of guests had been invited. The PMC made it clear that an 'aspic extravaganza' was required.

The pig was billed to make his sixteenth and last appearance.

He was past his best.

He smelled.

He was not nice to be near.

In a word he was ... putrid.

But ... he still looked good. His tail had the same jaunty curl, and in his newest coat of aspic he was pleasing to the eye. By now eight different Chefs had decorated him and he had proved to be, by any yardstick, one hell of a cost-effective pig. Paid for sixteen times, he deserved a place in culinary history.

Mrs Middleditch was a trifle liverish on the day of the Ball. She had held a Wives' Club meeting that morning, where one young woman had been under the incredible misapprehension that Wives' Clubs were democratic institutions in which the membership actually voted. Mrs Middleditch had had to make it clear that she was the sole arbiter of anything and everything – Judge, Jury and, if need be, Lord High Executioner. Surely everyone already knew that ... what on earth was the Army coming to? You don't have Wives' Clubs for fun ... really!

She snapped at the Colonel when he enquired about a clean dress shirt and following up by warning him that she would be displeased if there was no soft tissue in the Powder Room when she got to the mess. The Colonel made a mental note and then, whilst taking a swift noggin before setting off, made a phone call. He was assured that there was some rather attractive soft paper in the ladies' loo.

The Colonel and his lady wife made their way to the Mess. There had been a light dusting of snow and Mrs Middleditch demanded to be carried but the Colonel, twice decorated for gallantry, knew his limitations and declined. Mrs Middleditch was thus already furious when she reached the Mess and took, from the Mess Sergeant, her first glass of champagne.

In the dining-room Horsefall inspected, tasted, titivated, criticised and generally co-ordinated the final touches to a buffet fit to set before the Queen or, at a push, Mrs Middleditch.

The young soldiers fidgeted with their neck scarves and shuffled their feet. The NCOs affected boredom and told stories of bigger and better buffets they had worked upon.

All knew that the pig was a culinary time-bomb and could not be served under any circumstances.

The Mess Sergeant invited the guests to inspect the buffet and in the van came Colonel and Mrs Middleditch. There was an appreciative murmur, but above it the Commanding Officer's wife could be heard bellowing at her spouse.

'Violet is an awful colour – why do we have to have violet paper? Aren't you in command here? What's wrong with pink? or green? or blue? or white for that matter? Why violet?'

The party eddied and flowed around the buffet. As Mrs Middleditch looked at the pig for the sixteenth time her conviction was absolute. It was the eyes... The pig's eyes had been replaced by two green grapes, each rather tastefully decorated with a stuffed olive. They stared sightlessly into her face.

'It's the same pig,' she breathed. 'No wonder they won't carve it. No wonder it looks the same. It *is* the same...'

Mrs Middleditch turned on her heel, walked over to the group around her husband and pointed back towards the buffet. 'I know that pig,' she stated.

The Garrison Commander blinked and the Chaplain took a deep draught of sherry. Others in the group affected interest in Mrs Middleditch's porcine acquaintances.

'Yes, dear,' replied Colonel Middleditch soothingly.

'It's his eyes, you know, I've looked into them and they're the same... The same ... d'you hear? He's following me ... everywhere I go... What about his tail?'

Mrs Middleditch clutched at the arm of the person nearest to her. The arm belonged to the Chaplain, and at its extremity his hand was clutching a sherry glass. The agitated grip of Mrs Middleditch caused the sherry to evacuate the glass in panic and take cover on the inside leg of the cleric's mess-kit. Throughout the room all eyes were on Mrs Middleditch. The band, which had been producing appropriate music in the background, realised it had lost everyone's attention and petered out lamely.

Mrs Middleditch pointed an accusing finger at the buffet. She was wild-eyed, and hysteria was only just around the corner.

'The pig, that pig, I see him everywhere, it's his eyes. They are made of grapes, you know.'

She added the last sentence in a conversational tone that only served to accentuate the immoderation of her earlier remarks.

Someone – and it was never determined who – said 'Violet paper,' and giggled. Like measles the giggle spread, and within seconds the room was rocking with laughter. Mrs Middleditch looked around her; she had never *ever* been laughed at before and hysteria, just around the corner, came in and joined the party.

'Shut-up, Shut-up, Shut-up, all of you!' she shrieked. 'Don't you understand? Haven't you noticed? That pig is everywhere. The tail, you must recognise the tail?'All eyes turned to the pig. Several people swore that he assumed a Georgian demeanour and for a few seconds appeared to be clad in a suit of shining armour, with a lance under his right shoulder and a high-mettled steed beneath him. It was only for a moment ... of course hysteria affects different people in different ways. Mrs Middleditch paled to merest puce and beat the Garrison Commander on his chest. The assault was so violent that the Brigadier spilt his sherry down the Chaplain's other leg.

The evening was in chaos, and even after Colonel Middleditch had led his shrieking wife away the tumult continued. In the confusion, Horsefall snorted at Rix and Palmer, 'Get that pig out of here now and dump it in the swillbin. Fill the gap on the table with the stuffed pheasant.'

The partygoers were thus unable to view the pig that had been at the vortex of the maelstrom. Questioned by a member of the Mess Committee, Napier said, 'Pig? Oh! the suckling-pig? Oh yes, been taken away for carving. We do dozens, of course, and I know the Master Chef likes to carve them behind the scenes.'

Early the following morning, behind closed doors, Lieutenant Napier, accompanied by WO2 Horsefall, spoke to his men.

'Some of you were there last night when Mrs Middleditch was taken ... ah ... ill. Those of you who were not will have heard about it. The suckling-pigs we produced for all the various functions seem to have er ... er upset her, and she has formed the impression that a specific pig is following her around... I think that the least we say the better.

'Now Palmer, you prepared a pig didn't you? And you, Corporal Rix? I fancy you did one too, Sergeant Pilbeam? ... Yes, quite. Well, as long as we all are um, um, er...'

'Discreet,' supplied the SQMS.

'Discreet,' Napier agreed.

'Then there won't be any painful repercussions, if you all get my drift?'

There was a general buzz of approval, and in the euphoria SQMS Horsefall offered a cigarette to Lieutenant Napier, who was able to give up the facade of feeling in his pockets for tobacco that he knew he did not have. Oddly enough, the matter of the pig was never pursued, but the outburst by Mrs Middleditch was a talking point for weeks.

Just as British influence in the Far East was never the same after the fall of Singapore, so the influence of Mrs Middleditch was never the same after what became known as the 'Pig Palaver'.

Lieutenant Napier did make a substantial sum of money for the soldiers' messing account, having charged for a veritable herd of swine yet having purchased only the one.

There was, as I said at the beginning, only one fatality ... regrettable but inevitable. It was the pig ... of course, and he was laid to rest, his epitaph a single entry in the swill account. Cost-effective to the last.

⚔

Of course, all this happened a long time ago. Such a thing could never happen today ... never. If, however, you want to chance your arm, the recipe is on p.68.

T.N.

GETTING
DOWN TO
BASICS

Getting down to basics

For the want of a stock-cube the gravy was lost; the for want of the gravy the roast beef was lost; for the want of the roast beef the meal was lost; for the want of the meal a contract was lost; for the want of the contract a man's job was lost. For the want of a man's job, a marriage was lost. For the want of a marriage, contentment was lost – and all for the want of a stock-cube.

It follows that this section is arguably the most important part of our theses. If the screws in a new car are faulty, the whole wretched vehicle breaks down. The same might be said of a meal if the basics are wrong.

I have cited the example of the stock-cube. As you might have observed, the Colonel is largely unaware of its existence; he assumed that all gravy and sauces are home-made – like all pastry, ladies' knitwear and plum puddings. He would approve, without question, of everything in this section.

On the other hand, the Colonel does not cook. His contribution to this new age of equality has been to manage his household without a staff – and allow his Lady to do the work instead. If she, therefore – while he is not looking – reaches for the ready-made mustard, frozen pastry or sauce mix, who could blame her? As the Colonel rarely enters the kitchen, except by accident, who would know?

The moral of this story is that, while we show here how the best menus are prepared, we acknowledge that there are alternative short-cuts. A busy cook should not be deterred from his/her objective by the thought of having to do everything the hard way. There are times when the second-best suffices.

What matters is the overall result, which depends on how many short-cuts one is tempted by. No canned or frozen meal, however seductive its appeal on television, can match the succulence of the real thing. Few restaurants fail to disappoint their customers – unless the latter have abysmal expectations. This is largely because the cooks have lost their way; they have taken one short-cut too many.

One can of course go to the other extreme. Some years ago I went to a dinner-party where the hostess was so fastidious about fresh food that she not only cooked every course while we waited but cleaned the vegetables and scrubbed out the oven between them. Large saucepans containing great carcasses and bones boiled on every ring as she toiled away making stock as her mother had taught her. Steam drifted in cumuli clouds throughout the house, and every windowpane glistened with condensation.

The results of her lone dedication were impressive. The soufflé she bore proudly to the table at 2 a.m. was among the most exquisite I have tasted. But by that time most of her guests had fallen asleep, or had drunk so much that the masterpiece was lost on them.

There is therefore a middle way, and we hope that we have mapped it in this section. Follow the drill, do as the sergeant says, and the victory which will be yours will have been worth striving for.

H.S.

APRICOT GLAZE

Preparation and cooking: 10 minutes

Ingredients

100g (4oz) sugar
50ml (2fl oz) water
1tsp lemon juice
200g (7oz) apricot jam

Drill

1. Bring the sugar, water and lemon juice to the boil and strain.

2. Pour the syrup over the apricot jam and boil for 4-5 mins. Then pass it through a fine sieve.

ASPARAGUS SAUCE

Makes: 300ml (½pt)
Preparation: 4-5 minutes

Ingredients

175g (6oz) green asparagus, cooked
150ml (¼pt) fresh mayonnaise
1tbs lemon juice
100ml (4fl oz) double cream or yoghurt
pinch cayenne pepper
salt and freshly ground pepper

Drill

1. Purée the asparagus in a food processor.

2. Add the mayonnaise and lemon juice and blend until smooth. Pour into a clean bowl.

3. Add the cream or yoghurt and seasoning.

4. Strain, and use chilled.

CHICKEN MOUSSE

Makes: 450g (1lb)
Preparation: 20 minutes

Ingredients

225g (8oz) chicken breast (skin and sinews
removed and chopped)
pinch of mace
1tbs chopped tarragon
1 egg
pinch of salt
225ml (8fl oz) double cream

Drill

1. Process the chicken in a blender for 1
minute, together with the mace and tarragon.

2. Add the egg and salt and work the mixture in
the blender.

3. Chill the resulting mixture for 10-15 minutes
in the refrigerator before adding the cream or
work on ice adding the cream a little at a time.

4. Pass the mixture through a sieve to achieve a
very fine texture.

Note: The mix must be kept as cold as possible
at all times to prevent separating.

CHICKEN STOCK

Makes: 5 litres (8¾pts)
Preparation and cooking: 2½ hours

Ingredients

5 litres (8¾pts) water
1.5kg (3lb) chicken wings, or 1 large boiling
chicken
2 carrots
1 stick of celery
2 whole leeks
3 onions
bouquet garni

Drill

1. Put cold water in a deep saucepan and add
the chicken.

2. Bring to the boil and skim off any fat.

3. Wash and peel the vegetables, and add to
the stock with the bouquet garni.

4. Simmer for two hours, then pass through a
sieve. Keep any excess stock in a covered bowl
in the refrigerator or freezer.

CHOCOLATE SAUCE

Preparation and cooking: 10 minutes

Ingredients

225ml (8fl oz) cream
1tbs honey to taste
½ vanilla pod
200g (7oz) plain chocolate

Drill

1. Bring the cream to the boil with the honey
and vanilla pod and cook for a few minutes to
extract the vanilla flavour. Then remove the pod.

2. Melt the chocolate in a bain-marie (water
bath) and stir in the hot cream, a little at a time.

CHOCOLATE SPONGE

Preparation: 20 minutes
Cooking: 30-35 minutes

Ingredients

75g (3oz) flour
25g (1oz) cocoa powder
4 eggs
100g (4oz) caster sugar
50g (2oz) melted butter

Drill

1. Sift the flour and the cocoa powder together.

2. Whisk the eggs and sugar with a balloon

whisk in a bowl over a pan of hot water. Continue until the mixture is light, creamy and double in bulk.

3. Remove from the heat and whisk until cold.

4. Fold in the flour/cocoa mixture very gently and then add the butter in the same manner, taking care not to over-mix at this stage.

5. Place in a greased and floured cake tin or a Swiss roll baking sheet.

6. Bake in a moderately hot oven at 200°-230°C (300°-400°F, Gas Mk 3-4) for about 30 minutes.

CHOUX PASTRY

Preparation: 15 minutes

Ingredients

300ml (½pt) water
100g (4oz) butter
pinch of sugar (if the paste is being used for sweet recipes)
150g (5oz) plain flour
pinch of salt
4 eggs

Drill

1. Bring the water, butter and sugar (if used) to the boil in a saucepan.

2. Remove from the heat and add the sieved flour and salt. Mix in well with a wooden spoon.

3. Return to a moderate heat and stir continuously until the mixture leaves the sides of the pan. Remove from the heat and allow to cool.

4. Gradually add the beaten eggs, mixing well. The paste should have a good shine and be of a dropping consistency.

CLARIFIED BUTTER

Heat the butter until the salt and sediment have sunk to the bottom of the pan. Gently pour off the fat and strain through muslin.

Note: Clarified butter keeps well if covered in the refrigerator. It is recommended for frying because once the sediment has been removed it will not burn.

CRÊPE BATTER

Preparation: 10 minutes
Resting: 1 hour

Ingredients

270g (9oz) flour
pinch of salt
25g (1oz) sugar
4 eggs
600ml (1pt) milk (boiled and cooled)
200ml (7fl oz) double cream

Drill

1. Combine the flour, salt and sugar (if used) in a bowl.

2. Add the eggs, 2 at a time, mixing well with a spatula.

3. Stir in a third of the milk to make a smooth batter.

4. Pour in the cream and the rest of the milk.

5. Leave to rest in a cool place for at least 1 hour before cooking.

CURRY CREAM SAUCE

Makes: 300ml (½pt)
Preparation: 15 minutes

Ingredients

150ml (¼pt) double cream
1tbs curry paste
1 clove garlic, crushed
2tbs white wine (not sweet)
150ml (¼pt) chicken stock
1tsp lemon juice
1tsp fresh chopped coriander leaves

Drill

1. Bring the cream to the boil in a small pan and add the curry paste. Cook for a few minutes until well blended, then add the garlic.

2. Add the wine and chicken stock. Reduce until it just coats the back of a spoon. Add the lemon juice.

3. Strain the sauce and add the chopped coriander. Serve hot.

FISH CREAM SAUCE

Makes: 300ml (½pt)
Cooking: 20 minutes

Ingredients

25g (1oz) butter
2tbs flour
300ml (½pt) well-flavoured fish stock (hot)
1tbs dry white wine
1tsp Dijon mustard
2tbs double cream
1tbs fresh chopped dill

Drill

1. Melt the butter in a heavy-bottomed saucepan over a low heat.

2. Add the flour and cook until butter and flour are thoroughly mixed and give off a slightly nutty aroma.

3. Add the hot fish stock, a little at a time. When all the stock has been added, cook on the side of the stove for 10 minutes.

4. Add the wine and mustard and cook for a further 2 minutes.

5. Strain the sauce and add the dill. Use hot.

FISH STOCK

Preparation: 10 minutes
Cooking: 25 minutes

Ingredients

25g (1oz) margarine
100g (4oz) sliced onions
1kg (2lb) white fish bones (sole, whiting or turbot)
2 litres (3¾pts) water
¼ bottle white wine
½ bay leaf
squeeze of lemon juice
parsley stalks
4 peppercorns

Drill

1. Melt the margarine in a thick-bottomed pan.

2. Add the sliced onion and the well-washed fish bones.

3. Cover with greaseproof paper and a lid. Sweat for 5 minutes, then remove the paper.

4. Add the water, wine and the other ingredients.

5. Bring to the boil, skim and simmer for 20 minutes, then strain.

Note: To make a fish glaze, reduce the fish stock to a light syrup consistency. This can be stored in a refrigerator and used to enhance the flavour of fish sauces, or can be reconstituted with water and used in the normal way.

GAME JELLY

Preparation: 15 minutes
Cooking; 60 minutes

Ingredients

150g (5oz) game trimmings
150g (5oz) carrots
25g (1oz) leeks
25g (1oz) celeriac
25g (1oz) onion
2 small tomatoes
1 clove garlic
10 white peppercorns
1tsp salt
40g (1½oz) gelatine powder or leaf gelatine
1 small piece of bayleaf
3 large egg whites
1 litre (1¾pt) game stock
100ml (4fl oz) port or red wine

Drill

1. Mince the game, using a medium-large mincer blade.

2. Dice the vegetables. Crush the garlic and peppercorns.

3. Mix the meat, vegetables, salt, gelatine etc. with the egg whites. Work thoroughly together. Add the stock and the red wine or port. Stir this well and heat on the stove.

4. Stir with a spatula, taking care that this reaches the bottom of the pan. Stop stirring when it is simmering.

5. Simmer very gently for 40 minutes. The meat and vegetables should now look like a big hamburger floating on the top.

6. Filter the stock through sheets of muslin. Leave to set. Game jelly can be kept for up to a week.

Note: Both powder and leaf gelatine must be soaked before using. In the case of gelatine powder, add the stock and soak for 15 minutes. Leaf gelatine should be soaked in water until it becomes soft (about 4-5 minutes).

GENOESE SPONGE

Preparation: 20 minutes
Cooking: 30-35 minutes

Ingredients

270g (9oz) sugar
8 eggs
270g (9oz) flour
50g (2oz) melted butter

Drill

1. Pre-heat the oven to 190°C (375°F, Gas Mk 6).

2. Put the sugar and eggs in a bowl and whisk on a bain-marie (water bath) until the mix reaches about 30°C, 8°F.

3. Remove the bowl from the bain-marie and beat the mix for about 10 minutes, until it is cold.

4. Sift the flour and fold it gently into the mixture with a large spoon, taking care not to over-work it.

5. Add the butter in the same way as the flour.

6. Pour the mixture into two 8in cake tins which have been lightly buttered and floured. Bake immediately in the pre-heated oven for about 30 minutes.

Note: This mixture can be used for Battenburg cake. Simply flavour and colour part of it with raspberry essence and pink colouring.

MUSHROOM PURÉE DUXELLES

Preparation: 10 minutes
Cooking: 15 minutes

Ingredients

50g (2oz) butter
75g (3oz) shallots or onion, finely chopped
800g (1lb 12oz) finely chopped mushrooms or
mushroom trimmings and stalks
5g (¼oz) parsley, finely chopped
salt and pepper

Drill

1. Melt the butter in a saucepan. Add the chopped shallots and cook until soft but without colouring.

2. Add the chopped mushrooms, cover with a lid and stew for 5-10 minutes, allowing the liquid to reduce in quantity until the mushrooms are fairly dry.

3. Add the chopped parsley and season to taste with salt and pepper.

PASTA DOUGH

Preparation: 15 minutes
Cooking: 1 hour

Ingredients

270g (9oz) plain flour
1 whole egg
4 egg yolks
1 level tsp salt
1tbs olive oil
2tbs water

Drill

1. Place the flour in a mixing bowl and make a well in the centre. Add the whole egg, egg yolks, salt, olive oil and water to the well.

2. Mix with the fingertips, gradually drawing the flour into the centre. Work the dough until all the flour has been incorporated, adding another tablespoon of water if required.

3. Place the dough on a lightly floured work surface and knead thoroughly until perfectly smooth.

4. Wrap in clingfilm and leave to rest in the refrigerator for 1 hour.

Note: The dough can be made using a food processor by placing all the ingredients in the processor in the given order and mixing for about 30 seconds until just blended. Knead the dough and rest as above.

PIE CRUST PASTRY

Preparation: 10 minutes

Ingredients

450g (1lb) flour
225g (8oz) butter
1tsp salt
5tbs water
1 egg

Drill

1. Sieve the flour on to a work-top and make a well in the centre.

2. Cut the butter into cubes and place in the well. Sprinkle with the salt.

3. Pour the water on the butter and add the egg. Mix the egg, butter and water together, gradually working in the flour.

4. Knead the pastry as quickly as possible. If it looks dry and cracked, you may need to add a little water. Let it rest for 1 hour before using.

PUFF PASTRY

Makes: 1.2kg (2½lb)
Preparation: 1 hour
Resting: 4 hours

Ingredients

450g (1lb) flour
225ml (8fl oz) water
1¾tsp salt
25ml (1fl oz) lemon juice
50g (2oz) melted butter
400g (14oz) well-chilled butter

Drill

1. Place the flour on a work surface and make a well in the centre.

2. Pour the water, salt, lemon juice and melted butter into the well. Gradually draw the flour into the liquid and mix well.

3. Work the dough with the palm of the hand until it is completely smooth and firm. Roll into a ball and make a cross cut in the top. Wrap in polythene and chill for 2-3 hours.

4. Roll out the ball of dough from the four corners so that it looks like four round 'ears' around a small 'head'.

5. Place the chilled butter into the centre of the 'head' and fold the four ears over it covering it completely. Chill for 30 minutes to bring the butter and dough to the same temperature.

6. Roll out the dough gently away from you into a rectangle about 70 x 40cm (27 x 16in) and fold over the ends to make 3 layers, as if folding a long sheet of paper to fit an envelope. This is called the first turn.

7. To make the second turn, roll in the opposite direction and fold in the same way as before.

8. Wrap the dough in polythene and chill for 30 minutes.

9. Make two more turns as before and chill for a further 30 minutes.

10. Make two more turns to bring the total to six. The pastry is now ready for use.

Note: Puff pastry can be frozen and will keep for up to 3 or 4 weeks.

SALAD DRESSING

Makes: 150ml (¼pt)
Preparation: 5 minutes

Ingredients

½tsp English or Dijon mustard
2tbs red or white wine vinegar
1 clove garlic, crushed
squeeze of lemon juice
100ml (4fl oz) good olive oil
salt and freshly ground pepper

Drill

1. In a bowl, mix the mustard with a little of the wine vinegar. Add the garlic. When well blended, add the rest of the vinegar and lemon juice.

2. Add the oil, mixing well.

3. Season to taste.

Note: If not needed immediately, beat it again just before serving.

RASPBERRY SAUCE

Preparation: 5 minutes

Ingredients

300g (11oz) fresh raspberries
125g (4½oz) caster sugar
juice of ¼ lemon

Drill

1. Place all the ingredients in a food processor and liquidise.

2. Pass the sauce through a fine sieve and serve.

Note: This can be stored in a plastic container in the freezer.

REDCURRANT SAUCE

Proceed as above, substituting redcurrants for the raspberries.

STOCK SYRUP

Makes: 1 litre (1¾ pints)

Preparation and cooking: 10 minutes

Ingredients

450g (1lb) sugar
600ml (1pt) water
50g (2oz) glucose

Drill

1. Combine all the ingredients in a saucepan and bring to the boil, stirring occasionally with a wooden spoon.

2. Boil for about 3-5 minutes, skimming the surface if necessary.

3. Pass the syrup through a conical strainer and leave until cold before using.

Note: This will keep for up to 2 weeks in the refrigerator if covered with clingfilm.

SUET PASTRY

Preparation: 10 minutes

Ingredients

450g (1lb) flour
1tsp salt
225g (8oz) prepared suet
200-300ml (7-10fl oz) water

Drill

1. Sieve the flour and salt into a mixing bowl. Add the suet.

2. Mixing with the fingertips, lightly blending the suet and the flour. Do not over-mix.

3. Add the water, a little at a time, adding more if necessary to achieve a light dough.

4. Knead the pastry quickly. Do not over-handle at this stage. Leave to rest for at least 20 minutes in a cool place before using.

Note: This pastry will not keep.

TOMATO SAUCE
(*Tomato Coulis*)

Makes: about 300ml (½ pint)

Preparation and cooking: about 30 minutes

Ingredients

100ml (4fl oz) olive oil
3 shallots, peeled and finely chopped
450g (1lb) very red tomatoes, skinned and de-seeded
25g (1oz) sugar
15g (½oz) fresh tarragon
15g (½oz) fresh basil
salt and pepper

Drill

1. Place half the olive oil in a thick-bottomed saucepan and place on a medium heat. Add the chopped shallots and cook until soft but not coloured.

2. Add the chopped tomatoes and cook until they form a pulp.

3. Add the sugar and herbs. Cook for a further 3-4 mins, then take off the heat and cool.

4. Strain the mixture through a coarse sieve.

5. Place the strained sauce in a food blender and blend for a few minutes, adding the remainder of the oil at the same time.

6. Season to taste and use hot or cold.

VEAL STOCK

Makes: about 1 litre (1¾ pints)
Preparation: 45 minutes
Cooking: 4 hours

Ingredients

oil for browning the bones and vegetables
450g (1lb) veal bones
1 pig's trotter
2 carrots
1 stick celery
3 onions
900g (2lb) veal meat (neck or shin of veal)
5 litres (8¾pts) cold water
bouquet garni

Drill

1. Pour a little oil into a roasting tin, and brown the veal bones and pig's trotter in a hot oven for about 40 minutes.

2. Wash and peel the vegetables. Pour a little oil into a deep saucepan, place over a moderate heat and add the vegetables together with the meat to brown. Then add the cold water and bring to the boil.

3. Take the bones from the roasting tin and add to the vegetables and meat in the saucepan. Add the bouquet garni. Simmer for 4 hours.

4. Pass the stock through a sieve and let it stand for 10 minutes. Skim the fat from the top.

5. Boil the skimmed stock until it is reduced by half. Store excess stock in screwtop jars in a cool place or freezer.

Note: to make beef stock, replace the veal bones with beef bones and proceed as above.

VEGETABLE STOCK

Makes: 1 litre (1¾ pints)
Preparation: 45 minutes

Ingredients

2 courgettes
4 onions
1 bulb of fennel
2 leeks
8 cloves of garlic, crushed
14 peppercorns
50g (2oz) butter
1 litre (1¾pts) cold water
15g (½oz) chopped fresh chervil
15g (½oz) chopped fresh basil
15g (½oz) chopped fresh tarragon

Drill

1. Coarsely chop the vegetables, then sweat them with the garlic and peppercorns in the butter until soft.

2. Add just enough cold water to cover and bring to the boil. Skim and simmer for 15 minutes.

3. Add the herbs and cook for a further 2 minutes only. Strain immediately. Keep any excess in a covered bowl in the refrigerator or freezer.

Glossary of technical terms

Coulis: A liquid purée of fruit or vegetables, usually tomatoes, made without flour.

Balsamic vinegar: Originates from Italy and is made from grapes. This vinegar has a balance of sweetness and acidity. It is left to mature in oak cases for a minimum of 10 years.

Fillet: A prime cut of fish, meat or poultry with all bones removed.

Garnish: An edible decoration added to savoury and sweet dishes to improve appearance, to awaken taste, to add variety or colour.

Gelatine: Leaf and powder gelatine are used in the recipes in this book. One leaf weighs about 2g (just over $^1/_8$oz) so use the equivalent weight of powder. Both need to be soaked before use.

Glaze: To brown under a hot grill or reduce a liquid stock until it is like syrup.

Marinade: A seasoned liquid in which to soak fish, meat and game before further preparation, to give flavour and tenderise.

Medallions: Small rounds of meat, game, fish or shellfish evenly cut.

Supreme: Choice pieces of poultry, game or fish.

Garam masala: A sweeter and more perfumed type of curry powder, usually having no turmeric and little chilli. It is used to finish curries – simply sprinkle a little into the dish at the end of cooking.

Ghee: A vegetable oil used in Indian cookery.

Saffron: The dried stamens of a species of crocus, used for flavouring and colouring.

Measurements conversions

Abbreviations

g	=	gramme
kg	=	kilogramme
l	=	litre
mm	=	millimetre
cm	=	centimetre
°C	=	° Celsius (Centigrade)
°F	=	° Fahrenheit

Oven Temperatures

Regulo No	Centigrade	Fahrenheit	Definition
½	130	250	Very cool
1	140	275	Cool
2	150	300	Warm
3	170	325	Moderate
4	180	350	Moderate
5	190	375	Moderate
6	200	400	Hot
7	220	425	Hot
8	230	450	Very Hot
9	240	475	Very Hot

Note: It is important that the oven is preheated to the required temperature for at least 20 minutes before cooking the dish.

British/American Measures

Dry Measures

Metric	Imperial	American
15g	½oz	1 tablespoon
100g	4oz	½ cup
225g	8oz	1 cup

Liquid Measures

Metric	Imperial	American
15ml	½ fl oz	1 tablespoon
50ml	2 fl oz	¼ cup
100ml	4 fl oz	½ cup
225ml	8 fl oz	1 cup
300ml	½ pint	1 cup
600ml	1 pint	2½ cups

It is not practical to give exact equivalents when converting from metric to imperial measurements. To avoid complications, the conversions have therefore been rounded up or down to the nearest ounce or fluid ounce. Please remember that you must use *either* metric *or* imperial measurements, but not a mixture of both. All spoon measurements are level spoonfuls unless otherwise stated.

Index

cycle and her term of pregnancy with the lunar cycle brings woman and the moon imaginatively together. There is a woman in all moon myths. Even in cultures where the moon is a god, the imagery includes woman either as the mother of the moon, as mate, or as daughter. Over and over again the moon is a god and goddess together—symbol of the growth and change that govern all forms of life on earth. But as goddess alone, the moon has many forms. She may be woman herself who grows and dies and is born again as a maiden, bringing with her the hope for the rebirth. She may be "the old woman who never dies." To the Polynesians she is Hina, the great goddess who has the power to grant immortality. To the Slavs she is Libussa-Baba, who invented birth and death, and who, as Golden Moon, eases birth. Or the moon may be a worker at any of woman's daily tasks and so unite in symbol the worker and the dreamer.

Behind the beauty and the romance of moon imagery flashes the vitalizing idea that woman is the special manifestation of the driving, untiring, *active* force of life. Of this the primitive woman's symbols and musical rites remind her daily. She perceives in everything that flows, that lives and moves and grows, something akin to her own power of growing and giving birth. The very word "rite" means a stream, a flowing, a manner, and a way. All through her life, in company with other women, she is asserting the special "way" of her sex and showing what good for the whole people can come from her work and her thoughts.

The men of primitive tribes know that woman's way in the scheme of life brings good. This conviction comes primarily from the practical results of women's working and thinking, which in simple societies relate directly to the fundamental needs of existence.

When the various rites of the mother's religion with its music and dance ceremonies are pieced together, a kind of composite woman emerges—strong, wise, creative by right of her womanhood. She cannot be seen anywhere in her perfection, though in fortunate and well-educated tribes like the Maoris there are women who very nearly approach the ideal stature of musician-chieftainess. But even when she seems to a Western tourist to be poor, backward, and greatly overburdened with work and babies, she may still have a kind of inner spiritual assurance that the educated and pampered woman of our civilization lacks. For hers is the inestimable privilege of *authority* in religion and song. And so the chief priestess of the Kwakuitl Indians sings, as she fancifully catches superpower from the air and throws it among her people:

> "I have the magical treasure,
> I have supernatural power,
> I can return to life!" [14]

CHAPTER II

BRINGERS OF LIFE

1.

BEHIND the music of women, in the simpler societies outside our present "civilized" culture pattern, there is a truly grand idea. It is an idea so obvious that it seems to have occurred to women everywhere, almost as soon as they were able to think in general terms and imaginative symbols. It is so fundamental and so universal that much of it has been incorporated into all the great religious systems.

This is the idea: that the process of birth offers the key to the understanding of everything else in life. As St. Paul wrote the Romans, "For we know that the whole creation groaneth and travaileth . . ." As Christ said, "Except a man be born again, he cannot see the kingdom of God." As Buddha said, "The life of an individual on this earth is but one link or cycle in an endless chain of births and rebirths."

One cannot understand the relation of women to music in our culture today until one understands in detail how the primitive woman centers music, with its ritual and healing, in what is to her the primary fact of human existence—childbirth.

The circumstances and associations of childbirth set the pattern of the music and inspire other rites of the life cycle, such as puberty rites and wedding ceremonies. By a process of symbolic thinking, simple, profound, almost inevitable, music that has definite associations with childbirth becomes the music for death. For except as a seed fall into the ground and die, as Christ said, it shall not live. And beyond this death, there may be birth if she who gives birth will sing in the face of death the song she made out of the struggle of birth.

Marina Núñez del Prado has expressed this idea of rebirth in a

21

powerful statue. (See Plate 7.) The Bolivian mother Aymara prays to the Spirit of Life for her dead baby:

"Give back the smile of my dead son in the waving wheat!
For his flesh, flowers in the strengthening grain of my fields!"

From this faith it is a short step to the belief that everything good and desirable may be thought of as birth into a new condition. So the song of birth becomes a magic for the fertilizing of the fields, for the protection of men at war, for well-being and success of all kinds.

2.

For the woman, childbirth is a profoundly religious and spirit-bearing experience.

Where there are no physicians and hospitals to take over, anesthetics to be administered, and trained nurses to preside with impersonal routine efficiency, a woman must depend on spiritual rather than mechanical aids. Nothing mechanical and scientific stands between her and the dark glory of the moment when in labor and pain, face to face with death, she battles for the new life. But all the unseen mysteries of the universe are involved. Evil ghosts hover to inflict pain. Good spirits may be invoked by incantations and ritual. And over all presides the great, brooding mother spirit. So, as a woman's time approaches, there are preparations as for a supreme religious rite.

Almost everywhere, women banish men during childbirth. They resent any interference and have been known to kill men who spied upon them. But in some cases they compel a husband to remain alone in a hut and cry out, as if in pain, while his wife, on her part, bears her baby in silence. Whatever the local custom is, a professional midwife, who is often the high priestess or shamaness or a magician, takes charge. The mother or other feminine relatives and the woman's neighbors and friends gather round. In societies where the girl leaves her own home and joins her husband's family, the mother-in-law and her relatives are called in.

Midwives and relatives busy themselves loosening hair, unlocking doors, and untying knots in the effort to remove any impediment against birth. They swing and dance to keep in the rhythm of life. Among the Fans of Africa, the business is so important that a special enchantress hides in the bushes near the place of confinement and chants an elaborate melody for hours. Even the pregnant woman sings. And, over and above the human song, goddesses imitate with divine melodies the "low-lying" mother's voice.

A Fox Indian woman says of the birth of her son:

The child could not be born. The women who were attending me were frightened. They said, "We shall pray for help." My mother-in-law went to a woman skilled in birth. She boiled some medicine. She made me sit up and she spat upon my head. She gave me the medicine to drink. She began singing. She started to go out singing and went around the little wicki-up singing. When she danced by where I was, she knocked on the side. "Come out if you are a boy," she would say. And she would sing again. When she danced by she would again knock the side. "Come out if you are a girl," she would say again. After she sang four times in a circle she entered the wicki-up. "Now it will be born." Lo, sure enough, a little boy was born.[1]

In the Fiji Islands today women are famous as poetess-musicians and use their talents to help a woman in childbirth. At this sacred event they allow no man to be present. Escorting their friend to the bank of a river, they place her against a wooden support erected for the purpose. The chief midwife, who is also the high priestess of the tribe, kneels with palms upturned in magic gesture, as in Greece Eileithyia, the goddess of childbirth, is always depicted. She invokes the child about to be born. Around the two central figures the other women stand in a semicircle. They wave their arms to and fro in rhythm to her pains and sing with a sighing, wailing sound. The low notes are given first and then the sound swells up to a high tone. Another wail begins on the high note and drops down, to rise again in rhythm with the effort of birth until the child is born.[2]

Here is the model for that rite of symbolic birth which is to be found in so many religions. The wooden supports and the woman in labor suggest an altar on which is laid a token representing the re-birth—the bread and the wine, the flesh broken and the blood spilled. Here is not the derived symbol but the act itself—the agony of struggle for the perpetuation of life in the divine presence. For the mother looking up in her struggle to the soft tropical sky may feel that out of it an all-comprehending mother spirit supports her—an infinite mercy, who like the moon knows what it is to wax and wane, to go down into darkness and after three days to rise again. So nature, in this quiet place, makes of the birth chamber a church. The fronds of the coconut palms meet overhead like the intricately carved arches of a great cathedral. The still waters of the river amidst the jungle undergrowth are the baptismal font. The rich tropical odor of growing things—of ferns and flowers and ripe bananas and of the fertile earth itself—rises like incense. (See Plate 8.)

And because they believe that in themselves they have power to invoke life universal, these women have something of sacerdotal dignity. Clean-limbed and strong, authority in every line of her straight backbone and high-held head, dignified and formalized by the gold-tinted circle of hair, the high priestess is the intermediary between the real and the mystery. The attendants form the liturgical choir chanting the eternal affirmation of life.

3.

Unless deliberately stifled, as it is in the Fiji Islands, some audible expression of the muscular effort involved in child-bearing accompanies labor pains. In an Indian tribe of Northwestern America, the sounds made by women in childbirth are a kind of irregular crying or singing, half way between a whine and a melody. But whether a whine, a cry, a shriek, or a suggestion of a melody, the generic term for these sounds is "wail."

In the effort to insure propitious delivery, every power of invention is brought to bear upon the childbirth cry. For this is the cry of life, the woman speaking in her critical hour to the universal life. The proper management of the wail is thought to be so important that it is often strictly controlled by social and religious usage. The mother's sound may be re-enforced by the beating of drums, timed to strengthen the rhythmical contractions of birth. Sometimes the mother makes no sound but, instead, her friends or her husband cry out in her behalf. In Thrace and in some Celtic countries, the attendants, the husband, and all the family cry aloud when the child is born. In certain African tribes, women even pretend that a spirit mother is wailing when her child departs from the land of ghosts to become a human baby.

Everywhere in the world, women make their music by imitating all kinds of natural sounds—the songs of birds, the soughing of wind, the rippling of water. But the sound of the birth cry is the natural

1. Carl Lumholtz photographed native women for his book *Through Central Borneo*. The Dyaks believe that beating drums and singing attract good spirits. (See page 3.)

2. A photograph from Routledge's *With a Prehistoric People* shows Akikúyu women in a great assembly. According to the customs of this musically gifted people, solo singers improvise and the group responds. (See page 8.)

3. In a Russian painting, girls can be seen going from house to house, singing Christmas carols and *kolyádki*. (See page 9.)

4. A contemporary Pueblo woman of New Mexico depicts her companions performing the Wheel Dance, an ancient war ritual. (See page 11.)

5. Wearing silver ornaments like the horns of the moon, these singers of the Dahomey tribe of Africa represent the army of 10,000 women warriors, famous in former times. (See pages 13 and 40.)

6. Chorus of Russian mothers in the Esthonian village Gorodische sing their wedding ritual. The men listen but do not sing. (See page 13.)

7. Graven in stone by a Bolivian sculptress of today, Aymara is the symbolic mother raising her hands in the gesture that magically brings about birth. (See page 22.)

Courtesy of Marina Nuñez del Prado

Courtesy of Virginia McCall

8. Under the direction of an eyewitness, a Philadelphia artist has sketched a childbirth scene in the Fiji Islands. (See page 24.)

sound most distinctive of women, the most intimately associated with that supreme experience which is the climax of their physical life and the source of their religious thinking. The Fiji Island women —notable musicians as they are—bring to their incantations considerable technical skill and base their music accompanying childbirth upon a sighing, wailing sound.

In transforming the wail into melody, women have a great variety of methods. A musician may herself build a musical phrase around a recurring wail. Or she may make a recitative alternating with wailing by other women in unison. In Corsica, a chorus of women intone a chant. The leader leaps suddenly into the center of the group and wails: "Woe! Woe!" as was the custom in performing Greek tragedies. At death ceremonies, Iroquois women formerly divided into two choruses, one of which gave the long-drawn out sobbing wail while the other sang a melodious chant.

In this manner, women's dirges in primitive music were born. As an art form, they evolved from the cry of childbirth, and for musical existence, depend upon a sound natural only to women. Dirges and laments are noticeably absent from the repertoire of primitive men. It is the mother's business to bring life, even in death.

And for this purpose of bringing life women have also stylized the wail itself. One magician may give it a regular form with a crescendo to a climax, followed by a relapse into a slow, dragging drawl. A Nubian woman begins on a high note and drops her voice by thirds to a twelfth below the original note. Wailing may be considered an art distinct from singing and a wailer, often an official of high standing, may be praised for her appealing, or her grand, individual style.

The wail, in its stylized form, is used now by many primitive people and was used in ancient societies. It was developed by women for a particular purpose as an independent art but it is not music and never became music. From the simple wail, women also evolved the wail song. In company with melodies derived from other inspirations, this did become music and was employed with endless variation by countless women musicians for those many practical purposes for which primitive mothers need music.

4.

According to the imagery of women, all life is a series of births and rebirths that they are empowered to bring about. Sickness can be transformed into health; adoption can symbolically render a person a blood relative. Puberty, or mating, is birth into maturity; death is rebirth into another world; the annual growth of vegetation, or the new moon, is birth for other forms of life.

One kind of birth is similar to another, so that in some cases the imagery of the three great crises of a woman's life—birth, marriage, and death—become interchangeable. A dead Russian maiden is dressed in her wedding garments and her burial is attended by friends who come as if the ceremony were for the wedding. In a poem by a Greek mourner the bereaved parents implore their daughter to return to them but the girl answers:

"Nay, I may not, dear father mine and mother deep-beloved,
Yesterday was my marriage day, late yester e'en my wedding.
'Hades' I for my husband have, the tomb for my new mother." [3]

The human mother's womb changes into a tomb and death becomes a form of marriage. The idea of the poem was clearly inspired by womb imagery and derived originally from the reality of childbirth.

It is easy for us to misunderstand these primitive wail songs because, with our overintellectualized and overdepartmentalized approach to music and to life, we have lost the simple yet profound consciousness of the oneness of joy and pain, of birth and death, that is in them.

The wail alone, or in its elaborated form of lament and dirge, sounds mournful in our ears. To observers of primitive women who sing with tears streaming down their faces, as in the Maori *tangi*, it may seem an expression of inconsolable grief. But its intent is actually to ensure rebirth. The very word "dirge" comes from the Latin *dirigere*, which means "to direct." The dirge directs the vanished life on its way.

The peculiar mournfulness of this primitive wail music is due to two factors. Even for sophisticated audiences sadness is more artistically moving than joy. It touches deeper levels of the unconscious. It induces a more complete sense of release. The primitive woman early learned that an orgy of weeping brought relief—an idea later elaborated by Aristotle in his dictum that the function of tragedy is the purgation of pity and fear through representative pain and death. So the primitive woman artist makes the most of the wail song, prolonging it, building it up to climaxes of sorrow.

The other factor that makes the wail songs mournful is that life has in it much of pain, and pain translated by the woman musician becomes the wail. For the woman every change may be thought of as birth or rebirth. And every birth has its memory—or anticipation—of physical and emotional distress. Even at weddings, occasions for joy and hilarity, women sense the coming suffering inevitable to their altered state of life. Mating and childbearing, essential in bringing about fulfillment of life, have for women an aftermath of pain and sacrifice. Estonian bridesmaids sing:

> "Make thyself fine, O lovely maiden—
> and on thy head place the wreath of sorrow
> and on thy brow the wreath of pain—
> Quickly, quickly while still there is light
> gird thyself—for the twilight is coming on." [4]

But, sorrowful as women's wail songs may seem to our ears, they have two characteristics that make them anything but depressing when rightly understood. One is the intent, already discussed, to induce rebirth and the faith that this can be done. The other is the periodicity, the rhythmic alteration of mood, which is of the essence of a woman's peculiar vitality. So women combine lamenting and rejoicing in one rite. It is a common practice in primitive tribes for mourners at funeral rites to wail for hours, even for days at a time, but to break every now and then into sudden bursts of rejoicing. They find the burden of grief intolerable, possibly, and release themselves in the cry of joy. Or they rejoice in anticipation of the rebirth and so hasten it. Some Russian groups today also have the same custom. At the festival of Radunitsa, the goddess Ustara (whose name became converted to Easter) is invoked. The people mourn over their dead, over the decay of life in general. Then they turn toward the east and rejoice.

Women's expression of the mood of rejoicing seems universally to involve the sound of the letter "l." It is often formalized into the phrase *al-al-al, la-la,* or *lu-lu*—familiar to us as the "alleluia" of Jewish and Christian worship. In the primitive and peasant world, women give the "l" refrain in their songs of joy. (See Plate 21.) *Lully-lu* is often incorporated into lullabies, which are incantations to persuade children to sleep and also little proofs of joy in them.

Friends of a Jewish bride in Palestine sing a song of good luck for the new husband:

> "May the eye of God protect you.
> Lu-lu-lu-lu-lesch!" [5]

The high trilling tone they use, often pressing their hands on their throats to achieve it, suggests the origin of the word "ululate." But since "to ululate" actually means "to wail," it is the womb from which the cry of joy and the wail of sorrow both come.

In a remarkable example of the union of the cry of joy and the wail of sorrow, a Calabrian singer pictures death as crouching in a mountain defile and snatching a young girl.

> "Joy, I saw death! Joy, I saw her yesterday!
> I beheld her in a narrow way, like unto a great gray hound and I
>   was very curious.
> 'Death, whence comest thou?'
> 'I am come from Germany—I have killed princes, counts, and
>   cavaliers, and now I am come for a young maiden so that with
>   me she may go.'
> Weep, Mamma, weep for me, weep and never rest—no more shalt
>   thou await me." [6]

The idiom of the wail song, varied to suit the occasion but essentially the same in all primitive woman's music, is associated with a great variety of symbols and symbolic gestures. When the woman makes her rituals, she finds a thousand objects to reinforce with sympathetic magic the power of word and movement and tone. For almost everything about her tells of birth and rebirth. Everywhere she finds flowers—flowers that are buds, like little girls, and open and bloom like a girl into womanhood. They fade, but in fading set fruit, and out of the fruit comes the seed, which, when planted, grows and flowers again. In every way flowers are symbols, even to the many strange ways in which, in their shapes and their colors and their folds and secret places where the honey lies, they seem to be modeled after those organs which the primitive woman often looks on proudly as the seat of her power. So flowers are everywhere used in women's rituals. The Hawaiian girls, greeting the big ocean liner with song and singing it on its way out of port, wear great wreaths of fragrant flowers called leis, and hang wreaths about the strangers' necks as a symbol of loving greeting. In the Andaman Islands a young girl is given a flower name from the time of her first menstruation until her first pregnancy. And in Persian folklore, if a girl dies before her marriage she becomes metamorphosed into a flower.

Lights and water are, like flowers, full of meaning. Torches symbolize the light of the moon, which must never be allowed to die, for as the moon comes back, so life comes back. Mirrors imitate the still surface of a lake in which the moon can be reflected. Water flows from the mother's body. When the membranes rupture the child is born—hence the water of baptism and of other rites of rebirth. When the child is born, first comes the water, then the blood. Broken pots filled with red ocher symbolize the blood of the mother sacrificed at childbirth. Plumes and jewels are the child. That queer little figure which is the peculiar mark of the Maoris, with its eyes of gleaming blue-green *paua* shell, is the unborn child with the moonlight in its eyes. In shape, bells suggest the womb. Flutes blow the breath of life. Drums give the beat for the rhythm of the universe.

The movements of the dance often frankly glorify the seat of the woman's power—with that circling movement of the pelvis and rhythmic rotation of the hips which is the distinguishing technique of the woman's dance in the Pacific islands and southeastern Asia. Susceptible young men often find these dances seductive, and so, when danced by young girls, they are often meant to be. For it is the right of woman, young and ripe for motherhood, to attract her man. Yet the real concern of the girls is often only to perform the traditional movements well enough to escape the artistic criticism of the older women and often of the older men, who become connoisseurs in these women's ways. So many hours of tiresome practice have usually gone into the acquisition of this hip and belly movement that it often seems to the girl a chore the elders expect her to perform, with very little relation to her own personal desire, which is naturally to attract a lover.

So the Roratongan girl, clad only in a brief skirt of shredded bark, a brassière, and a flower, lifts her pelvis as high as she can and then keeps it circling to the accompaniment of her chant. It is as if her pelvis were an instrument on which she were playing. It is a kind of invisible music similar to the visible and complex patterns of movement with which the Maori girls often accompany their songs.

Whatever conscious seduction there may be in the girls' dancing, there is none in that of the real experts in the pelvis technique. When one of those middle-aged or really old women who greatly excel the girls in the skillful manipulation of pelvis or feet performs the dance of the pelvis, she has no notion of attracting any man's eye. It is to her the lusty assertion of the glory of her womanhood, the triumphant flourishing of the seat of her power. And when under the fantastic gold lacework of the Shewe Dagon pagoda, on those marble courts smooth as glass, the Burmese women dance with circling movements of hip and breast, while the torchlight flickers on their smooth, earnest faces and the scent of trampled flowers and fruit rises like incense around them, they are dancing not to please men or women or even the impassive gold Buddhas sitting in golden shrines, but rather to realize something greater—their own part in the rhythm of the universe.

Out of the importance of birth, which is the center of the woman's religion and the source of her power to invoke rebirth, grow the various rites of the woman's life cycle—puberty, marriage, family or tribal celebrations of birth, and, finally, death. Since a woman has such important functions to perform, she must be carefully trained and provided with spiritual aids in all the crises of her life. So the little girl learns her pelvic dances. It is even more important for her to have this seat of her power well exercised and well trained, flexible, powerful, rhythmically responsive, than it is for her brother to learn to flex his muscles, clench his fist, strike straight from the shoulder, brandish his weapons, or leap and jump in the war dance. The tribe might get along very well if men did not go to war. It could not get along at all if the women did not bear children. So the girl must learn to move her pelvis freely and powerfully and dance the pelvic dance as the sign of her fitness for womanhood.

5.

When a girl becomes physically capable of womanhood, she needs spiritual instruction, a ritual induction into her new responsibilities, a new attitude to herself. Running around, often playing with her little brothers, she is sexless, immature. These traits she must now shed as the snake sheds its skin or the butterfly its cocoon, and emerge a true woman, with a woman's personality.

Girls' puberty rites are held at new moon and the initiates dance all night and every night while the moon is waxing. Dancing, instrumental music, and special songs quite generally accompany the rites.

Just as for childbirth, women have their own hierarchy. The mother, the eldest sister, and other female relatives play their part. High women officials lend dignity to the ceremonies. The queen of the Ashantis, for example, has a silver stool modeled on the type of stool used by women in labor. Seated on this throne, she presides at the rites of the rebirth.

In some parts of Africa, puberty rites are controlled by the women's secret societies. The Bundu, in Sierra Leone, is one of the most powerful of these associations. Women called "Soko" know the secrets of life—of which music is one—and pass them on to the next generation. (See Plate 9.)

Certain musical instruments are associated with the girls' puberty rites. According to local custom, girls play drums, rattles, xylophones, horns, and musical bows. The Bavenda girls, who belong to a very musical race, have an orchestra made up of different instruments. They perform at the Phala-phala Dance, one of the initiates' rites.

Whenever women assume responsibility for the girls' initiation into womanhood, they have also the incentive to invent the rites, the dances, and the songs. They make the ceremonies a time for chanting long stories in which heroines abound, a time for singing incantations, invocations to deities, a time for lamenting the loss of their little daughters and rejoicing that a new woman has arrived in their midst. The time, the occasion, and the symbolism inspire creative musical imagination.

A typical ceremony of puberty, interpreted as rebirth into womanhood, is that of the Intonjane in Africa. This is usually in charge of the aunts on the father's side, who choose girls and women to help them. When the old moon fades, the initiate is led, with much ceremony, to a small thatched hut that symbolizes the womb, and there she is left alone during the dark of the moon. On the second day girls go out early from the village to cut soft grasses for the ceremony. The women and girls left in the village sing and dance from dawn till sunrise, celebrating the coming of a new woman, invoking all good upon her. On the morning of the third day they dance again.

After sunset on the night when the new moon will appear in the sky, women and girls cover the girl with a blanket, wrap her head in a veil, and surround her in a dense crowd so that no man may see her. They take her with singing and dancing and clapping of hands away to a distant hill. In the dusk, just as the slim, silver crescent of the young moon gleams over the African bush, they come back with her to the village, singing and rejoicing as if a new person were being welcomed to the kraal, and from that night to the night of the full moon she sings and rejoices with them. Both the older women and the girls are musicians. No man has made for them the music they sing to the moon. They have made it themselves, out of their own hearts, with their own skill, for their own woman's need.[7] (See Plate 10.)

Where girls have ritual preparation for womanhood under women's leadership and are adequately trained in music, their poetic-musical compositions are rich in imagery, full of allusions to the various devices employed to bring about the rebirth, especially flowers. The girls liken themselves to a bud, which only the warmth of love can open. Or they look longingly at a meadow and ask who will make them a wedding wreath. The songs are often made in the form of a duet between mother and daughter. The mother asks the girl what is troubling her and the daughter confesses her desire to rest in her lover's arms. Many laments voicing disappointment or loneliness and many love lyrics expressing devotion to the beloved belong to this group. Known as "maiden songs" among European peasants, they form an important and particularly beautiful group of folk music.

6.

Marriage, like puberty, calls for the women's talent in music making. A typical primitive wedding is one among the Pygmies of Africa. These slender little black folk—four feet high, weighing only about eighty pounds—are thought to be one of the oldest races on earth. Though they never arrived even at the agricultural stage of society, and live by hunting and fishing in the great, hot, tangled forests along the equator, explorers have testified that their intelligence is of a high order. They have a rich lore of ceremony and music; they are vivacious and witty, cleanly and fond of decency, order, and beauty in the details of their very simple lives.

When a girl is to be married, the clan of the fiancé comes to her village to take her away. The men set up enormous tom-toms. As the drums begin to beat, the bride retires into a hut with her mother-in-law and as many of her girl comrades as can crowd themselves in. The mother-in-law places in the bride's arms the latest-born baby of the village. The bride says nothing. Silently she gives the baby back and turns away. At this all the bridesmaids begin to sing and the bride bursts into tears. Her bridesmaids keep on singing the whole night through. And while they sing, the bride must weep, even though to keep the tears flowing after long hours she puts a pimento seed in the corner of her eye. The songs of the bridesmaids are long, and among them there are strains of great beauty, in which after the manner of all ancient poetry the music is of one piece with the verse form, conceived with it in a single impulse of the imagination.

Song of the Bridesmaids, African Pygmy Tribes

Counting your steps and turning no backward glance,
Reluctant your feet and with the slow tears falling,
Today with a troubled heart, with a heavy heart you are leaving,
The Bridegroom is waiting, maiden, reluctant, advance.

Here is the home you loved, your girlhood companions,
Here you played as a child, here you trod in the village dance,
You must leave it now, turning no backward glance,
With a heavy heart you must say farewell to your loved ones.

The Bridegroom is waiting, maiden, reluctant, advance.

Counting your slow steps, go, but keep with you ever,
Keep in your heart the treasure, the sandal flower
Plucked from your mother's garden, it will tell you:
"There they love me still and will love me forever."

Counting your steps and turning no backward glance,
Maiden, reluctant, maiden, reluctant, advance.[8]

There are tears throughout these wedding songs, like the soft rhythmic sound of falling rain on the awakening earth in spring.

At a Russian bride's farewell party—her *devíshnik*—which she gives for her bridesmaids the night before the marriage, the leader starts to sing in a low voice and the others pick up her melody:

"Why are you here, my sisters? Why are you here, my white swans? You have come, my sisters, for my last girl's party.

"My dear friends, maidens fair, the golden crown will be taken off
    my head, the red ribbons will fall out of my fair braids,
My freedom will cease to be." [9]

The bride herself, seated in the center surrounded by the brides-maids, repeats the words of the song, but instead of singing she wails —the stylized wail that is one of the earmarks of women's expression from time immemorial.

Bridesmaids' songs are both numerous and beautiful. There are the flower songs, sung while the girls are picking flowers and greens to decorate the house and to make the bridal wreaths. In the Cyclades they sing:

> "Adorn the crowns with pearls and flowers,
> The bride and bridegroom are the moon and stars." [10]

There are songs ridiculing or extolling the bridegroom; songs praising the bride's beauty, songs rejoicing over the bride's new estate; and always songs lamenting the passing of girlhood.

> Happy she may be again,
> But never more a maiden.[11]

The older women and the professional song leader have their opportunity, too, for musical expression. Songs are sung while the food for the wedding feast is being prepared, while the bride's bed is made, while she is swinging and dancing her way into her new life, while they are waiting for the bridegroom to come, while the house is being decorated. while the bride is being washed and dressed. In Syria, when the professional hairdresser has finished her work she beats her little drums and sings:

> "O bride, be silent, your mother weeps,
> And your bridegroom and his friends rejoice!" [12]

Finally, the bride herself must sing, and in her song her joy is tempered with unfeigned grief and longing. A Greek girl realizes that her family will miss her as she will miss them—especially at the hour of waking, at mealtime, and at family celebrations. She sings:

> "I leave my blessing on my home!
> Neighbors and friends, adieu!
> Three vials filled with bitterness,
> Mother, I leave to you!
> The first to drink at dawn of day,

The next in noontide heat,
The last and worst in festive scenes,
Where all but one will meet." [13]

Wedding music is women's music, made by the bride, her brides-maids, her feminine relatives, professional attendants, and the special singers. In any age, in any culture, including our own, music to accompany the marriage is a comparatively unimportant category of men's compositions. All wedding songs by Greek and Roman men were modeled on those of Sappho. Among primitives and peasants today—especially in Russia—men rarely sing during the long-drawn-out marriage ceremonies but are satisfied to listen for days to women's endless repertory. (See Plates 6 and 11.)

7.

When the woman feels the first sign of new life in her body, she rejoices, again often with elaborate and interesting rituals. After the child is born, women have a series of celebrations at which they dance, play on instruments, and sing.

The desire of parents to present their offspring in some formal manner to other men and women of their group and to whatever deity they worship seems to be universal. In primitive societies the mother, who has admittedly played the larger part in this new creation, participates actively. Sometimes the ceremony is a joint affair between men and women. Often women exclude men and conduct the rites alone, according to their own interpretation.

The Pygmies have both types of ceremony. When a son is born, the fathers celebrate and sing their own songs of rejoicing. The women join in the refrain with their cries of jubilation. The young mother herself is, however, the most important person of the group. Custom decrees that she perform the dance of life, not only for the purpose of giving life to her own child but to bring symbolic regeneration to the whole tribe. To the accompaniment of the shouts of exultation given by the other women, she dances into the center of the open plot and imitates every movement of her recent experience.

For every child, son or daughter, the musically minded Pygmy women have a special ceremony to present it to the moon, the symbol of the rhythm of life. Among the Pygmies, the moon is feminine —Generatrix, She Who Creates. To unite the mothers with the moon spirit, the women paint their bodies white and yellow and dance the dance of life. They sing their sacred songs to Mother Moon—songs that have never been heard by men, even by those of their own tribe. This is a secret ceremony, women's own business to make the life they have created secure on earth.

In the Baltic States—Estonia, Lithuania, and Latvia—antiphonal choruses of women welcome the newborn child. Among the Latvians, two groups of girl singers vie with each other and compete for the praise of the guests. Sometimes two girls sing sitting face to face and holding hands. The listeners accompany them. These choruses are renowned for their excellence and represent the most finished type of peasant art. (See Plate 12.)

One of the most common ceremonies for women after childbirth is the rite that reintroduces her to her normal life. As practiced in primitive tribes, it is associated primarily with the idea of a mother being a potent manifestation of the life force. At the time of childbirth the life force is believed to be present in such power that it might injure other people. Like a live electric wire, it is dangerous. Primitive people have a feeling that they must detach themselves from the supernatural after any event that seems to suggest supernatural agency. When, for instance, strangers insist upon photographing them, they hurry afterward to bathe in flowing water. Most primitive women have a special ceremony to detach a mother from her close contact with the life force. At such ceremonies they employ the customary rebirth techniques—drumming, dancing, and singing magic songs. Owing to the distortion of these particular rites in "civilized" societies, the original significance of the idea behind them should be understood by everyone interested in women's spiritual growth and in her opportunities to be a creative musician.

A mother in the state of confinement, and even a menstruating woman, is often called "unclean." This word is used in the sense that she has disturbed the ordinary course of events. Butchers are also "unclean," because they handle live blood; those who tend the dead are "unclean"; men and women who have just had sexual intercourse are "unclean." All of these people and their actions have had contact with the life force. But a woman giving birth has had the closest contact and has the most profoundly disturbed the normal course of events. It is a general custom, too, to allow a longer period of time to elapse between the birth of a girl baby and the ritual detachment of the mother from the life force than in the case of the birth of a boy.

This is probably because a girl baby must derive added strength from her mother in order to carry on with women's business. But in any case, the word "unclean" has not the significance of an unhygienic or dirty condition, nor does it have any connotation of evildoing. The rites of primitive women, invented by them and presided over by them, are definitely associated with the holiness of woman as the bringer of life.

8.

It is in the presence of death that a woman's singing is called to its highest functioning. To the primitive mind, death is rebirth into another world. Because women bring life, they are needed to assist the spirit along its destined path. Without their ministrations, a soul might be lost and remain suspended in mid-air without rest forever.

Mothers, sisters, wives, midwives, priestesses, and especially the professional singers are in demand as purveyors of life. In the Hebrides the midwife is called upon to close in the sleep of death the eyes she opened at birth, and to sing her incantations for the rebirth. According to locality, the professional mourner has different names. In Russia she is "the sobbing one" (*voplénitsa*); in Corsica, *praefica*, like the ancient Roman woman mourner; in Calabria and Sardinia, *reputatrica*, or the one who tells the story of the dead. The Irish women's leader takes charge and, calling her companions around her, begins the chant: "Cease now your wailing, women of the soft, wet eyes." [14] (See Plate 13.)

In many places men are excluded from death rites. In others, men participate but without the authority of women, who are generally called upon to beat the drum of life, to act out the mimicry of birth, to pour the libation, to swing, to dance, to wave flowers and green branches, to tell the history of the departed, to wail, and especially to create and sing the dirges.

Mourning ritual usually includes dancing and often swinging. Death is the principal one of those events in human experience that disturb the even flow of life. Affirmation of the will to live is therefore important. Swinging and dancing keep one in touch with the rhythm of the universe, and at the same time can be employed as devices to bring about the rebirth. Among the Dyaks of Borneo the professional wailer sits on a swing near the corpse and begs the spirits to guide the soul in the right direction.

The dance is capable of infinite variation and has been developed into many forms by the fertile imagination of primitive women. Among the Baronga, when a chief has been dead for three months the oldest woman of his family connection is called in as leader of the ceremonies. The men demolish the hut that was the former home of the chief and prepare a flat place for dancing. The old woman then dances the womb dance and imitates every movement of generation and childbirth in order to deliver his soul. Likewise, on the shores of the Gulf of Carpenteria (Australia) certain relatives of the dead person have the duty of performing the mourning dance around the body. Weeping and singing all night until they fall exhausted, the women stretch out their arms as if to lay the body in the earth and thud their feet upon the ground in rhythm. (See Plate 14.)

Of all the devices to bring about rebirth, the wail is the most important. In the Jabo tribe of eastern Liberia the wail is developed into a long and elaborate composition by the mourner, who is an official of very high rank, lawyer and historian of the tribe. She stands with the white sunlight and black shadows of this equatorial land playing on her polished black body. She is stately and tall, full of poise and dignity, for in her land women are persons of power. In the absence of written records, the vast store of tribal information is kept in the head of this woman official—historian, lawyer, and singer at funerals. Since she knows the background of all present events, what she asserts becomes the law of the land. No funeral of a man of property can be conducted without her.

At the funeral this personage presides while a chorus of women wails for hours. Then she takes the stage and, performing solo, builds around her own wail an elaborate composition. She chants the virtues of the deceased, describes the status of his family, enumerates its prerogatives, and reports on the extent of his property, modifying her wail and transforming it into a melody. She sings the names of the living men and women of the tribe; she sings the names of the ancestors, both men and women, from the beginning. She sprinkles the many proverbs in which the life wisdom of the tribe is concentrated at appropriate intervals throughout this musical discourse, and always she builds out of the wail her melody. To her, as to Fiji women in their childbirth rites and the Russian women at the *devíshnik* or bridal ceremony, the primitive wail is an inspiration to musical composition.

In the effort to make the wail a living and developing art form,

satisfactory to their artistic instinct while performing its more practical purpose of invoking the rebirth, women are stimulated also to
poetic imagery. The best performers try to avoid stereotypes and to
make words and music specifically apply to the one who is mourned.
In Albania, when they mourn an unmarried girl they sing:

> "O joyless woman who hath never known joy,
> Who hath never fulfilled thine own life." [15]

When they mourn a mother they sing:

> "O spirit of the house within the very walls where you sat—
> There you left shining glory!" [16]

In Dahomey (Africa) the oldest member of the family has the
duty of watching the dead body with the widow. It is also her duty
to compose the burial song at the grave and another special song
when the grave is later revisited by the family.

An old woman weeps, amidst the leaves;
A white haired woman—O—weeps amidst the leaves of the forest,
And she says, the birds in the bush,
The life of these birds is to be envied.
How is it that man born into life has no more generations?
He has no more! [17]

Laments return again and again to the imagery of the rhythm of
life. An Arabian mother mourning for her son slain in battle sang of
days and nights endlessly alternating. A famous Polynesian poetess-
musician, when two hawks bore her tidings of her son's death, compared him to the moon:

> "Thou art a moon that ne'er will rise again,
> O son of mine, O son, O son of mine!" [18]

The poetic imagery includes the representation of divine feminine
beings who sing and wail. In the Hebrides a goddess called Grainne
personifies the "Love of Women." She it was who kept the death
watch over the hero Dearg and made the famous lay, still considered
a masterpiece of its kind:

See, O God, how I am—
A woman without heart forever,
A woman without son, without husband,
A woman without gladness or health.[19]

This is the model for the many songs of sea sorrow in the northern isles, always composed by women when their men are drowned at sea. Like dirges the world over, its air has the form of a wailing chant.

Beautiful and touching as these individual songs may be, the meaning of them is missed entirely if one thinks of them as lyrics of personal sorrow. The grand fact is not that the woman weeps, but that she has the privilege of a representative position at death for her family and her community. And she has this because, in herself, as the bearer of life, she is the symbol of life. This is a position to call out any woman's talents, to give spiritual power and cohesion to the women functioning in groups or choirs at a state funeral or memorial service.

In Dahomey, for example, an important occasion for music is the memorial ceremony held before the tomb of a former king. A woman's choir of fifty singers officiates. It was heard by Dr. and Mrs. Herskovits in 1935. (See Plate 5.)

From the point of view of musical style [writes Dr. Herskovits], the most striking songs [of the Dahomean culture] are undoubtedly those which glorify the names and deeds of the dead kings and living chiefs. Here is no impromptu performance, but rather singing of a quality that can only result from long periods of rehearsal . . . the leader conducts very like a choir master in our European civilization conducts his singers. Songs are sung in unison to the accompaniment of only a gong, and, to the European ear, the tessitura is almost incredible, particularly in view of the length of the skips which take the singers abruptly from the highest to the lowest tones of their range. The training of the chorus is also to be remarked, for judged by any standards of *a cappella* singing the technical proficiency of these groups of women in unison of attack and in dynamics of shading is of the highest.[20]

Such singers have technique. But they have something more—a deep spiritual composure. For there is something in death that brings out a woman's talent and peculiar quality of imagination. And to the communal celebration of death, to the great concourse of

9. While her husband made anthropological investigations, Frances Hall painted a Sherbro tribe initiation rite. (See page 31.)

10. For his book *Sex, Custom, and Psychopathology*, Laubscher photographed Bavenda mothers inducting girls into womanhood. (See page 32.)

11. On an old cloth painting, Norwegian bridesmaids swing the bride into her new life. (See page 35.)

12. A seventeenth-century miniature shows professional women singers called "Domin" performing songs of congratulation to an Indian princess and her newborn son. (See page 36.)

From Mrs. S. C. Hall, Ireland, 1841

13. At a wake in nineteenth-century Ireland, the men listen while women perform the ritual wailing and singing that brings new life. (See page 37.)

Courtesy of the Australian National Research Council

14. In an article on certain Australian mourning rituals, Ursula McConnel describes how women dance, sing laments, and make gestures as if to bury the dead. (See page 38.)

15. In Borneo, mothers swing their babies to sleep. (See page 43.)

16. Stone figurines from archaic Greece represent women bakers, led by one playing the flute. (See pages 43 and 101.)

men and the gathering of official personages, they bring their natural authority. Having created and practiced their wail songs of rebirth in rites from which they exclude men, for their own spiritual support, they are in a strategic position to be called in, in power, under their own leaders. Theirs is the privilege of adapting their own music to the high occasion when their community as a whole wishes to make the woman's natural affirmation of life in the face of death. Other songs they may make for themselves; many of their dances and rites may never be known except to other women. But here they are called to perform a public duty for the spiritual reassurance of all. So the dirge, as elaborated by women out of the childbirth wail and out of their faith that all life is one, becomes women's most important and distinctive contribution to music.

CHAPTER III

WORKERS AND DREAMERS

1.

THE great moments in the woman's life are not many. Rituals may be called for only once in a year or once in a lifetime. But a woman's work goes on all the time. If she did not work, her family could not live. In many primitive societies women work too hard. The hours are too long, the work often heavy and monotonous, performed against the discomfort of extreme heat, extreme cold, or, as in the rice swamps, in a perpetual state of dampness.

But whatever the work is, it goes more quickly and easily if a woman sings. Most primitive people sing at their work for the practical purpose of easing the burden, as all who have watched—and heard—the coolies unloading the cargoes of steam liners in Shanghai or Calcutta or Singapore know.

In the African community of M'Komis, women are known to be poor and inefficient workers if they do not sing. Among the Bantu, the organization of groups for communal work is definitely stimulated by the opportunity to sing in chorus. Tibetan women work harder and longer when they lighten their labor with songs. In Lithuania, where the lyric poetess-musican flourishes, a young man in search of a wife will spy upon the girls while they are working to find one who can sing especially well, so fixed is the idea among these people that a good singer is also a good worker.

Spirits and goddesses who reflect woman's power and woman's activity are often singers and workers. When Tibetan women draw water at the wells, especially during the ceremony of the Great Prayer, the Goddess of Government incarnates herself as one of them. In the guise of a working woman, Pal-den-Tha-mo teaches her companions the topical songs. Holda, a Teutonic goddess, was a spinner who sang loud and long as she sat at her spinning wheel. Those feminine spirits that appear in so many myths representing fate, destiny, and fortune are always spinning and singing. Men workers are apparently not deified as singers.

Women's work songs are legion. Though they frequently rise out of the patterns and rhythms of a woman's work—as in the case of spinning songs, for example—their real inspiration are the associations and symbols centered in the woman's deepest personal experience. All art is the unleashing of the unconscious. Save as the unconscious is released, there is no true inspiration. And the primitive woman deftly fits the words and musical tones that come spontaneously to her lips to the pattern of what her hands happen to be doing. In this process she has one great advantage over her civilized sisters. She works in her own time, in her own way, under the leadership of women. So no male philosophy stops the welling up of emotion from her woman's unconscious, and the same musical idiom that has been developed for the rituals of birth and rebirth serve for the work songs.

In some kinds of work, women sing alone. In others, they sing and dance together. Since most mothers rock their babies in solitude, lullabies are solo songs. The work of grinding corn at a hand mill is also customarily a solitary task. The songs sung at this occupation are solo and, as a rule, sad. But when women work in groups at tanning hides, making pottery, milking cows, making butter, harvesting grain, mowing, gathering nuts and berries, washing clothes, spinning, weaving, fetching wood and water, and many other tasks, their songs are gay and spirited. (See Plates 15 and 16.)

Often the workers enliven their task by a singing game. In some European districts, for instance, the spinners sit in a circle with the best singer, who is usually the most expert spinner, in the center. She improvises a verse and then throws her spindle to one of the girls, who must add another verse to the song started by the leader. Whatever the mood and the form of the songs, however, they are women's own production, flowing freely from a natural ability for self-expression in terms of music. (See Plate 17.)

It is a general custom for the work leader and the song leader to be the same person. Sometimes strangers are brought in with the idea that they will suggest new songs and, by imparting new life to the music, will also speed up the work. Mary McLeod, a famous seventeenth-century singer, used to row around in her own boat from one little island of the Hebrides to another in order to assist the women with their "waulking." In the islands today, women are still waulking, as the task of tossing and circulating the cloth that comes woven from the loom is called. Descriptions of the business show how Gaelic women combine work and music.

At this waulking we were women only. . . . An old woman, one of the two song-leaders, began to croon softly. And, as one listened, a quaint refrain shaped itself, a theme fashioned in strong rhythmic and melodic outlines, calculated, like a fugue subject, to impress itself easily upon the memory. This was caught up and repeated by the workers *tutti*. A verse phrase of more recitative-like character, perhaps consisting of only eight notes to eight syllables, was then intoned by the leader, and this was followed by a second refrain, longer than the first, but again of a strongly rhythmical character. This, in its turn, was caught up and repeated in chorus. And now the leader sang the alternating verse portions only, leaving the refrains to the other women. But the musical interest was not yet exhausted, for the leader skilfully varied the verse themes, and I have tried in vain to catch and note all the changes sung on a few notes by one of these capable, practised folk-singers of the Isles.[1]

Women of the primitive and pagan cultures are remarkably rhythmical in their movements. It has been noticed that they walk more steadily than men and that they move with measured motion while engaged in work. In Madagascar, for instance, women working in the field, making long furrows for planting rice, move all the time evenly as if to a fixed beat. In the majority of primitive communities women work under their own leaders apart from men, at tasks that are their own by custom and tradition. The pace they set is their own pace. The movements are convenient to them. The tempo adopted by men in marching and rowing, for instance, would not suit women, and the tempo of songs sung to accompany marching or rowing would be different for men and for women, and therefore quite individual for each sex. Every work song takes its form from the rhythm of the work. The leader's signal is often incorporated into the text of the song. Words like "ho" or "oi" or the repetition of numbers—one, two, three, four—mean that the leader is setting the pace for the work.

To make the work go well, it is wise to have a verse that is the charm, or rune. Meaningless words like *ko-ko-ko-ko, ninna, ninna,* or *lully-lu* constitute the magic added to the verbal and musical command. Women use these charms for everything that they do—for quieting children and sick people, for healing wounds, for bringing milk into the breasts, for tattooing, for building, for making and washing clothes, for tanning hides, for making baskets or pottery, for bringing their men home safely, and finally, most important of all, for charming the good and evil spirits believed to be perpetually hovering about.

The charms and incantations that a woman may employ are sometimes enumerated in stories of supernatural women who guard the incantations and bring them out on occasion. When the hero Siegfried woke Brynhild from her magic sleep, she gave him a reward in the form of a magic kit containing her incantations. "This enchanted box," she said, "is full of secret power; full of enchantment, of prayers, and of joyous words. With it, you can learn the runes to bring you victory, the runes of the philters which will ensure you the fidelity of the captive wife, runes to bring about pregnancy, runes for plants which will heal wounds and cure sickness. Such are the runes whose power will endure until the day which puts an end to the reign of the gods." [2]

2.

Many different types of song are created by women as they work. There are the lullabies; the satiric songs, in which women make fun of men; the lyrics, either love songs or nature songs; the laments; and the ballads and epics.

Lullabies and other songs to entertain children form one of the largest groups of women's songs. They are composed not only by mothers but also by nurses and elder sisters, who in many societies are charged with the care of babies while their mothers do more productive work. Songs to induce sleep invariably take an even, rocking rhythm and often associate the rocking with swinging on trees.

> Rock-a-bye, baby, on the treetop,
> When the wind blows, the cradle will rock.

Dyak mothers actually suspend their babies on the branches of trees, where they swing to and fro and listen to their mothers' voices blending with natural sounds of wind, water, and the trilling of birds.

The subjects selected by women for the lullaby poems are usually directly related to the child or to themselves. Some mothers and nurses praise the baby and assure it of undying affection and protection. A Hottentot mother touches each part of her baby's body and commands it to grow strong and big. Many mothers compare the child to a flower or to a jewel or to the moon. Some sing of their own experience at childbirth:

"Peace, my child, be still and sleep, my love, my tiny one.
Pain I learned from you, learned such pain as only God and I can
　　　ever know, and she who stayed beside me and saw you born.
Peace, my child, and cease to weep. Peace, my child, be still." [3]

In describing Eskimo music in Greenland, Thalbitzer refers repeatedly to the drumming, dancing, and singing of the women. And when he gives an example of the musical aptitude of these interesting people, he uses a woman and the song she sings to her baby as an illustration.

Much more art is required in the rendering of a little children's song than one would think from looking at the notes or words. The whole of the singing is marked by the deepest feeling in the voice. The singer makes use of the finest modulations in appealing to the fantasy of the listening child. . . . A bewitching charm lies in the East Greenland's mother's lullaby tones which she hums as she rocks her child. She sways her body and croons a simple song of two notes, one very long and one short which is higher—the most primitive song in the world which may have remained unchanged from the earliest childhood of humanity. Generation after generation has been introduced with those tones which have formed themselves in the soul of the Eskimo woman out of the loneliness and wild monotony of the desert land.[4]

The Pygmies, too, have a rich spiritual and musical life with fully developed rituals for the life cycle. As we have seen, Pygmy customs provide incentives for both men and women to develop creative musical imagination. But nothing that the men produce in music has impressed the historians of these extraordinary people as favorably as the women's songs. The high point of musical achievement stands out in the lullabies created and sung by the sisters and mothers.

Satiric songs form another large group of women's musical expression. An illustration of good-natured raillery can be seen in a Serbian folk song that describes girls and boys at work gathering in the harvest. After the work is done the boys fall asleep exhausted, only to wake hours later and to find the girls knitting and singing, not tired at all! Songs sung when women and men work together are usually gay and cheerful, with sometimes a suggestion of sarcasm or playful derogation. The satiric songs of bridesmaids often insinuate that the bride is superior to the bridegroom or that the new husband will not dare to mistreat his wife on account of the loyalty of her family—a fact in many primitive tribes. In Dutch Guiana an established form of social criticism is maintained through poetic-musical compositions. Women publish their opinions of men by means of song. The fact that society gives a name—*lobi singi*—to the custom endows the women's music with importance.

Laments of various kinds are sung by women while they work. In the Cyclades the professional mourners practice their dirges and plan the improvised verses they expect to sing at the next funeral. Or a musician may express her own sorrow. An Osage Indian woman has a special lament she sings while weaving the rush mat that is to be used on the new shrine. Softly and flowingly she gives her cry of longing for her dead relatives:

"You have left me to linger in hopeless longing—
　　Ah; the pain, the pain!" [5]

In India, women have a set of laments that they sing while grinding corn. These belong to the group of incantations known as *raga* and *ragini*, which are believed to have a direct influence on the weather, the change of night and day, and even the shift of the seasons. In these laments, called *Bārah-Māsas,* the singer mourns the absence of someone she loves and devotes each verse to a month of the Hindu year, describing the particular kind of woe she feels at that season. In this way she lightens the labor of her work, and by causing symbolically the rebirth of the year, hastens the return of her beloved.

Work is a time for storytelling. The world over, women are famous for their ballads and epics, which they usually chant with interludes of song and instrumental music. Russians are particularly adept at this type of musical expression. On the huge Lake Oñéga in the far north, women rowers are employed by the government for mail delivery. While making their rounds, which take many hours, they chant long sagas. Long ago other women like them were symbolized by Wotan's daughter Saga—divine storyteller.

The topics of these song-stories vary in accordance with varying folk customs or folk experiences. In a lovely Russian folk song a girl describes how she makes a flute:

> In the field, a birch tree stands,
>   *Lyóuli*, it stands,
> I will cut three sticks from the birch tree,
>   *Lyóuli*—
> I will make three pipes—
> The fourth one will be the balalaika.[6]

A Chinese tea picker sings the whole story of her life—how she is awakened by the sun, goes to work in the fields, looks forward to the evening, and so on. A large number of the ballads and epic poems sung by women refer to historical events such as battles, floods, famine, and to the deeds or love affairs of ancestral heroes and heroines. The whole of peasant life is portrayed in the Lithuanian lyrics (*daina*). Songs of the family cult have a name of their own in Russian—*semeíniya*. Songs relating to the ways of the people also have a name—*bitovíya*.

Another type of story is pure fantasy. Whenever an African Valenge woman starts to improvise, she says, "*Karingani was karingani*," which means "Story of stories." The audience repeats these words over and over, as if to remind themselves that the tale is only make-believe. These are the legends in which mythical creatures appear. We call them myths or fairy stories. Flowers, trees, and animals talk. Heroes and heroines become identified with them or with supernatural beings and then perform incredible deeds. In the stories, the superhuman and the human women too are continually singing in the most beautiful way imaginable.

The Ibibios have a legend in which the naiad of a pool sacred to women came to the help of one of these skillful singers. There were certain days, so says the legend, when no one was allowed to go near the spring. But a mother was forced to break the taboo in order to get fresh water for a sick child. She was blocked on the way by the spirit of the trees. She made a song appealing to the tree to let her pass: "I pray you, open the road, and let me pass to the spring!"

When the spirit heard her lovely voice, he swept his branches aside. She hurried on but was stopped by a leopard. She charmed him, too, and induced him to move out of her way. At last she came to the spring, and she sang again more sweetly than ever, entreating the goddess to forgive her for breaking the rule. Moved by the magic singing, the naiad guarding the pool rose from the water and gave the mother permission to fill her pitcher.[7]

A favorite fantasy appearing in all parts of the world is the bird-woman, who may be either a wailer, a warrior, a dancer, or a singer. She is always endowed with magic power. It is common for mourners in myths to turn into birds. In Lithuania the verb "to cuckoo" signifies "to lament." In Africa the honey bird, or *schneter*, is said to be an old woman who, wailing, pursued her lost son until she was changed into a bird. Among the North American Indians there is a myth of a girl who, grief-stricken over her lost lover, became a songbird. In Russia the bird-women Sírin and Alkonóst rejoice and lament. Feathered creatures, half women, changing miraculously from one state to the other, have different names. In Russia they are called *vili*. They perform all kinds of superhuman feats and are akin to the Valkyrie, who, in Teutonic myth, bear the dead warriors to Valhalla. *Vili* steal the apples (symbols of fertility) from the magic trees that grow golden fruit. They have long golden braids; they dance, sing, and always love music. (See Plate 47.)

Other spirit women live in faraway lands where men can never go. On the mythical island of Tuma, near the Trobriands, there are hundreds of women ready to dance all night. In the Hebrides, the beautiful Binnevale, who was called the "Mouth of Music," lived in her own specter world where the sun never set, the wind never rose, and singing never ceased.

These mythical retreats for women have actual counterparts. Many primitive women have their private islands and mountain haunts to which they retire at times of menstruation, puberty rites, and child-bearing. The fantasy is an idealization of primitive custom.

3.

After the work of the day is finished, people everywhere turn to recreation and entertainment. Especially on holy days and at festival times, men and women congregate in the public place. There they play games, dance, swing, tell stories, and sing. Village dances in the

Hebrides are often accompanied by an old woman singing the *port à beul*. This is a type of vocal music that the Gaels find more exhilarating to dancers than any instruments. Often as the merrymakers dance around a May pole or a bonfire, drums are beaten and gay songs are sung. But always music of some kind is indispensable.

Choral singing or instrumental playing by women frequently entertains men. (See Plate 18.) The Trobriand Islanders, who are devoted to music, have song festivals called *kamroru*. Women dress themselves gaily and sit on new mats spread out in the central plot of ground. Swaying rhythmically, they sing all evening while the men look on and listen admiringly. In Kamchatka, too, the women were once wonderful singers. A traveler, Stellers, who visited the peninsula during the eighteenth century, noticed that the women had unusually musical voices, that they made extraordinary modulations while singing, and that they sang in parts. He described how the women sat on the rocks, like sirens, and sang to attract traders coming from other tribes. Stellers was so much impressed with the women singers that he said their arias could be favorably compared to those of Orlando di Lasso. "As they sing, they become very calm and well-poised. From this can be seen their special genius for music." [8]

Swing festivals are another type of amusement enjoyed by girls and boys together, but with girls taking the lead. Wherever the swinging games are played, girls and women are the chief celebrants and the creators of the songs. In Lithuania, especially, where the poetess-musician is so conspicuous, the lyric poetry contains a large number of girls' swing songs.

Swinging is, with many people, a rite performed at times when a symbolic threshold is being crossed. The bride swings into her new life, men and women swing at funerals, when seed is being planted, when rain is needed. The Dyaks of Borneo use swinging in connection with both daily life and religious ceremonies. Mothers swing their babies on trees; professional wailers swing at a burial and sing the songs that will direct the soul to its heaven; old women swing at the planting season in order to secure the soul of the rice.

Even if the swing festival is dedicated to amusement, it is usually a seasonal affair, suggesting its ritual origin. In India the women swing during the rainy months. (See Plate 19.) In Korea swing songs are sung on the fifth day of the fifth moon of the year. In the Cyclades the swings are put up in Lent. In the region of the Seven

Mountains (Germany) flax harvesters swing at the end of October and the girls play a singing game:

> Where does the moon rise?
> Blue, blue, little flax flowers!
> It rises over that linden tree.
> Flowers in the valley,
> Maiden in the dwelling,
> O, gallant Rosa! [9]

This verse is repeated as many times as there are girls present, and the home of each one is indicated as the rising place of the moon, thus connecting the song with the moon rituals common to so many primitive and peasant societies.

Another set of swing songs incorporates the wail into the even, rocking rhythm. In Karpathos, Greece, a festival is celebrated on each of the four Sundays preceding Easter. Swings are suspended between the windows of the houses bordering the narrow streets and on them the women sit. The whole village watches, but only women and girls swing and sing the death wails for the crucified Christ.

Primitive women and girls also have their own amusements apart from men. Beginning at an early age, the little girls play singing games similar to our "ring around a rosy," or the pantomimic type like "Here we go round the mulberry bush." Those invented by the young Pygmies are quite remarkable. Some are imitations of the mothers' work, such as fishing. One especially fine exhibition of talent is a singing game imitative of a partridge calling her young.

Older women, too, play, dance, and sing for each other's amusement. They frequently have secret societies, or women's clubs, where they meet with their friends. Bushwomen entertain each other for hours dancing the *kokucurra*—flute dance—and playing their flutes. In Dutch Guiana the women celebrate with dancing and singing at birthday parties—*mati*. Formerly, specialists made stirring toasts of congratulation, using this incentive to develop their poetic-musical talent. In many societies women are famed as storytellers. Among the Valenge Africans the relating of both true and imaginary events is one of women's chief pastimes. The Baronga are particularly good at it and begin singing tales and legends when they are little girls tending the babies of the family. Names and photographs exist of more than one "distinguished historian." Primitive women often act out their stories like a play. The women of the Caroline

Islands have a mock war, when they paint themselves red, brandish spears, and dance, not as if in sympathetic magic to help their men to victory in battle, but as if in a drama.

In the peasant groups there is the same kind of play and entertainment. The Russians have their *besédi* and their *posidélki*—words meaning "conversations" and "sit-down parties." These are always gay affairs at which the girls spin, embroider their trousseaux, and play games. With infallible memories and boundless enthusiasm, thousands of songs are sung.

Games played by older girls generally involve courtship, love, marriage, and ideas relating to rebirth. In Russia they tell each other's fortune on Christmas Eve. They place a dish (*blyoudo*) on the table and put in it their rings, earrings, bread, salt, and three pieces of charcoal. The charcoal signifies the house spirit and sacred flame of the domestic hearth. Then they sing the dish songs (*podblyoudniya*) and take one object out of the dish with each refrain. If the ring is drawn out first, it means marriage. If the charcoal, it means death. Another game song (*igorniya*) describes the hiding of the gold. "I am hiding, hiding the gold," sings the leader as she places a gold ring, which symbolizes the sun hidden in the winter. A girl in the center has to find the ring and bring it to life again. From Easter until midsummer, Russian girls perform their rebirth rites. In one of these, Kastróubonka impersonates the sun. To imitate the natural decline in the sun's vitality during the winter, a girl falls down pretending to be dead. She is buried in a mock burial by the other girls and bewailed by them. They move around her in a circle lamenting. After a time, the dead girl comes to life and they all rejoice with special songs.

Where there are games and singing, there must also be a leader, and in the women's groups the leaders are women. One singer mentioned by a collector of Russian folk tales in 1934 was Doūnya, a young girl twelve years old. Her repertory consisted chiefly of fairy tales which she told to two little children of whom she took care. Doūnya inserted songs, spiritual verses, and dirges into her stories. Anna Antónovna was another song leader. This old blind singer had no home of her own but went around to the different houses in the village to help the housekeepers. She earned her board and lodging by spinning, but it was her singing that made her welcome in the morning while the work was going on and in the evening when the games began.

Here are the keepers of traditional lore, re-creators of the musical heritage of the past, composers of new rhythms and melodies in their own right—artist folk singers in the making. They might well serve as guide and inspiration for some of the new social and artistic stirrings of our own day. Theirs is a kind of music that women might well bring back, in a great fertilizing flow, into the music of tomorrow.

CHAPTER IV

VICTIMS OF TABOO

1.

WHAT has happened to the women of our civilization? Why are we not matching in creative output the simple women of cultures much less developed than our own? Everywhere in the world, outside the highly civilized centers of Western culture, there are women whose participation in music is active and creative. Women's contributions in the form of love songs, lullabies, dirges, ballads, and epics are among the musical treasures of an art that itself has recognition in the annals of human achievement.

Are we less women than these singers and musicians? We love, work, play, bear children, seek reassurance in a sense of oneness with the life force. We inherit a magnificent art of music. Why, then, do not women as composers make, on the level of our highly developed culture, symphonies, requiems, songs, dances equivalent to those that are created by women everywhere in other cultures? Why are we so inhibited?

Before we seek the answer to our own specific problem, we may look again at the primitive and peasant cultures. Even there we can see that women are not everywhere performing their own rites and making their own music. Tradition or custom determines what forms of ritual, dance, and music shall develop. Frequently, customs seem to be followed without reason. They are fixed by what is called "taboo"—a social habit that, once established, becomes absolutely binding. Taboo means that something or other "just isn't done."

Primitive people all have the same general approach to life, the same conception of what the right relation of men and women to the laws of the universe ought to be. Their customs, their ways of living, however, vary radically from group to group. Some, for instance, believe in monogamous marriage. Others permit a man to have several wives, or a woman to have several husbands. In some communities the birth of twins is regarded as a sign of good luck. In others it signifies some evil influence at work and the mother is forced by unwritten law to leave her husband and her other children and to go to a settlement where only women who have borne twins may live. Custom determines what kind of work is suitable for men and for women. In some societies women milk cows and make butter. In others only men tend the cattle. Sometimes women do all the fishing; sometimes they neither fish nor eat fish that is caught by men. Everywhere people abide by local custom, local taboo.

2.

In the large majority of societies both men and women make music and dance. Both have their ceremonial dances, songs, and instruments in connection with the work and the rites customary to any given group. It frequently happens that certain instruments are played only by men and certain others only by women—taboo being equally strong against either group. There are some tribes, however, where *only* women are the musicians. Because men are *not* of the female sex, they have an inferior status with the spirits, and are therefore not in the class preferred to make affective music.

Such a tribe is the Tuaran Dusun of British North Borneo. Among these people, women only are the priests. Upon them alone falls the task of performing the rites that, with music, are thought to be capable of propitiating evil spirits. Priestesses conduct ceremonies at the planting of rice, for producing rain, and for blessing the villages. Dividing themselves into two groups, the women dance back and forth as in an antiphonal chorus and sing songs in a secret language. In a neighboring tribe the women use a sacred rattle. It is hung in a bamboo receptacle at the door of each house. Only the women may handle it. The men are actually afraid to touch it. Men play a subordinate part in all religious ceremonies, their only function being to accompany the songs and dances of the women by beating the drums. Although these particular men are inherently as musically capable as men of other races, they do not break through the barriers imposed by custom.

The Wanyamwezi in Africa are people of a different race and cultural level from the Borneo tribes, and among them, too, men are at a distinct musical disadvantage. The word Wanyamwezi signifies "Land of the Moon," and this tribe is part of the great Bantu family in which women in general hold high position. Wanyamwezi women are very strong physically and from a distance can hardly be distinguished from men. They have the right to be elected chieftainesses. They have the right to be magicians and witch doctors; and as wives of chiefs, they have great influence on all public matters. Religion with the Wanyamwezi consists in worshiping the spirits of the dead mothers and fathers. It is the women's business to keep the living tribe in contact with these unseen powers. This makes them important and necessary in the spiritual life of the tribe, and out of their spiritual function grows their music.

Wanyamwezi women sing more songs than the men and institute more ceremonies at which music is required. They celebrate secretly at puberty rites with songs and dances. Men have no corresponding rites. Women make music for the marriage ceremony, music for funerals, and music for prayers in which mother and father spirits are invoked. They sing lullabies and have special songs to celebrate the birth of twins. As women do most of the work, they have many work songs, especially for the preparation of the beverage *pombe*. Choral dances for war, for traveling, and for the greeting of visitors are particularly beautiful. Moving their bodies back and forth, waving green branches, clapping their hands, these magicians charm the assembled company. Only predestined women are poet-musicians. Famous as composers of songs, some of them are very influential and richly paid by the chiefs. Women alone rank as official songsters and lead other women singers in chorus. Accordingly, they are encouraged from earliest childhood to cultivate their natural talent. There is obviously no reason why men should not have the same high musical status, but they do not. Men never attain the status of official poet-musician and do not compete successfully with the women. In every branch of music making, women excel.

In other tribes where men are in no competition with women, they frequently raise barriers between their musicians and a free expression in music. Among the Omaha Indians, for instance, men singers are trained to adhere rigidly to a rhythmic model for the chants of the Hon-he-wachi Festival. Since the Omahas are a very musical people, quite capable of inventing new melodies and rhythms, this restriction is clearly a taboo and has nothing whatever to do with innate ability.

From Ján Hála, rod Tatrami

17. A contemporary writer and artist has sketched girl spinners of the Slovak village Vežee at work. Boys, waiting to walk home with the girls, listen to the spinning songs. (See page 17.)

18. Nineteenth-century Cambodian women of the royal household play orchestral music to entertain the king and his guests. (See page 50.)

19. Swinging is universally a rhythm to insure life. A miniature of the Kangra School depicts a seventeenth-century lady on a swing and her companions playing musical instruments. (See page 50.)

20. Arctic explorers see women musicians in action. A Koryak mother of northern Siberia beats her drum to protect her family from evil spirits. (See page 59.)

21. "Al-al" or "lu-lu" generally express rejoicing as in "alleluia." While hunters drag in a white whale, Koryak women dance on the beach and sing, "Ah, a guest has come, la, la, la, lo." (See pages 27 and 59.)

22, 23, 24. Rock paintings from the preliterate age depict women performing ceremonies similar to those in many primitive tribes today. (See pages 62 and 63.)

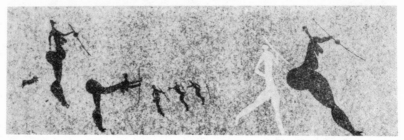

Taboos of all kinds surround women and can often be traced to fear of their supposed contact with the supernatural. In some tribes women are officials, such as queen, chieftainess, priestess, shamaness, blian, doctor, rain maker, or magician, wielding real power, both temporal and spiritual. In others their responsibility is limited to the women's group and they are not called upon as public officials to translate their feminine power into benefits for the whole society. In still others women's organizations are comparatively weak. Women and girls have but little opportunity to work together in symbolizing their experiences.

Customs for women and music also vary greatly from group to group. It is frequently the custom for women to sing the songs in honor of ancestors. In other places they never sing them. Sometimes there is a taboo upon their playing the flute, or the particular type of drum used by men in secret ceremonies. In Surinam, for instance, women, the principal singers, never play drums. They believe that if they break the taboo their breasts will grow down to the ground. On Manam Island (New Guinea) girls are called upon to sound the single death beat but do not use drums at any other time.

The Caraja tribe of Bananal Island, Brazil, places a complete barrier between women and music. In this tribe it is the custom for women not to sing at all—not even lullabies for their babies. According to the cultural definition of singing, men only are the singers. When women wail and keen over the dead, the Caraja describe the sound—which we would call singing—by a word analogous to "croaking," a word used by them for the raucous calls of unmelodious birds. The Caraja word parallel to our word "sing" is used for the singing of men and of songbirds. Occasionally when women are working in the fields they attempt to imitate the men singers, but generally end by joking and granting that women cannot sing. Yet they have larynxes like other human beings and the same natural ways. Simply because they live in a society that does not expect them to be musicians and that deliberately discourages them from receiving training in music, they are forced by custom to pretend that music is outside women's sphere.

3.

Barriers arise from various causes. In some tribes, occupations around which music formerly developed have fallen into disuse and the accompanying songs are forgotten. "Meta, the Rikatha potteress, has given up the manufacture of pottery. All her pots cracked because, she said, she was the only woman practicing the art. In her former home, everybody made pots and the potteresses strengthened each other. When a pot was heard cracking in the furnace, somebody ran to the hut and collected a little of the dust on the floor and threw it on the other pots. It was too far for Meta to run to her old home." [1] And so no more pots are made. No more pottery songs are sung.

Or a taboo may be in force against introducing innovations in a traditional musical form. Such a restriction does exist among some of the African tribes where, although a woman has authority as a priestess over initiation ceremonies, she is under the prescription of a native law that deadens her imagination.

In other tribes particular types of song are never needed. Rowing songs, for instance, are not made by mountaineers. War songs are not necessary to peace lovers. Bridesmaids' songs are never sung where people make light of the marriage ceremony or omit it altogether.

Restrictions on sexual freedom before marriage naturally prevent a girl from composing wooing songs. When sexual freedom is allowed, however, girls may become the aggressors in courtship. In this role they create courting songs. In the Trobriand Island groups of girls with their faces tattooed make ceremonial expeditions to a neighboring village and, singing a ritual courting song, give signal to the boys of the village to approach. The two groups mingle and smoke and sing all night. Obviously, these courting girls, with no inhibiting tribal tradition of sex passivity, have incentives to compose love songs of their own.

Marriage is often a barrier that prevents women from either creating or performing music. The moonlight dances of the Akikúyu girls (east Africa) are never danced by married women, who express great surprise when the suggestion is made that one of them do so. A husband might say: "I have bought you and you want to go to dances!" Among the Annamites, girls are professional singers and dancers and are very much in demand at banquets or festivals, where they improvise for hours at a time. But opportunity for such performance disappears the day they marry.

A more formidable type of barrier between women and music in particular primitive tribes arises because women in those tribes are not in positions of authority and responsibility. It may be that men only are the chiefs, the priests, the shamans, the magicians, or the doctors. Men, therefore, have the incentive to invent appropriate songs and dances for the occasions where music is required. Among the Mescalero Indians, for example, priests rather than priestesses do all the singing at a girl's puberty rites. The same prohibitive factor operates in Bali, where the girls, although famous dancers, are taught and directed by men. Bali women are expected to perform, but not to create. Loss of leadership, or lack of a chance to lead, is a barrier to creative work that ranks second to none. The value of leadership to the composer cannot possibly be overestimated. It is the musical leader who has the opportunity to display artistic ability. It is the leader who can select significant poetic and musical phrases out of the many expressed by the less talented. It is through the leader that incoherent, incompleted utterances of immature artists are filtered and refined until they become art forms, acceptable to the whole group. Free and active participation in music making is, of course, a necessary condition to the possibility for leadership. But the mere singing, dancing, and playing of instruments in a group will not of themselves result in substantial creative achievement without the added opportunity of commanding the situation.

In the shamanistic cults authority may shift back and forth between the sexes. Shamans are individuals especially endowed with supernatural power to control the good and evil spirits. Shamanism is often identified with mothers, who, as chief guardians of family welfare and as chief interpreters of the supernatural, have the responsibility for controlling spirits who might harm or benefit their mates and offspring. Among the Koryaks of Siberia every woman has her own drum and her own individual drumbeat. Whenever any untoward event threatens to disturb her family affairs, she beats her drum and chants her magic formulas to frighten away the evil spirits. In this same tribe women are the official shamanesses, notable for their ability to keep in contact with the spirit world. Their primeval ancestress, Miti-Miti by name, brighter and more glorious than her husband, Big Raven, excelled him in cunning inventions and especially in the making of incantations. The real and the ideal women correspond. (See Plates 20 and 21.)

Among the Maidu Indians today, women are still the only shamans, and with their drums officiate as doctors and magicians. There are many other places, too, in which women are the shamans, notably in Kamchatka, where they are such fine musicians. Even in civilized Korea today a sorceress called Mu-Tang goes from house to house and by means of charms and music benefits the sick. Frequently both women and men know the art and are qualified to perform magic and to sell their musical formulas as we would sell medicine. In some places men have usurped the power of women, have taken over women's functions, and have become professional magicians. When shamanism becomes an affair affecting the welfare of groups larger than the family, men often exclude women from the professional group. They confess the higher qualifications of women for dealing with spirits, however, by dressing as women and by even imitating women's voices.

The North American Indians are an example of a large cultural group that regard music as the function of men rather than of women. There are many exceptions to this general rule, in the case both of individuals and of tribes. North American Indian women often dance, sing, and create music, but not to the extent that men do. When women are musicians, their music equals men's in quality and is often reproduced or mentioned by musicologists. There is no lack of musical ability, therefore, in North American Indian women, but a certain type of taboo prevents them from developing native talent. This taboo may be traced to the general custom of receiving dreams from the spirit world. These Indian men are expected to have contact with spirits, especially at the time of their initiation into manhood. When they fast and pray in solitude, they conceive music. These women, on the other hand, are not expected to receive messages from the supernatural. They are capable of it and frequently do, but just as frequently they are actively discouraged from such contacts. Among the Papago, girls who begin to show signs of mantic powers are forced to have their "shamans' crystals" removed. In this manner, a girl is directed away from developing creative musical imagination for no reason except that she is not a man.

How the different traditions for capability in music originated no one knows. Both men and women, however, made the customs in the first place or allowed certain prescribed manners to develop into tradition. Women, for instance, are not compelled by men to carry out puberty rites, which in many tribes involve some practices definitely damaging to the individuals concerned. Mothers and girls submit to being shut up in a cage for months after the first menstruation or after the birth of a baby. Nor is the separation of men and women in work and worship a state forced upon women by men. Women at times are aggressively antagonistic toward men and have been known to maul men unmercifully and even kill them for daring to intrude upon childbirth or other rites.

In connection with music, women sometimes themselves uphold customs that deter them from being musicians and probably often establish such customs. The Iroquois Indian women, for instance, who have a remarkably high status as mothers and tribal leaders, call upon men to be the singers at certain of the women's dances. Before the men begin to sing, they say: "We do this for our mothers." It has been suggested that long ago women needed the men's protection from enemies during the performance of the religious dances, and secured the men's services as watchmen by allowing them the privilege of singing.

Without the consent and approval of women, no cultural pattern could endure for generation after generation. Nevertheless, women often uphold cruel and senseless taboos that could be removed at will but which, while they are sanctioned, act as a bar to the free use of human energy.

The natural aptitude of men and women for musical expression is self-evident. But whether or not this natural aptitude is allowed to develop or to lie dormant depends upon local custom. As flowers flourish in bits of soil between rocks, so will musicians grow where even the least incentive exists; but where tribal custom dwarfs and obstructs, neither men nor women can create music, any more than flowers can grow under the shadow and weight of stones.

Has tribal custom dwarfed and obstructed the musical talent of the women of our society? Let us go back to the beginning of human records and allow the unfolding pages of western European civilization to tell the tale.

CHAPTER V

THE FIRST MUSICIANS

1.

*T*HE day that men and women danced the first dance, sang the first song, and beat the first drum will never be known. Who the first musicians were, where they lived, what motives and incentives led them to make rhythms and melodies, will forever remain a secret.

When the last of the great glaciers that had covered Europe for thousands of years was melting away, the warmth that came into the sunshine and the green that grew in the valleys made that age the real beginning of our history. The oldest monuments of human achievement that have survived are the paintings and carvings on rocks. Found in many parts of Europe and Africa in caves and on rock surfaces, protected by overhanging ledges, the finest ones date from about 10,000 B.C. Not all, however, are so ancient. Some, in Africa, are of quite recent origin. Yet the recent ones are so like the old that only an expert can tell the difference. A remarkable similarity in custom between very early peoples and those living in the same region today can be deduced from the illustrations and also from the testimony of the people themselves. The Bushmen of Africa, for example, interpret one rock painting as representing their Dance of the Blood—a charm against sickness. (See Plate 22.)

In some paintings women without men can be seen performing ceremonies of the sort that in present-day primitive tribes is accompanied by women's music. The women might be conducting a puberty rite or initiating a priestess. (See Plate 24.) One African rock picture seems to correspond accurately to a myth of the Australian Wikmunkan Ghost Clan, in which only the women know how to sing the mourning songs. According to legend, the ancestral husband and wife came to a tragic end and assumed the form of ghosts.

The wife sat weeping by a lagoon and made laments that her women attendants heard and passed down to generation upon generation of women.

The habitual secrecy with which our primitive contemporaries conduct their rites and the recognized authority of women in matters of birth and rebirth indicate strongly that designing and painting were also an evidence of women's magic powers and that many of the rock paintings were women's work. In certain North American Indian tribes of today, girls who are secluded during their puberty rites occupy their time painting pictures on the rocks. The midwives of Malacca, too, trace mystic designs—mainly flowers—on the bamboo tubes that hold the water they use for washing their patients. Only the erroneous notion of many nineteenth-century scholars that women do not function imaginatively has established the fiction that the pictures were all the work of men artists. (See Plates 22, 23, 25, and 26.)

2.

Everything that we can deduce by working backward from the present to these rock paintings suggests that the art of music may have begun in the singing of magic by women, and that women were the first musicians, and perhaps for some time the only ones. In general, the earliest forms of human society seem to have resembled those of the tribes that today have the least developed cultures. Some of the most primitive people today are very musical people— the Pygmies, the Bushmen, certain of the primitive Siberian tribes, some of the North American Indians, the Semangs in the Malay Peninsula, some of the Australians, the Tierra del Fuegans, and the now extinct Tasmanians. Semang men do not dance but are content to watch the women repeat their very primitive dance steps. Among the Seri Indians, only the women perform music. They have been heard singing simple melodies as they construct their rude huts of branches. They beat drums at puberty rites for girls and at death ceremonies. Bushwomen make drums and beat them. They play flutes and compose songs—especially lullabies and flower songs. The Kamchatkans and the Pygmies, as we have already seen, stand out conspicuously as creative musicians. Women of the Ona tribe (Tierra del Fuego), led by their own "kloket mother," perform a dance accompanied by a chant that is considered one of the rare examples of genuinely primitive music.

It is a striking fact that the women of the simplest cultures are more interested in religious ceremonies than are the men. In some tribes women only are the religious officials. In many, puberty rites for girls are conspicuous while corresponding rites for boys are lacking.

Again, observation of these primitive tribes today confirms the opinion now generally held by scholars that the earliest form of religion was moon worship, and the earliest religious ritual was a dancing and singing magic performed by women, with a view to influencing the potent power of the moon over life on earth. Today among the Pygmies the moon is feminine and is thought of as Generatrix, or initiator of life. The women of the Ona tribe (Tierra del Fuego) believe that Kra, the Moon Woman, came down to earth, lived with them, and taught them the ways of all women. This myth suggests that formal worship of the moon originated when women first observed that their own monthly cycle was synchronized to that of the moon and that the term of pregnancy could be counted by lunar months. There is, indeed, no explanation of the similarity of women's rites in all parts of the world except that they sprang from natural causes, common to all women.

Several myths represent a forcible determination on the part of men, at some point, to take over the women's magic moon rites. The Ona tribe has a myth that appears also in many other places. According to it, women had originally a pre-emptive right over the life of the spirit and over music. They once possessed the secrets of birth and death and spent their time discussing rituals and organizing choral dances. Often they dressed up like ghosts and deceived the men into thinking them supernatural beings. Finally, the men discovered the ruse and killed the women's leaders. Ever after, the men performed the women's ceremonies, excluding women from the stolen rites.

While this type of myth cannot be taken in the strictly historical sense, it reveals a state of envy—by no means limited to the primitive level—on the part of men for women's closer association to natural forces. Where men are known to have taken over mimetic rites that were originally the activities of women, as well as in many other cases where the history of the rite is not known, men often dress like women and imitate women's voices. This constitutes a clear recognition by men that they had adopted the magic devices, including the music that is inseparable from the rituals.

Just as religious music was probably made by women first, so the form of work songs probably originated with women. Such a development of musical imagination may be assumed from the fact that women are believed to have worked in groups long before men organized themselves for pursuits other than hunting and fighting—neither of which adapts itself to rhythmic action.

Whatever men may have done with music to suit their own needs in these earliest times, there is no question that all evidence points to the complete independence of women in music and ritual and to the general recognition of their special authority as life bearers in the making of singing magic.

<h3 style="text-align:center">3.</h3>

After the rock paintings, the next historical evidence of human activity is found in pottery vessels used for domestic purposes, mortuary urns, and little idols of men, women, and children. These have been excavated in the Indus Valley, in Sumer, in Egypt, and in Europe. They are frequently decorated with male and female symbols. The umbilical cord as the life line is a favorite design. Others are the triangle and spiral, which are also feminine symbols. Often vases were made in the form of a lyre—one of the oldest of the moon-woman symbols—or in the shape of a woman actually giving birth to a child. There are many figurines of women holding musical instruments—clappers, drum, cymbals, or flute. Other figurines represent women weeping or wailing. Most significantly, the images of musicians are generally female. Scholars suggest that the people of those times believed the images, when placed in a grave, to be capable of bringing about the rebirth by means of magic music.

These are often the earliest remains of truly civilized society, which began to be firmly established about 5000 B.C. in a few great river valleys.

Between 10,000 B.C. and 5000 B.C. the last ice melted in Europe. The shores of the Mediterranean were like a great garden. Where now there are only deserts in the Sahara and in parts of the Near East, there were meadows and flowing streams. And in Asia and Africa, as the earth settled into the warmth of our present time, great rivers built wide flat areas out of silt brought down from the mountainous centers of the continents. On these rich flats great numbers of people could live together and grow food for all. So in these river basins the early primitive tribes, each clustered around its tribal mothers, combined into large societies. These societies began to develop all those skills and comforts that are possible only where there is a pooling of the power of many people for the needs of subsistence and a specializing of skills. Instead of one primitive woman cooking and weaving and raising food, people began to have cooks and bakers, weavers, herdsmen, and farmers.

Between 10,000 and 5000 B.C. such great communities were forming in four great river basins—in Egypt, where the Nile River brings the black silt of the far-away mountains down to the sea, making there the flat lands of the Nile delta; in the Near East, where the two largest rivers of western Asia, the Euphrates and the Tigris, roll down their topsoil and spread it in a great reedy, marshy swamp and plain called Mesopotamia (or "Between the Rivers"); in China, where the clayey yellow mud is brought down by the Yellow River from the high peaks of central Asia and spread for hundreds of miles, making soil of inexhaustible fertility; and in the Indus Valley, where the earth from the Himalayas is rolled westward to the Arabian Sea. Here the tribal families of the primitive mothers began to coalesce and to build on a larger and larger scale, in more enduring materials. The dried brick made of the river mud (what we call adobe) took the place of reeds and wood; and then stone brought a long distance down the rivers from the mountains took the place of adobe. By 5000 B.C. people were making things so enduring that one can find today the remains of large cities and societies. In the same period several forms of writing began to develop, and from that time we know more and more about the past.

But what happened in those years when the primitive mothers were uniting and linking their families to make cities and states? Did they keep on singing to the moon and weaving songs of lamentation and of triumph? Did the primitive mother evolve with evolving society into the queen and priestess? And when there began to be great religious ceremonies, with thousands of people participating in vast temples with massive pillars of carved stone and hundreds of lights at the altar, was there still a singing to the moon? And were women as priestesses leading it? We have every evidence that this was so, even in some cases down to Christian times, for in the first picture writings, statues, and paintings there is the Moon-Mother-Musician goddess in the full flower of her glory.

4.

This goddess, as she appears at the time when written and pic-
torial records become numerous, is the climax of a long development.
She sums up and crystallizes what women did, what they wished to
do, and what men believed they could do in the preliterate period
when ancient mythology was being elaborated and handed down by
word of mouth.

When about five thousand years ago unknown scribes began to
write the first histories (in the form of stories designed to be sung),
they told about superhuman beings who created the world, founded
civilizations, and performed heroic deeds. In these epics women
played a lively part, frequently a greater part than that attributed to
men. To many people these deities of ancient times seem to be crea-
tions of poetic imagination with no relation to actual conditions.
Gods and goddesses were ideal images, it is true, but the ideals expressed in them indicated existing values. A goddess standing on a
crescent moon, for instance, represented the close association of
women with new life. But at the same time the deities were generally
reflections of the people—real men and women being prototypes of
gods and goddesses.

The great driving energy that is the fount of all life was to many
Hindus a female force. They gave it a name—śakti. In later times,
in this section of Hinduism, every god had to be acompanied by his
śakti and was often so depicted. Her energy manifested itself with
particular power in the persons of the Great Mothers. They were
sevenfold—the Seven Mothers, whose cult exists among many of the
more primitive groups today. The large number of female figurines
that come from the Indus Valley civilization suggests that a goddess-
mother was worshiped three thousand years ago. In Egyptian history
no time is known when four of the mighty mothers were not already
there. Néït, the Weaver, thought to be of Libyan origin, had for title
"The Old One Who Was When Nothing Was," or "The One Born before There Was Birth." Cat-headed Bastet had a name that meant
Love. Nekhbiyet—Eileithyia to the Greeks—was the goddess of
birth. She was the moon, the bringer of life. The Egyptians honored
her by calling one of their towns after her. Hat-hor was "The Great
One; eye of the sun-lady of heaven; mistress of all the gods." With

the same authority, the Sumerian Innanna carried civilization and the arts to new centers. And under another name, the Great Mother in Sumer created the world and everything in it. The idea that woman gives the final touch which endows human beings with capability is also found in primitive tribes. It is an exciting one for a girl to realize and might well be incorporated into the teaching of history.

These goddess-mothers were generally represented as giving speech, music, and the art of gesture to humanity, and as being themselves dancers and musicians. The reason why the mother was thought of as the giver of speech and music may be easily understood if we again work backward from what we know of simple societies today. For where life is very simple, the baby is almost inseparable from the mother until after the age when it can speak and can begin to sing and imitate patterns of gesture. Mothers often carry their babies on their backs while working or while dancing and singing in religious ceremonies. The child drinks in speech and music with its mother's milk. So Bhāratī and Sarasvati, divine representatives of the dark-eyed women of early India, were thought of as giving all their people speech, music, and ritual. Sarasvati gave poetry and music and arranged musical tones into scales. Bhāratī taught the union of dancing with singing and is often called the Mother of the Bards.

In certain ancient invocations to deities, these two goddess-musicians were summoned with Ilā, goddess of the rite itself, and were spoken of as a group of three. Since they were deities of speech, gesture, music, and ritual, it seems clear that poetry, dance, and the occasion were enhanced by music and that they were integrated then, as they are now in India when the temple dancing girls add songs to their rhythmic gestures. The fact that these ancient deities were goddesses, not gods, implies that before their time women had been active in the making of rites, dances, and songs.

In Egypt, cat-headed Bastet held the sistrum and delighted in dancing and in music. Hat-hor, the Great One, was "mistress of the dancing, lady of music and wreathing of garlands, mistress of songs." They were matched by Innanna in Sumer, who was described as organizing rites, wailing to bring new life, lamenting over the dying year, and rejoicing over the rebirth. "She of the Beautiful Voice" made the lamentations and the incantations for the magic rituals. "O singer" are the words with which people began their appeals for mercy and compassion. The link between the real woman and the ideal in these representations was such a goddess as the Chinese Nukua. With her fine gold-tinted skin and tilted eyes, she has been identified as an empress, wife of the emperor Fohi. About 2500 B.C. these two interested themselves in making musical reforms, and to the Empress is attributed the creation of a tonal system for the use of musicians. In legend, the real woman became a goddess who mythically performed what the good Empress had already achieved.

5.

These oldest goddesses, spirits, symbols, and even names represent the type of woman normal for the period *before* written history begins. The women of the ancient world of seven and eight thousand years ago—in China, India, and on the Mediterranean shores—were themselves the prototypes of the deities. The hierarchy of divine and semidivine spirits represented the institutionalized role of women in that type of society. If a goddess was supreme in her circle, a queen and high priestess had previously had authority in her tribe or clan, settling a new territory, perhaps, selecting a sacred grove, finding times and places for the cult dances and songs. As the goddess Isis did, so might a queen have led the people to abandon cannibalism and to eat the bread she taught them to bake. If a goddess was able to help a woman in childbirth or to make grain grow by means of her incantations, then women had previously been skilled in medicine and in agricultural magic. If many goddesses danced and sang, lamented and rejoiced over the waxing and waning moon, or over decaying and sprouting vegetation, then many more priestesses had contributed to the development of those elaborate rituals and had been singing and dancing in choirs. There can be no doubt that women were creative musicians in that age which preceded the epoch of written history. Superhuman or human, women had economic and spiritual authority and could do what people expected to be done with music.

Women's religion, women's customs in primitive tribes, traditions handed down by men's secret societies, and the symbols of divine women in early mythology all point directly to the conclusion that men had not yet seriously put their minds upon the development of rituals, domestic work, and music until after women had established their own conception of a life of the spirit, including expression in music.

CHAPTER VI

QUEEN AND PRIESTESS

1.

*F*ROM about 5000 B.C. there are more and more indications of the way in which women were functioning as musicians. In the two greater river civilizations from which we draw our social and religious ideas—Egypt, whose culture was filtered to us through Greece, and Sumer (including Babylonia, Assyria, and Chaldea), whose heritage came to us through the Jews—the woman chieftainess and priestess-musician retained her high power for many centuries.

The spirit of the great civilizations of antiquity was the spirit of the primitive world, not of our modern world. Like simple people today, the ancients worshiped nature in its various manifestations as moon, as sun, as plants and animals, as the life-giving power of their great rivers. And like primitive people, also, they used music in a practical way to control their environment with sympathetic magic. Above all, they revered the special harmony of women with the rhythm of nature.

As civilization developed, religion, music, and the functions of women in connection with them were elaborated and refined. The forces of nature were personified by many goddesses and gods. Chief among them were the great goddesses, representative of woman's unity with the life force. When communal storehouses for surplus foods were built as a primitive form of social security, it was natural that the music and ritual for invoking the life force should center in these food houses. Gradually they developed into great temples, keeping down to Christian times some traces of their original structure and function as food houses.

Since woman's place in the scheme of life had purpose and dignity, public institutions were built around her natural functions, as well as around those of men. Women then represented in an official capacity the principle of female energy. Priestesses with their choirs of dancing, singing votaries functioned in the most important temples and in the most important rites, worshiping nature's rhythmic laws and striving to keep in touch with them by the techniques of primitive times, particularly by the dance and by music. But whereas in primitive times women appear to have carried on their rites separately from men, as civilization developed the tendency was for men and women to carry out their rites together. Many depictions of religious ceremonies represent a procession of men advancing from one side and of women from the opposite side, meeting before the altar in perfect equality.

2.

It is fortunate for our understanding of the early Mediterranean culture, in which our own civilization began, that its spirit and way of life have survived to this day in a mountainous region of the Sahara Desert. Here live the Tuareg tribes, thought to be the descendants of the once mighty Libyan nation, and believed to retain customs formerly prevalent in Egypt, in the Near East, and in Crete.

"She walks with her head high" [1]—a native proverb thus characterizes the strong-minded, gifted, and intelligent Tuareg woman, who is respected by the men of her nation in a manner that has no parallel in the Western world. These women have complete authority over the home and the rearing of children. They own property over which the husband has no rights. It is the custom for them to take an active part in public life, to be asked for advice in the tribal councils, to rule as chieftainesses, and even to lead the warriors into battle. Women are the preservers of tradition and learning. Where the ancient script, which has a similarity to the old Minoan script of Crete, is still used, women are more versed in it than men. Before marriage, girls enjoy great freedom. They are the wooers and often ride all night on their camels to visit their lovers. No household tasks are expected of them, but rather dancing, making poetry, and singing.

Music pervades the life of Tuareg women. When the explorers Denham and Clapperton visited the tribe over a hundred years ago, they reported: "In the evening, we heard numerous bands of females singing . . . this custom is very common among the people and is one of the principal amusements in the mountain recesses. They go out when their work is finished in the evenings and remain till near midnight singing and telling stories. The males seldom sing." [2]

At the present time it is the custom for noblewomen to organize the meetings at which songs are performed and judged. The texts of these songs are extremely varied, ranging from the love lyric to ballads of war and travel and to hymns of thanksgiving. Although men and women both create the music, women are the more famous. Some of them are known throughout the Sahara as the great creative artists of this region. Women are at the center of these *ahaals* and have evidently taken the lead in establishing them, just as the famous *salonières* of Europe attracted the brilliant men and women of the eighteenth century to their own private houses. An *ahaal* often takes place in the moonlight under a large tamarisk tree. The company gathers around the great fire. The women, clad in graceful veils and heavy ornaments that might have come from the Bronze Age, sit in a circle. Young men stand behind them and camels loom in the shadows. A stringed instrument called *amzad* is played by the women as they sing haunting melodies in a rhythm unknown and indefinable to Europeans.

> "The heart thou lovest, and which loves thee not,
> Whatever thou do to strain towards him, he flieth.
> A sad torment for a thing it were better not to ponder.
> But if two hearts meet, it is heaven!
> It is better than all friends;
> It is better than the whole world!" [3]

The status of the woman musician and the attitude of men and women toward the poetess suggests what musical customs were actually in force in an age when goddess, queen, and high priestess had a pride and spiritual independence comparable to that of the present-day Tuareg poetess-musicians. (See Plate 34.)

3.

Protected by mountains and living off the main highways of aggression, the Tuareg probably represents a survival into modern times of a fairly typical example of the light-brown race of northern Africa that appears to have given our Western civilization its earliest institutions. This race was widespread both in north Africa and in

From L. Frobenius, Mdsimu Dsangara

25. On the extreme left of this prehistoric rock painting, a woman holds her arms in the conventional pose of mourners. The Australian Wikmunkan Ghost Clan believe that the first lament was made by a wife for her drowned husband. (See pages 62 and 63.)

26. One hand of the prehistoric priestess rests on the seat of her power. The other holds a bison horn shaped like a crescent moon. A similar instrument is used today by the musical Valenge women to deflower girls. (See pages 62 and 63.)

Courtesy of The Hispanic Society of America

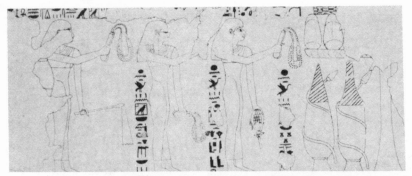

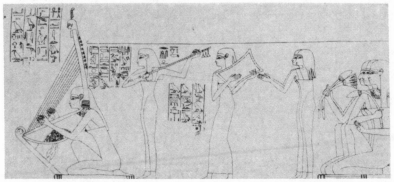

27, 28, 29. Egyptian wall paintings represented scenes of real life. Women musicians can be seen officiating at religious ceremonies. On the extreme right of Plate 28, the choirmistress holds her hand before her mouth, probably making the ululating trill. (See pages 76 and 78.)

30, 31. Cretan priestesses perform a religious dance before a great concourse of people, possibly invoking a feminine spirit to ensure the continuation of life. (See page 85.)

32. Cretan frescoes, like the Egyptian, reveal ancient customs. These choristers are boys, dressed like girls and led by a priestess. (See page 84.)

33. On a Greek vase, a chorus of women stands enveloped in a cape, the leader holding a tambourine. (See page 92.)

such Mediterranean islands as Crete. To it belonged the Egyptians, who have been called Hamites and are assumed to have been of the white race.

No civilization, not even that of China, has had a longer continuous existence than the Egyptian. From about 4000 B.C. to the conquest by the Moslems in the seventh century A.D. it had not only a continuity of life but a relative harmony and freedom from internal disturbance that indicated something very sound in its social organization. Egypt was distinguished for the high degree of comfort and beauty attained in household furnishings. All the arts of daily living were brought to a state approaching perfection. In some kinds of manufacture the Egyptians have never been surpassed, and rarely equaled. On the bodies in the Egyptian tombs there is linen of an exquisite sheerness. There was cloisonné of exquisite delicacy and perfection of finish. There were beautiful glazes on tiles and pottery of many colors—green and blue, purple, violet, red, yellow, and white. The manufacture of glass and the artistic use of it in inlays and mosaics was remarkable for skill, beauty, and originality. The same high standard may surely be assumed for music, especially since music was regarded by them as a direct and powerful magic for influencing spirits.

Egypt was also distinguished for the very high status of its women. As if reminiscent of a former matriarchy, royal power was transmitted through the female line. Every daughter of the Pharaohs was born a queen and possessed the prerogatives of royalty from the day of her birth. A man became king only by marrying a princess. In the later days of Egypt none of the sons of the royal house, however powerful, was allowed to forget that he held his right through his queen.

The custom of matrilineal inheritance made the queens legal and spiritual heads of the people. From the earliest times they undoubtedly had a large share in government and in affairs of the external world. As high priestesses, queens were identified with a local goddess, homage being paid to them in death as well as in life. Upon the death of the beloved Egyptian queen A'h-mose Nofret-iri (Eighteenth Dynasty), a special priesthood was organized to burn incense in her honor and to recite the formulas of prayers used in addressing the gods. When her mummy was excavated it was found to have dark-blue skin, the attribute of Hat-hor and Isis, goddesses of life and death. Immediately below the queen in rank were the other women whose husband was also the king. Custom allowed the king and other important men a number of lesser wives, who were princesses from neighboring countries. Some of the great kings had as many as three hundred concubines in their royal households. But these women were in a very different position from the concubines of later times or of some Oriental societies, for their relation to the queen as assistant priestesses gave them an institutionalized role in religious ceremonies and therefore a certain state dignity that can be acquired in no other way.

The position of ordinary women, who did not partake of the divinity of the women of the royal house, was, on a smaller scale, a replica of that of the priestess-queens. In the many legal documents that survive from ancient times in Egypt, this is emphasized again and again.

I acknowledge thy rights of wife [so runs one of those contracts]; from this day forward I shall never by any word oppose thy claims. I shall acknowledge thee before anyone as my wife, but I have no power to say to thee: "Thou art my wife." It is I who am the man who is thy husband. From the day that I become thy husband I cannot oppose thee, in whatsoever place thou mayest please to go. I cede thee . . . [here follows a list of possessions] that are in thy dwelling. I have no power to interfere in any transaction made by thee, from this day. Every document made in my favour by any person is now placed among thy deeds, and is also at the disposal of thy father or any relatives acting for thee. Thou shall hold me bound to honour any such deed. Should anyone hand over to me any moneys that are due to thee, I shall hand them over to thee without delay, without opposition, and in addition pay thee a further twenty measures of silver, one hundred shekels, and again twenty measures of silver.[4]

"Thou assumest full power over me to compel me to perform these things," [5] declares a similar contract.

It was the custom for women to mingle in the general life of town and country, taking part in industry and agriculture as well as in trading. One of the boasts of Rameses III in the period of prosperity about 1200 B.C. was: "I let the woman of Egypt walk out to the place she wished, no vile persons molested her on her way." [6]

From the spiritual point of view, woman was generally regarded as being close to the invisible powers behind life and death. She could see and hear that which was beyond the perception of man. She could control the spirits with her flexible and piercing voice. Without a wife to influence the spirits, a man could not enter the gates of the future life. Many women, and not merely a few, therefore, played an active part in public festivals and in religious ceremonies. During the period of the New Kingdom (c. 1800 B.C.) scarcely one could be found who was not, or had not once been, a priestess or at least a minor official in the service of the deities.

The queen, as leader of women, was followed by an independent hierarchy of women—prophetess, spiritual teacher, priestess-musician, and choirs of dancing, singing attendants. The prophetess was regarded as divinely inspired; the priestess was the actual embodiment of the goddess she represented.

The priestess served both goddesses and gods. If priests served too in a goddess cult, they ranked lower than the women officials. It was the custom for priestesses to receive salaries from temple property and to be members of societies of scribes. They did not live in seclusion but attended to other normal duties. Many of them had titles such as "Worshiper," "Clothier," "Mother," "She Who Suckles." These names denote a high antiquity, an identity with the natural woman, and a precedent for the descriptive names frequently given to goddesses.

While the Egyptians were building their great civilization, making life stable, beautiful, and comfortable, they were never allowed to forget that the end of life is death and that beyond death is rebirth. Their genius and their wealth spent themselves lavishly on the tomb. Their religious feelings were expressed chiefly in rituals, incantations, and musical ceremonies intended to direct the soul on its way and to invoke the rebirth.

In conducting the rites for the rebirth, the indispensable priestess used the magic devices common to women the world over—holy water, the sacred ear of corn, incense, flowers; musical instruments, especially the sistrum; dancing, wailing, and singing. (See Plate 35.)

That the priestesses were trained musicians can be seen from their titles. A Fourth Dynasty name was Mrt, meaning priestess-musician. Another name given the woman conductor—Hnyt—signifies "Chief of the Female Musicians." Still another name was Phylarch, used in the time of the New Empire, when the priestess-musicians divided into *phylae*, or watches, for the purposes of attending to the music of the temple. From the time of the New Empire on for many centuries, chantresses increased in number and importance, being mentioned more often in the records. There were the "Great Players with the Hand"—always the hieroglyphic for singing; there was the "Great Chantress." Throughout Egyptian history she never failed to "content Amun with her voice." One of the most important, as well as one of the oldest, of the rebirth rites was the celebration of the Osiris mysteries. For this, priestess-musicians had special hymns of mourning for the death of Osiris in which his resurrection was anticipated. The priestesses impersonated the goddesses Isis and Nephthys— divine composers of all laments. They carried tambourines and sang both solo songs and duets.

Another important rebirth ceremony took place during the Sed Festival. This was celebrated for a dead king or other prominent man. According to an old custom practiced before the days of mummifying, a statue was made in the image of the deceased. While the statue was still in the workmen's shop, before it was dragged through the streets with crowds of wailing, mourning people, the priestess-musician was summoned to perform the rite of "the opening of the mouth" by means of her magic incantations.

A festival to ensure the continuation of life was the one named after Hat-hor. On the day chosen for its celebration, a choir of priestesses marched in procession, holding out emblems to bring health and wealth, blessing the people within their houses. In wall paintings these priestesses were depicted and designated especially as "the female musicians of Hat-hor, Lady of Dendera, Mistress of all the Gods." The inscriptions also convey the words they were supposed to be singing: "I offer to thee the *menat* necklace, the *sistra*, in order that they may give to thee a fair and long-lasting life." (See Plate 27.) Many religious ceremonies were conducted by priests and priestesses together. In the temple at Karnak bands of men and women musicians are depicted clapping hands and singing. Choirs of male and female musicians who daily sang hymns in the worship of Berenike are mentioned in a decree of Canopus. Celebrating the accession of Rameses IV is a line in a poem: "Maidens rejoice and repeat their songs of gladness. . . ." [7]

Throughout Egyptian history there is evidence in written documents, in pictures, and in statuary of women participating to the fullest extent in the religious ceremony and in the music accompanying it. As goddess, as priestess, as magician, as wailer, as choir leader, as choral singer, as dancer, and as instrumental player, women were there in the temples on an equality with men and often in a superior position to men. Often, indeed, the great temples, with their thick walls and massive columns, reproduced in stone the pattern of those huts made of reeds tied together that African women everywhere still construct with their own hands for their homes. And the elaborate ceremonies conducted in them retained a homely memory of the household life of women. More than one scholar has quoted the hymn:

> Awake in peace, thou cleansed one, in peace!
>
> .   .   .
>
> Thou sleepest in the barque of evening,
> Thou awakest in the barque in the morning [8]

as an example of similarity in practice in ordinary living and in temple service. These are supposed to be the words sung by the women of primitive Egypt for the purpose of rousing their chief in the morning. In later centuries, when the king impersonated the sun god in the temple, the same hymn was used by the priestess-musicians in the "House of the Morning" as a ritual for the ceremonial morning rebirth.

A similar association between the temple service and home practice can be seen in childbirth rites. In the pyramid temple of Sahuri —where the pyramid form itself resembles the female symbol of the triangle—priestesses impersonated Nekhbiyet, goddess of childbirth like the Greek Eileithyia, with whom magic formulas and incantations for aid in childbirth were immemorially identified. Egyptian women must have made such incantations, just as primitive women do today, or royal births would not have been described in legends in which Isis, the cunning magician, and three other deities appeared disguised as musicians to assist the queen in her need.

Songs sung by women in connection with other home events have been preserved and show the same belief that characterizes all primitive music in the magic properties of an incantation:

> Keep away from his teeth—they will bite you!
> Keep away from his navel—it is the morning star! [9]

Every part of the little body is mentioned in this long charm to protect a baby from evil spirits.

In personal as well as in the symbolic life of the spirit, the wail and the incantation were required to bring about the rebirth after death. A funeral was a great religious ceremony at which women, whose particular and unique function was mourning, always participated. They followed the bier in a procession, throwing ashes on their heads, waving green branches, scratching their cheeks, holding tear cups to their eyes, and screaming themselves hoarse. The wailers were sometimes members of the family, but they could also be professionals who made wailing a specialty distinct from the musical lament or dirge.

Often the dead body was borne on a barge across the Nile, followed by other barges carrying wailers and choirs of women singers. Statuettes of Isis and Nephthys, goddess composers of both wails and laments, might be placed at one end of the boat and surrounded by women performing the rite of wailing. At the other end another group of women led by a choir mistress might officiate as singers. (See Plate 28.)

At home, the funeral feast was accompanied by music. Women played the lyre and the flute, beat their drums, and clapped their hands to the rhythm of songs invoking the blessing of a goddess whose function it was to receive the dead. "Put balsam in the locks of Ma'et; for health and life are with her. . . ." (See Plate 29.)

In old Egypt both the love lyric and the song-story reached a high point of development. There is a flower song in one of the famous collections similar in imagery to other women's flower songs in all parts of the world. A maiden is weaving a wreath. Each flower she adds reminds her of her love:

Blush roses are in it [the wreath], one blushes before thee—
My life depends upon hearing thee.
Whenever I see thee, it is better to me than food or drink.[9]

Did not some woman there use her musical talent to express her personal emotions and to compose "the beautiful gladsome songs of thy sister whom thy heart loves"?[10] Penthelia, we know, was one who described in song and story the events of the Trojan wars. Her technique is said to have inspired Homer, or other Greek bards, to imitate her treatment of this epic material.

As a priestess of the god Phtha, Penthelia may be regarded as a

symbol of the woman who was both a religious official and an entertainer. She was only one of many Egyptian women musicians
trained for service in the temples who was also expected to use music
upon other occasions than the temple ceremony. The large groups of
women living in the palaces danced, played, and sang at banquets
and other entertainments, employing the same musical ideas and
idiom that were appropriate to the rituals. A certain Rahonem was
at one time the chief woman manager of the lesser wives, and in her
capacity as directress of the female players of the tabour (drum)
and of the female singers, had the same title as that given to the
priestess-musician.

The princess-musicians were assisted by girls drawn from social
classes beneath the rank of royalty and trained in regular music
schools. Many pictures show graceful dancers and instrumentalists
playing lyres, flutes, and drums in combination. During the Eighteenth Dynasty these professional women musicians competed successfully with the blind harpers. In singing, the trained musicians
had an undeniable advantage over men. Their voices, believed to be
so potent in affecting spirits, combined also the clarity and flexibility
for making subtle and delicate melodic variations. Ideals in religion
and art converged to bring the woman musician forward in a manner unparalleled in the modern world where women and music both
have different values.

Women's association with music in Egypt reached a brilliant
climax in the Eighteenth Dynasty and continued to be a vital one
until the priests converted religion into an organized system of sor-
cery from which all but they were excluded. Women's music can be
traced back to the earliest days of Egyptian history. In the beginning
it was chiefly dancing and singing, especially lamenting, in which
they excelled. The oldest goddesses symbolized these early women
musicians. In instrumental music women apparently did not participate extensively until about 2700 B.C., after the passing of the Old
Empire. Men are depicted as the usual performers on instruments.
Some kind of a taboo evidently existed preventing women from being trained in a field in which they later showed so much proficiency.
Significantly, the oldest goddesses hold the sistrum but not other
instruments. If this negative reflection of women's musical activities
has verity, so then must the positive reflection be true to life. And
the predominant part taken by these old goddesses over gods in

dance and song strongly indicates that real women, whose interests and activities became integrated into divine characters, were in fact leaders in ritual and in music.

4.

Simultaneously with Egypt, peoples of the Near East, allied to the Jews in language, customs, ideas, and physical type, were building another great civilization in the low flat land between the Tigris and Euphrates Rivers. The most southern part of this region, where the rivers come down to the Persian Gulf, was called Chaldea. The northern section, composed of the lower slopes and valleys of the high mountains whence the rivers came, was called Assyria. The great central area—lying low and flat between the rivers—was called Babylonia and was dominated by its great city, Babylon, whose ruins are about seventy miles south of the medieval and modern city of Bagdad. The three sections of this great region are referred to together as Sumer.

The life of Babylonia was the life of merchants and small farmers, busy, prosperous, with widespread education and general comfort and luxury in the arrangements for daily living. It was regulated by an elaborate system of law that guaranteed justice and, in general, favored women and especially mothers. For example, if a free woman married a slave, her children were guaranteed to her and could not be made slaves by the father's master.

Almost everybody in Babylon, both men and women, learned to read. Writing was done with a pointed stylus on tablets of wet clay and baked. Women even had the first woman's college mentioned in history. In the district of Cappadocia, tablets have been found that mention a lady's college in a "women's city." The studies appear to have been arts, letters, and crafts.

As in Egypt, princesses were priestesses and women carried out religious rituals with music and incantations in which the wail was made the basis of a great variety of music. Both men and women played instruments and gave the chants. In Akkadian, the language of north Babylonia, the word for the liturgical psalmist and chanter was *zammertu*, of the feminine gender. Convents of women religious officials called "virgins" were attached to, the temples. Though said to be vowed to chastity, actually, under Babylonian law, they were allowed to marry. They were not supposed to have children of their own but might give their husbands a concubine, whose children were regarded as their own. Possibly there is some misunderstanding of the various laws regulating the women religious officials who had a high status and many prerogatives. Possibly the word virgin as applied to these married priestesses means only that they were expected to be persons of decorum or good character. The statement that they were to have no children but might give their husbands a concubine whose children were to be regarded as their own means merely that their duties to the temple must be set above those to their home. In compensation for which they might very properly get another woman to manage their households!

Temples were great storehouses of surplus products under the administration of the state, for which people in privation might make application. A tenth or tithe of all products was contributed to the temple—whence comes the practice of tithing in the Jewish and Christian churches. A similar plan of making the temple the storehouse of surpluses to help the people in famines was followed in early Persia. It seems a natural expression of a mother's forethought.

In the temples there was an elaborate music by women, under the direction of the queen and princesses as priestesses. Queen Shu-bad of Ur made music on harp and tambourine with her ladies in waiting or with professional musicians. In her society, too, the word *nartu*, meaning "chanter," is feminine. Lipushiau, the granddaughter of King Naram-Sin, was appointed player of the *balag-di* drum in the moon god's temple at Ur. This drum was used not only for the liturgy but at feasts. Its other name, *balag-lul*, has a connection with singing. We can fancy this girl of 2380 B.C. drumming and making incantations to hasten the rebirth of the moon and then dancing and singing with her companions in the palace.

In Ishtar's temple at Erech, troops of dancing priestesses chanted their laments in a dialect used only when a female deity was supposed to be reciting. Although the word "wailing" is repeated in every line, the tradition of Ishtar as "She of the Beautiful Voice" and other references to "sacred music" point to some form of singing accompanying the utilitarian magic of the wail. Choral dancing in connection with national victory or defeat was a widespread custom. When the Sumerians and Akkadians were being oppressed by their Gutian conquerors during the third millennium B.C., the women of several towns assembled to mourn their fate. Dividing into two choruses, they gave the lament antiphonally, each group singing, in alternation, appropriate verses. At a much later date a document from Babylonia records that a certain group of women musicians were to assist in the celebration for a victorious army. Such performances, of which many other examples could be given, were by no means an impromptu or an individual expression of emotion but an organized, studied affair demanded by public opinion.

The tendency of all this religious and musical ritual under the leadership of singing women in Babylonia was toward an intellectual and monotheistic religion that had an influence for many centuries over religious thought. But the soul of the universe, as the Babylonians saw it, was not the male warrior god on which the monotheistic imagination of other near-by Semites, the Jews, later fastened, but was instead an all-encompassing mother principle, generally personified as Ishtar. Ishtar was Life—the teeming life of the rich Babylonian plain. She was in the waving grain, in the figs and the olive trees, in the fat cattle and sheep, in the inexhaustible waters from the high mountains that watered the garden lands the Sumerians had made for themselves. She was in the bright fostering sun by day and the moon and stars by night. Ishtar was not a goddess like the other gods and goddesses of Babylonia. She was something above and behind them, the ultimate explanation, universal being, life itself.

Between the superhuman woman-being and earthly men and women the imagination of the Babylonians created not only a pantheon of deities, but a host of intermediary spirits. Spirits were everywhere. The unseen world was full of imagined beings, both female and male, local and specialized representatives of the ultimate life, who might be influenced by the singing magic or incantations. Women had their special wisdom, which was revered by men. The oracles at Arbela were always regarded as being divinely inspired. And always the singing women continued to invoke the fertile power of Ishtar. If her power appeared to fail them, they created lamentations that sometimes have great poetic beauty and remind us of many passages in the Bible. The intention of these, as in all wail songs of women, is to invoke the rebirth.

The wailing is for the plants, the first lament is, "they grow not."
The wailing is for the barley; the ears grow not,
For the habitations and the flocks it is, they produce not.

For the perishing wedded ones, for perishing children it is: the dark-
headed people create not. The wailing is for the great river: it
brings the flood no more.

. . .

The wailing is for the forests; the tamarisks grow not.

. . .

The wailing is for the garden store-house; honey and wine are
produced not.

. . .

The wailing is for the palace; life unto distant days is not.[11]

5.

The mountainous island of Crete, only a hundred and fifty miles
long and from seven to thirty-five miles wide, is a small place to have
been the seat of a great civilization. Though its lower valleys are
well-watered and fertile, the land growing lemons, oranges, pears,
grapes, and olives to perfection, it could hardly have sustained a
large number of people. But, from about 3000 to 1200 B.C., the
Cretans traded far and wide with people on the shores and other islands of the Mediterranean Sea. They seem to have made these
contacts without much fighting. Few civilizations of which we have
record are so unmilitary or have lasted so long. The culture was, in
every way, an example of a beneficent type of matriarchy, with
women as goddess-priestess-musicians.

The immense and remarkable remains of its "hundred cities" reveal that artistic and engineering talent were devoted, not to temples
and tombs, but to details of household life. In the palace at Knossus,
there was plumbing such as Europe did not know until the nineteenth
century. The town of Knossus was crossed by a well-paved street
with a stone sewer and was flanked with fine private homes. The
frescoed walls show women dancers and gymnasts, as well as priestesses in costumes similar to those in the rock paintings of Spain. (See
Plate 37.) Yet in other pictures, the clothes are surprisingly modern.
In their flounced skirts, trim waists, and decorative sleeves, these
Cretan women seem to move and sing. No other ancient paintings are
as lifelike.

Crete, like Egypt and Sumer, illustrates the principle that in that
period of history, women were the inspirers and the chief ministrants

of spiritual life. Gods were rare and inconspicuous, goddesses numerous and important. This society, which has left such charming records of polished and refined daily living, shared with some African tribes (especially the Bantu) many of the regular female symbols. Among these, either wholly female or combining female and male characteristics, were the moon, the double axe, pillars, rocks, trees, flowers, shells, snakes, and birds.

In the service of the deities and other symbols of life, priestesses predominated. Many frescoes depict women conducting a sacrifice attended by men porters. When the men attendants carried musical instruments, they dressed like women. When youths joined a choir, they were led by a priestess and imitated the dress of maidens, as if to deceive the spirits into believing them members of the stronger spiritual sex. (See Plate 32.)

The spiritual superiority of women was manifested also in the small images of musicians made for the purpose of accompanying the dead in their graves. The manufacture of these figurines—invariably feminine—was a regular industry, especially in the nearby Cyclades Islands.

It is a striking fact that nothing remains of an overemphasis in the glory of man as king, priest, or husband. Polygamy evidently had no vogue in Crete. Monogamous marriage was the custom. In a betrothal scene, depicted on an ivory cylinder near Knossus, the man and the woman, both the same height, raise their right arms for a handclasp. They stand as equals.

The presence of small chapels in the women's quarters of the palace indicates that informal and formal rites were indistinguishable. The queen—high priestess—probably burnt her incense, poured out holy water, lit her torches, and arranged her flowers in vases of her own making on her domestic altar. Being both a normal mother and a representative of a goddess, such a worshiper would repeat at home her incantations for protecting her family and for controlling spirits.

Girls had their swings hanging between pillars topped by the sacred doves, symbols of love and fertility. At their first pregnancy, they may have been called to their rites by a mother blowing a seashell trumpet as girls today in South Sea islands are summoned by the priestess in charge. (See Plate 36.) When rain was needed, women sprang in ecstatic motion around the great rock which represented Rhea, spirit of flowing water and goddess of the dance. The fame of such dancers spread far beyond the borders of their own land and long after their own time. Sappho sang: "Thus of old did the dainty feet of Cretan maidens dance pat to the music beside some lovely altar, pressing the soft smooth bloom of the grass." [12]

Public religious festivals were probably staged out-of-doors in an open stadium. Plate 30 shows a ceremony conducted by priestesses and attended by a large assembly of women and men. The object of adoration is unfortunately missing, but Sir Arthur Evans suggests that it may have been the day-spring from on high in the shape of a tiny goddess. (See Plate 31.) One can imagine hearing the voices of the priestess-musicians chanting hymns, songs of praise, laments, and joyful songs of the birth. Hymnos, paen, elegoes, and dithyrambos are Greek terms for poetic forms which, with the skillful use of melodic norms, derived from Crete.

This choral dance on the "Isle of Women" seems to be the fore-runner of the Greek tragedies in which men dressed as women and acted the part of women characters. What would give clearer evidence of the fact that men first imitated, and then developed for a purpose of their own, rites which had been invented and utilized for centuries by women in the mother's religion?

6.

No names of individual creative musicians have survived from those far-off times. There is no way of knowing whether men or women excelled in the invention of dances and music. But women's relation to music and to a religion, based on the sense of the glory and power of woman's function as life bearer, was very different from that of the woman of today, outwardly free but spiritually devitalized, with no faith in her womanhood to inspire her to song.

All these ancient religions were based on the primitive woman's grand idea that she who gives birth can invoke the rebirth—that, as mother, she has authority over life and death. And this authority she exercised by making music. The intimate relation in ancient societies between goddess, queen, priestess, and ordinary woman meant that the collective body of women was drawn into a musical life that had its origin in connection with institutions and occasions planned in previous centuries by women themselves. It meant that the woman with creative musical imagination had behind her a long tradition of capability on the part of women and that she started composing on an already high plateau of experience and achievement.

Occasions for the development of musical talent had already been formalized in the regular events of living—in the birth of a baby, rebirth at adolescence, marriage, death, and springtide, in the work of feeding, clothing, and manufacturing needed articles, in caring for children, and in amusement. All the ancients recognized and valued woman's bond with the life force. There was no denial of the imaginative faculty. Institutions existed for the purpose of directing her beneficent power into the proper channels. Music was regarded as a direct extension of the functions of women. As in primitive tribes, the barriers between women and music were merely local limitations upon specific occasions when women were expected to function as musicians. As long as there were goddesses, queens, and priestesses, as long as there were women leaders holding positions of responsibility in musical life, women were adapting and arranging the inherited songs and dances, or creating variations on them for new occasions. And they were doing this on their own inspiration, in the proud consciousness that, as women and mothers, they sang with voices that the great powers of life would be bound to heed.

CHAPTER VII

THE LYRIC POETESS

1.

$\mathcal{S}$OME time between 2000 B.C. and 1000 B.C. our modern world began. For on the great plains of Russia, north of the Black Sea and the Caspian, another people—the Aryans—began stirring. During the next centuries they moved outward in all directions, traveling great distances, riding on horses, and driving their cattle before them. They went down into India, pushed back the older Dravidians into southern India, took over the north of India, and began to tell their own story in the *Rig-Veda*. They came down into the Near East and established Persia, whose present name, Iran, means Aryan. They spread westward into Europe and gave their language and customs to whoever was living there at the time when they arrived. Above all, they took over, one after another, the isles and peninsulas of the eastern Mediterranean and put themselves to school amidst the Cretans, choosing and modifying and usually simplifying the charming civilization they found there. Greek civilization did not originate as a single country or culture. It began among little groups of rather rude, hardy people who settled in amidst the decaying luxury and splendor of richer and brighter days, and who in their own plain way civilized themselves by borrowing from their betters.

The one bond among these early Greeks was that they spoke the same language. This was a bond, more or less, among all Aryan peoples, from the misty shores of Ireland to the sunburned banks of the Ganges. This was and is the only bond. Aryan does not refer to a race or a color of skin. It refers only to a kind of language. An early Chinese writer who saw these Aryans in India mentioned their distinctive appearance, however, as well as their widespread language

87

and their attitude to women. "From Wan westward to An-si the languages of the people, though differing slightly from one another are generally similar so that they may understand one another when conversing. All these people have deep eyes and a rich growth of beard. They hold their women in high honor, for whatever a woman says, her husband invariably agrees to it." [1]

Wherever people speak the same language, they tend to have common ideas and social attitudes. The first of the Aryans to write down their ideas about life were those in India. In the *Rig-Veda*, written perhaps about 1200 B.C., there are references to women and to their authority in religion, music, and social life. "From of old comes the wife to the public sacrifice and to the festive gathering; as orderer of the sacrifice comes the noble woman attended by men." [2] This record from the sacred books indicates that the wife was essential to the ceremony.

An especially beautiful service was one performed at the hearth-altar. "O gods," says the *Rig-Veda*, "the married couple, who together intend to present to you libations—who together come on the grass to place there the sacred food—[grant that] this couple, surrounded by little children and growing sons and daughters, pass a happy life. . . ." [3]

At the marriage ceremony, the company chanted hymns to Agni, the fire god, invoking perfection of the well-knit bond between husband and wife. One such hymn, in which only feminine adjectives appear, has been ascribed to the poetess-musician Visvavara, a member of the priestly family of Atreya.

> Show thyself strong for mighty bliss, O Agni,
>
> .   .   .
>
> And overcome the might of those who hate us! [4]

With these Aryan people, marriage ensured the mother and her children protection from the native enemy hordes but apparently did not limit her personal liberty beyond the natural prescriptions of physiological laws or pervert the relationship into a degradation of woman's natural powers. In ancient India a boy was thought to be blessed eightfold if his mother presided at his initiation into manhood. Institutions through which woman's authority in matters of rebirth rituals could be maintained continued to hold people's respect.

As Pandy says to his wife, Kunty, in the Indian epic, the Mahab-

Courtesy of Ernest Benn, Ltd.

34. Raishallala of the Tuareg tribe of northern Africa, photographed in front of her tent, is a modern example of the ancient Mediterranean poetess-musician. (See page 72.)

From C. Sachs, Die Musik der Antike

Courtesy of The Macmillan Co.

35, 36, 37. Women musicians of ancient Egypt and Crete.

(See pages 75, 83, and 84.)

38. On a small bas-relief from ancient Greece, the goddess Eileith-yia protects the mother in childbirth. (See page 96.)

39. In ancient Greece, the swing festival was a woman's rite associated with the rhythm of life. (See page 100.)

From Perrot-Chipiez, Histoire de l'art dans l'antiquité

From O. Benndorf, Vorlegeblätter fur Archaelogische Ubungen

Musee de Louvre

40, 41, 42. Greek artists often decorated their pottery with representations of women working, rejoicing at weddings, and mourning at funerals. (See pages 98, 99, and 101.)

From A. Furtwängler. Griechische Vasenmalerei

43. Greek girls learned their religious dances from women musicians. (See page 103.)

Courtesy of G. Routledge & Sons, Ltd.

44. Sappho, honored by her pupils, sang, "Mark me, the after days shall see, those that will still remember me." (See page 107.)

harata, which reflects the life of a later day, "I shall tell thee about
the practice of old indicated by illustrious Rishis fully acquainted
with every rule of morality. O, thou handsome of face and sweet
smiles, women were not formerly immured in houses and dependent
upon husbands and relatives. They used to go about freely enjoying
themselves as best they pleased." [5]

The next records we have of the way the early Aryans felt are the
poems of Homer, which began to be sung (perhaps as early as 1000
B.C.) all up and down the islands of the Aegean, and the shores of
Greece and Asia Minor, where the Greeks were settling. All these
Greeks traced their ancestry to Helen, the daughter of the moon. The
hero of one of the two great Homeric poems, the Iliad, is Achilles,
grandson of the lunar goddess Doris, the Engenderer. Doris had fifty
daughters known as the Nereids. One of them, "silver-slippered
Thetis," was the mother of Achilles.

These early Greek stories concern the kidnaping of their beautiful
Helen by the Trojans, also Aryans, who carried her away to Asia,
and the attempts of the kings of Argos and Mycenae and innumerable heroes, sons of goddesses, to get her back. Woman is such an
all-pervading, all-protecting spirit in the Odyssey, the other great
Homeric epic, that it is not unlikely that the poem was fashioned
by weaving together lays earlier composed and sung by women.

2.

Throughout Greek history until about 400 B.C., when the drama
began to absorb public interest and the theater usurped the mimetic
rite, singing, dancing, and playing on instruments had the same
significance and the same utility that they have today for our primitive and peasant contemporaries. Music was deemed by them a
thing divine, the breath of life, a tremendous power for influencing
the thought and actions of people, for controlling nature and supernatural beings.

Like other ancient peoples, the Greeks placed a high value on the
art of the dance, which they regarded, like swinging, as a means for
keeping in the flow of life and for ensuring equilibrium to the soul.
Many of the dance movements had come from magic gestures intended to awaken life. The high leap and the wide sweep of the leg
won immortality for the dead or made the corn grow tall. Scooping
imaginary dewdrops with the hands, arching arms like the moon

were techniques to stimulate growth. Holding hands and forming a circle conveyed the strength of the group to each individual.

With the art of manufacturing musical instruments capable of fine gradations of tone still in its infancy, the voice was naturally the favorite medium for musical expression. In the golden ages of Egypt and Crete, emphasis was placed upon melody—a development that the Greeks later carried far toward perfection. But behind this art was practical magic, revealed by words in several of the ancient Aryan languages besides Greek. In Sanskrit, for instance, the word *mantra*, which means a verse of praise to a deity, comes also to mean a magical invocation to compel that higher power to grant some human appeal. The old Indians had charms known as *rāga* and *rāginī*, Aryan words that have survived in the Lithuanian language as *ragana*, meaning one who makes magic formulas or incantations. In Latin, the words *carmen* and *ode* both have the double meaning of "song" and "charm."

Music, indeed, to the Indians of former days, was regarded as being conformable to cosmic laws when it was brought into juxtaposition with certain seasons and hours. Were every rule about the performance of music strictly obeyed, the six male *rāga* tunes and the thirty female *rāginīs* were then considered capable of producing some desired effect. Should they be used in defiance of tradition, a calamity, such as the turning of day into night, might ensue. (See Plate 45.)

In Greece, the conception of the universal life force operating through music was given a beautiful expression by the fifth century B.C. philosopher Pythagoras and his wife Theano, a poetess-musician. They taught that the spheres and the stars of heaven move to music in an eternal song and dance. And so they organized rites for their followers, to the end that each person, by taking part in the music and the dance, might achieve an inner harmony of spirit.

Later Greek educators and philosophers employed the various musical "modes" which had developed through centuries of musical experience to induce a state of mind or "mood." A certain arrangement of tones in a scale was believed to be capable of inspiring soldiers with courage; another was used to inspire worshipers with reverence; still another stimulated passion. Plato later proposed that music for young people should be limited to those modes that would strengthen their characters. He desired to imitate the Egyptians in the creation of melodies that had the capability of calming human passions and purging the soul. The seriousness with which he advanced his theory shows that the most highly educated men believed in the *affective* power of music and of music as an accompaniment to the other arts.

Of such social and religious uses for music, professionalism and the training of professional performers of music were by-products. For many centuries the important music of that great Greek culture remained in its primitive milieu—in the religious rite, for the purpose of placing the worshipers in accord with the life force; in the home, for work, recreation, and magic; at the banquet and formal social gatherings, for entertainment. Consequently in early Greece women were at the center of these three types of music. They danced, sang, and played instruments, especially flutes and cymbals and drums. From childhood to the grave, at home, in small group gatherings, and in formal public ceremonials, early Greek women had opportunity and occasion to use music, and incentive to compose it. The result of such a setting was a rich musical experience for women in general and a great wealth of songs composed for women and by women.

Throughout the period of ancient times until the Christian Era, and even long after, the Greeks like other ancient creators of music usually followed the primitive custom of associating their songs, dances, and instrumental playing with a specific occasion and purpose. Musical art reached its climax when it enhanced the emotional value of some event—a victory over enemy armies, defeat in battle, a wedding, a funeral, a religious festival, a public or private entertainment. The same musical idiom served for all occasions and purposes; one cannot tell from the picture whether a religious rite is being celebrated or whether an entertainment is being staged. This is because the function of music had not changed since the most primitive times. People believed that music was for the purpose of heightening emotional reactions. No matter what the occasion, the artist employed the same techniques.

3.

As in all goddess-worshiping cultures, priestesses in Greece were valued and respected members of their communities. They usually came from noble families and held their offices by hereditary right. Priestesses were assisted in their duties by the so-called *hierai*, sacred women, and the girl choristers. These remained an integral part of the religious and musical life of Greece until long after the beginning of the Christian Era. Members of the choir received training in their youth for the proper performance of the dances and religious songs, often spending the year before marriage within the precincts of a temple under the guidance of a priestess.

Priestesses assembled in societies or hierarchies. Some of the best known were the Oleiai of Orchomenos, the Dysmainai of Mount Taygetos, and the Dionysiades of Sparta. Most renowned of all were the Thyiades, a society whose origin is shrouded in the mists of antiquity. Its members claimed descent from Ino, mother of the Danoi, who, legend tells, brought women's rites from Egypt to Greece. Ino herself was the Horned Cow, like the crescent moon. The Thyiades had colleges in several different places, notably Elis, Pisatis, Sparta, and Delphi. They served both Hera and Dionysos; and when celebrating rites for the rebirth of Dionysos, they were led by the mythical mother of Dionysos, Semele. Though Dionysos was the god of wine and later was worshiped by drunken votaries, his rites in Crete and old Greece were not orgiastic in the sense of intoxication from drink. The women who belonged to these important religious institutions sang their hymns and danced their dances in sobriety. Their ecstasy was a ritual, performed in imitation of the maenads of immemorial tradition and for the same immemorial reason—to become one with the rhythm of all life. (See Plate 33.)

The cult of Dionysos, which was widely and enthusiastically accepted throughout the classical world in the pre-Christian centuries, represented a religious idea that seems to have had an extraordinary popular appeal—the idea that a woman might bear a child without the interposition of a human father, in ecstatic union with a god. This child might be a son or a daughter, and in some cases the divine infant was thought of as of both sexes. But whether son or daughter, the young divinity born like a human baby, nurtured at a human mother's breast, growing up as a human being, beautiful and beloved, demonstrated that through the woman's body alone, with no help from the human male, the universal life force might be incarnated in a young being who was both human and divine. This idea, which appears in various forms in Greek mythology, was best represented by the young god Dionysos, son of Semele and Zeus.

It is important to emphasize the fact that in the earliest times all Dionysiac cults were exclusively women's cults and that they came from the Cretan culture where only women were the priestesses. The

song of the birth (dithyramb) was the song of the mothers, and by
tradition the women choirs of the tribe of Akamantis had used the
primitive cry of joy—alleluia. Priestesses of Elis, probably the distinguished women who belonged to the college of the Thyiades
priesthood, sang the oldest dithyramb preserved in Greek literature:

> In springtime, O Dionysos,
> To thy holy temple come,
> To Elis with thy Graces,
> Rushing with thy bull-foot, come,
> Noble Bull, noble Bull! [6]

From these symbolic mothers singing their dithyramb invoking the
divine child to birth, back to the midwife chanting her incantations
to hasten the arrival of the human child, we see the extraordinary
continuity of Greek ritualistic practice, the carry-over of personal experience to group emotional expression.

The most usual name for the worshipers of Dionysos was the
Bacchae or the bacchantes. Both words mean "the mothers." With
Dionysos were associated also ancient mythical women called
maenads. We know much about these singing, dancing societies of
women and their secret rites in the mountains. For in a later century
an inquiring and sensitive man named Euripides happened to escape from the rather conceited circles of the male intelligentsia of
Athens in his day and to catch a glimpse of them. He was profoundly
stirred and wrote a beautiful choral drama, *The Bacchae* (or *The
Mothers*), about them. Had Euripides known more about the primitive origins of his own civilization, he might have avoided a groping
indefiniteness in his beautiful verse. But he believed, in his poet's
soul, that these women, with their ringing cry, "Oh, wild white
maids, to the hills, to the hills!" [7] had something men might well try
to understand.

Their rites, he thought, came from Crete, and he represented the
Bacchae as singing:

> "For thee of old some crested Corybant
> First woke in Cretan air
> The wild orb of our orgies,
> Our Timbrel; and thy gorges
> Rang with this strain; and blended Phrygian chant
> And sweet keen pipes were there.

"But the Timbrel, the Timbrel was another's,
And away to Mother Rhea it must wend;
And to our holy singing from the Mothers
The mad Satyrs carried it, to blend
In the dancing and the cheer
Of our third and perfect year." [8]

Casting an interested masculine eye over their attire, but not apparently aware of the age-old meaning of their symbols, Euripides noted that the Bacchae wore long white dresses and had fawn skins flung over their shoulders, and that some of them carried wands with serpents wound around them. "The Songs of Serpents sound in the mazes of their hair." [9] Perhaps he had never heard that the snake is from immemorial time the symbol of rebirth. All the maidens carried oak wands wreathed in ivy. Most of them had ivy wound in their hair. They had outposts to warn all onlookers away. A maiden went ahead of the procession chanting:

"Who lingers in the road? Who espies us?
He shall hide him in his house nor be bold.
Let the heart keep silence that defies us;
For I sing this day to Dionysos
The song that is appointed from of old." [10]

And when the women, seeking the still dell of the Muses, had climbed far into the hills (as primitive women in Africa do to this day), a shepherd saw them in the dawn, sleeping after their night-long songs and incantations.

"Our herded kine were moving in the dawn
Up to the peaks, the greyest, coldest time,
When the first rays steal earthward, and the rime
Yields, when I saw three bands of them. The one
Autonoe led, one Ino, one thine own
Mother, Agave. There beneath the trees
Sleeping they lay, like wild things flung at ease
In the forests; one half sinking on a bed
Of deep pine greenery; one with careless head
Amid the fallen oak leaves; all most cold
In purity—not as thy tale was told
Of wine-cups and wild music and the chase
For love amid the forest's loneliness." [11]

While there were a few mysteries in which men and women jointly participated, most of the secret rites were conducted by women alone, and only by initiated women. Those that concern women's mysteries have never been fully understood since their meaning was not disclosed to any uninitiated person. The whole subject of the women's hierarchies—their secrecy, their mythical association with goddesses and with the moon—takes us back into the farthest realm of primitive times and shows the force of those old beliefs even among people as highly educated as the Greeks.

4.

The expression of religious feeling by means of rites was an integral part of Greek daily life. The Greeks had inherited belief in the power of magic, and they placated their numerous deities at every turn—in their homes, at wayside shrines, in sacred groves and caves, and later with formal ceremonies in the great temples of the classical age. Before a meal a Greek family would place on its hearth a few bits of food in offering to Hestia, goddess of the hearth, and would pour a few drops of unmixed wine on the floor to placate the good daemon of the house. Women made obeisance to Eileithyia and to Hekate, goddesses of life and death, at shrines erected at the thresholds of their homes. In his "Ode to Theron," Pindar tells of the maidens who danced and sang before his door through the night.

Divine protection was particularly required for the special events in human life—for birth, presentation of the child to society and to the spirits, puberty, marriage, and death—and for the normal changes of nature—the birth and decay of vegetation. In the main, Greek religious rites centered around these rhythmical crises. The character of the rites varied all the way from simple house cult practices of primitive times to elaborate festivals involving many people and lasting for days.

The most striking aspect of Greek religious practice is the continuity of its expression—the constant carry-over from the real to the ideal; from actual experience to a deity who symbolized the experience. To women, this constant carry-over was extraordinarily important. All their activities, all their physiological crises had feminine impersonations to whom they could voice their needs. In these symbols women projected their own strength and capabilities, their own value in the life scheme. In the worship of the goddesses, women had opportunity and compulsion to express with ritual and music their own deep emotions, their own creative urges. Help for a woman in childbirth, for example, was not confined to incantations sung by a midwife to ease and speed her actual labor. In congregation, at shrines—such as the shrine at Olympia that Eileithyia, goddess of childbirth, shared with the snake-child Sosipolis—women sang formal hymns to their protectress. At the great festival of the Thesmophoria, sacred to married women, it was customary on the third day for the women votaries to sing a hymn of invocation to Artemis Kalligenia, or Prothyraia, to her who would grant an easy birth to mothers. (See Plate 38.)

To Artemis Prothyraia

Hear me, O most majestic goddess, spirit of the many names,
Deliveress from the pangs of birth, sweet presence to those in travail,
Savioress of women, you who alone love children, goddess of the
     gentle mind,
Giver of a birth that is rapid, deliveress from mortal sorrows,
Prothyraia, you who are before the Door!
Who hold the keys, beautiful to meet, kind to all,
     who love to feed and keep animals,
Of the homes of all you are mistress, you rejoice in the gladness of
     feasts,
Loosener of girdles, invisible, yet manifest by your works to all!
Through sympathy you suffer along with women in travail,
And with those who bring forth easily you rejoice,
Ilithyia, goddess of childbirth, releaser from the throes none can
     escape!
On you alone they call in travail, O resting-place of the soul,
For in you the pains of childbirth are forgotten.
Artemis Ilithyia, and Prothyraia, hallowed in beauty,
Hear, blessed one! Give the fruit of seed, coming as a deliveress,
And saving us, even as you were born eternal Savioress of all! [12]

The woman's singing magic of birth and rebirth was used in the various rites of the life cycle as it still is among primitive peoples. At puberty, Greek girls were inducted into maturity with various minutiae of ceremony. As with primitive tribes, flowers, the holy bath, games, foot races, festivals at the new moon, and always dancing and singing were characteristic features of these ceremonials. For example, girl initiates serving Hera, in whose cult flowers were always used, would gather spring blossoms and twine them around a statue of the goddess as they danced to the music of flutes and invoked the holy one in song. In ceremonies of Artemis at Sicyon, where the Crete-inherited feminine influence was especially strong, a statue of the goddess was annually carried down to the sea and dipped into the water for the sacred bath. The most beautiful girl initiate was chosen to impersonate the goddess, and a choir of dancing and singing girls led the procession to the sea. In the rear followed a choir of boys, also dancing and singing. These boys probably represent a relatively late addition to a ritual in which originally only women and girls took part. The great festival of the Heraea, held under the direction of the Thyiades in the month of Parthenos, when the moon was new, was also a puberty rite, a festival of games for girls like the Olympic games for boys, and probably of older origin. The music for the Heraea was made by the Thyiades. Under their organization and leadership, two choirs of sixteen women sang the sacred hymns.

Little is known of the Heraea, but it is not difficult to guess the character of the rites or to infer the leadership of women. These women's rites are alike the world over. Among the Tusayan Indians in New Mexico, for example, the La-la-konta Festival lasts for ten days and has a deep religious significance for the whole tribe. Its chief purpose is to induce the germination of seeds. The girls run a race, a common practice at puberty rites and certainly a feature of the Heraea. There is a procession to the spring—water is always the source of life—and a dance. The priestesses hold their office by heredity. After ceremonially calling the women together at the shrine, they lead them in wonderful choral singing. As we have seen in many places in the primitive world, as well as in Egypt, the priestess is also musician. Undoubtedly in Greece, women with the same status also composed their own music for their own rites.

Marriage rites in Greece, like those of puberty, were rites of transition from one state of life to another, celebrated both at real and at symbolic marriages. Real weddings usually took place just before full moon. Before the ceremony, sacrifices to the goddesses were made and the bride was given her sacramental bath. At the festivities the bride was veiled to signify rebirth from a symbolic womb and also to signify dedication to her new life. The two mothers lit the torches that symbolized the light of the life-giving moon. Accompanied by flute players, the wedding procession marched to the

bridegroom's house. The wedding feast was the ideal time for felicita-
tions. (See Plate 41.)

Bridesmaids greeted the bridegroom:

> "Raise high the roof-beam, carpenters,
>   Hymenaeus!
> Like Ares comes the bridegroom,
>   Hymenaeus!
> Taller far than a tall man,
>   Hymenaeus!" [13]

The hymn-call was to bring forth the daemons of fertility. It was always shouted at weddings as a kind of good-luck motto by the
friends of the bride and groom. Bridesmaids at a Greek wedding always lamented the passing of the bride's girlhood. In Sappho's words
they sang:

> "Maidenhood, maidenhood, whither art thou gone from me?
> Never again will I come to thee, never again." [14]

Then groomsmen would praise the bride: "O fair, O lovely!" and the
wedding guests would praise the bridal pair:

> "Hail, bride!
> Noble bridegroom!
> All hail!" [15]

It was the bridesmaids' duty and pleasure to prepare the bridal
bed in a bower garlanded with flowers, and to conduct the bride to
it. The epithalamium, accompanied by dancing, was sung outside
of the bridal chamber at night by bridesmaids and youths. At dawn
came the last benediction of the friends:

> "Farewell the bride,
> Farewell the bridegroom." [16]

In temples and at festivals, sacred marriages, symbolic of the union
of the sexes, were performed on many occasions, often with other
rebirth rites. At the Heraea festival, for example, the girl victorious
in the foot races, olive-crowned, would be married symbolically to
the boy winner of the Olympic games. At the rites of Dionysos in

Athens the wife of the second archon officiated regularly as bride to a symbolic Dionysos. Sometimes, as in the cult of Hera at Samos, the rites of the sacred marriage were performed without men, but they were never performed without women—a fact that clearly suggests a feminine origin of the marriage rite as a *"rite de passage"* for a woman about to enter a new state of life. In Greek religion the rites of the sacred marriage and of the birth of the holy child or of some symbol of the rebirth were indissoluble and represented the central mystery of religious ritual.

Greek funeral rites, like other rites of the rebirth, were held for both real and for symbolic deaths. When a person died, the family and the professional women mourners would gather around the bier. It was the business of the professional mourner to give the wailing necessary to hasten the rebirth of the dead soul into the spirit world. The mourner was expected to remain for several days, during which time she sang one dirge after another. A mourner was not worth her pay if she repeated herself. She probably behaved very like the present-day professional singer at funerals in Mykonos. In old Greece the group of family mourners burst out with a refrain. The men exclaimed in their own characteristic fashion and the women gave the *evoe*, "Alleluia," similar to the cry of joy given by priestesses in the bacchanals. Sometimes a flute player, also a woman, accompanied the cortege. There was a great demand for these women artists and they had consequently a strong incentive to create music that would be considered good among professionals. (See Plate 42.)

Part of the funeral ceremony was often conducted very like a drama. The cortege consisted of a chariot, or men, bearing the coffin, of women walking in front, at the sides, and in the rear. It was the custom to display grief. The women beat their breasts, wailed for a time, then walked in silence, then wailed again. When the procession halted, the mourners grouped themselves in dramatic attitudes. Sometimes there would be formal choirs. Following a very old custom, the people of Megara used to send fifty maidens and fifty youths to Corinth whenever a death occurred in the Bacchiad family. In all types of death ceremonies women played their classic role.

At the symbolic deaths, mourning for the dead vegetation of the year, or for a hero, a heroine, or a god, a goddess took the place of mourning for a real person. During the Thesmophoria, married women stood at the crossroads and lamented in spirit with Demeter, goddess of the grain, who was searching for her lost daughter, Kore.

In the Adonia, women wailed on their housetops for Adonis, a vegetation god. At all the festivals, after the lamenting came the cries of
joy in anticipation of the resurrection, be it of nature, the moon,
or the deity.

5.

Religious festivals in Greece showed many traces of a matriarchal
origin. In the great periodic rites known as the Thargelia for transferring the force behind vegetation to the new harvest, men and
women celebrated together, as do those of many primitive tribes in
similar fertility festivals. Men and women both joined, too, in those
for Adonis as well as in the requiems, from which our idea of All
Saints' and All Souls' Days came. Connected with the rites of the
Anthesteria were the Eumenides or avengers of a mother's wrongs.
Women sang as they walked along carrying flowers and green
branches. In Aeschylus' drama *The Eumenides* is a description of
what was probably the actual rites:

Pass to your house thus augustly estated,
Come, O mysterious maidens, come, offspring of night!
And silence all for our sacred song.
Come ye with sacrifice offered, with worship and with rite.

Some festivals celebrated by men were modeled on women's festivals. The Apatouria—Festival of the Same Fathers—was, for example, an adaptation of a far older form, Festival of the Same Mothers.

Many rites of rebirth were practiced by women alone, or with
men playing a secondary role. Korythalia was the women's version
of the various May-pole dances (*eiresione*). The Aiora, or Swing
Festival, was distinctly a women's ritual, bound up with the moon
and the rhythm of life. (See Plate 39.) Besides the Heraea,
which had the primitive girls' puberty rites in the race at new moon,
there were other festivals of Hera. One was the Anthesphoria, celebrated with flutes amidst bowers of greens. Various Artemisia belonged to women. In them the features were processions to a sacred
spring, bronze tympani, and laments called *oupingi*. At the Herse-
phoria the dew-carrying maidens refreshed the bloom of their own
youth. The Tithenidia was a festival for the nursing mothers of
Sparta, who danced and sang to Artemis as they ate loaves of bread

shaped like a woman's breast. Like the Eleusinian mysteries, the Thesmophoria concerned agricultural magic—woman's ancient prerogative. It was conducted by married women.

Many festivals of Dionysos belonged to women originally, as well as the Adonia, in which Aphrodite's son, or lover, was first mourned for as dead and then rejoiced over as resurrected. Three festivals made up the Ennateric group. The second of this group was the Herois, in which the women invoked Semele, mother of Dionysos, and called upon the dead heroines to return and help them in their colossal task of bringing life to the earth. The third was the Charila and involved carrying out death, preparing for new life. At Orchomenos, where the Thyiades had one of their colleges, the priestesses sang to the Charites, the gift-bringers of plenty.

Greek songs, both religious and occupational, were divided into categories and had generic names. There were songs of winnowing, songs of reaping, mill songs that women sang as they ground grain, songs of the water carriers, and rope songs sung at the well in imitation of the gurgling water. (See Plate 40.)

Nursing mothers had songs of their own—*katabaukaleses*, which means literally to lull to sleep. The bakers sang to Demeter: "Send forth a sheaf, a plenteous sheaf, a sheaf send forth!" [17] (See Plate 16.)

6.

Out of the rich musical life of Greece, with its many opportunities for women to sing and to make music, came a substantial number of poetess-musicians whose fame has carried down to our own day. A Greek compiler lists forty such poetesses by name. These women won numerous prizes in public competitions, had statues erected to them, and some were likened to the Muses by their men competitors. Phantasia, who came to Greece from Memphis, Egypt, in pre-Homeric times, was one of the early story-singers. It was the custom in those days for men and women to gather after supper in the great hall of a dwelling and to amuse themselves by chanting and listening to stories. Phantasia, being a skilled storyteller, like many women in primitive tribes today, entertained her companions with music. She and her friend Themis are reputed to have invented the heroic meter, the hexameter. Certainly they made a compound measure out of two lines of the Linus, that song of lament for Adonis sung by so many choirs of women.

Individual women artists sang laments in public not only in pre-classical and classical Greece but long afterward. In one of his most charming idylls, Theocritus mentioned a skillful singer from Argos who sang in the market place of Syracuse at the festival of Adonis. Two members of the audience, Praxinoe and Gorgo, are speaking: "Silence, Praxinoe! She is preparing to sing the Adonis—the girl of Argos, the skillful singer who carried off the prize of Sperchis, she is preparing to sing the lamentation. She sings, I know well, with talent." The singer modulates the hymn, and Gorgo exclaims: "It is more beautiful than I ever thought; fortunate woman to be so well informed! Altogether fortunate that she sings so softly!" [18] This professional musician was carrying on a custom of immemorial antiquity. She was giving the wail that would hasten the rebirth of Adonis, the god who personified the vegetation of the year. And, according to the way of the woman artist-musician, she had converted the wail into an art form—the musical lament.

Perhaps the two most important categories of women's religious songs were the hymns of invocation composed and sung by the hierarchies of priestesses—notably the Thyiades and the Elean priestesses—and the lyric poems sung by the girl choirs, known as *parthenia* or songs for maidens. The girl choirs were famous for the excellence of their performance. Pindar wrote of them: "Round Parnassus high cliffs, the bright-eyed Delphian maidens enter the fleet chorus and sing a sweet song with clear voices." [19] And Alkman spoke of his delight in the Spartan "maidens of honey voice, so loud and clear." [20]

The songs that the girl choirs sang usually had for theme some myth or legend of god or goddess, hero or heroine. As the girls sang, they would dance and gesticulate and more or less act out the story of the legend. Obviously, this was simply a development of the age-old mimetic rite and a forerunner of the later complicated Greek drama. About the seventh century B.C. a form of choral dance developed, called the *hypercheme*, in which the dancing and gesticulating chorus was reinforced by a stationary group of singers. In this way, more difficult and more complex music could be performed and more attention paid to the melodic element in the music. Favorite subjects for *hyperchemata* were such tales as Bacchylides' myth of Ida and Marpessa, a kind of wedding cantata, or the myth of Theseus' victory over the Minotaur of Crete. In the latter, dancing boys joined with the girls of the dancing chorus. The participation of girl choirs and of actors in this type of ritual dance drama—definite precursor of Greek classical drama, in which only men were allowed to sing or to perform—illustrates the extent to which women took part in the musical life of the preclassical Greeks. (See Plate 43.)

A Greek woman artist—this one distinguished for her singing, her dancing, and her lyric poetry—was Megolastrata of Sparta. Called the beautiful blonde, she led the Spartan girl choirs and composed music for their performances. Unfortunately, not one of her compositions has been preserved, but her fame as a leader and as a composer has come down to us from the seventh century B.C., a time when the girl choirs were especially active and important in Greek life.

Telesilla of Argos was a heroic figure, one of those courageous militant women who through quick decision save their countries in moments of great danger. When the Spartans threatened her city-state, Telesilla is said to have gathered weapons from homes and temples, to have given them to the women of Argos, and to have led them against the enemy. A poetess-musician as well as a warrior, Telesilla is especially famous for her hymns and for her political songs. Only two verses are left from her poetry, a call to maidens, obviously part of a hymn.

Corinna, a poetess-musician of Boetia, was Pindar's teacher and won five times over him in poetic competition. So lovely were her songs that the poet Antipater named her as one of the nine women whom he selected as earthly muses. Corinna's work consisted of epigrams, lyric poems, and choruses for women. Unhappily, only a few fragments of her poetry are extant and none of her melodies. As she herself explained, she sang of native myths and legends, of heroes and especially of heroines—"But I, I am come to sing the prowess of Heroes and Heroines, in fair old-wives' tales for the white-robed daughters of Tanagra!" [21]

Sicyon, a city-state that kept on conspicuously with Cretan customs and in which women played a leading part in both religious and musical life, was the home of the poetess-musician Praxilla. She was famous also for her *skolias* or table songs—later called drinking songs—sung at banquets, sometimes solo, sometimes in chorus; for her dithyrambs; and for an epic poem entitled "Adonia." Praxilla's songs were so well thought of in Athens that they were compared with those of Alkman and of Sappho, and were sung at banquets of the nobility.

Of all the poetess-musicians of Greece, the most famous, the one whose very name is almost synonymous with the words "lyric poetry," is Sappho of Lesbos (seventh century B.C.). Lesbos is a triangular island, lying a few miles off the shore of European Turkey— one of those garden islands of the Aegean, full of mountain dells and fresh streams rushing down to the sea, where the small gray olive trees cling to the hillsides, fruit grows sweet and ripe in the valleys, flowers bloom, birds sing, and the sun shines most of the days of the year.

In the seventh century B.C. Lesbos had built up quite a trade with the other Greek islands and the half-Asian, half-Hellenic cities of Asia Minor. And since it was so prosperous, its talented citizens found time and opportunity to bring the art of singing to the lyre to a very high perfection and to take great pains with the music and ceremonial of religious processionals led by women. Here in this tiny island city-state of Lesbos, women had the high social, political, literary, and religious status then common in the Aegean world. They owned their own property and were free to come and go as they pleased. Well educated, especially in poetry and music, they enjoyed the companionship of both men and other women, taking part, as a matter of course, in political and literary discussions. As priestesses in the temples of Lesbos, they served especially Hera, Aphrodite, Demeter, and Artemis. Perhaps no place in all of Greece was more favorable than Lesbos for the flowering of a woman's creative talent, and in this environment Sappho was born, matured, and asserted her leadership.

A woman of independent wealth, highly respected and greatly admired, not only in her own community but throughout Greece, Sappho lived all of her life, with the exception of about five years, in the beautiful surroundings of Lesbos. After her return from her period of political exile in Syracuse she founded a girl's college, or art school as we would call it, to which young women came from far and wide to study poetry and music.

The most gifted of these girls was Erinna. Erinna's mother is said to have chained her to her spinning wheel in order to make her spin rather than sing, or perhaps only to spin while she was singing. But Erinna appears to have found a way to study with Sappho with such

45. The Rāginīs of India represent the ideal graces of womanhood.
Bhairaveen, a beautiful maiden, places her flowers on the altar of "Linga"
at dawn, when Rāginī Bhairaveen may be sung. This, and other symbolic
paintings showing the relation of women to old Indian music, were recently done by Fyzee-Rahamin for his wife, who can sing the six Rāga
and the thirty Rāginī melodies and who knows the history of their power
of enchantment. (See pages 47 and 90.)

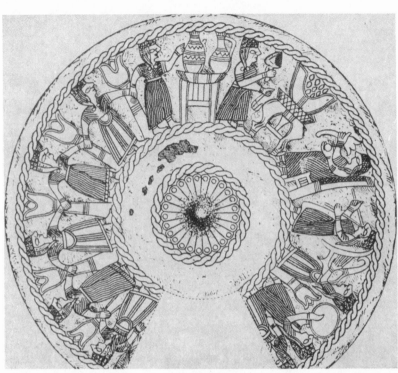

46. On a decorated goblet from old Cyprus, the goddess Astarte can be seen with her priestess-musicians. (See page 117.)

47. A modern Russian painter has portrayed the music of his country as personified by two birdwomen: Sírin and Alkonóst. (See pages 49 and 118.)

48. In Latvia, where women's songs enrich the musical literature, the pagan goddess Laime is represented on a wood-cut receiving a woman's sacrifice. (See page 110.)

C. Lenormant, Elites des monuments céramographiques

E. Gerhard, Auserlesene Griechische Vasenbilder

49, 50. History is told on pottery. Artemis, accompanied by the dog as symbol of healing power, played magic music but was superseded by Apollo. (See pages 120, 122 and 142.)

success that when she died at nineteen, her poems were already known and admired. It was even said that she could write hexameters better than Sappho. Only one fragment of her work remains, a beautiful lyric song in honor of a dead girl, also a singer—Baucis. Improperly entitled "The Distaff" by later critics, this poem is really a lament, written in hexameter with no refrain but with recurring cries of sorrow.

There appears to have been much affection and pretty displays of endearments among these girls and between them and their slight dark-haired leader and teacher, Sappho. These ways, which are natural enough in any group of girls, later received an unpleasant interpretation among the fourth-century male intelligentsia of Athens, who were openly carrying male homosexuality to a high degree of refined exhibitionism and celebrating it even in works as dignified as the dialogues of Plato. Most modern scholars believe the so-called "Lesbianism" of Sappho and her girls to be only the gossip over wine cups in Athens, where middle-aged literary gentlemen and men about town toasted their own boy flames.

The actual records of Sappho seem to indicate a normal woman's life. She had a little daughter named Cleis. She did some social and poetic sparring with the other most famous poet of Lesbos, a man named Alcaeus. What she and Alcaeus seem to have done is to sing between them a *tenso,* which is a sort of poetical dialogue between kindred spirits. The *tenso* has been an art form from earliest times all over the world, among the Chinese in the pre-Confucian age, among ladies and lords of the medieval court of the Japanese emperor in Kyoto, and among the Tuareg today. The Song of Solomon in the Bible is a *tenso* representing King Solomon's dialogue with Arabian queens whom he courted.

So Alcaeus sang to Sappho: "violet-weaving, pure, sweet smiling Sappho, I wish to say something but shame hinders me."

And Sappho replied, in song: "Hadst thou had desire of aught good or fair, shame would not have touched thine eyes, but thou wouldst have spoken thereof openly." [22]

No one has ever questioned Sappho's genius as a lyric poet. Her fame has lasted for more than twenty centuries. Plato called her the Tenth Muse and Ausonius named her the Muses' Sister. Unfortunately, only a few fragments of the poetry upon which Sappho's fame primarily rests have come down to us; and all of the music with which she accompanied her songs has been lost. But from her own poetry and from relatively contemporaneous accounts in Greek literature, we know her high reputation as a player and singer. She was called "a nightingale of hymns." Her favorite instruments to accompany her songs were the "golden lyre" and the "sweet-toned flute." "Come now, O lyre of mine," she herself sings, "lift up thy voice divine." [23]

Besides accompanying her songs with lyre and flute, Sappho is reputed to have developed for her own use a special kind of stringed instrument called the pectis and to have introduced into musical usage the plectrum, or quill, for striking the lyre's strings. Her creative genius is further illustrated in her invention of new melodies, new forms of music. She is credited with having evolved the mixolydian mode and with having invented a new style of music by breaking up the meter. "This feature," writes one modern admirer, "the Greeks called 'contrast of accent.' In her verse it was like silver things clashing against each other. She buckled together these clashing feet by the golden bands of rhythm and by this means made havoc of emphasis. . . . But when she chose to make symmetry of emphasis, she could. The sapphic meter is a woman's hexameter. It is the feminine heroic." [24]

Sappho and her pupils officiated at public religious festivals as well as at weddings, and Sappho herself may even have been official conductor of the temple choirs. "Come to the splendid temple grounds of Hera of the gleaming eyes, you girls of Lesbos," she writes, "and trip lightly with whirling measure, performing a beautiful choral dance for the goddess; and Sappho shall lead you, her golden lyre in her hand." [25] We have fragments of the beautiful wail laments that Sappho and her girls sang to hasten the rebirth of the child god at festivals to Adonis:

Maidens: Tender Adonis lies adying,
    O Cytheria, what were best to do?

Cytheria (Leader): Go, beat your breasts, ye maids, and crying,
    Rend ye your robes in sign of rue!" [26]

The subjects of Sappho's lyrics were the subjects important to women, the everyday happenings of their lives. She sang of her love for her little daughter; she wrote love songs and marriage songs; hymns and laments to be sung at religious ceremonies. So famous were her epithalamia or wedding songs that Sappho and her pupils were frequently and widely employed as musicians at weddings. And the poetic form of her epithalamia was the model which other writers used for nearly a thousand years in Greece, Rome, and even Europe. Knowing Sappho's authority in one type of art-song, can we not assume the same for the Egyptian poetess-musicians who created the laments and dirges attributed to the goddess Isis?

In order to judge the quality of Sappho's music, it is unnecessary to have samples of it. Her verses, her melodies, and the strains that accompanied them on flute or lyre were regarded by her contemporaries and by critics of the golden age as bearing the stamp of perfection. Her work had the same quality as the poetry and sculpture of the Periclean Age in Athens. Unquestionably, the music composed by Sappho and her companions, while of course very different from that of our times, was creation of the very highest order by trained musical talent.

Sappho was not a "sport"—a woman gone masculine—as many people have considered her, or an extraordinary deviation from type that might never occur again. She was simply an extremely talented individual, a woman with a great aptitude for poetic-musical expression, who lived in an environment peculiarly favorable for its full development. For her there existed a juxtaposition of the three factors *always* essential to the full unfolding of creative musical imagination. She developed in a culture in which music was an integral part of both informal and formal life. She belonged to a class of people from whom, in that culture, music was expected. As a member of the Aegean society, she inherited melodic impulse. Every artist of the islands had the background of Egypt and Crete for musical assertion in lyric song. Finally, Sappho had training and experience in the technique required by the standards of her community—an outstanding woman, it is true, but intrinsically no different from other exceptionally talented women of her own and of many other communities. What made Sappho the peerless lady of music and song was the fact that she had behind her an immemorial past of experiment by women in poetry and music. Hers was the last perfect flowering of thousands of years of women's song. (See Plate 44.)

CHAPTER VIII

ARTEMIS

1.

*F*OR creative expression in music there must be a free flow between the plane of daily experience and the plane of thought and fantasy. One must be able to transfer into universal and ideal terms one's vital personal experience. To the extent to which the ideal plane is restricted or distorted, the creative energies of the individual are devitalized or even poisoned.

Women in pre-Christian times all over the world had simply and naturally evolved a grand religious idea out of their greatest experience—the experience of birth. And just as simply and naturally, they assumed that the life of the universe could be expressed in terms of a woman's experience. Surely, they thought, the universal life must be a mother. It might unite with a father. But the motherhood of the deity was to them more obvious and more really important than the fatherhood. They were not restricted, as Western women later were for nineteen hundred years, to a single male god. On the contrary, they had a representation of what they, as women, knew of life. They had a means of idealizing and universalizing their own highest impulses.

Women were pre-eminent in the creation of music in these early times. They are not pre-eminent now. For in those days, they were also pre-eminent in the formulation of religious ideas. They did not take their religion from men, or leave it to men to make their music.

To understand what happened to women later, one must understand the kind of religious images that women had as an inspiration for the outpouring of their songs. In all the myths, rituals, sculpture, painting, and literature of antiquity, there is an all-pervading woman

108

presence. Whether she is called Cybele or Ishtar or Isis or Hera, or some name foreign to our ears, she represents woman power as an active beneficent principle in all life, sometimes as life itself, the ultimate being, mother of all living things. A realized truth generates creative power. From these noble images of women, energy flowed back to the individual woman, releasing and strengthening her imagination and her artistic impulse at this deep level where music is conceived.

Behind the rites of primitive people everywhere today, and in all very early religions, there is the woman spirit. In the great early civilizations of Egypt, Babylonia, and Crete, the Great Mother acquired a grand, all-embracing personality, and was loved and worshiped with a passionate faith. In Rome the cult of the Great Mother persisted and resisted the powerful onslaught of the growing Christian Church until the fifth century. In Greece, where the tendency was to bring all gods down to earth and turn them into human beings, the personality of the Great Mother was split up into a number of divine feminine figures and lovingly individualized, by the Greek talent for character delineation, into ideal women, clearly distinguished from each other in temperament, appearance, and the kind of interest they took in human affairs—but all of them noble, benignant, all-powerful.

The great goddesses, by whatever name they were called, had their own rites, in which music and dancing were always conspicuous, their own liturgies, their own myths, and their own insignia. One had the spiral; others carried the plume, jewels, an ear of corn, the three-stalked flower, a musical instrument. One was crowned with the sun's halo, one held the sky cape above her, another a sea shell. One stood surrounded by the swiftly flowing rivers of the world. Many were accompanied by lions—symbols of the strength inherent in womanhood. All the great goddesses represented the rhythm of life and the moon.

These goddesses, in their many beautiful impersonations, with their various symbols, represent three mighty facts of nature, akin to each other in their character and manifestations, which seemed to these early human beings, and especially to women, to hold the key to life. One was the waxing and waning of the moon, its three nights of darkness, its effulgent period of resplendent light making night for the brief period of the full moon a kind of heavenly day full of mystery and magic. The second was the fact that, in nature, death is the prelude to new birth. When the flower petals fall, there remains the seed from which new flowers will spring. And the third was the kinship of the woman—in all those biological details that distinguish her from the male—to the moon cycle and to the something that gives birth throughout all nature. Hence the divine life was naturally and inevitably feminine and woman was its natural priestess. She knew how to speak to it in her incantations; she knew the rhythms, the gestures, and the symbols, the spirit behind all things that would understand and heed. (See Plate 48.)

2.

As time went on and many, many women worked to perfect their understanding of the ultimate woman power, different goddesses, or different phases of the one great woman spirit, came to represent the woman in her different characters and functions—as mate, mother, worker, musician, and "virgin," or free, unattached to a mate, untrammeled with children.

All the goddesses represented to some degree the woman's life span. But there was one great spirit, the Greek Hera, who represented this the most clearly. She had three distinct forms, corresponding to the three phases of changing life. In the first she was the girl-child, young, fresh, free, having not yet come to maturity. In the second she was a woman of the childbearing age, in the fullness of her peculiar power of womanhood, as mate and mother. In the last she was the woman past childbearing age, but not old, free again, in the ripeness of character, in the profound knowledge of life that motherhood and wifehood nobly fulfilled have brought her.

In the beginning, when Hera first came to Greece from goddess-ruled Crete, she was entirely independent of Zeus. Even in the Olympian age she kept her own temples, priestesses, girl choirs, and rites, in which music and dancing were integrated. Hera was primarily the matron, guardian of marriage, mistress of the home, noble, dignified, and wise. A famous artistic representation of her, of which only a description now remains, showed her seated on a throne, carrying the scepter of world dominion in one hand and in the other a pomegranate—symbol of life.

The concept of mate as distinguished from that of mistress of the home received other impersonations. A dignified god symbolizing mating or sex is rare in the ancient pantheons. The Oriental gods usually represent unbridled male energy. The little boy Cupid or Eros was a frivolous conception of late Greek literature dominated by male intelligentsia, and very trivial and silly in comparison with the mighty, all-powerful goddesses of sex in earlier times, who symbolize the *rhythm* of sex desire.

Of these, one of the oldest was Sumerian Innanna, later Ishtar. In her resided the rhythm of sex desire. When she rested, all procreation ceased. Even the urge for it died until she gave the signal for the rebirth. An ancient myth represented Ishtar descending into hell, or darkness, for three days, corresponding to the three nights of the dark of the moon. On the third day she was revived by two goddesses impersonating the bread of life and the water of life; then, clothed in splendor and beauty, she emerged and roused all living things to mate.

Ishtar was one of the mightiest superhuman powers of all time, known as "Directress of Mankind." She was worshiped in many temples by both women and men. Troops of dancing, singing priestesses and many women officials served her. On the monuments and seals of Sumer she appeared in a long robe with a crown on her head and an eight-pointed star in her hand. From this same Ishtar, beautiful Venus in Rome took her name and her characteristics. In Greece, Ishtar and the idea of deifying sexual love were impersonated by Aphrodite, whose real home was the island of Cyprus. Here, where Cretan culture took early root, Aphrodite was a moon goddess and specifically the bearer of the life-giving dew, or mist, which comes at night. This refreshing moisture was thought to be, like the life-giving seminal fluid, the gift of the moon. Hence Aphrodite was the goddess born of the sea, and also the moon, which influenced, in some obscure magnetic ways, its tides and the sexual rhythm in women. Like other Great Mothers, Aphrodite lamented and made songs of rejoicing over the death and resurrection of her son, Adonis. Everywhere in Greek culture the mighty goddess of the rhythm of life itself and of music was the inspiration of festivals at which the whole populace shared her grief and joy.

In most of these deities of sex there was a recognition of the sex urge as the basis for a higher development of the life of the spirit. But without woman's authority in regulating the rhythm of sex life, spiritual life also lay dormant. As if to symbolize woman's life-giving power in affairs of the spirit, one of the old Oriental goddesses was depicted holding the material substance of the world encased in a spiritual essence. This image may be regarded as representing the meaning of all ancient feminine deities—unity of the higher human faculties with the natural and real things of the earth.

3.

Nearly all great goddesses were mothers and often passed on the torch of life to the next generation by their own power. Many of them had names whose roots indicated their function. The last part of the Greek Demeter's name means mother. A present day South Indian word for "nurse" or "mother" is "amma," and it is incorporated into the Great Mothers' names, such as Nukalamma. In representations of the mother goddess, her maternal functions were universalized by associating various symbols of life and the rhythm of life with the figure of the woman. In picture after picture the Great Mother sits on her throne holding, not a child, but the more comprehensive emblem of the phial containing the water of life. She beats a drum, not only because real women use a drum as a magic device to assist childbirth, but because her life is bound to rhythm. She sings, not only because real mothers sing to their children, giving them their first impressions of melody, but because the music of the spheres resounds to human ears only through the door of life she opens for both body and soul.

With only local variations in the different countries, the Great Mother was the focus of celebrations for changes in the seasons and for the reappearance of the new moon.

The goddess gave a child to the world, fashioned out of her own body and blood. She gave nourishment that her child might thrive—first her own milk and then cultivated foods. The child was sometimes a son and sometimes a daughter. Demeter gave Kore, a beautiful clean-limbed, clear-eyed maiden. Other goddesses had both a maiden and a youth. Cybele's child, Attis, was double-sexed. The offspring of the Great Mother was often identified with the fruits of the earth and became the symbol of regeneration, to be lamented and rejoiced over by the goddesses and their semidivine attendants. Every year or so, at great national festivals, Ishtar mourned for Tammuz, Isis for Osiris, Cybele for Attis, Aphrodite for Adonis, and Demeter for Kore. Rites for the rebirth were the most important rites and they were ceremonies of the goddess-mother, not the godfather. It was the mother's sacrifice, the mother's power for bringing life, the mother's point of view that gave the religion of those times its character and appeal.

As mother, the goddess created the world in co-operation with a male deity, to whom, with a grim feminine realism, the early priest-ess-theologians assigned the lesser part in this mighty achievement. It would have been impossible, in those honest early days, to convince a woman who had borne children that the father's part in projecting life was the greater part and should be so represented in the creation of divine images. Running through all the early stories of the creation there is also the idea that a male god can never do much until a woman puts real life into him or his work. Prometheus once made a youth, but it was Athene who pressed the spiritual substance into his brain. The shepherd boy Endymion led a passive existence on Mount Latmos until Selene, the Full-Moon Mother, embraced him. Inspired by her magic touch, he began to dream of noble thoughts and deeds. Again, in one of the Nile legends the river is a male spirit that flows between two banks represented by a goddess. She stands with outstretched arms, as though begging for the water to come and fertilize her. But the mighty river swelled and flowed only when Isis let fall her tears of mourning for Osiris, the Nile god. The goddess had to make the wailing and the weeping that always brings about the rebirth.

In a hymn of remarkable vigor, Indrānī, one of the Seven Mothers in India, chanted the dogma of her superiority over her husband: "I am the banner and the head, a mighty arbitress am I! I am victorious and my Lord shall be submissive to my will. I am victorious o'er my Lord, my song of triumph is supreme." [1]

The women theologians did not generally assume that even a goddess could create the world without a mate. The oldest company of Egyptian deities consisted of four pairs of consorts with equal powers. Throughout Egyptian history most of the well-known gods had their female counterparts functioning in exactly the same way. The old Babylonian creation myth told of the primeval ocean flood containing male and female elements. Oriental gods still have their *śakti*—their female half without whom they would be powerless.

As mother, the goddess could compel rebirth. Rites for the rebirth were the most important features of early cults, and in them emphasis was placed on women's attitudes rather than on men's. Ishtar rejuvenated her son Tammuz by holding him on her knees. Demeter displayed an ear of corn as the symbol of power to bring about rebirth. The woman's power of self-sacrifice for the sake of others, the mother's authority in regeneration is beautifully expressed in the story of the rebirth of Osiris. This popular Egyptian god, who personified the life-giving river Nile, was murdered by Set, the Typhoon, and cut into fourteen pieces as a symbol of the waning moon, which takes that number of nights to disappear from the sky. His mate, Isis, Creatrix of Green Things, determined to save his life. Alone and exhausted almost to the point of death, she persevered until she had found the scattered pieces of his body. Nūt, the Sky Mother, united and regenerated the dead god. "She gives to thee thy head and thy legs, she joins the limbs together, and replaces thy heart in thy body." [2] Then Isis conceived by Osiris and bore the child Horus. Without her persistence in the face of dire distress and her overpowering love, life on earth might have remained dormant— symbolically speaking—forever.

Of all the goddess-mothers, Isis was the greatest, just as Ishtar was the greatest of all goddesses of sex. In her the idea of mother love was sublimated into an altruistic, civilizing force capable of leading men and women to a higher level of intelligent living. Springing from other earlier mother-spirits of the preliterate age, she was more widely worshiped in Egypt by both women and men than any other goddess there. She survived until the sixth century A.D., spreading her influence in Greece and Rome. An old Greek inscription shows the reverence accorded her in magnificent terms:

I am Isis, mistress of every land; I laid down laws for mankind and ordained things that no one may change; I am she who governs Sirius the Dog-Star; I am she who is called divine among women; I divided the earth from the heaven; I made manifest the paths of the stars; I prescribed the course of the sun and the moon; I found out the labours of the sea; I made justice mighty. I burdened woman with the newborn babe in the tenth month; I ordained that parents should be believed by their children; I put an end to cannibalism; I overthrew the sovereignty of tyrants; I compelled women to be believed by men; I made justice more mighty than gold or silver; I made virtue and vice to be distinguished by instinct.[3]

4.

The woman as mate evolves into the woman as mother. The woman as mother is a worker for her family, and as such she evolves into the presiding spirit of community work and welfare. There were many women spirits in all parts of the ancient world who reflected women's work and activities as extensions of the functions of motherhood. There was Ishtar, the potter; Nëit, the weaver; the spinning and singing Fates; Athene, worker in the art and crafts of civilized life. Innanna, the great Sumerian mother and goddess came to the aid of women in childbirth with the words: "Maiden of the place of begetting am I; in the home where the mother gives birth, a protecting shadow am I!"[4] Many goddesses had the power of healing and carried the magic wand entwined with serpents later held by Aesculapius. Egyptian Taweret, called The Great One, presided over family affairs and symbolized ancient woman's authority in the home—the focal point for bringing life and for making music.

The most remarkable example of the way the ancients were thinking out the relation between private home and community was to be found in the impersonation and functions of the goddess Hestia in Greece and of Vesta in Rome. Since primitive women today are generally the keepers of a perpetual fire, these goddesses probably symbolized a very old association of woman with authority over the hearth. Hestia and Vesta were the guardians of the hearth in its twofold aspect, as symbol of the internal unity of the family and of hospitality to the stranger. As impersonations of hospitality, they were hostesses of suppliants and fugitives who might invoke the sacredness of the family hearth where they had taken refuge and so be protected. Hestia's home was in the prytaneum, where a fire, representing the common hearth for the whole city, was kept ever going. Colonists traveling from the city to settle elsewhere received a coal from the fire, as symbol of the continuity of life in their new home with that in their old. Similarly the Roman Vesta, a very ancient goddess, became an important state deity whose vestal virgins guarded the sacred fire and the Sybilline books with their treasured secrets of the way to live.

The Greeks expressed their sense of the communal importance of woman's work and authority by adopting a specific goddess as the guardian of a city. Of these personifications of woman as worker and manager, the most complete and authoritative is that of Athene, guardian of Athens. In this noble figure was concentrated the highest qualities of the feminine personality as shown in work and public leadership. She was the goddess of the pure ether, the dawn and the twilight, and goddess, in her moments of righteous wrath, of the

thunder cloud and the lightening bolt. She was the guardian of
women's arts and industries, protector of family and community life.
As guardian of peaceful industry, Athene was goddess of peace. But
to ensure peace she would go to war, resolutely and thoughtfully. In
war she was goddess of counsel and prudent strategy as opposed to
her reckless brother Ares, who represented brute courage and violence. The heroes like Odysseus whom she led and protected were
"wise." They used their heads. They exercised forethought, they
strove to overcome brawn and violence with intelligence and management.

In the many statues of Athene power and benign authority seem
to be guiding the hand of the artist in the molding of the noblest
kind of feminine face, with its broad, open brow, candid, thoughtful
eyes (which in the Greek statues were carefully painted in), and
firm, kind, resolute mouth. She stands with helmet on her head,
shield and lance in her hand, the leader of states, the supreme authority in civilized life, the sure, unruffled, unflinching guardian of
all that is under her care.

Such authority as Athene wielded might even be conceived of as
extending beyond private hearth and city hearth to the whole world
and to the universe itself. As a mother weaves her children's clothes,
Nëit in Egypt wove the warp and woof of the world's fabric. The
Fates (the Teutonic Norns) occupied their time in spinning. The
threads they span and cut were the threads not of garments, but of
life.

5.

As mate, mother, provider for the household through industry,
and guardian of home and community hearths, the woman sang at
the altar to invoke the universal life for the protection of lives under
her care. So she was, by necessity of her motherhood, a musician.
In every country of the ancient world, divine symbols represented
women in their role as dancers, instrumental players, and especially
as singers.

The dance had many feminine and few masculine impersonations.
All nymphs, fairies, and forest mothers danced. In India the Apsaras
were in perpetual motion. In Greece the Horae danced to mark the
march of time. The Charites, the Horae, and the Graces—symbols of
the bloom of youth—moved with measured steps under their own
leader, Thalia. The Greeks portrayed religious dance as a matron.

In Crete the great Mother Rhea "invented" the steps that made the Cretan youth famous for centuries. In Egypt, Hat-hor was goddess of the moon and goddess of the dance.

Musical instruments were often the property of spirits and goddesses. A certain type of drum was sacred only to Sarasvati, giver of speech and music to humanity, but various types of drums, tambourines, and cymbals belonged to the company of deified musicians. The Bacchae always carried them, and Cybele, the All-Begetting Mother, beat a drum to mark the rhythm of life. Flutes were also played by the Bacchae and by many others. A legend tells that Athene invented the instrument that blew the breath of life. To Isis was attributed the invention of the sistrum, a glorified type of rattle. Lyres and harps of different types were associated with supernatural musicians, especially Artemis. In Persia the spirit of the harp was personified by Azada, whose music echoed the harmony of the spheres. (See Plate 46.)

Singing was the genius of goddesses. Each separate step in the making of magic song became deified. The wail, the cry of joy, the imitation of natural sounds all had feminine impersonation. Every type of song—incantation, epic, lament—had a special feminine spirit.

As a result of its constant use upon occasions of birth and rebirth, the wail received impersonation. Little figures of clay or marble, representing women as wailers and weepers, have been found in the graves and on the sarcophagi of many peoples. When her son Ruadan was born, the Celtic goddess Anu gave the first wail ever heard in Ireland. Ishtar wailed "like a woman in travail" in her effort to bring about the return of creative energy to the sleeping earth. Isis invented the wail and taught it to the women of her country as a magical device to bring about birth. The Great Wailer herself, accompanied by Nephthys, her sister, the Less Wailer; Neget, a goddess known as the crier; Neït and Nūt, two of the Great Mothers; Selket, protectress of the dead; and two lesser deities, Ibwet and Tayet, stood in the temple of Hat-hor at Denderah in the room consecrated to lamentations, ready to wail the image of Osiris back to life.

Wail songs, or laments, were composed by many supernatural women. All nymphs, forest mothers, and other semidivine creatures sang laments. The sirens, as playmates of Persephone, goddess of death, personified death lamentations—incantations to bring about rebirth. But whenever sirens appeared upon tombstones, they were depicted as both lamenting and rejoicing. In the earliest times they assumed the form of bird-women, and as such may be relatives of Sírin and Alkonóst, the two Russian bird-women from whom came all laments and songs of joy. (See Plate 47.)

A link between fantastical bird-women and real women singers is the common myth of women turning into birds. In Greece there were two such legends. In one, Aedon killed her son by mistake and prayed to be turned into a bird. "Daughter of Pandareus, the brown bright nightingale," wrote the poet, "pours forth her full-voiced music, bewailing her child." [5] In the other myth, two sisters are turned into birds and bemoan their sorrows. Philomela became a swallow and Procne a nightingale. (Ovid twisted the names—probably on purpose, as Philomela is the prettier sound.) Both bird-sisters lament. Pausanias, always interested in the origin of myths, explained: "The tradition of the change into the nightingale and swallow is, I think, because these birds have a melancholy song like a lament." [6] The significance of Pausanias' interpretation is that neither he nor anyone else, apparently, thought it odd for a woman to be identified with a songbird when in reality only male birds sing.

The same association is found in Lithuania, where the verb "to cuckoo" signifies "to lament" and where the cuckoo is nearly always compared to a woman. The reason this identification did not seem incongruous is undoubtedly because the association of women with the singing of laments was so strong that the sex of the bird dwindled into unimportance. All mother-goddesses, too, sang the laments and the songs of rejoicing. In Egypt, Isis and her sister Nephthys composed the laments that became the models for both informal and formal dirges. In other countries the name of the mother is mentioned in the lament as the one who is mourning and rejoicing.

Other types of incantations—those for achieving any purpose— often assumed human guise. The singing Sirens, for example, could influence the behavior of people, animals, and even natural phenomena. They could inspire some men to great and noble deeds; they could lure others from their chosen pursuits and chain them fast. Only the Great Mothers surpassed them in the art of making incantations. Nearly every one had a subtitle such as "Lady of Incantations."

In the mythology of ancient Rome, the Carmentes were pesonifications of the fortune or luck of the mother in childbirth, but they were also projections of the incantations made by midwives, whose chief means of assistance at childbirth was music. The Carmentes got their name from the word *carmen,* meaning a charm, and incantation or song. *Carmen* is derived from the name of a real person, Carmenta or Nicostrata, an ancient poetess of Latium, who is said to have introduced religion, poetry, and agriculture. She seems to have been a prophetess, bard, and cult heroine. To us the translation of *carmen* is more familiar as "song" than as "magic formula for aid in childbirth." The shift from the original specific meaning to the more generic one must have resulted from the innumerable incantations or songs made through the ages by women for aid in childbirth.

Not only each separate department of music had a special goddess, but the art itself was generally given a feminine impersonation. As we have already seen, some of the very ancient goddesses combined music with their other life-giving functions. Hat-hor, Bastet, Sarasvati, Bhāratī, Innanna, Artemis, and the Muses were all identified with singing and dancing and the playing of certain instruments.

The Muses, at first only three in number, had names that indicated their business. One was called Invention, or She Who Invents the Words and Musical Phrases. Another was known simply as Song, or The One Who Sings. The third Muse answered to Memory, or She Who Remembers, an important quality in an age when song and story were passed orally from singer to singer. This one inherited her name, her faculty, and her function from her mother, Mnemosyne. One very old set of their names was Nete, Mese, and Hypate. These also signify the low, middle, and high tones in the Greek system of scales. Such designations would not have been associated with feminine spirits if an identity with music had not been intended. In the oldest depictions of the Muses, they stand with a woman leader, sometimes Mnemosyne, sometimes Athene, sometimes an unknown figure—possibly Artemis. Throughout their long history the Muses, from whose very name the word music is derived, kept their musical authority. Around Zeus's altar they alone chanted the epic of the world's origin. Thamyris, the bard, was struck blind for daring to challenge them in song. Even after Apollo had acquired the title "God of Music," he rarely dared appear without their encircling support.

Taking the music deities from many ancient countries as a whole, we can thus reconstruct a complete hierarchy of women whose prestige and authority survives to the present day in painting and in literature. Chief among them were the Great Mothers. They were surrounded by specialized deities of lesser rank. Then came groups like the Bacchae—the mothers who brought Dionysos to birth—various grades of Forest Mothers, Heroines, Nymphs, Seasons, Hours, Nereids, Graces, Apsaras, Gift-bringers of Plenty such as the Charites, Fates, Sirens, other bird-women, even witches. These creatures were eternally dancing, playing instruments, and singing. When male spirits are found in their ranks, they come as consorts. The Gandharvas, a group of Indian spirits, were husbands of the beautiful dancing Apsaras.

When and where the first of these spirits of women's music was projected is a mystery. Many of them appear as fully developed and powerful musicians in the earliest strata of literature. In India, there were Sarasvati and Bhāratī; in Egypt, Bastet and Hat-hor; in Sumer, Innanna. In Greece, the Muses belong to the oldest company—Artemis, too, has been traced to the most ancient times. With various attributes, she was widely worshiped long before her so-called brother Apollo entered the scene and usurped her authority in music. (See Plate 49.)

In the beginning, these oldest goddesses undoubtedly reflected the musical activities of real women. In later times, when primitive naïveté gave way to sophistication and to what is called learning, they often became glorified into abstractions. The Muses, their number augmented to three times three, came to represent wisdom and knowledge. Terpsichore, She who Loves to Dance, became the abstract choral dance. Calliope, the One who Loves to Sing, became abstract epic poetry; Euterpe became lyric poetry; Melpomene, tragedy; Erate, erotic poetry; Klio, the storyteller became history; and Urania, from She who Dwells in the Heavens, meaning the moon and the stars, became astronomy. From images of the waxing, full, and waning moon, Artemis, with Selene, Hekate, and the dancing nymphs became the symbols of harmony and order in the universe. Anahita, Aphrodite, and Venus, from being personifications of sexual love became symbols of life—and symbols of music.

From the historical point of view, the music goddesses as abstractions, although very grand and noble figures, have tended to obscure rather than to fortify the former association of women with music. It requires a mental effort to accept an image such as Urania, muse of astronomy. In our culture, women astronomers are too rare to warrant their idealization. But Urania as She who Dwells in the Heavens is readily comprehensible to anyone. It is less difficult to accept the Great Mother, creatrix and ruler, because in everyone's experience, there is somewhere a mother giving birth and managing a baby. But if we can recognize a real woman in a divine Mother, why can we not recognize a real musician in a divine Music-Maker? Only because, in our culture, women have not so distinguished themselves. Without being oversublimated, Calliope, the One who Loves to Sing, and Klio, the One who Tells Stories, are obvious enough as reflections of reality. To them and others of their kind we must turn for an understanding of the woman-musician's past. Divested of vague and visionary attributes, the goddess-musicians are historical evidence, revealing real musicians of high creative intelligence and power.

6.

A woman, by reason of her sex, is mate and mother, and in performing her functions as such evolves naturally into worker, community manager, and musician. But even so, she must remain a human soul, free, unenthralled to sex, an individual self, which is a single expression of humanity. This idea of the freedom of the self in womanhood was very precious to women of ancient times, overburdened, as they tended to be, by work and maternity. The determination to keep some freedom is expressed in the secret societies, among women everywhere, for whose rites women escape from children and household to the hills.

The supreme example among goddesses of this ideal of free selfhood is Artemis. She represents at once the creative individual who meets life with a proud, positive attitude and the creative freedom of collective womanhood. Artemis, the Maid, had no mate; she was not a mother, and remained forever "virgin," that is, herself, reflecting the value placed by the ancients on womanhood as an independent spiritual power. Coming from societies in which women predominated in religious and musical life, and in which men musicians admitted their debt to women by wearing feminine costumes, Artemis carried the lyre, an old moon-cult female symbol. Until late in Greek history, Artemis Hegemonia (leader) or Artemis Hymnia accompanied the lyre-playing Apollo, who dressed and wore his hair like his mother, Leto, or his great sister. (See Plate 50.)

Artemis as the protector of all young things and guardian of wild life was the protector also of women against the too insistent demands of Aphrodite—of sex and childbearing. She was woman, free, fleet of foot, strong of limb, serene of soul, woman as a creature of nature, forever untamed, able to slip out of the grasp of any man and take herself on her swift feet to the hills. Nothing could bind her. In many Greek representations of her she stands with her robe girt up and her hair bound for swift movement, with a hind, symbol of all fleet-footed wild life, at her side, and bow and arrows in her hand, ready to shoot a dart at anyone who would stop her.

Today Artemis is often misrepresented as the goddess of chastity —a sterile title indeed for the great moon spirit. When Sappho sang about herself, "I am forever virgin," [7] she knew that Artemis was integrity, the self; the part of the individual soul that must preserve its independence or perish. And as such she received the sacrifices of many women of Sappho's age. Among the most inspiring of these votive offerings is the small ivory figurine of the triple moon goddess holding the torch of life for the lovely dancing Daughters of the Moon. (See frontispiece.)

7.

Mate, mother, worker, communal guardian, musician, and free soul—such was woman's picture of herself in the thousands of years in which she worked out her own idealizations of her own functions and sang freely at altars of her own building to the great goddesses and their hosts of spirit attendants. Mirrors of woman in her different natures, avatars of the strength that can alter—as the moon alters— and yet preserve the feminine core,[8] they also symbolized life in its many manifestations. What the natural woman was, what she did, became the highest object of religious devotion, and so idealized and universalized, became an ever revered inspiration to effort and invention.

Before these spirits, the holy hymn of an ancient faith was chanted. Worshiping nature's rhythmic laws and striving to keep in touch with the life force, which is beyond human comprehension, men and women set a spiritual value on woman's natural way. Men and women both lived according to the principle that woman is creative in body and spirit. In the independence and originality of the spirit of collective womanhood, which was and remains the glory of primitive religion, a woman may have faith and courage —and the heart—to sing. When Artemis strikes her lyre, she sings no man's composition, and lifts her eyes to no man's heaven. She sings for herself, out of the deepest truths she knows as a woman, in the reassuring and lovely splendor of the moon at its full.

THE DARK OF THE MOON

CHAPTER IX

THE TWILIGHT OF THE GODDESS

1.

ABOUT 500 B.C. there fell on these hopeful civilizations of our earth a kind of creeping blight. It did not come all at once, but slowly in a change here and a change there that may have seemed at first a great improvement in the organization of life or a correction of a local abuse. Indeed, the Chinese, who went further than any other people in carrying out the new ideas, say flatly that real civilization began at the moment when men determined to know who their own children were and to assume responsibility for their care and education. This was, indeed, a change for the better—or might have been for the better if more intelligence had been shown in carrying it out.

But the men, in taking over, did it crudely. Their idea of making sure that their children were their own was to shut the women up from the moment they could bear a child, out of sight and hearing and contact with any man but a predestined father. In China they achieved this in the end by so crippling the women that they could not move beyond their own homes and courtyards unless they were carried. The long slow process of foot-binding began in childhood and continued through years and years of torture. At puberty, shame and fear descended on the girl, for now she was really a menace to society. She must be watched with all eyes and barred with all bars.

How different from the customs of the mothers, even among very primitive tribes, with their incantations to the moon, their holy baths, torch races, songs, dances, and flowers! Primitive mothers sometimes put the girls through very trying ordeals. But behind these ordeals is the grand sense of destiny, the taking up of the women's burden with pride and congratulation, the initiation into the sense of oneness with all birth and being.

The new attitudes were formulated in the hard, clean-cut maxims of Confucius, which became the official religion of China and the foundation of its education. Confucius was a wise man. But he was also the world's worst prude. He thought it immoral for a man's coat and a woman's dress to hang side by side on pegs on a wall. No wonder that Mme Sun Yat-sen, the great wife of the great leader of modern China, says that if China is to live, Confucianism must go. Yet even in China there are indications of an earlier and better day, astonishing to one who knows the pruderies of Chinese life even now wherever it is not yet touched by the spirit of such women as Mme Sun Yat-sen.

What life in China was like just before Confucius became its law-giver one may guess from the lays of Che-king, which Confucius edited. These lays represent the ancient customs of country people. As among primitive people today, the men and women were like two separate tribes and had each their own functions and collective activities. The men were farmers, the women weavers, having learned the art of raising silk worms from the wife of Huang-ti. This separation is indicated in a Chinese legend in which two stellar deities represent the female weaver and the male ox driver. Between them spreads the milky way, the Celestial River.

But according to the legend, this Celestial River could be crossed once a year. So, also, the peasant girls and boys had a spring festival to relieve the hard, monotonous toil of daily life and to awaken in them the joy of living. In the province of Honan they used to have a celebration that was very different from anything allowed well-brought-up Chinese girls after Confucius reformed China for the benefit of men.

This great seasonal celebration was the time for social intercourse and the sanctioned hour for the young people to meet and mate. At the spring rites the girls first bathed in the life-giving river, then exchanged flowers with the boys and played games that suggested the flight of birds as they pursue each other seeking a mate. The boys and the girls challenged each other in song, the girls drawing from their own experience as they gave the invitation. Since they were accustomed to weave both plain and flowered material, they sang:

"In a flowered skirt, in a plain skirt—
In a flowered robe, in a plain robe—

"Come, sirs! Come sirs!
Take me in the chariot to your home!" [1]

The boys prepared their own mind for courtship by suggesting that spring was in the air:

"Withered leaves, withered leaves,
The wind comes to blow upon you."

The girls expressed their longing:

"Until I have seen my lord—
My restless heart, ah, how it beats—
But as soon as I am united to him,
Then my heart will be at peace." [2]

The two groups danced and sang in antiphonal choruses, each group having its own leader and each group bringing to the festival its own musical contribution.

In this primitive festival, the origin of the symbolic sacred marriage of so many ancient societies is suggested. What was at first in the childhood of humanity a natural way to sanction sex intercourse became dignified in many ancient societies into a formal religious ceremony performed as a symbolic act by kings and queens to bring health and wealth to their people.

2.

While China was thus "civilizing" itself, by repressing women's rites and music, a great change had already come over India. As we have seen, the early Aryan people there had worshiped a trinity of great goddesses—Sarasvati, Bhāratī, and Ilā—who symbolized women's participation in both the religious rite and in music. At first the Aryan conquerors had held women in high esteem, and women had performed the sacrifices at the altars and had sung their hymns. It may be that the tendency to lock women up was intensified by the rabid color prejudices of the Aryans, who were determined not to mingle their blood with the darker native race, a prejudice that also created the great evils of the caste system. However this may be, Indian women fell under the blight of a peculiarly fanatical male fear of their sex.

Even before the spirit of Confucius froze down upon the early naturalness and joy of China, an old pedant named Manu in India had decided to put the singing women in their place and let man take over and perform the sacrifices, including those that women had invented out of their own intimate and unique faith as child-bearers and life bearers. Manu's regulations said, among other things: "No act is to be done according to her own will by a young girl, a young woman, or even by an old woman, though in their own houses. In her childhood, a girl should be under the will her father; in her youth, of her husband; her husband being dead, of her sons; a woman should never enjoy her own will. . . . Though of bad conduct or debauched, or even devoid of good qualities, a husband must always be worshiped like a god by a good wife." [3] This attempt to silence women was followed by a resolve to curse her very nature. Manu insisted upon woman's intrinsic wickedness. She was spiritually inferior to man—identified with the Sudra, the lowest order of life, akin to brute beasts. She must not participate in religious ceremonies, she must not study the sacred books, she must not even hear them read. Manu announced: "No religious ceremony for women should be accompanied by mantras (except marriage)—with these words the rule of right is fixed; for women being weak creatures and having no share in the mantras, are falsehood itself. So stands the law." [4]

Among the Brahmans, then, women ceased to function as a beneficent power. Although some of the goddesses survived in Hindu theology, woman as a living creature became associated with insignificance and even with evil. She existed merely to serve her husband and to bear the son who alone could open for the father the door of eternal life. Her marriage meant not a fulfillment of her individuality, but a sacrifice of herself even to the point of ending her own life when her lord died. This absorption of her personality into another's was reflected in a famous epic sung by women while grinding corn at the hand mill. Innumerable verses describe how Basti Singh's wife was wooed by a dishonorable brother-in-law who had murdered her husband; how the wife pretended to submit in order to ensure a proper burial for her husband; how, when she saw his corpse, her purity ignited the funeral pyre and burned not only the dead body but herself as well.

Manu's law for women resulted in the erection of a barrier between women and music entirely different from the taboos existing in the primitive tribes. There the barriers consist of local taboos upon special activities and almost never a denial of ability. Manu's barrier was different, too, from the limitations placed upon women by the Egyptians. In Egypt, woman and her goddess were always regarded as a dynamic and a beneficent influence, indispensable to the common weal. But the Brahmans established a theory that woman was not merely insignificant in the scheme of life but was actually a malignant force. Here was the sinister threat to self-reverence, to dignity, and to integrity of spirit. Here was a body blow to the principle that feminine urges are a dynamic power for advancing civilization. This took away from women the expectation that they would collectively develop their confidence in their powers and in their importance as a beneficent influence on humanity, backed by a sincere and universal respect by men for them as such. No one with such a handicap can become a creative musician.

3.

The threat to women musicians gathered tremendous momentum in the religious ideas of the Jews. Their history, as it concerns the relation of women to the life of the spirit, is strikingly similar to that of the Brahmans.

The Jews of the Biblical age had inherited some of their beliefs from the ancient Sumerians, who were worshipers of moon deities and especially of Ishtar and her son Tammuz. Other ideas and customs came to the Jews from the Hittites, also a goddess-worshiping people who identified Ishtar with the sun. Still other traditions came from the nomad tribes who wandered with their flocks and herds around the Arabian desert, slowly drifting into Palestine. In the very early days of this migration—about 3000 B.C.—the god of the Hebrews was Yahveh. Like so many other deities of that period, Yahveh was man-woman together. In some tribes he was male with a wife called Anat.

The women of these tribes displayed a strength that corresponded to the woman power represented in the male-female deity. In the oldest part of the Bible, women appear as chieftains, judges, and magicians. Deborah was a prophetess and a judge in Israel. She also possessed magic powers, as Barak well knew. When Deborah commanded the warrior to go against Sisera, the Canaanite, Barak refused to go unless she went with him and lent him the authority of her presence. The oldest existing fragment of Hebrew literature tells of the murder of the enemy of Jael and finally of Deborah's song of triumph.

> "Hear, O ye kings; give ear, O ye princes;
> I, even I, will sing unto the Lord:
> I will sing praise to the Lord God of Israel." [5]

Although the whole hymn is clearly Deborah's, there are some verses that seem to have been chanted antiphonally. Possibly Deborah led her rejoicing women and Barak led his warriors:

> "Awake, awake, Deborah, awake, awake, utter a song!"

To which the reply is:

> "Arise, Barak, and lead thy captivity captive."

And one chorus sang:

> "At her feet he bowed, he fell, he lay down."

Answered by the other:

> "Where he bowed, there he fell down dead." [6]

The chorus was a medium through which the patriotism of the entire tribe could flow. As long as the Jews continued to be a nation of warriors, women were expected to rejoice over victories collectively with their own leaders. When Moses and Aaron led the Hebrews out of Egypt and when the hosts of Pharaoh were drowned in the Red Sea, their sister Miriam, as prophetess and leader of the women, "took a timbrel in her hand; and all the women went out after her with timbrels and with dances." [7] And Miriam sang in triumph antiphonal response to the chorus of Moses and his men. "Sing ye to the Lord, for he hath triumphed gloriously; the horse and his rider hath he thrown into the sea." [8]

Years after Miriam we find Judith, with courage and craft, seduc-
ing and slaying Holofernes, captain of the invading Assyrians. On
her return, and after the defeat of the enemy, all the women of
Israel, in gratitude and thanksgiving, ran together to see Judith
"and bless her, and made a dance among them for her . . . and she
went before all the people in the dance, leading all the women: and
all the men of Israel followed in their armour with garlands, and with
songs in their mouths. . . . Then Judith began to sing this thanksgiving in all Israel, and all the people sang after her this song of
praise. And Judith said, Begin unto my God with timbrels, sing unto
my Lord with cymbals: tune unto him a new psalm: exalt him and
call upon his name." [9]

Women's and girls' choruses are mentioned all through the Old
Testament. Girl choirs, organized for the antiphonal singing of
Psalms—such as Psalm 9—performed at public festivals. In this connection, the three daughters of a certain Levite priest are mentioned
as being excellent musicians. Under King Solomon, an enthusiastic
lover of music, the girl choirs performed in his second temple and
also in his court orchestra. "I gat me men singers and women singers,
and the delights of the sons of men as musical instruments, and that
of all sorts." [10]

Like all other women of ancient times, Jewish women participated, as a matter of course, in religious ceremonies and in formal
secular music. They also carried on their ancient rituals common to
women the world over. Wailing to bring the rebirth was expected
of them. The prophet Jeremiah called for the mourning women that
they might come with their cunning and their knowledge. Sometimes to make their wailing more effective, they sat on drums—
symbols of the rhythm of life. Dancing and singing, these natural
musicians were creating, as they still are today, beautiful songs for
christenings and weddings, for work and for play.

But as it was with the Brahmans, so with the Jews. Men's superior
physical strength, necessarily emphasized and developed for aggressive warfare, began to dominate in the life of the spirit. Women
gradually lost their prestige and authority. As the years passed, barriers between women and the affirmation of womanhood became
firmly established. The ark—always like a ship, a symbol of the
womb—remained the holy of holies for the Israelites, but it was
guarded by men only. Women, excluded from the priesthood, were
forbidden to enter the inner temple. The girl choirs did not sing

in the most sacred place. Eventually, women became associated with spiritual inferiority and even with a definitely evil influence. In men's invention of the story of creation, the female was represented as having done humanity a gross disservice. Theologians could not deny that Eve possessed the secret of life and that Adam learned it only by receiving the apple (or pomegranate)—symbol of life and knowledge—from her. But they satisfied their craving for superiority by ordaining that Eve, instead of being reverenced for her power, should be humiliated for her audacity. Jewish men, to this day, thank God in public prayer that they are not born women.

No feminine attributes were mirrored in Jehovah, the fierce warrior God, who guaranteed never to change the rhythm of life. The numerous passages in the Bible alluding to Jehovah's unchanging character refer to the difference between him and the mother-goddesses of the moon cults, whose energy waxed and waned like that of the moon. The ancient practice of lamenting yearly for Tammuz, son of Ishtar, was branded as heresy. No wailing, no rejoicing with the Great Mother was to be tolerated. Much of Old Testament history deals with the struggles of the grim followers of the male warrior god Yahweh to keep their people from straying off to the more attractive altars of the kindlier feminine deities. There is no god but Yahweh, they said. All other idealizations of life, all personifications of the life force, were to be barred. If one could not lift one's soul in faith and adoration to this harsh, unforgiving, unchanging male, the soul must die. "For I the Lord thy God am a jealous God"—so spoke God to man and man to woman.

When women's rites did survive in formal religious ceremonies, men directed them. A good example is the rite of reintegration into normal life after the great experience of childbirth. Instead of being celebrated by women alone, as it always was among primitive people, it passed into the hands of men. The mother required "purification" by a priest.

Exclusion from the intellectual life of their times, exclusion from the spiritual life of men, identification with the unwanted, the undesirable, and the inferior, all contributed to the establishment of a diametrically opposed relation of men to music and of women to music.

Men had, in the male god, a symbol of their own sex; they had officials to perform their rites. They had, furthermore, the sanction of the group to regard their own activities, rites, and modes of expression as the proper expression for all the community. Women's divine images were banished with fire and sword, and women's rites revised or distorted into worship of the male god as the only God.

So Jewish men became the group expected to create the national literature and music. Jewish women did not lose their inherent power to express emotions in the language of music; but they were gradually excluded from the group preferred to make the important music of their times. Women's songs of joy and songs of sorrow ceased to have value for the religious leaders, ceased to be inscribed in the national annals. These leaders even said that for a woman to be seen with her hair uncovered was a disgrace, for a woman to sing verged on unchastity, and that the very hearing of a woman's voice was indecent.

Beginning with Ezekiel (26:113), the prophets warned women: "And I will cause the noise of thy songs to cease; and the sound of thy harps shall be no more heard." [11] And for many centuries the rabbis held to this murderous attitude. "Music in a house must bring that house to destruction." [12] As a consequence of such ideas, the artist singer did not perform solo songs in public from about 300 B.C. until long after 100 A.D., nor did the association of the natural strength and beauty of women's voices with seduction and lust lose force for many more centuries.

The fact that Jewish women had reached this low estate at the time of the birth of Christian culture has a direct bearing upon the relation of women to the music of our times. St. Paul, the first great doctrinaire of the early Christians, saw through Jewish eyes the immediate solution to many of the social problems of his times. It was largely Paul who took the lead in transmitting the prejudices of the ancient Jews toward women to the Christian world then in the making.

4.

In Greece the revolution was slow. Up until about 200 B.C. some women were attending the old colleges for priestesses and some were even organizing new colleges for the study of philosophy and music. Nevertheless, by about 400 B.C. Greek women were feeling the strong impact of male aggression in the institution of the state. School, church, art center, amusement place, and forum became integrated under one control, wholly masculine. Men cultivated a sex solidarity and favored men teachers, men religious officials, men artists, men dramatists and actors.

As a part of this usurpation of authority, men attempted to take over the art of healing, which like magic and music had always been, and is still subconsciously, regarded as an evidence of supernatural power. An Athenian decree, for example, forbade women to function as midwives. Since it was the prerogative of upper-class obstetricians to sing the hymn of exorcism that banished evil spirits from the presence of the mother and the newborn child, the decree, as far as it was observed, erected a barrier between women and an age-old incentive for the composition of incantations. Men were successful, too, in dominating the formal religious ceremony. Priests often took the place of priestesses and led the thiasos or congregation of women. Men took over the women's religious rites, gradually belittled the power of the mother-goddess, and altered the character of the rites to suit their own needs. They took over the training of the girl choirs and the task of composing music for the choirs to sing. We can see this shift, this transition going on; men taking over women's rites at first dressed like women. For example, at the great Pyanepsia, a food festival or bean feast in which the participants ate a common meal out of a common pot, the men porters dressed as women.

With the taking over of religious festivals—always accompanied by the mimetic rite and music—men removed from women's control the activity that had been since time immemorial the principal incentive for the development of musical imagination. Although women continued to practice rites and to sing religious music in organized choirs, their spiritual activity had but little significance for the group then in control. Even priests had lost some prestige, having defaulted in favor of philosophers and the now rising dramatists.

The most remarkable result of this taking over of the women's rites was the development, out of the choral dances of women's bacchantes at the festival of Dionysos, of the great art form of the Greek tragedy. The Greek tragedy is a choral drama built on the singing and dancing choruses of women. The collective reaction of these choral participants, their philosophical interpretations of each stage of the drama, and their invocations to the deities from time to time make the drama. The actual story of a Greek tragedy is slight. The participants are few and the whole is, from the point of view of modern dramatic technique, rather static. A Greek drama represents what would be only the last act of a modern play. All the preliminary material, all the emotional build-up for the dramatic action, is provided by the choruses. The subject matter is traditional and religious, representing a sophisticated secularization of themes, moral and philosophical concepts and stories, some of which were of immemorial antiquity in the women's rites, many of which had long before been given a finished art form in the women's rituals of Crete.

When men took over the whole basic material of the women's festivals, they made some remarkable changes. In the first place, they transformed them from religious rituals into great popular shows, performed not in the sacred place but on a large stadium. In the second place, they took them entirely out of women's hands, even though to do this, numbers of men performers had to dress as women, to cultivate women's voices and women's ways, and to sacrifice their own virile attributes to a silly feminization of their personalities. Men impersonated the women characters; only men and boys sang in the dramatic choruses. Outside of Athens, in small country communities, women may have participated, but in Athens they possibly did not even attend the performance.

In the third place, the writing of plays and preparations of choruses was thrown open to competition, from which the social seclusion and educational limitations imposed on Athenian women naturally barred them. Hundreds of men playwrights, artists, performers competed in putting on plays. The best were selected by the state and given a great public performance. Here, in the public performance before huge masses of nonparticipating spectators and in the intense competition in technical performance, is the characteristic form of much of modern musical and artistic production. It is in every respect a contrast to the original women's rituals on which Greek tragedy is based, performed often in secret, by women, in the sincere religious outpouring of feeling.

The fourth change the men made when they turned women's choral dances into tragedy is the most remarkable. As has been so often said, it was characteristic of women's sense of pain and sorrow that, while they made the most of it artistically with weeping and wailing, there is also implicit in every woman's ceremony the idea of rebirth. This, from time immemorial, had been the faith of women, the essence of their own observation of other living creatures.

The men who took over the choruses and gave them grandeur,

substance, and a kind of solid dignity had no perception whatever of the woman's faith, because they did not have the unique experience on which it is founded—the monthly cycle, pregnancy, and the supreme agony and triumph of childbirth. They saw the emotional effect of the wail songs and wished to keep it. They devoted a great deal of sound masculine logic to explaining the psychological value of a bath in sorrow. It was, said Aristotle, a form of emotional purification, a purgation of the two great fundamental emotions of terror and pity—terror of one's own fate, pity for that of others. But these men, for all their able and earnest efforts, missed the vital point in the women's sorrow—the hope and the intention of invoking the rebirth. There is no rebirth in Greek tragedy. There is really very little faith. Substantial, solid, and somber, the story moves to its climax in death or destruction.

All that remains in the handling by Greek tragic poets of the material they borrowed from the women's rites is the nobility of the women's characters. Many heroines appear in the dramas. Women characters in the great Greek plays are as numerous, as noble, and as intelligent as the men. They reflect the former power of the principle that female energy is creative and the traditional respect accorded it by the men and women of earlier times. Women's spiritual influence was still recent enough to be a suitable topic for the state players, but women themselves were excluded from this development of their ancient rites.

Sensitive men, who saw what was happening, felt that the stilling of women's voices might be the end of the true life of Greece. And so it actually proved. For after the great age of drama and art, which was the first flowering of men's taking over of women's rites, there was but little more inspiration. Euripides thought the women should not allow this usurpation. He even protested against the physical enforcement of chastity. It is deadly, he said, "to hold maids pure perforce."

"In them it lies, in their own hearts; no bawdy throng can soil the soul of her who knows no wrong!" [13]

He implied in *The Bacchae* that they might rise in their might and take back what was their own. One of the leaders of his rebelling Bacchantes sings:

> "With fierce joy I rejoice,
>   Child of a savage shore;

For the chains of my prison are broken, amid the dread
        where I cowered of yore!" [14]

And he represents the maidens as singing their lament and their protest for what men have done to the great inheritance of Greece. The
women who have broken the chains with which men are trying to
bind them sing as they fly ahead of pursuing men and hounds:

> "Will they ever come to me, ever again,
>   The long long dances,
>   On through the dark till the dim stars wane?
>   Shall I feel the dew on my throat, and the stream
>   Of wind in my hair? Shall our white feet gleam
>   In the dim expanses?" [15]

5.

As exemplified by the Chinese, Hindus, Jews, and Greeks—four
widely separated peoples of the ancient world—women's authority
for music making waned at the same time that it weakened for emphasizing her special way of life.

The primitive belief that woman's power to bring life was at least
as strong as man's gave way to an illogical exaggeration of man's
authority. A new theory was persuasively expressed by Aristotle to
the effect that *only* men transmitted the spark of life and that
women were merely incubators carrying the male seed. "The Father
alone is Creator; the Mother is but the Nurse." [16] He even taught
that woman was man in arrested development—a deficit of nature.

But in biological truth, it is the male who is the deficit. In the dis-
tribution of the great gift of life and life-giving, nature discriminates
against man in denying to him the high sense of destiny, the heroic
struggle of flesh and blood, the triumphant wresting of the new life
out of pain, followed by the joy and harmonious happiness of holding
the baby at the breast. Nothing in man's life can touch the ennobling
experience of bearing a child. For man, sex remains but a casual
matter, unless he shares the woman's responsibility for the offspring.

Woman's fundamental assumption for symbolic thinking has always rested upon a faith in herself as a creative being, pre-eminently
potent in the making of both children of the flesh and those of the
imagination. Accordingly, if she could not create life and if she were

inferior to men in nature's scheme, she had no purpose in performing rites which would enable her to transmit the strength of her sex to the community. Women collectively must have lost their primeval faith in their power to bring life or they would not have abandoned so many of their own religious ceremonies.

No one can deny that it was a great advance in civilization when men began to challenge women's natural monopoly of the higher values of sex, of the child, and of the home. There is no substitute for the permanent marriage tie or for a father's leadership over children. But when men, in their laudable determination to establish paternity and to know who their own children were, started shaming girls and locking them up at puberty and when men undertook to manage women's secret rites for them, they trespassed on holy ground.

This sin by men is poignantly expressed in a Persian myth about the beautiful Azada, Spirit of the Harp. As the favorite singer of Prince Bahram Gur, she often accompanied him to the hunt. One day, she taunted him for his cruelty to animals. He, riding his camel —symbol of unbridled male energy—turned upon her. In the vanity of his superior physical strength he killed her, though he loved her and needed her.

In real life, men's unbridled energy wounded women to the quick. For the mother-musician, singing naturally in rituals of her own making, out of the fullness of her own vital experience, they substituted young boys, castrated males, and the courtesan.

The whole romantic love life of Athenian upper-class male society was transferred to boys, dressed in imitation of girls and idealized by the immature son of Aphrodite—the little Cupid. One does not have to go up any dark alleys and by-ways of historical research to discover this. The refined homosexuality of the Greeks, coincident with the taking over by men of women's rituals, choruses, music, and dancing, is written large in the Dialogues of Plato. There one can see exactly how it functioned to the last social detail. And in some of Plato's greatest passages on love and life, one can still feel it in all its decadence and utter ridiculousness.

The castrati, whose singing was later utilized for many centuries in the services of the Christian Church, carried to an equally morbid extreme the attempt to turn men into women for the purpose of singing religious music. As early as 1000 B.C. in Sumer, eunuchs known as "kali" substituted for priestesses. A result of this change in custom was that a god Lumha emerged as the patron musician of religious song and replaced the earlier goddess, "Singer of the magic ritual."

Wherever women as childbearers have been locked up at puberty and kept out of male social life, the musical and highly educated courtesan has flourished. In Japan she became the geisha. In China she is the singsong girl, hostess of the gaily decorated floating restaurants, the "flower boats" on the great Chinese rivers. In Greece she was the hetaera. In the great age of Greece, when the men were taking over the long tradition of women's musical rituals and stimulating them to their last magnificent flowering, Pericles' social establishment was managed by a famous hetaera, Aspasia. She entertained for him, made herself the center of musical, artistic, intellectual, and social life, and functioned socially as the wife of a statesman in America might do today.

In some respects the musical courtesan was the happiest survival of the free woman-musician of antiquity. She had a certain liberty, status, and inspiration to do well which women immured in homes completely lacked. As entertainers everywhere, and especially in the Orient, women retained and even developed a fine musical art of their own. But the courtesans were nevertheless artificial creatures. For motherhood in its full honor and glory was denied them. Children, if they had them, had no status. They were borne furtively, concealed if possible, and were at best a hindrance and inconvenience to women who were entertainers and musicians. Beautiful as the singing courtesan's music might be, intelligently as she might serve as the transmitter of the social and cultural traditions of her race, she could never bring music to the highest point of her culture because she was denied a normal relation to life.

It was only gradually that the serious consequences of women's altered value to civilization affected women musicians. Changes in religious and musical customs did not occur everywhere at the same time, nor did women suddenly lose their prestige in the religious ceremony. For a long time, also, even after the loss of their prestige, women continued to have a theoretical ritual function. With it went the right to participate actively in the sacrifices. This was because ritual generally hangs on long after the hierarchy which developed it has ceased to have influence. Women continued as priestesses in the temples but often under the leadership of men. Women continued to dance and to sing in groups and to play instruments but, more and more, men taught and led them. Women continued to hold hereditary offices but often were not trained sufficiently in current standards of musicianship to compete with men in creating new art forms. The lyric poetess appeared again in Rome, but the sources of her inspiration for creating new forms had by that time run dry. In both Greece and Rome, naturally talented girls who might have developed into creative artists settled down into being mere performers of men's music, mere instruments for men to play upon.

Finally, when the mother-musician became denuded of her musical heritage, wedding songs and laments—always women's greatest contribution to song—no longer appeared in the lists of new compositions. And it is an undeniable fact that the quality of music was vitiated for several centuries until men developed another idiom from an entirely different inspiration.

6.

Inevitably the question arises—why did so many people allow this spiritual mutilation of women to happen? As with all great religious and social upheavals, it was undoubtedly due to the converging influence of a large number of factors—many of them imponderable—no one of which could have been determinative by itself, but which in juxtaposition were irresistible.

One of the direct results of the revolution, and one which profoundly affected the relation of women to music, was the twilight of the goddess.

When the lyric poetess was silenced, Orpheus usurped the power of the Sirens. Apollo assumed the leadership of the Muses and took the lyre from Artemis. (See Plates 49 and 50.) Zeus became the lord over Hera—she who had had a longer past than he and had always been an independent deity. The Father of the Gods even took upon himself the functions of a mother and after having swallowed, or absorbed, a pregnant woman, gave birth to Athene from his forehead.

Not only did many of the powerful old goddesses become subservient to the gods, but more than a few suffered degradation of character. Hera, for example, appeared in story after story as a quarrelsome and jealous wife instead of in her noble aspect as the reflection of woman's life span with its marked rhythm. Aphrodite, heiress of other older goddesses of sexual love and its higher values, once proudly displayed her natural body. In the later stages of Greek art she is depicted in an attitude of embarrassment and shame, trying to cover her female form with her hands. In the metamorphosis of Pan-dora, feminine strength became diverted into a menacing weakness. Originally one of Greece's great earth deities, giver of plenty and beneficence, she changed to a woman consumed with curiosity. With a child's mentality, she opened a chest and let out trouble and evil.

The Jews disposed of goddesses by simply ignoring them. Ishtar, one of those very powerful Semitic deities, became merged with various male divinities of near Eastern mythology. Hymns, formerly addressed to the Great Mother, later invoked the gods first.

Still more significant for us is the change in the text of an old Sumerian legend. In recently discovered tablets, a certain goddess is called Nin-ti. This name has a double meaning, as *tee* in Sumer meant both "rib" and "to make live." Nin-ti had been created—made to live—by the great goddess-mother to cure a pain in her son Enki's side caused by eating forbidden fruit. When this ancient paradise story was taken over by the Jews, they chose the title "Lady of the rib." In Hebrew the words "rib" and "to make live" have nothing in common. The legend then became transformed into the familiar Bible story—the lady became Eve, created by a god-father out of Adam's rib.[17]

From the psychology of the Jews came the omnipotent Father-God of our own religion today, with no daughter, no mate, and even no mother.

CHAPTER X

MARY

1.

AFTER the age of Pericles—with its drama, its beautiful archi-tecture, its noble and lifelike sculpture, and its philosophy which rationalized the old popular myths—the real vitality of Greece rap-idly declined.

The Greek states became involved in the long and exhausting Peloponnesian War. Finally they were organized in the fourth cen-tury by Aristotle's bright young pupil Prince Alexander of Macedon. He started on a career of conquest, in which he took under his rule practically the whole civilized world eastward as far as China, in-cluding Egypt and India. Everywhere he went, he carried Greek custom, language, and art. And everywhere he liberated the deities of the ancient world—such as Cybele, Isis, and Mithra, the Persian god of light—from their localities. When he brought these deities back to Greece, people enthusiastically grasped at variations of the principles of divinity and organized many religious associations for the worship of foreign gods and goddesses.

In these religious groups men and women banded together, ignor-ing ties of national or social rank, emphasizing the relation of the in-dividual rather than the relation of the state to religious observance. The members themselves paid the expenses of the cult practices and allowed office bearers to serve in rotation. Greek women were always eager votaries of the new deities, and by taking a vital interest in the new art of proselytizing, they prepared the way for the missionary work of the early Christians, soon to make their appearance.

Meanwhile a new and powerful state was rising in the Italian pen-insula, where some Greeks had settled and mixed with the Aryan-speaking peoples already there. They in turn had spread outward and eventually took over Greece as well as a good part of Alexander's eastern empire, adopting the Hellenized forms of Eastern religion along with much that was purely Greek. So at the beginning of the Christian era the ancient world was being ruled from Rome. Everywhere Roman engineers had built roads connecting different parts of the empire; everywhere Roman soldiers and governors were stationed and local customs of many sorts were being integrated under a universal, remarkably intelligent Roman law and political government.

Of religion the Romans were generally tolerant. The Romans intended to keep public order. But so long as public order was kept, they did not think what people believed or worshiped was of much significance one way or the other. So under the Roman aegis all sorts of religions flourished and some of the old goddess religions began to get a new lease on life.

Cybele, as the Magna Mater, had thousands of worshipers in Rome and in the Near East, the place of her origin. When the Persian god Mithra, with his secret rites for men, became popular, the women of a family served Cybele, the earth goddess of Phrygia. Shrines have been discovered showing a kind of combination cult of Mithra and Cybele. Romans knew that daughters of noble Phrygians who worshiped Cybele carried torches and tympani and wore the miter later associated with Christian bishops. A great Roman mother-goddess, representing food and fertility, the Bona Dea, received homage in a temple at the Porta Carmentalis, said to have been built in ages past by women's own hands. Her rites were celebrated by women alone in secret ceremonies. Isis, as the goddess who lighted the way of souls to the spirit world and who symbolized divine mother love, had many followers. Her attendants symbolically roused the goddess at matins, laid her to rest at vespers, mourned with her at the annual death of her son, rejoiced with her at his rebirth.

Many noblewomen in Rome and in the Roman provinces served as priestesses. Roman women, indeed, never lost the sacerdotal prestige they had inherited from their feminine forebears of the goddess age. Until the passing of Roman grandeur, the vestal virgins remained hallowed as guardians of the Sibylline books and of the sacred fire. In the goddess cults, it was the custom, too, for rites to be celebrated in the home at private altars. Every woman could offer sacrifice, burn incense, pour the libation, play instruments, dance, and sing magic formulas for all the rites of the life cycle. She could play the flute, double flute, lyre, zither, horn, and trumpet, especially at weddings and funerals. Accompanied often by hired female mourners (*praeficae*), she could participate in the important ceremony of waking the dead, she could sing the dirges (*nenia*) and make the gesture (*planctus*) appropriate for calling out to the deceased (*conclamatio*). She could carry on the immemorially old customs of primitive faith. (See Plates 51, 52, 53, and 54.)

2.

While the goddess cults were thus reviving, something much more momentous happened. In a small province of the Roman Empire, in what had formerly been the kingdom of Israel and Judea, an obscure young woman bore a child and laid him in a manger. He was born in Bethlehem in Judea, but he grew up in his mother's home town of Nazareth—which was a very different place from the grim, semiarid land around Jerusalem, dominated by the equally grim and arid male intellectualism of Jewish teachers and leaders, who were called Pharisees. Jesus grew up in the sweet garden land of Nazareth, where spring comes with a sudden mantling of fresh green grass and a burst of flowers, not far from the port of Haifa on the Mediterranean. All the winds of Greek and Oriental thought blew across Nazareth. Life was much pleasanter here than in Jerusalem and semidesert Judea. So Jesus grew up in his mother's house with a clear-minded, sunny indifference to the Pharisees and the extremes of male intellectualism and dogmatism they represented. When he set out to challenge the Pharisees, in the three intense years of his ministry, they finally killed him. But not before he had become the representative of a great new hope for the human race.

When Mary brought the savior of mankind into the world, the majority of people in the Roman Empire were still imbued with the primitive religious idea of keeping in touch with the flow of all life. To this idea Jesus gave a new meaning. Jesus believed in a life force of which everyone was a part. To him, this life force was God, the Creator of the universe and of every living thing. He taught, "Thou shalt love the Lord thy God with all thy heart, and with all thy soul, and with all thy mind." [1] This, he said, was the "first and great commandment." Having identified himself with God, the Creator and the life force, he, being the son of God, told his followers that they, too, were one with him, saying: "I am the vine, ye are the branches." [2] By using imagery to which the people of those times were accustomed, Jesus showed that he did not belittle the old beliefs or deny their validity. His criticisms were directed only against the Jewish scribes and Pharisees, "hypocrites," caring for the dead letter of the law and overemphasizing the dogmas of the priests.

The superlative contribution of Jesus was what he added to the old idea of keeping in touch with the life force—of "loving God." He introduced a new idea associated with that force. He taught that human beings—children of God—were also to keep in touch with each other. They were to cultivate a new and a more mature idea of what the ethics of human relations should be. "Thou shalt love thy neighbor as thyself." This, said Jesus, was the second great commandment—to have a dynamic sympathy for one's struggling fellow creatures. In this ideal is inherent a faith as dynamic and as enduring as the old ideal of unity with a higher power. The principle of keeping strong a bond of love among human beings of different races is as independent of dogmas and as widely applicable as the principle of keeping in touch with the flow of life. Each age, every people can use whatever symbols correspond to the thinking of its age and of its people. And so can each group shift to new application as events change. In the beginning, under the direct rays of Jesus' magnetic personality, the validity of that ideal must have been understood by his followers. Otherwise they would not have been believers and would not have gone out into the world as a great civilizing force.

Jesus' two commandments were both compatible with the life of women's spirit. Women had always been conspicuously active in the cults of the life cycle. Women had always been active in the cultivation of unselfish human relations. It has often been admitted that mother love is the basis of all altruism. And goddesses, symbolizing mother love, had been worshiped by both men and women aeons before Jesus called his Father the God of Love. Jesus' nature itself had none of the overmasculine characteristics, such as physical strength and aggressiveness. Rather it reflected qualities common to civilizing motives in both men and women. Jesus clearly intended his commandments to be accepted by both sexes. He never intimated in any way that he considered woman less able than man to understand his message. In the Gospels and in the other traditions, Mary Magdalene is represented as excelling all the disciples in her understanding of the life of the spirit.

Throughout the period of his life on earth, Jesus was surrounded by women. A mother bore and nurtured him. Women were his friends and disciples. Almost five hundred years later, Bishop Cyril of Alexandria wrote about seven Marys—Magdalene among them—who were the intimate companions of Jesus. Mary and Martha, the sisters of Gospel fame, have long been regarded as symbols of many women followers. Martha represents the woman who is interested in the practical details of fostering life. Mary reflects the ever present longing in women for spiritual development. In this symbolism the intense natural spirituality of women has been emphasized.

Women followed Jesus to Calvary, bewailing and lamenting in anticipation of their Lord's death. His mother watched him die, and according to the custom of her people, made her own lament:

> "My Lord, my son, where has the beauty
> of thy form sunk? How shall I endure
> to see thee suffering such things?
> For this I weep, my son, because thou
> sufferest unjustly, because the lawless
> Jews have delivered thee to a bitter
> death. Without thee, my son, what will
> become of me? How shall I live without
> thee? What sort of a life shall I spend?
> Where are thy disciples, who boasted
> that they would die with thee?
> Where are those healed by thee?
> How has no one been found to help thee?
> Bend down, O Cross, that I may embrace
> and kiss my son—
> Bend down, O Cross, I wish to throw
> my arms around my son.
> Bend down, O Cross, that I may bid farewell
> to my son like a mother." [3]

After Jesus' body had been placed in the sepulcher, Mary Magdalene, Mary the mother of Jesus, and Mary Salome went there to see whether the body had been properly cared for. Again the women acted according to custom and so were the first to see the risen Lord and to rejoice over his resurrection. At birth, in the intimate circle of friends, at death, and at the rebirth—at all of the rites of the life cycle—women were beside the Lord.

3.

Supreme among the women associated with Jesus was his mother, Mary. She was always held in great esteem by the first friends and disciples of Jesus. Women followed her all her life, saying: "We will not separate from thee, O Mary, blessed Mother, except through death." [4] The apostles revered her, too, and were at her bedside when she died, watching the women burn incense and listening to their laments. In this universal honor to Mary, the harsh and fearful barriers men had placed about her sex were quietly swept away. Joseph, as husband, became the woman's best friend, her shield against scandal, the first and most ardent believer in her divinely inspired mission. So the holy family, Joseph, Mary, and the child, emerged as a beautiful collective image, full of tenderness. It wanted only a daughter to make it complete.

The new religion of Jesus gathered into itself many of the beliefs of the old goddess cults. Although the first friends of Jesus—the first Christians—were of course Jews, worshipers of the great gods and goddesses of the countries visited by missionaries soon came to believe Jesus' message. Christians then became a larger group of people with very different religious backgrounds. Owing to the variations in race and in temperament, men and women could not avoid giving Jesus' parables different interpretation. Sects, or "heresies," as schools of thought were often called, developed in different localities, each one with its own idea of what Jesus had intended, each with its own version of a Christian religion.

In the days before Christ was born, one of the favorite attempts to represent the relative values of men and women was the personification of the life force as mother, with a young or male god, often but not always her son. The son-mother concept was the most appealing of these because it was the most readily understood by the human heart. It was natural that Mary, with her son, should step into the place prepared by these old popular beliefs. John of Damascus even spoke of Mary as "the soverign lady to whom the whole of creation has been made subject by her son."

Many early Christians saw in Mary another great goddess-mother. Among these were the Copts, who lived in Egypt and whose church was founded by St. Mark. A statue of a woman holding a child has been recovered from that region. It is so like the old Egyptian representations of Isis holding Horus that one can see in it the eternal theme of mother and child. In the Coptic spell known as the "Prayer of the Virgin," Mary sings her own holy dogma in the attitude of affirmation familiar to the great mothers of earlier times: "I am Mariham, I am Maria, I am the Mother of the Life of the whole world!" [5]

A variation of the new thinking about man and woman was that of the Gnostics, who carried reverence for the beneficent power of women over from the old world to the new. They professed a belief in the union of a world mind (masculine) with a world soul (feminine). Since each principle represented resources that they assumed not to be possessed by the other, they thought that contact should be made with both. This is similar to saying that, to a satisfactory theology, a goddess is as important as a god. These people worshiped Sophia, divine mother, and her two daughters, who, as the spirit of wisdom, were represented by a dove, exactly like the old dove-goddess of Crete. The Gnostics also kept to the ancient way of expecting women to have official positions in the priesthood. Women and girls invoked Sophia in choral hymns:

"Thou Mother of Compassion, come—
Come, thou revealer of the Mysteries concealed!
Come, thou who art more ancient far than the five holy Limbs—
Mind, Thought, Reflection, Thinking, Reasoning.

"Come, thou who givest joy to all who are at one with Thee;
Come and commune with us in this thanksgiving (eucharist)
Which we are making in Thy name in this love-feast (agape)
To which we have assembled at Thy call!" [6]

A sect called the Marianites (also called Priscillians, Kollyridians, or Montanists) agreed with the Gnostics in deifying female power. Two prophetesses from Phrygia, Priscilla and Maximilla, had been among the founders of this sect. They came from the east with a legend that Priscilla had met Jesus in a mystic embrace by which she had been inoculated with a superior wisdom. From the scanty records that remain about the Marianites, women's authority and activity stand out with more force than in any other early Christian group. They, too, had a hymn that they sang at death in anticipation of the rebirth:

Grace goes with the round-dance,
I wish that the double flute might continue!
Let us all dance with all our hearts—Amen.

Whenever one dances the mourning dance!
Beat your breasts—Amen.[7]

The significance of these verses, entirely aside from the evidence that instruments and dancing accompanied the singing, lies in the word "grace," which was interpreted as meaning "mother," "regeneration," or "alleluia"—the ancient cry of joy for the rebirth. Somewhere the alleluia received an impersonation as a symbol of feminine potency and appeared during the Middle Ages as a tangible object. At the alleluiatic offices for Saturday in Septuagesima, it was buried in the earth while a verse closely resembling the Marianites' hymn was sung:

"Alleluia, joyful Mother,
Alleluia, voice of rebirth,"

to which a response, similar to the hymns of longing for Ishtar, was given:

"Alleluia, while she is present, they
entertain her, and they greatly long
for her when she withdraws herself." [8]

To this day, the alleluia is never sung in the Roman Catholic Church during Lent, the time of mourning and waiting for the rebirth.

4.

In time the figure of Mary, who was replacing the old goddesses in popular love, became the storm center of the battle between the male intellectuals, who wanted to assert the dogma of exclusive male supremacy in heaven, and the people, who wanted to feel that they could open their hearts to a divine mother. The Jewish element in Christianity was naturally opposed to a goddess-mother, since one had been ignored by the Jews for centuries. So, also, was a certain kind of Greek and Roman intellectual trained in the precepts of Aristotle. Sermons delivered to the congregation were frequently devoted to a discussion of Mary's status. According to fifth-century custom, the people applauded or hissed as the preacher pleased or displeased them. When Dorotheus shouted, "If anyone says that Mary is Theotocos [Mother of God] let him be anathema," [9] the congregation made a great uproar in protest and stampeded out of the church.

Finally the popular determination to have Mary as the divine mother with Christ caused Bishop Nestorius to be brought up before a council of the Church at Ephesus in 431 on charges of detracting from the glory and sacredness of Mary. No more dramatic setting for a trial on such a charge could have been chosen than the city of Ephesus. For in Ephesus the worship of Artemis, under her Roman name of Diana, had flourished from of old. Here in Ephesus, Mary herself had died, according to one legend, and had been carried to heaven by choirs of singing angels.

The council was opened by Cyril of Alexandria, who made what we would call the keynote address. In terms long sacred to Artemis, he described Mary as both "virgin," or free and independent in her selfhood, and "mother." Through her as virgin and mother, he said, "Heaven triumphs; the angels are made glad, devils driven forth, the tempter overcome, and the falling creature raised up even to heaven." [10]

While the Church Fathers were thus debating, the crowds surging outside cried, "Hail, Mary, Mother and Virgin," as crowds in Ephesus had once surged and sung, "Great is Diana of the Ephesians." And when the judges determined to excommunicate Nestorius for his heresy in denying the glory of Mary, the crowds with a great uproar picked up the judges and carried them through the streets with torchlights flaring, incense floating in fragrant clouds. The whole city sprang into light and music with illumination and the cries of alleluia.

Elsewhere the controversy settled itself by merging a pagan goddess with Mary, and henceforth devoting to Mary, as mother, many of the old rites of rebirth and the women's symbols of birth. The union of Artemis as guardian of the crops with Mary as the blessed one who protects the harvest took place in the celebration of Mary's assumption into heaven on August 15, the day formerly dedicated to Artemis in Syria. Among the Celts whom Christian missionaries were converting, the moon goddess Bridget was transformed into Mary. The Celtic woman's festival, which had to do symbolically with sacred fires and the torch of life, became the Christian festival of

Candlemas, and was merged with the celebration of Mary's ritual purification after childbirth.

5.

With Mary thus established as queen of heaven, in the glory of the old moon goddess, there was a precedent for keeping lesser feminine spirits. More than one specialized goddess became a Christian saint; many pagan shrines on a holy mountain or beside a sacred spring became the site of a church or monastery; many feminine symbols of creative power endowed Christian edifices with holiness. The water of life became the holy water, and its container, which primitive women thought of as the womb, became the baptismal font. The old flower symbol, which had seemed to women to represent her own organs and the seat of her power as mother, became the rose window. There were rivers of life and trees of life in the new Christian symbolism—new images that were also as old as woman's faith in birth and rebirth. Without these, Christian art would have lacked much of its beauty. Without the alleluia, triumphant cry of women's ancient rites, Christian music would have been deprived of its most gracious song.

Women gave the new religion their goddess. They also gave it their rites. From the beginning, the old rites of the rebirth were of the very essence of the Christian ritual. None of the sects broke completely with the past and all of them adapted old rituals and familiar forms of music to the new Christian ideals. Of all the ceremonies of the early church, the most sacred and the most characteristic was the partaking of bread and wine—symbols of the body and blood of Christ, the tokens of the rebirth. From time immemorial, human mothers had offered their bodies and their blood in actual childbirth. Goddess-mothers had done the same in symbolic births of the fruits of the earth, of the new moon, or of the life-bringing child. Epiphanius, one of the early bishops (second century), tells of a prayer about the bread of life used by the Kollyridians, a sect that took its name from a loaf of coarse bread. The prayer was taken from one of the cults of Cybele, the Magna Mater: "Bread of Life, the eating of which brings immortality." [11]

Probably no primitive rite has been more closely associated with women than the one connected with grain or bread. Women, as wielders of agricultural magic, had a long tradition of symbolic representations of feminine food bringers and also of ritual in honor of the various grain goddesses. In Spain, women of the Marianite sect held secret rites at which the eating of sacrificial bread, dedicated to Mary, was the principal feature. Baskets filled with loaves of bread featured in the annual grape festival at Aquileia and were carried by certain elderly Christian women who had an official position in the hierarchy of that sect. Old Russian sermons describe ritual meals served by women for *Rod* and *Rojánizi,* a pair of words meaning birth or race or family. *Rojánizi* means women in labor. Sometimes the same rite was performed in honor of the Virgin Mary, who had inherited the attributes of the old goddesses of the family cult. "White bread and cheese were served, the goblets were filled with wine or drinking honey, and the troparion to the Holy Virgin was sung. Passing to each other the bread and wine, the women drank and ate, thinking that they were praising the Holy Virgin and the birth of mankind." [12]

But in addition to the traditional ritual of eating and drinking symbolic sustenance, early Christian women had a real association of feasting with Jesus. Nothing in the gospels bears a greater stamp of human reality than the reports of the moments when Jesus sat down at the table to break bread with his friends. At the home of Lazarus, Mary and Martha were with him. His mother, Mary, was at the marriage of Cana. Gnostic Christians included women in the list of the faithful who gathered at the last supper. Catacomb pictures show a woman seated at the Lord's table. [13]

Many of the other primitive and pagan devices to bring about the rebirth survived—incense, the holy water for baptism, the torch of life in the guise of candles, the dance, the cry of joy as the alleluia, musical instruments, and song in the form of incantations or litanies. According to variations in practice among the different Christian sects, many are used today with the intent of bringing about resurrection and spiritual regeneration.

In the early days, women participated fully in the rites of the rebirth. All Christian men and women were baptized, confirmed, and given extreme unction at death. All communicants partook of the sacrament. Women continued to officiate at times when devices for the rebirth were needed with their old symbols of incense, lights, and flowers. Mary burned incense when she visited the sepulcher, and so did her women followers use the censer at her deathbed. Many other references can be found relating to the burning of incense by women, enough to give the impression that its use was quite customary. In one of their formal ceremonies the Marianite women carried candles or torches to symbolize the light of the world, and the idea of women guarding the light of the world persisted for many centuries. The Brigittine nuns of the Middle Ages in Ireland kept the sacred fire of Kildare burning and evidently were the successors of priestesses who had been officials in a cult of Bridget, the moon goddess of the Celts. It was a general custom for women to wear flowers and to wave green branches at the rites of birth, marriage, death. Is it not still usual in most Christian churches for women to have charge of arranging flowers on the altar?

Just as the old power of the mother-goddess was transferred to Mary, so women retained in many places the positions as priestesses, officials, and musicians they had held in earlier days. The Arabian Christians counted a symbolic disciple, Helena, or Selene the moon goddess, among the chosen of Christ. The Gnostics recognized the three Marys—the mother, Salome, and Magdalene—as members of Christ's inner circle. Extant fragments of Gnostic literature reveal that women participated in the religious ceremonies of that group as representatives of the divine mother, just as the priestesses did of old. Some of the groups made women bishops. Some allowed women to baptize converts—the rite of the rebirth. Many recognized the prophetess. The four daughters of Philip the Evangelist were lauded by historians long after the first century, the era of their high activity, and the mantle of their age-old power fell finally upon the shoulders of the deaconess. The Arabian Christians appointed women as readers and chanters of the holy word. More than one sect must have invested women as regular priestesses, and in some places women as priestesses must have continued to function for many centuries. Otherwise, Roman women holding office in the ninth century could not have been visited by Alcuin and urged on by him to greater activity in preaching.

6.

The old religious associations of women, against which men as fathers of families had battled so long, both by passing laws against them and spreading scandals about them, were revived in associations of Christian women pledged to further the new religion. All accounts of early Christian activities agree that women's wholehearted espousal of the cause was a determining factor in enabling the first Christians, a mere handful of people, to survive in a hostile, military-minded world. Rich women were donors of wealth, of their houses, and of their time. They supported and comforted traveling missionaries. They distributed alms and nursed the sick. Women and girls startled the civilized world by their steadfastness to Christian ideals and by their ready consent to martyrdom.

Among these first Christians, organizations of dedicated women developed more than a century before monasteries for men were started. This was a natural outcome of women's priestly and ritualistic function. For centuries there had been organizations of women in attendance on the temple and generally vowed to chastity, at least for the period of their service. Immemorially old in women's religious life was the idea of escape from men and children for certain periods. Such escape involved, naturally, a period of release from the demands of sex. This was very different, in essence, from the lifelong vow of chastity later taken by women, for that was founded on an idea of her biological functioning that degraded women. But their earlier assumption of, or assertion of, their right to freedom in the service of the goddess, at least for periods, was an assertion of spiritual dignity.

The earliest known Christian leader in organizing girls was Thecla, who traveled with Paul as a missionary. About 50 A.D. she settled with a large following of women in the caves of a mountain near Seleucia, Syria. From beginnings such as these the great monastic system eventually developed.

Women and girls who voluntarily chose to develop the life of the spirit enjoyed a prestige comparable to that of the priestess. St. John Chrysostom estimated them as high above other women as the angels are higher than mortals. The word "nun," as such a woman came to be called, is a translation of *nonna,* which means "a holy person" and also "mother." Curiously enough, the masculine term *nonnus* was never used by the men celibates. They were called monks (*monazontes*). A fourth-century writer, Basileus, in describing Thecla and her followers, said that he could not enumerate the holy women of the first century without making a book as large as that of Hesiod. Over and over again, until late in the Middle Ages, nuns were credited with miraculous powers of healing and with prophetic vision. Many of them attained the rank of saint.

Aside from the purely religious reason of wishing to save their souls, women were undoubtedly attracted to the monastic ideal by the reverence to their persons. They found in monasticism a counter-action to the growing tendency to exclude them from the governing group. By joining the ranks of the select, they remained in the sacred circle. Christian women by becoming nuns raised themselves from the status of Jewish women. Apparently they were approaching the status of the pagan priestess. Still another reason for the Christian woman's support of asceticism was the practical advantage offered her. In those turbulent times, the convents provided not only social security for the timid but a career outside of marriage for the bold. Women found scope for energy and talent, opportunity to cultivate intellectual, spiritual, and especially musical tastes. It was here in the convents, where women and girls assembled in the name of the Lord, that they participated in the evolution of the ritual and music of the new culture.

For this they surrendered the right in which primitive woman had founded her sense of spiritual dignity—the right to bear a child. They did this more easily because they were under a delusion almost universal among early Christians—the idea that Christ would come back to them shortly, in all his heavenly might, and they would all be caught up with him into glory, where there is no marrying or giving in marriage, but male and female are "as the angels in heaven."

So women transferred from physical birth to spiritual rebirth their sense of their mission as women. It was a hopeful beginning of what was to prove ultimately a devitalization of their power as women. But women were not to realize this for many centuries.

7.

In these early Christian centuries, in many places, dance and ritual remained much as they had been in the mother's ancient religion. Most of the Christian sects retained the religious dance with its long social and artistic history. The Therapeutae, the Kollyridians, the Marianites (also called Priscillians or Montanists), and the Gnostics were groups who danced at ceremonies that were identical with primitive and pagan ceremonies. The reborn disciples of the Marianites, a sect in which women had great influence, were united to Jesus by means of performing a sacred dance called the Hymn of Jesus (incorporated with the Leucian Second-Century collection of Acts of John). A surviving form of this choral dance was performed by village boys and girls in Cornwall up to a hundred years ago. Dancing to stimulate fertility was usual at weddings, at spring festivals, and at funerals. The custom of dancing at funerals was kept up by the Christian Bogomiles until the fourteenth century. Sarcophagi have been discovered in the south Slavic region of Bosnia showing dances in which men and women holding hands and singing dirges stepped backward instead of forward. That women participated in the religious dances of the first Christians until the fourth century is certain from St. Chrysostom's question: "If neither girls nor married women may dance, who then will dance?" He answered himself with the words: "No one." [14]

To all Christians, dance and song had the same significance that it had to the ancients and that it has for the primitives to this day. None of the early Church Fathers doubted the divine origin of music or its magic power. They thought that music affected the mind and pushed the will into action. "Without music, no discipline can be perfect," [15] said Isidore of Seville. And Theodoret attributed to music the faculty of changing the mood of the soul and of inducing any desired emotion.

Christians authorized the use of music to enhance the affective power of their rites and their prayers. At death, especially, they believed that the purpose of music was to lead the departed spirit to the grave and that music had a necromantic influence on the souls of the dead. In the beginning they naturally lacked original Christian music for these vital needs. Just as the ritual and the liturgy had to be developed, so did the appropriate music.

In its learned and studied aspect, music met Christianity chiefly in the great pagan cities like Rome, Alexandria, Edessa, Antioch, and Byzantium. These centers were inhabited by thousands of prosperous people, many of whom belonged to the most noble families of the pagan world. Music was an integral part of social and religious life and women were expected to be musicians. The Roman historian Pliny said of his wife, Calpurnia: "She takes my verses, sets them to music and sings them to the harp." [16] Lucian of Samosata, second century, described the musical customs of his times. The musicians he mentions are almost exclusively women, both amateur and professional. In developing their music, the early Christians of pagan origin could hardly avoid the woman musician. As we shall see presently, the most renowned of the choirs in the first centuries consisted of girls.

Early Christian annals are filled with references to the participation of women in music. The leaders clearly wished to utilize this musical talent to further Christian ideals. With the idea of binding music to Christian texts, many of them composed litanies, work songs, and hymns for women and girls to sing. The mother Mary herself was held up to them as an example: "None was found before her . . . more elegant in singing!" [17] Young people were taught to greet their father upon his home-coming by singing alleluia. Widows were "to sit at home, sing, pray, read, watch, and fast, and speak to God continually in songs and hymns." [18] St. Chrysostom exhorted fathers to sing daily with their wives and children: "I tell you this: that you should not only sing praises yourselves, but that you should also teach your wives and children to sing canticles, such as these psalms and hymns, while they are weaving and doing their work, and especially while they sit at meals." [19]

In the early church services, when men and women often had to meet secretly in underground catacombs to avoid detection by the authorities, and when the co-operation of women signified life to the sect, congregational singing was a feature of worship. Even among people of Jewish affiliation, the women evidently took part. Philo, the Jew (first century), gives a vivid description of the vigils of the Therapeutae, Jewish people who had become converted to Christianity.

The vigil is conducted on this wise. They all stand up in a crowd, and in the midst of the symposium first of all two choirs are formed, one of men, and one of women, and for each, one most honoured and skilled in song is chosen as a leader and director. Then they sing hymns composed to the praise of God, in many metres, and to various melodies, in one singing together in unison, and in another antiphonal harmonies, moving their hands in time and dancing; and being transported with divine enthusiasm, they perform one while lyric measures, and at another tragic plainsong, strophes and antistrophes, as need requires. Then when each chorus, the men separately, and the women separately, had partaken of food by itself, as in the feasts of Bacchus, and quaffed the pure God-loving wine, they mingle together and become one choir out of two—the mimetic representation of that of yore standing on the shore of the Red Sea on account of the miracles wrought there. To this (the singing of the Son of Moses) the chorus of the male and female *Therapeutae* afforded a most perfect resemblance with its variant and concordant melodies; and the sharp searching tone of the women together with the baritone sound of the men effected a harmony both symphonious and altogether musical. Perfectly beautiful are their motions, perfectly beautiful their discourse; grave and solemn are these carollers; and the final aim of their motions, their discourse, and their choral dances is piety.[20]

During the fourth and fifth centuries many of the Church Fathers spoke of the congregational singing and of women's part in it. St. Jerome, St. Augustine, St. Zenobi, and St. Gregory of Naziana all praise the beautiful choral singing of women. St. Ambrose of Milan said: "The women sing the psalm well." [21] He was one of those bishops who exhorted the faithful to let antiphonal singing delight them, being particularly interested in the artistic effect that could be procured by using to musical advantage the different timbre of male and female voices—the men having a choir with their own leader and the women having a choir with a woman conductor. Singing at funerals was also often performed in the antiphonal manner, psalms having been substituted for pagan songs and instrumental music. Among the Marianites, men and women had separate choruses. In behalf of the departed soul, the women sang, "Lord, have mercy!" and the men responded, "Christ, have mercy!" Another favorite mode of group singing was the custom of having people give a response to the celebrant. In the Mozarabic rite, used principally in Spain, the Lord's Prayer was given in this way: "Our Father who art in Heaven"; the congregation would respond, "Amen," to this verse and to the three succeeding verses. After "Give us this day our daily bread," they chanted, "Which is God." To the celebrant's "And lead us not into temptation," the people voiced their appeal, "But deliver us from evil!" [22] Upon occasions when special invocations for mercy seem to be required, the amen to special prayers was repeated three hundred times, then two hundred, and finally one hundred. Evidently, there was no objection to the mixed group of singers, and women were eagerly solicited to enhance the affectiveness of congregational singing with their rich voices. In many Christian communities, men and women together chanted the Kyrie Eleison—the worshipers' own plea for mercy—and the Alleluia—their own hymn of praise.

From the middle of the second century, some of the church leaders sponsored the singing of women and girls in liturgical choirs. So proficient an instrument for furthering Christian ideals was at first highly valued, always, of course, with the understanding that Christian words and melodies be provided. Clement of Alexandria was one of the first leaders interested in establishing an official status for girl singers. He explained clearly how he intended to transform the old women's rituals into a Christian ceremony. "This is the mountain beloved of God . . . consecrated to dramas of the truth. . . . And there revel on it, not the Maenads, the sisters of Semele, the thunderstruck, but the daughters of God, the fair lambs who celebrate the holy rites of the word, raising a sober choral chant." [23]

The "sober choral chant" was raised as early as the year 150 by the girls of the Arian sect. Bardasanes and Harmonius made their church famous by the lovely singing of the young women, and drew thereby many converts. One of the most renowned of the girl choirs sang in the parish of Bishop Paul of Samosata. Leader of the sect known as Marcion, he had his headquarters at Antioch. The Marcions gave women a high status and allowed them to have positions of responsibility. During the second century, Antioch belonged to the kingdom of Zenobia, one of the masterful Arabian queens. Women there evidently enjoyed a liberty and independence similar to that of their queen. Elected to the office of prefect and president of the games that occurred there annually, they took an active part in social life. Antioch was a rich community, the home of some of the noblest people of pagan society. It was also filled with women musicians, both amateur and professional. Obviously, in order to satisfy the requirements of a musically cultured society the church choirs must have been the finest. They were formed of girls, both because women musicians abounded in Antioch and because the Marcion Christians sanctioned the woman musician.

Girl choirs are mentioned by Aetheria, a Galician lady who made a pilgrimage to the Church of the Holy Sepulchre in Jerusalem in 392. "Every day before cockcrow all the doors of the Church of the Resurrection are opened, and all the monks and virgins, as they call them here, go thither, and not they alone, but lay people also, both men and women, who desire to begin their vigil early. And from that hour to daybreak, hymns are said and psalms are sung responsively, and antiphons in like manner. . . ." [24] The practice of training women and girls to sing psalms is also referred to in other early documents.

By the fourth century a girl choir had become a well-established institution. Any group that did not have one fell behind in popularity.

The good Bishop Ephraem of Edessa in Syria frankly organized his
"Daughters of the Convent" as a counterattraction to the Arian choirs
that had been functioning successfully for three hundred years.
An anonymous Syrian biographer described Ephraem's ardor in
training his girls and mentioned the fact that he "arranged for them
different kinds of songs." Besides singing odes and responses every
morning, the "Daughters" often journeyed to the dwelling of a dead
woman, even far away into the mountains. According to the Syrian
custom of the times, they acted there as professional mourners.

In the Jewish Christian portion of that population today, women
are still singing dirges and often go as trained groups—the *lattâmât*
—to the house of the deceased. Sometimes there is a special solo
singer, and after each verse of the *kauwâla's* dirge, the chorus utters
its lamentation. In the country districts the trained choir of women
is often absent, and the chorus is then made up of all the women,
who form a ring around the tent. They are called the *reddâdât* or
neddâbât—the sorrowing women who sing the response to the solo-
ist.[25] The dirge sung by Ephraem's nuns was probably an adaptation
of the Syrian poetess-musicians':

"Tears are in the eyes, in the ears are sounds of woes,
In the mouth is wailing, and sadness in the heart:
Comfort me, Oh Lord!
This day separates a woman from her house.
Her soul hath gone away, as Thy command hath decreed!
Behold, she hath become dust, as Thy command hath decreed!
Lord, make her live anew!"[26]

8.

In the early centuries of Christianity, when Mary was becoming
established as queen of heaven, there is every indication that women
participated more fully in the ritual and in the music of the various
groups than they did in the period following the fourth century. In
the beginning, they accompanied Jesus in close intimacy. Nor were
their natural ways ever condemned by him. Consequently, women
were welcomed by men as co-operators in establishing the struggling
faith. Some groups gave women positions of authority. Women
frequently celebrated secret rites in a manner similar to goddess worshipers. Evidence is not lacking that they were initiating their own

rites, recasting their own music, and preparing in their own way for a renaissance.

In music, mothers joined in congregational singing. For about four hundred years nuns functioned as liturgical choirs in important churches, notably those in Edessa, Antioch, Jerusalem, and Alexandria. These choirs have been traced back to the second century and were regarded by many Christians as fitting instruments for the performance of sacred music.

The teachings of Jesus appeared to have arrested the threat of universal male dominance. Women were released by this touching new faith, which kept the best of their original religious practices while regenerating them and making them more simply and appealingly human. The idea of mother love, of women as the bearers of life and invokers of rebirth, could be insensibly transformed into Christ's definition of divine and human love and spiritual rebirth into life everlasting.

There was everything inherent in the ideals and practices of Jesus' immediate followers for the institution of a way of life patterned on the two great commandments. There was the Saviour, incorporating in his sublime person the noblest and most lovable characteristics of both men and women, symbolizing the rebirth from childhood into maturity, showing the way, the truth, and the life. There were the men and women believers, led by the mother, symbol as always of love and the good life. An organized theology, hierarchy, and system of rites with both male and female symbols and with men and women representatives of the divine symbols should have been the natural result of Christ's teaching and example, the normal way to interpret the new commandment of love and the new ideal for the rebirth of the spirit. And although the very first Christians were Jews, the worship of the Father-God of the Jews was from the beginning combined with the worship of the beloved son and his holy mother.

Above all, in the early days of Christianity the benign woman spirit began to live anew in the beautiful personality of Mary. The people of those times perceived that the ultimate life of the world is not exclusively or even predominantly male. No father, even a Father in heaven, can give all the heart craves. But Mary was not an old goddess revived. She was a unique spirit, with a place peculiarly her own in the love and memory of the earliest Christians. Independently of any attributes inherited from the goddesses of ancient times, Mary rose by virtue of her own power to be the symbol of the Christian virtues love and mercy. In medieval times she was regarded by men as the spirit that drew them irresistibly heavenward, by women as their special guardian, and by all as the chief mediator between sinners and divine mercy. Mary received the prayers of those who craved tolerance and love, the very qualities Jesus had sponsored and the very essence of the Christian ideal. Her authority rested on the human appreciation that these attributes are qualities native to women and that a feminine image of them is essential to a Christian way of life.

Theological edicts can settle a theoretical dispute but not a psychological reality. No theologians could destroy Mary. They could, however, and they did prevent Mary from securing for her women followers their normal function of representing her as priestesses and singers. For side by side with this promise of the resurrection of women's spirit and song there was, in early Christianity, another power working to imprison and degrade women. So the story must move on to the fateful end, in the so-called Dark Ages of Europe, when Artemis was at last completely gagged and bound.

CHAPTER XI

ARTEMIS BOUND

1.

"DAUGHTERS of Jerusalem, weep not for me, but weep for yourselves, and for your children. . . . For if they do these things in a green tree, what shall be done in the dry?" [1]

On his death march, Jesus turned to the wailing women with these pregnant words. Was he not presaging the tragedy that was to befall the Christian way? He had shown the people the way to rebirth—"death unto sin, rebirth unto righteousness." He had explained that the primitive child must mature into the civilized adult, into a new state of humanity in which tolerance and love for others were to be the controlling force. Far in advance of his time he had forecast the unity of male and female, pointing out that in the realm of the spirit, in "heaven," there would be no distinction of sex and implying an equality on earth in human ability to cultivate the life of the spirit. But already, as the heaviness of his mood indicates, he had sensed failure in drawing disciples into a unit sufficiently strong for the realization of his ideals.

From the beginning there had been dissensions in the ranks of Christians. Questions of doctrine having nothing to do with the principle of "death unto sin, rebirth unto righteousness," had interfered with the practical application of Jesus' ideals.

The most important of these barriers against the full flowering of Jesus' ideals arose from a misunderstanding of certain of Jesus' sayings. Men and women were firmly convinced that the end of the world was coming immediately. Judgment Day, with its system of rewards and punishments, they thought was close at hand. This belief led them to regard the material world as of no importance and to think of the spirit as separate from the body. On the ground that

165

procreation was useless in view of the approaching end of the world and also that sex intercourse bound the body to the earth, they condemned both and set up an ideal of chastity and continence. Marriage between men and women was tolerated only of necessity for those who were less pure in heart. A real union with Christ was deemed possibly only by the chaste. The ideal was for the individual, perfected soul, and for the whole church, to become the bride of Christ. Generally, people began to believe that no one could be truly holy without forsaking the natural urges to love and to reproduce life.

And so the ascetic ideal took root and quickly grew to fantastic proportions. Some devotees, in fanatical enthusiasm for mortifying the flesh, retired to caves in the mountains, ate only the minimum amount to sustain life, and denied themselves all human intercourse. A little later, others established communities and organized their lives for the rites, prayers, and music that were to save their souls. In the beginning, these enthusiasts were not interested in or moved by our ideas of Christian charity, which we have derived from Christ's second great commandment. They were concerned solely with a technique for gaining life everlasting.

Thus there was a split in the ranks of Christians. Only some took the vows of obedience to the antinatural way. The majority of men and women kept on mating and having children, but even they accepted as more holy the idea of the negation of life.

This morbid idea was woven into the warp and woof of early Christian thinking. Instead of birth being a holy thing, a symbol of the human being's share in the creative power of the universal life force and of humanity's link with all living things, it became a symbol of man's "fall from grace." Children henceforth were to be born "in sin," and "redeemed" only by the Church. Mothers, after this fall, must be "purified." One version of this idea is the foundation of the first great formulation of Christian thinking by an old bachelor of genius who, by his own account, had some chronic malady of the flesh, possibly epilepsy—the apostle Paul. Paul believed—as a rhymed version of this doctrine later put it—that "in Adam's fall, we sinned all." Adam had fallen because Eve gave him an apple (symbol of life and knowledge). Because of this "sin" of Adam's, all human beings are condemned and can be redeemed only by the grace of God through Christ. Out of this concept evolved the belief that the spirit could be enriched only by denying the flesh. Thence came the tendency to identify the female with the flesh and to call it low and ignoble. This sequence of ideas represents the spiritual catastrophe whose repercussions still influence our thinking and feeling about women.

The identification of women with the flesh was based, of course, on the obvious fact that women bear children. In their natural ways, women embody and symbolize the idea of a human tie with earth and nature. Always recognized by men of pre-Christian times as being the stronger manifestation of the life force, women were still recognized as such. But now the strength inherent in women was distorted into a weakness—worse than a weakness, a menace. Instead of opening the door to life, women, because of their association with physical birth, closed the door forever.

"Woman, thou art the gate of Hell—thou ought always to be dressed in mourning and in rags—thine eyes filled with tears of repentance to make men forget that thou art the destroyer of the race." [2] Tertullian's estimate of women forcibly illustrates a point of view held by certain second-century groups. The giver of mortal life became the withholder of the spiritual life, instead of the symbol for both, as in times past.

Woman's integrity and honor quivered in Clement of Alexandria's devastating blast: "Every woman ought to be filled with shame at the thought that she is a woman." [3] This was the inevitable result of the distorted idea that the living world is evil. And it proved to be the doom of the goddess. Sex was no longer a fateful and august force, to be exercised or not, in accordance with a woman's natural rhythm, as symbolized by the great goddess Ishtar. Motherhood was no longer a holy participation in the mystery of creation, allying all mothers with the creative power of the universe as represented by Isis. Virginity meant no longer the service of the inviolate personal self as represented by Artemis, free, courageous, and creative. Woman no longer had a self in this sense. Her inmost being as a woman was "evil."

2.

Theoretically, the period of early Christianity ended in 325, when the emperor Constantine recognized the faith of Jesus as the hope of the world. Practically, of course, the period of indecision and experimentation ended at an earlier date in some localities than in others. But eventually, the goddess and the principle that women are creative lost authority.

When Constantine, in 325, recognized Christianity as the official religion of the Roman Empire, the heresies were forced to combine and to declare a common creed. At that time the strongest group was dominated by antinatural views on life. To that group of leaders, who had always shown enmity to the interest of women, Christian affairs were entrusted. If at first one or two abbesses sat in their councils to determine the form and content of the organized church, women soon ceased to be represented in the governing body and allowed the new hierarchy to be formed without a recognition of their highest values.

The arbitrary laws of the theologians and not Jesus' love established the godhead. Contrary to the timeless female-male combinations, God became idealized in a trinity of male power—Father, Son, and Holy Ghost.

The word "god," which in Gothic and old Teutonic had been neuter, now became purely masculine with masculine pronouns. The Holy Ghost had a similar metamorphosis. Derived directly from the dove-goddess of antiquity, it had formerly signified a spiritual possession of women by the śakti, their own female life force. Although some of the very early Church Fathers taught that the Holy Ghost was the feminine principle in God, the later theologians neglected to emphasize the natural man-woman concept of a creative power. Eventually the Holy Ghost came to signify the spirit of love passing between the Father and the Son—the spirit that led to the incarnation. In pictures of the Anunciation the Dove is usually seen hovering over Mary's head, but it came to be associated, of course, with the male element in generation, and so the Holy Trinity materialized without a divine woman spirit.

The beautiful figure of Mary that was drawing into itself and regenerating the old popular faith in the goddess became in the teachings of the theologians something of an anomaly. In the conception of Mary as both mother and virgin, there was an opportunity to crystallize an idea that had run through much of the thinking of the creators of religious imagery in the pre-Christian era. This was the idea that a woman as "mother" might be "virgin"—that is, she need not be the helpless slave of sex in herself or in the male. She could accept motherhood as a holy responsibility, ally herself with universal mother power, and still retain a proud freedom of the spirit. "I am forever virgin" meant something much deeper and more universal than physical abstinence from sex intercourse.

This idea, after which Christian thinking has constantly groped through the centuries, might have been represented by Mary. It may be that it could have been formulated if women themselves had taken the initiative in a matter of which they should know something! But the thinking about Mary was checked and somewhat distorted by the conflicting idea that women were evil and motherhood a disgrace, and by the determination also to assert that a male God must be the one and only divine image to which humanity might look. The result, so far as the divinity of Mary was concerned, was a series of compromises.

The mother Mary was never a goddess in the same sense that God is a god, or in the same sense that the old mother-goddesses were superhuman. She was not a creator of life in her own right. Only God the Father was supposed to have created the Holy Child. The term "only begotten son" does not mean "this *one,* or *only* son." It means "alone-begotten," that is, begotten by the Father without any mate—a reversal of the emphasis upon the goddess-mother of an earlier age who, as "whole," "complete," *alone* created life. Mary was not even the counterpart of God, the role of the Great Mothers when they lost their original supremacy. She no longer possessed even half of the responsibility or honor for bringing to birth the Saviour, the deliverer of humanity. Mary the mother lost her active and primary part in creation. Although in picture after picture she wears the sky cape of azure blue bequeathed her by Cybele and Artemis, she sits beneath it as if it were the cover of the sky god. Humble and passive, as Christian women are supposed to be, she sings her new song: "Behold the handmaid of the Lord." [4]

Mary, as projected by the theologians, lacked the independent power of Cybele, Ishtar, Isis, and the other Great Mothers of the pagan faiths. On the other hand, she rose from the anonymity accorded women by the exaggerated Jewish patriarchy, in which the creating Father-God triumphed. A compromise was effected by recognizing her presence in the holy family. But in the family circle she was shorn not only of creative power but of the essential female attributes that made the old goddesses symbolize the normal woman. Her virginity, instead of meaning independent creative power—such as Artemis idealized—came to mean chastity and continence from sexual intercourse. Even the value of her motherhood was be littled. Bishop Epiphanius (second century) went so far as t maintain that the glorification of mothers was a morbid feminin sentiment—"silly and devoid of reason." [5] And St. Chrysoston (fourth century) also scorned motherhood as an ideal for women He called only the chaste nuns "imitators of Mary." [6] The woma spirit of the Christians made no claim to represent the natura woman.

With no symbol for an active, creative womanhood, there was n need for a hierarchy of women. The oracles, seers, and prophetesse officially vanished. Of that group, the deaconess alone remained with only a suggestion of mantic power surviving in her prayer o dedication. The priestess was demoted to nun. In 367, the forty fourth canon of the Council of Laodicea contained the first forma limitation of the priestess' age-old sacerdotal functions:

"It is not fitting for women to draw near the altar nor to toucl things which have been classed as the duty of men. . . ."

Measures to restrict women from exercising priestly power wer extended to include the celebration of formal rites at home. In 39 the laity (men and women both) gave up the custom of sacrificin at private altars and performing other ritual acts that had, of course preceded any organized church service by many centuries, anc that had been the inspiration for so much of women's music. Afte the establishment of the orthodox church in 325, the formal funera "wake" was transferred from home to church. The rulings affectec women far more adversely than men, since women now could no become priestesses, whereas any man who wished could enter th priesthood.

By excluding women from the priesthood, the Church Fathers sep arated women from men. They allowed only men to be sponsors fo the life of the spirit. They denied women a similar prerogative Woman never received from organized Christianity her authoriza tion to re-create the spirit according to her own feminine conceptior of Jesus' teaching. Christianity theoretically dedicated itself to a cultivation of the incorporeal quality of existence. It denied woma an official status of equal rank or value with man's in the quest fo this spiritual existence. It thus closed the door to the state from whicl artistic imagination had formerly evolved.

The prohibition preventing women from entering fully into th life of the spirit was not merely a deterrant to activity. It went fur

her than a negation of power. It took a positive direction toward the
dentification of women with the undesirable and the unwanted.
Without the slightest foundation of evidence in the Gospels, Mary
Magdalene—once regarded as the most spiritual of all the disciples,
he most sympathetic with Christ—came to be the personification
of carnality, the state despised by the Christians. She symbolized
sexual desire. And sexual desire itself, a re-creative power, was given
an evil, destructive significance.

In primitive religion, women had symbols signifying all of the
creative attributes of normal womanhood. Ishtar, for instance, re-
lected creative energy—that driving female urge to bring to birth.
She was the re-creating mate and the creating mother, giving both
physical and spiritual life. In the Christian religion, Mary the mother
and Mary Magdalene the spiritual friend were reduced to models of
he passive and the corporeal with no possibility of ever regaining
he active, noble, and spiritual forms of the great goddesses.

Not content with fixing the spiritual status of women for the future,
he Church Fathers turned to the past in order to obliterate every
race of woman's soul at work. Churchmen displayed particular
animosity against women's poetry and music. As they tossed Sappho's musical poems into the flames, they manufactured the in-
famous reputation of the Lesbians. All priestesses, led by Bacchae—
he Mothers—became lewd and obscene. All free musicians became
branded as sirens of seduction.

Sections of written accounts of Christ's contacts with women were
methodically expurgated to suit the ideas of the ecclesiastical authorities. On the ground of inauthenticity, Mary's lament did not appear
in the New Testament. Even in the manuscripts omitted from the
Bible, falsifications in translation invariably tend to belittle the tremendous influence exerted by women in the early days of Christianity. Thekla's activity in the first century as a Christian teacher,
preacher, and baptizer of converts has vanished from the extant copy
of the Acti Pauli et Theklae. The account of the "Greek women of
honorable estate" in Macedonia who flocked to Christian standards
has been changed to read "men and women in considerable numbers." So flagrant and so numerous are these misrepresentations of
the truth that a modern historian has summarized them in accusing
words: "Christian writers, from Eusebius Bishop of Caesarea down-
wards began to enter into the domain of falsehood . . . And the
19th century has witnessed . . . the most senseless and shameless

attempts to re-establish ancient and modern fraud, falsehood, and nonsense, and pass it off as orthodoxy." [7]

Backed by the authority of the Emperor, the orthodox group undertook to disband the other sects and to destroy their records. Heretics were portrayed as immoral and undisciplined, outside the pale of sanctity. While undoubtedly Roman society had degenerated and while the aristocracy had fallen from their high estate of setting the fashion for noble conduct, still there were many groups of people who led normally good lives. The Marianites of Bordeaux in the early centuries of the Christian development were austere and dignified, very much like the Puritans of colonial America. They respected women and sanctioned the participation of women in the larger life of the community. Several women are recorded as doctors and as scholars. It was within this sect that Christian women conducted secret rites and took official part in the regular ceremonies. And yet no heresy has been censured more strongly by the orthodox Church Fathers than the Marianites. Because they—and many others —did not conform to the ideas of the orthodox group and especially because they admitted the creative power of women, they were condemned to annihilation.

While the integration of the Christian sects was progressing, the formal rites of the new church quickly adapted themselves to the ideals of the dominant group. The story of the Christian year unfolds like the mighty drama of life and death and rebirth so dear to the nature worshiper's mind, but this is a drama in which women play an inert instead of a dynamic role. There was every reason in tradition and history, every social and psychological reason, too, for giving women a part equal to that of men in the Christian story as developed in the seasonal rituals of the Church. But the power of a group of fanatical leaders was such that to this day women's symbolic participation consists almost wholly in their being adjuncts to men—now the possessors of the superior "mana."

By mimetic rite, by verbal description, by symbols, Christ's life on earth is rendered vivid to the worshipers. During the period of the shortest days of the year, his advent is longed for. With the first sign of the sun's renewed activity, Christ, as the light of the world, appears on Christmas Day. Then comes Epiphany, the manifestation of Christ, when the Wise Men bring their gifts. Later in the Church year is Lent, the period of repentence and mourning when Christ retreats to the wilderness. Then the entrance into Jerusalem and the last supper, the vigil at Gethsemane, the trial and condemnation. Good Friday is the day of death, the Crucifixion. The time between the death of Christ and his resurrection on Easter Day is three days and corresponds exactly to the time that the moon is invisible. As the moon god and goddess always resurrected themselves, so did the new light of the world rise on the third day from the dead. Easter signifies the rebirth. Ascension Day marks the miraculous translation of Christ into heaven, and Whitsuntide signifies the descent of the Holy Spirit as a comfort to mankind. Through the summer months, until Advent comes again, the Trinity is worshiped.

Although Mary has festivals given in her honor, the only one in which she has complete independence is the feast of her assumption into heaven. Otherwise, she is not the principal figure. In the rite of Christ's birth, celebrated as Christmas for the first time in 395, the focus of interest centers upon the Child of the Divine Father of Love, rather than upon the collective mothers whose self-sacrifice and effort had brought the longed-for Saviour into the world. In the rite of the Resurrection, interest revolves around the Son's transfiguration rather than upon the collective mothers who had made the rebirth possible and who had themselves experienced transfiguration in the process. In the rite of Pentecost—the descent of the Holy Ghost— the Holy Spirit becomes a symbol of the love between Father and Son. Mother love, or woman as a beneficent power, had representation only in the antinatural symbol of Mary. Even in the rite of the last supper women were forgotten, and according to the interpretation of Christian artists, only men received the symbol of rebirth from Christ's own hand. When even a nun went to receive Holy Communion—symbol of the initiation into the life of the spirit— she was not allowed to receive the sacrament in her bare hands as men did, on account of her inherent impurity (Council of Auxerre, 578).

3.

Women's own rites of the life cycle, which they had invented themselves to affirm the natural way peculiar to their sex, became altered to suit the Christian idea of life negation for the natural woman.

In the mothers' religions, puberty rites signified a crossing of the threshold to maturity. Girls prepared themselves physically and spiritually for mating and for motherhood. In the Christian religion, on the other hand, emphasis was placed upon a denial of natural functions, upon *chastity*. From the days of early Christianity until the sixteenth century, the state of marriage was theoretically despised and the state of continence dignified. Innumerable treatises, sermons, and letters upon the topic were addressed to girls. Voicing the long existing sentiment, the author of "Holy Maidenhood" in the thirteenth century called a wife the slave of the flesh, contrasting her with the free nun, who in his eyes was alone able to follow the spiritual way. But since the large majority of girls married, the precepts could not be followed and merely served the purpose of creating an irreconcilable emotional conflict in a normal girl's mind.

But however men may try to banish women and the image of the natural relation of woman to man from the human mind, it cannot be done. All that can be done is to offer an unnatural substitute. Just as homosexual love for young boys had been developed when the romantic love of young girls had been banished among the Greeks, just as castrated males or boys in women's dresses had to be substituted when women were banished from religious choirs, so when natural marriage was condemned or degraded to the position of an ignoble necessity, an unnatural marriage was substituted. The woman keeping herself from physical sex intercourse is dedicated to a rapturous union with Christ. In the Christian description of this marriage the most sensuous details are borrowed from the songs of earthly love and sex. Not so did Artemis assert, "I am forever virgin!"

An example of the transformation of women's wedding rites into Christian poetry was the hymn written by Methodius, bishop of Lycia, in 303, for the members of his flock. It was entitled "The Banquet of the Ten Virgins" or "Concerning Chastity." The style imitated the partheniads—songs for maidens—written by Alkman and Megolostrata for Spartan girls. Its theme was borrowed from women's wedding rites still used in Adrianople today, where it is the custom for a Jewish bride and her women companions to sit for hours in their wedding garments while waiting for the bridegroom. At last the cry is raised: "Behold, the bridegroom cometh!"

This hymn was written by Methodius to be sung by girls—an early example of the now prevalent custom for men to formulate what women think and feel about their most intimate personal lives, and women, parrot-like, to repeat the words in song.

So in singing this hymn, according to the statement in *Prolegom-*

ena de Poetis Christianis Graecis, girls impersonated Thekla, the first virgin martyr, and others of the noble band. "We give the name 'Parthenion' [song of Virgins] to the hymn of Methodius because it was sung by virgins. . . . The ten virgins are introduced after a cheerful and modest repast, during which they discussed the merits of inviolate virginity. Afterward, they all rose as though inspired by a divine spirit and dedicated their lives to Christ as though to the noblest spouse." [8] Thekla, named by Arete (Virtue) as the chief of the virgins, sang the versicles of the virgins' song. The other virgins, standing in a circle around her under the willow tree—symbol of chastity—entoned the response. The hymn has twenty-four stanzas, of which we give two:

Stanza

The Bridegroom cometh! overhead
The shout descending wakes the dead!
 Go forth to meet the King,
 The gates just entering!

Virgins, white-robed, with lamps haste
 eastward forth to meet him,
Haste ye, O haste to greet him!

Response

With holy feet, the lamps bright burning,
I go to meet my Lord returning.

Stanza

My home and country for Thy sake,
And maiden dance, I did forsake,
 And mother; pride and race,
 And thoughts of rank and place;
For Thou, O Christ the Word, are all in all to me;
 I long for naught save Thee!

Response

With holy feet, the lamps bright burning,
I go to meet my Lord returning.[9]

When the ideal of marriage to the heavenly bridegroom was dramatized for nuns, something was offered them—morbid, silly, but a kind of substitute for normal living. The greatest crime consisted in modeling the religious instructions for girls of marriageable age, who would normally become wives and mothers, upon the ideas of marriage to the heavenly bridegroom. Music as well as sermons impressed upon young minds the value of an unnatural mode of life. So was a Christian girl forced to repress her natural instincts or to accept the guilt of sin.

Marriage rites for goddess worshipers emphasized the holiness of sex relations and reproduction. Women played the major role, symbolically passing on the torch of life to their daughters and also impersonating a goddess in the rites of the sacred marriage. But in the Christian religion, the holiest thing in the world for women was not regarded as such. Marriage was not even made a sacrament by the Church until 1550. For fifteen hundred years, married women were held to the monastic ideal, being told that sexual intercourse was sinful. In one of the first-century documents, our Lord is made to assume the disguise of Judas Thomas and advises a young couple on their wedding night with these words: "Know that as soon as ye preserve yourself from this filthy intercourse, ye become pure temples, and are saved from afflictions manifest and hidden, and from the heavy care of children, the end of whom is bitter sorrow." [10]

Rites for a mother after childbirth have a particularly arresting history. As practiced in primitive tribes, they are ceremonies for re-integration into normal life conducted by women themselves. Among the Jews, these rites were conducted for women by priests—women being excluded from the priesthood—but the idea remained identical. The so-called "purification" was a ritual detachment of the mother from her close contact with the life force. No blame on the part of the women was suggested, rather a superholiness. Among the Christians, the rite of the "churching" of women, as well as that of presenting her newborn child to God, became completely distorted. A Christian mother was told that her child was born "in sin," that she herself had erred, that she required absolution. She was made to kneel outside the church and be "purified" before she could again share in common worship. Thus she was given a sense of guilt rather than a sense of fulfillment.

No rites were ever instituted in which fathers were required to apologize for their natural ways.

The godhead, the priesthood, the rites, and the liturgy as established by the Church Fathers during the fourth, fifth, and sixth centuries had the primary purpose of saving the souls of the cult members for life everlasting. The idea of salvation and resurrection was carried over from primitive and pagan religions. Although the Christians pretended to despise birth and the earth, they kept most of the primitive magic devices for bringing about birth and rebirth. Music especially was regarded as the same important magic it had always been.

In the performance of the formal rites, and even in the privacy of their homes, women were forbidden to touch the symbols that they themselves had invented. They could not burn incense or light the sacred fire symbolizing the light of the world. They could not watch the torch being plunged into the baptismal font—symbolic act of sex union. They could not even baptize their own babies with the holy water, symbol of the life-giving fluid surrounding the child in their own bodies. Pope Zacharias (741 A.D.) in interdicting the celebration of mass by an abbess, made a classic statement: "We were indignant to hear that a series of holy ceremonies were degraded by suffering women to read the Mass." [11] So the very touch of women, which had always been regarded as life-giving, became transformed into a contamination.

Let Mary stand at the bar of heaven and ask if any symbol of the rebirth could be degraded by a mother's touch!

From a disinterested point of view, the whole theory of woman's spiritual incapacity as depending upon her motherhood seems to have been a mass neurosis. The enormity of the accusation that a woman's touch could contaminate any symbol of birth or rebirth has been belittled by time and habit. To the modern mind, such men as Pope Zacharias appear as almost mythical characters who can be blown away like a phantom. But in the eighth century—indeed, until the eighteenth century—they were powerful realities and loomed like giants in establishing customs that denied women leadership in the Church and so in Christian music. And the effect of what they did survives in our culture today to a degree that should shock both men and women.

The participation of either men or women in the musical life of the newly forming Christian culture depended primarily, as it must in any age and among any people, upon the ideas of the group concerning the utility of music. Christians believed in the power of music. They sanctioned its use with the religious ceremony in order to enhance the affective quality of the rites and prayers. Music was

held, however, within certain bounds prescribed by the ecclesiasti
cal authorities.

The dance was absolutely forbidden and has never been reinstated
in Christian worship. Dancing is too much associated with the body
to permit its transformation into a purely incorporeal state. For sev
eral centuries the wail laments disappeared from choral literature
intended for Church use. Laments were too actively associated with
women to be divorced suddenly from their begetters. Instruments
were probably allowed, but did not play an important part until
later. Singing was the method employed to affect the deity. In mel
ody to accompany the liturgical texts, Christian musical art devel
oped.

There was a fierce struggle to suppress all singing outside of
church and monastery. Religious canticles could be sung at home
but only those with Christian texts. Choral spring and love songs,
wedding songs, and especially songs based upon the wail assumed
a sinful character. When the bishops issued prohibitions against the
choruses of men and women who were carrying on age-old customs
of song and dance at the seasonal festivals, they alluded invariably
to the character of the songs and dances as being "erotic," "obscene,"
"scurrilous," or "the Devil's songs." Bishop Caesarius of Arles (Serm
XIII) made the complaint in 542: "How many peasants and how
many women know by heart and recite out loud the Devil's songs
erotic and obscene." [12]

Except for religious canticles in the home, song—Christian musi
—existed only in the churches and monasteries. At that time, n
other institutions functioned. Because a woman could not ente
religious institutions in honor without trailing with her the fancied
dishonor attached to human birth, her performance of instrumenta
and vocal music fell into the same category of evil that she hersel
assumed.

Because prostitutes played instruments of music, Christian girl
were never to play them. The great teacher Jerome wrote in hi
letter *Ad Laetam,* concerning the education of girls: "Let the mai
of God be, as it were, deaf toward instruments. Let her not know
why the flute, the lyre, and the zither have been made." [13] Basileu
said that it was a pitiful sight for pious eyes to see a woman singing
to the lyre instead of weaving. This attitude is taken by Arnobius
Commodian, Basil of Caesarea, and others. That the notion per
sisted is evinced by numerous medieval representations of the wis

and foolish virgins in which the foolish ones hold musical instruments in their hands as an indication of their levity. Nothing was
said about boys not playing instruments. It was not that girls were
incapable of playing the cittern and the flute and the lyre; it was not
that they played less skillfully or with less musicianship than boys;
it was simply that the risk that their music might distract men—the
chosen leaders for developing the life of the spirit—could not be
taken. (See Plate 52.)

The liturgical choirs of girls, who had preceded the boy choirs,
eventually became cloistered in their own monasteries and no longer
served in the public churches.

Choirs of laywomen and girls, as well as of professional musicians,
were absolutely forbidden. Congregational singing by women was
also forbidden, even when they were in church with their families.
The converted Jew St. Paul, imbued from childhood with a distrust
of women, commanded them to be silent in church. A little later,
Cyrillus of Jerusalem, also a bitter enemy of women, taught that they
were to read and pray softly with the lips, without sound: "For I do
not allow a woman to speak in church." [14] In the Didascalis of 318
the singing of women in church was forbidden; in the Council of
Laodicea (367), congregational singing was abandoned and the
musical portions of the service were placed in the hands of a trained
choir of men and boys; in the Synod of Antioch (379), women were
forbidden to join with men in chanting the Psalms. Mothers could
not give their own thanksgiving for motherhood in imitation of
Mary. Mothers could only listen to little boys or nuns singing the
song of rejoicing for the birth of the Saviour. As already shown, such
customs had at first only local authority, but they gradually came to
be accepted as proper by the whole Christian body.

Professional women musicians submitted to regulations that practically prevented them from pursuing a musical career and remaining
respected members of the Church. St. Chrysostom (fourth century)
despised the professional mourners. "Anyone who hires these
wretched women shall be excluded from the Church for a long time,
like an idolater." [15] Bishop Hippolytus (fifth century) had the same
feeling: "A woman who attracts people with her beautiful but delud-
ing sweetness of voice (which is full of seduction to sin) must give
up her trade and wait forty days if she is to receive communion.
Then only may she receive the mysteries." [16]

Finally, the authority of several sects began to disapprove of the girl choirs unless the girls had taken the vow of chastity and had become nuns. Women and girls were expected to sing their religious canticles in humble tones or with a sexless quality like that of immature boys. The natural, rich, low-pitched voice of the mature woman was absolutely tabooed, and was not introduced as a vocal instrument for many centuries. The musical terms used now to designate vocal parts that are higher than the normal range of men's voices developed from men's usage, not women's. Soprano means *superius,* or the highest, no matter what the pitch. Its feminine form—never used —would be soprana. Alto means *altus,* or high—high for men. The form "alta" would be meaningless and never appeared. Neither term, soprano or alto, had originally anything whatever to do with women, and there is still no word for the woman's natural voice.

The training of little boys to sing the high vocal parts of Christian music was the beginning of a practice that has persisted to this day in the Church, and that perpetuated the morbid idea of the Greeks at the beginning of their decadence—that the innocence of young boys could be made a healthy substitute for the natural purity of girlhood. The whole conception symbolizes the movement to degrade the natural woman and to limit her opportunities to be a musician merely because she was a woman.

The Church Fathers themselves made an explanation and an excuse for their attitude. The charm of women, the appeal of their voices, and their whole emotional life as expressed in music had unfortunately been associated with a kind of ritual that in the fourth century had fallen from its former high estate. At various times it had been necessary to regulate the extremes of orgiastic worship associated with the old goddesses and with primitive religion. Exaggerated demonstrations of grief at funerals had fallen into this category. Early in the history of Athens, one of Solon's laws had forbidden citizens to hire more than ten professional mourners and flutists to perform music at funerals. And in 185 A.D. the Romans, usually tolerant of any religion, suppressed the order of the Bacchantes after women had held a three-day secret celebration that seems to have caused public protest. There had long been denunciations on the part of all decent people against the sexual orgies and other vulgar exhibitions of some of the aristocratic Romans. Music by women had always accompanied and stimulated the obscenities. A reaction to such excesses was both inevitable and healthy, to be regretted only because Christian leaders allowed the incurable human failing of immoderation to becloud the issue.

Despite their belief in the power of music as practiced by *men* to enoble character, the Church Fathers apparently never made any provisions for *women* (except as nuns) to integrate music with formal religious devotion or for women to take the lead in finding spiritual sustenance through Christian music. After about the fifth century, laywomen dropped out of the organized musical life of Christianity. The singing and dancing of peasants and of the noblewomen in their castles continued, as we shall see, in spite of and in successful revolt against the plans of the priesthood for the use of music. Whether women made any formal protest against the rulings that fixed their relation to music for a thousand years to come and more, whether they realized at the time the full extent of the repression, is unfortunately not recorded.

This movement reached its height as the whole civilized world was falling into decay. Just as the brief brilliant triumph of classical Greece in taking over women's rituals and music and in suppressing women's part in them was followed by the long slow decay of Greek creative talent, so now the triumph of the Church leaders in eliminating women from all authoritative participation in ritual and music coincided with the beginning of general social darkness in Europe. The Roman Empire fell. The old civilized life of the Mediterranean cities was overrun by barbarians, or decayed of itself. It was to be several centuries before the fresh energies of the still primitive and pagan north of Europe could become effective in reviving Western culture. Under such circumstances it was hard for women to unite and make a stand. Isolated as individuals and groups, amidst general social chaos, they had to make the best of things as they were.

The unfortunate thing is not that all this happened long ago. The unfortunate thing is that, fundamentally, it has not yet been undone.

When men departed from Jesus' way of love and tolerance, they broke with women and created a situation that has never ceased to be death-dealing to woman's imaginative faculty. The Church, which should have enabled the noblest men and the noblest women to seek spiritual regeneration for all humanity, became primarily an institution for men's point of view, men's imagery. From the fourth century to the twentieth, Church leaders have given no serious thought to the needs of women for ritual and music created by women themselves—ritual and music both being capable of nourishing that part of the spirit known as the imagination. Although men would not be satisfied without their own symbols, rites, leaders, and their own spiritual sustenance, they have expected women for nearly two thousand years to feed their imaginations on crumbs from the men's table.

Women lost their symbols, their rites to emphasize their own strength, their leaders. They lost more than that—self-confidence in their own powers to be a dynamic, beneficent influence on humanity backed by the reverence of men for them as such. It was because women were regarded as a menace to the life of the spirit and as interfering with the quest of their men for salvation that they were forbidden to be priestesses and choristers. As recently as 1928, bishops of the Church of England gave the reason identical with that of the early Church Fathers for refusing the petition of women for ordination. Men might be emotionally disturbed, they said, by women's presence near the symbol of spiritual regeneration.

Barriers between women and music did not arise from any lack of natural musical talent, skill, intellect, or imaginative faculty on the part of women. Merely because nature had fashioned her body for the purpose of carrying a child, a human being was deprived of the use of the mimetic rite and music—two of the basic means of expression and communication. The inevitable result has been slow spiritual starvation.

Instead of entering the Christian way in the pride of womanhood, in affirmation of her "Artemis value," woman approached it in negation. Instead of glorifying her existence, she started apologizing for it and so killed the spirit in which imagery gestates. "Daughters of Jerusalem," said Jesus to his followers, "weep for yourselves and for your children."

Weep for yourselves, O Daughters of the Moon!

NEW MOON

CHAPTER XII

THE NUN

1.

I N THE darkness that had fallen on women at the end of the fourth century A.D., in many parts of the Christian world, even in its highest councils, and in the silence that had been laid on their music, there began to gleam again a faint, thin crescent of light. Like the moon in her nights of darkness, the music of women had not really vanished. It was only obscured. And to this day it is still only a crescent, with the full moon still a long way off. Nevertheless, the waxing had begun.

This new moon rose over rude collections of huts and clumsy farm buildings surrounded by walls, in which some rough, stormy princess of the north gathered the more rebellious and self-assertive women of her circle and defied men to marry them against their will or keep them married, by putting themselves under the protection of the Church. For as the Roman rule over the forests and farmlands of France and Germany crumbled, the missionaries of the Roman Christian Church took over and began to organize the turbulent north.

The first to see the many advantages these polished, cultured, and subtle persons from the old civilized world had to offer were often the wives or women relatives of the so-called "kings" and "nobles" of the northern tribes. One of these, the high-spirited Chrotield, adopted Christianity, and was then, with some adroit persuasion on the part of the Christian bishops, married to the leading German barbarian, King Clovis. She forthwith required him to become a Christian and all his people with him. Thus was Christianity established among the Franks. In the next three centuries this Germanic tribe took over the rule of all Europe and produced a great emperor,

Charlemagne, who was crowned in Rome in 800 A.D. as emperor of New Roman Empire—the Holy Roman Empire. Chrotield, in order to assert her independence of any man, even the King, established a religious house for women near Rouen, but she was no model of Christian meekness.

The example of Chrotield was followed by "princess" after "princess" among the conquering Teutonic tribes. No man of the royal Frankish house entered a monastery. But the women formed religious establishments everywhere. In so doing they were able to reassert the ancient power and independence that women had held among the uncultured Aryan-speaking tribes of Europe from time immemorial. Big, blunt women, strong of limb, downright of speech, resolute of will, most often flaxen-haired or red-haired and blue-eyed, splendid in fur mantles and heavy gold ornaments, these princesses were still of the race of the old mother-chieftainesses and priestesses. They did not intend to be broken by men if they could help it. So, one after another, the noblewomen, with the help and connivance of the Roman bishops, set up their own religious establishments, often on lands they themselves owned and flatly refused to transfer to a husband.

In the centuries to come, succeeding generations of "nuns" were slowly broken to the rule of the Church. But meanwhile they were given at least a limited opportunity to develop their talents in literature and music.

One of the early religious houses for women was founded at Poitiers by Radegund, the high-tempered wife of King Cloathcar, who ruled all of France, Burgundy, and Thuringia, and some lands in Italy and Spain. But he could never rule Radegund. When he objected to her failure to have his meals on time and her neglect of his company for that of any scholarly man who came to her court, she appealed to the bishop to consecrate her a deaconess and let her set up her own monastery for women. And thereupon she offered up her embroidered clothes, her girdle heavy with gold, and all her gems in the oratory of St. Jumer, and went forth clad only in thick flowing robes of a brownish, undyed wool. When King Cloathcar appealed to the Church to send her back, she said she would die rather than return to him. Since Cloathcar had seven recognized wives, of whom she was the fifth, she may have thought he could find feminine company for himself.

As head of her own religious establishment, Radegund led a vivid public life in touch with bishops and various turbulent kings. She left an equally vivid literary record of herself, including three poems in the form of elegies. One of them told the tragic story of her young friend Galeswith, who was murdered shortly after her marriage to King Chilperic. The lament in this poem is intoned by several women in turn. "The cry which sounds through these lines is the cry of a woman—the expression of tender and fiery passion . . . a suggestion of the strength of a woman of all countries and for all time." [1] When Radegund died in the year 587, the women who had left homes and families to follow her crowded around her bier, wailing after the immemorial pattern of the women's dirge, "To whom, Mother, hast thou left us orphans? To whom shall we turn in our distress? . . . The earth is now darkened to us . . . Woe unto us who are left by our holy mother." [2]

Radegund could not only read and write but was as well educated as any man of her day. For it was one of the great attractions of these monasteries that in them women could acquire the mysteries of reading and writing and learn the spiritually beautiful music of the Church. Women set themselves to learn the church music with much eager experiment over pitch and tone and with hours of devoted practice.

In the time of Radegund this music was reaching its climax in the marvelous art of Gregorian plain song. From Italy the churchmen who were converting and organizing the barbarians were bringing it to the north.

2.

To understand the relation of women in convents to this church music, it is necessary to review what had happened to music in the Church. As has been said, dance music, wedding music, laments, and many types of social and ritual music formerly composed by women, as well as men, had been forbidden. This was a barrier to the creative musical power of men composers as well as women. Since the religious dance was forbidden, men gave up composing dance music. For centuries, musicians avoided the laments that had been so rigorously prohibited by the Church. They did not compose music for weddings, since the marriage rite was not, at first, a part of the religious service. It is possible that men suffered no great deprivation by abandoning the dance, the wedding songs, and the laments. These forms of expression had always been associated with women and were never used as freely and consistently by men. This fact may explain why the prohibitions against pagan music were largely directed against women.

However, despite the many prohibitions against women's music and their exclusion from priestly offices, women in convents in the more civilized south and east had cultivated Christian music. This is evident from what Bishop Gregory of Nyssa wrote of his mother, St. Emily of Cappadocia, and his sister Macrina.

St. Emily of Cappadocia and her daughter Macrina are striking examples of leading Christian women. These two fourth-century saints were hereditary Christians of noble family. Macrina was both beautiful and brilliant. When she was still a child she knew all the Psalms by heart. Later she instructed her brother Basil in philosophy. She would not marry, but settled near her mother and gathered young women around her, teaching them to pray and sing in the Christian manner. Macrina was regarded by the whole countryside as a holy person, possessing supernatural powers. She miraculously cured a distinguished soldier's daughter of blindness and caused corn to grow in her own fields in time of famine. Upon the occasion of her last illness, her great brother Bishop Gregory of Nyssa hurried to her, and afterward wrote an account of her death and burial. In his book *Life of St. Macrina*, Gregory mentions first of all, in enthusiastic terms, the spiritual qualities of his mother and sister. "Such was the manner of their life, so great the height of their philosophy, and so holy their conduct, day and night, as to make verbal description inadequate. . . . These women, Emily and Macrina, fell short of the angelic and immaterial nature only in so far as they appeared in bodily form." [3]

All through the account, Gregory alludes to the singing of the nuns. "The voice of the choir was summoning us to the evening service . . . Macrina wished to repeat the thanksgiving sung at the lighting of the lamps." [4] Gregory describes the mourning rites: "Virgins' voices singing psalms mingled with the lamentations were filling the place; somehow the news had quickly spread throughout the whole neighborhood, and all the people that lived near were streaming towards the place, so that the entrance hall could no longer hold the concourse." [5] When they were all assembled Gregory ordered the psalms to be sung by both sexes in the rhythmical and harmonious fashion of choral singing.

The most significant part of the account is the description of the all-night vigil preceding the funeral, when the nuns, alone with their abbess' body and their own grief, cried and bewailed in the manner customary at Christian wakes:

> "The light of our eyes has gone out,
> The light that guided our souls has been taken away.
> The safety of our life is destroyed,
> The seal of immortality is removed,
> The bond of restraint has been taken away,
> The support of the weak has been broken,
> The healing of the sick removed.
> In thy presence the night became to us as day,
> Illumined with pure life,
> But now even our day will be turned to gloom." [6]

These Cappadocian nuns were only one community out of hundreds established in Christendom. In many monasteries the holy women were adapting old pagan rites into Christian ways and were contributing their own expressions to the stream of song that was to be liturgical music. The lament of Macrina's followers is merely a link in the chain of dirges that extends from Mary's own song of mourning to Queen Abbess Radegund's magnificent epic six hundred years later.

Men did not begin to create music for the religious ceremony until after Christianity had been established as the official religion of the Empire, until the persecutions had stopped, until a hierarchy had been organized, and until the circumstances gave them an objective upon which to focus their musical ideas. Then singing was authorized as the direct extension of the functions of religious officials. Musically minded churchmen directed their imaginations toward creating the liturgical song known as plain song.

Plain song had no utility except as an integral part of the religious rites and the liturgical texts. The melodies followed exactly the rhythm and intention of the words, just as much as any primitive song ever did. Only these persons who celebrated the rites and who repeated the prayers had the proper qualifications to be authoritative musicians. Christian music makers were the members of the hierarchy—pope, cardinals, bishops, priests, clerics, monks—and nuns.

For many centuries the composition of music was limited to liturgical song. The laity, although undoubtedly as talented as their brothers and sisters in the hierarchy, were not expected to compose the liturgical music. If one did not belong to the class chosen to make the music, one had no opportunity or incentive or training to do so. In the early days this barrier applied to men as well as to women. The names of robber barons do not appear among the composers of church music. Only later did the work of professional men musicians—trained, of course, by monks, the only educators—begin to be acceptable to the ecclesiastical authorities. But although the class of chosen musicians was later enlarged to include the professional who was not a member of the hierarchy, all churchmen at first submitted to barriers against a free use of music.

The limitation on the composition of any music except liturgical music by churchmen was increased by the social disorder that prevailed everywhere except in a few religious retreats. Until about 800 A.D., Christian Europe struggled against the inroads of the barbarians from the north and the Saracen invasions from Spain. Only gradually did the medieval castles and their walled towns become permanent centers for civilization. Universities, theaters, and other public forums were as yet unorganized. Learning and music lived only in church and monastery. Christian music was religious music, created and performed under the authority of the Church.

3.

Plain song was introduced into the convents for women, and became an earnest expression of their own spiritual life. In the early days some abbots and abbesses observed perpetual adoration, keeping shifts of singers on duty day and night. In later times certain orders prescribed only the recitation and not the singing of prayers and psalms. Between these two extremes, customs varied. From the fifth century until about the thirteenth, when many other orders arose, the rule of St. Benedict and St. Scholastica attracted the majority of the noblemen and -women who entered monasteries. Benedict and his sister advocated the use of music. Monks and nuns of the numerous Benedictine monasteries often spent from five to eight hours daily in the practice and performance of liturgical song.

The life of the monastery revolved around the performance of the prayer service and the celebration of mass. The rites were conducted and the liturgy recited at regular intervals during the day and night. Mass was celebrated once, and often more than once, every day. Its choral portions are the Introit, Kyrie eleison, Gloria, Gradual, Alleluia or Tract, Sequence, Credo, Offertory, Sanctus, Agnus Dei, and Communion. The prayer service consisted of matins, at about two A.M.; lauds, at about four-thirty A.M.; prime, tierce, sext, and nones during the day; vespers at twilight; and compline before retiring for the night. The whole set of devotions was known as the *horae*, canonical hours, or the offices.

The singing of nuns was a serious religious matter, sanctioned chiefly for the purpose of enhancing the value of prayers to the Almighty. Provisions were made for the singers to be properly trained. Each convent had its own nun-teacher. She was called *cantrix, cantorissa, Sängerin,* or *Singmeisterin* according to the language of her country. At Syon (England) the chantress had to be "cunning and perfect in reading and singing." [7] Women conducted the services at the canonical hours by themselves, under their own leadership, but a priest always intruded upon their privacy for the purpose of celebrating mass, thus limiting the opportunity for them to make innovations in the service as the monks did.

With a few strokes of the pen, one can describe the number of hours spent by medieval nuns in the pursuit of music, or depict a group of them in action. But a whole volume could scarcely do justice to musical life in the convents. To begin with, it is no insignificant achievement to assemble a group, large or small, eight or nine times a day for the purpose of singing to God. With no thought of an earthly reward, for almost two thousand years, in the dead of night, in cold, unheated chapels, these dedicated women have been earnestly striving to save their souls and those of humanity. Throughout the centuries the excellence of nuns' singing has been commented upon by their contemporaries. The beautiful, clear voices rising and falling to the incomparable melodies of Gregorian plain chant seem to have given musical satisfaction to all who heard them. The nuns functioned in a narrow groove, but they deepened it by genuine devotion.

4.

Plain song reached its greatest beauty in the sixth and seventh centuries, and again in the ninth when it first began to be written down. During these years the skill and inspiration that flowed into it were anonymous. So we have no way of knowing how much of it can be credited to the women in the early religious houses. If their music was as fresh and real as some of their writing, their contribution was considerable.

Nevertheless, despite the scope given to women's talents in the convents, it must be recognized that they were under severe repressions, which did not affect men, in the development of their talents. It is true that on the practical and material side, all Christians respected the abbess, who, as leader of women under monasticism, inherited many of the prerogatives of the primitive queen and priestess. St. Macrina exemplifies the high status of many abbess-saints whose advice was sought in the early synods and councils. Throughout feudal times these aristocratic women had the power of a bishop within the limits of their monastic precincts and carried the crozier as a sign of their rank. Again and again they demonstrated themselves to be the intellectual and spiritual peers of their relatives the popes and bishops, emperors and kings.

But ecclesiastical ideals in the Middle Ages, firmly established by men and acquiesced in by the majority of women, stood uncompromisingly against the emancipation of women from the stigma of spiritual inferiority. For all her proven ability and her acknowledged beneficent influence, any abbess stood *potentially* lower on the rungs of the hierarchal ladder than the most obscure little boy. She could never be a Christian priestess. Even for her own nuns, whose spiritual mistress she was, she could never celebrate mass. The rich abbess of Las Huelgas, supreme over twelve monasteries of noblewomen in thirteenth-century Spain, was deprived of her revenues and finally excommunicated for defying this inexorable law. Church annals are filled with such edicts.

Between all nuns and monks lay a great gulf. The monks belonged potentially to the upper ranks of the hierarchy; a monk could become a priest, a bishop, even pope. The nuns were ranked in the lower bracket only. And instead of being liberated from the distorted ideals of the early Church Fathers (as well as of their women followers), the sisterhood became tainted through and through with the devaluation of women's collective potentiality for good. Singing had been authorized as a direct extension of the functions of the religious officials. But music in the churches was performed by men and boys —not women. Nuns, therefore, lost the prerogative of being the liturgical choir in public as they had been in early Christian times. Nuns became more and more cloistered in their own precincts. Even there, they sang out of sight, behind a grille or curtain.

Women in the hierarchy were both outnumbered and outranked by men, being excluded from the enormous company of Church officials, from pope down to humble clerk. Until the thirteenth century, the clergy could be married men and so had the advantage of being able to lead normal lives. Nuns had the same status as monks, but were not nearly so numerous. The majority of women married and from them no music was expected. The total number of women from whom music might come was far less than the number of potential men musicians.

Particularly pertinent to the development of creative imagination is the fact that a monk was always in the position where he could exchange ideas with his fellow men, some of whom were leaders of the Christian group. A nun, on the other hand, was rarely admitted to the inner circle of authority. The convent was not the highest forum for discussion and women did not freely enter the men's forums. A nun, therefore, was given no broad chance to test experiments in symbolic thinking, or to match artistic effort, or to prove the validity of such effort by trial before auditors who were at the same time sympathetic, skilled, and also of the highest authority. Before original work could be accepted by the whole society, it was subject to the approval of men, who openly announced their scorn of everything feminine. In a handbook of canon law, the principle of women's subjection is clearly stated: "The very nature of religious life demands from the sisters submission to the ecclesiastical hierarchy." [8]

There was a further difficulty, and one that strikes at the very root of the matter. This was the ideal of virginity, as elaborated by men and preached into the ears of women in their tender and impressionable years. Since for men sex begins and ends in a swift impulsive release with no further effects or consequences, save as a man assumes them vicariously, the Christian preacher tended to think of sex as the sex act only. And having determined, in pursuit of peace and self-discipline, to deny or limit this in their own lives, they feared and distrusted the attraction of women. Women were to be suppressed because men's own impulses toward women were to be suppressed.

But for women, sex is only the beginning of instinctive movements of mind and feelings which, so far as the deepest unconscious life is concerned, they have entirely to themselves. The true soul of woman, her unique psyche, distinct from that of the male, is that of the woman who grows a child in her own body, bears it in sweat and blood and tears, and nourishes it with milk from her own breast. The total experience is so tremendous that it dwarfs all others of the physical and emotional life. It involves the depths of pain, the heights of triumph. However woman may try to put the subconscious aware‑ ness of this from her she never can, because month by month she is relentlessly reminded of it.

When men talked of sexual abstinence or of the glories of vir‑ ginity in terms of their own biology—which in comparison with women's is a deficit of nature—they completely ignored the psycho‑ logical necessity for women to respect these great life facts. They further injured women's psyche by taking over the imagery of wom‑ en's lives and elaborating it into allegory and theology. Christ, God, or the bishop nourishes something or other "as a mother." Something or other flows as "milk from the divine breasts." There is no end to this ingenious pretense. To this distortion of their own woman's ex‑ perience, and to a man's terror lest he should be turned from his way of salvation, women, as virgins dedicated to God, were subjected.

Sometimes the effort to tell women how they might sublimate their own impulses, instead of permitting them to find the far nobler and grander way to which nature had pointed them, approached downright indecency. Imagine some lone male priest, of the sex that alone was allowed to officiate at the altar, coming into a convent of women, some of them very young, and exhorting them in these words: "After the kiss of peace in the mass, when the priest conse‑ crates, forget there all the world, and there be entirely out of the body; there in glowing love embrace your spouse, Christ, who is come down from heaven into the bower of your breast, and hold him fast until he has granted you all you wish." [9]

Between the suppression of woman's every normal impulse, the identification of her sacred power of giving birth with the evil and undesirable, and the feverish tendency to interpret religion to women in terms of their own repressed male impulses, the domi‑ nance of men in the higher offices of the Church kept women's real soul in a position in which it could not really function. What a woman was offered and what she accepted in the nunnery was an artificial and inferior and crudely imitative substitute for her own real spiritual life.

Yet the temptation to accept this was very great. In the Europe of that day the opportunities for lifelong monogamous marriage with dignified and free motherhood were very few. The monastery was freedom from the rude dominance of some unloved man. It was freedom, too, from very crude physical toil. "And now I ask," ran one apology for the life of nuns, "how does the wife stand when she comes in, hears her child scream, sees the cat at the flitch, and the hound at the hide? Her cake is burning on the stone hearth, her calf is sucking up the milk, the earthen pot is overflowing into the fire, and the churl [or servant] is scolding. Though it be an odious tale, it ought, maiden, to deter thee more strongly from marriage, for it does not seem easy to her who has tried it. Thou, happy maiden, who has fully removed thy self out of the servitude as a free daughter of God." [10]

The way in which the tendency of men both to suppress women's musical artistic expression and to take over and perform themselves what women had thought out is shown in the case of two inventions that are natural expressions of women's life, but not nearly so natural for the men who appropriated them. One was the liturgical play, which turned upon the experiences of such women as Mary, the mother of Jesus, and the other Marys who were his friends. The other was the ceremonies associated with the death of their own women friends and leaders in the monastery. Over and over again, nuns were forbidden to act in the liturgical plays. Women could not even reproduce the scene in which the three Marys visited the holy sepulcher on Easter morning. In all Europe and England, the Easter drama has so far been found in only six monasteries for women, whereas in the monasteries for men the play was never suppressed. Monks elaborated the idea, imitated it for other feasts, such as Christmas, Epiphany, Palm Sunday, and Pentecost. They took it from monastery to church and finally to the public market place. Freedom to develop the events of Christ's and Mary's lives in forms of the mimetic rite according to their own interpretation was consistently withheld from women.

Yet there is evidence that women participated in the forerunners of the medieval liturgical play. The very character of the people— accustomed to display feelings of joy or grief in church, drilled for centuries in the mimetic rite—implies that action was often integrated with worship. The *History of the Blessed Virgin Mary* records that Mary and her women followers used to talk about Jesus all day long and that they mourned for him at regular intervals. *Feminae Sanctores* of the Marcion sect, marching in a procession into the hall where the congregation sat, carried lamps and gave laments for the sins of the world. Bishop Methodius' girls impersonated the characters in his play *Concerning Virtue*. A first-century fragment of a story about Seilah, Jephtha's daughter, suggests that some early writer had planned another play for girls. Men and women worshiping in the church at Gethsemane during the fourth century acted out the events of the day of Crucifixion—probably the original form of the Stations of the Cross. The few surviving traditions about the powerful Marianite women of Spain and Bordeaux (France) indicate that they imitated, at their secret ceremonies, the grief and joy of Mary and her disciples. In at least six medieval monasteries nuns performed the Easter rite of the visit of the three Marys to the sepulcher. In the version presented at Origny St. Benoîte, one verse of Mary's lament is unique; in the Barking text, there is a special verse for the lament and another for the cry of joy that appear nowhere else.

It is surprising to find that the dramas developed by monks in medieval times were so frequently scenes in which women characters dominated. The visit to the sepulcher was the oldest and the most frequently performed by men. Monks acted also the visit of the pregnant Mary to the pregnant Elizabeth, the lament of Rachel for her children slain by Herod, the episode of the wise and foolish virgins (Sponsus), and the Christmas story. How very odd that they so rarely dramatized events in which men had had the foremost place, such as the last supper! One might reasonably infer that the first Christian women had been inventing their own rites for two or three hundred years and that men had been impressed through these centuries with women's interpretation and selection of material for use in the religious ceremony. Some abbots did perceive that it really was not suitable for men to take the women's parts in these plays. It was degrading, they said, to pose as women. Others objected to the falsetto voice—it reminded one of the evil inherent in women's voices. But it was not suggested that women be allowed to take the women's parts in representing episodes in a woman's intimate life, which, badly played in a crude, secondhand way by men, were still the most moving episodes in the religious drama.

The refusal to accord women their immemorial privilege of officiating in the rites of death was another example of the appropriation by monks of women's rituals and women's musical inspiration. As early as the third century, when the first convents were being established in Egypt, St. Schenute of Atripe and St. Pachomius ordered that funerals of nuns were to be conducted by monks only. The sisters could merely listen to the praying and singing. Pachomius moderated the rule by allowing six nuns to follow the cortège at a suitable distance.[11] In the double monasteries housing both monks and nuns, such a direction from the abbot in charge was indeed a cruel deprivation to the women and is a striking example of the unwillingness of men in authority to give qualified women responsibility for correcting abuses in their own affairs. To cut them off arbitrarily from participation in the rite that had been since time immemorial the chief incentive to women's most notable musical achievements meant the erection of a high barrier between the second-century nuns and the composition of music. That the custom of having monks take the lead at nuns' funerals persisted can be seen in the account of Abbess Hathumoda's funeral in ninth-century Saxony. In the great, rich abbey of Gandersheim, where the famous Hrosthwitha wrote her plays and her music, the nuns had to send for the monk Wichbert to compose the funeral chants and merely give the response themselves to his verses. That such limitations upon the freedom of nuns to create existed in some, even if not in all monasteries, lowered materially the possible number of nun composers at the same time that it raised the possible number of monk musicians.

Unfamiliarity with this aspect of Christian Church history is largely responsible for the general failure to understand the relation of women to music in the convents. On the surface, monastic life appears to have provided the necessary incentives to all musically minded nuns. Certainly many women in the convents were able to ignore the prohibitions and went their own way. Hundreds of edicts repeated again and again through the centuries prove the active resistance of women to their prescribed status. Undoubtedly, many individual churchmen were Christlike in their attitude toward women and had no deliberate intention of denying them the right to think in terms of music. But on the whole, organized Christianity—Church and priestcraft—effected a repression of the natural woman. Even those men who appreciated the value of womanhood to Christianity failed to take a militant stand against the profaners of women. If some few did favor giving women recognition as officials in the Church, they were greatly in the minority. On the whole, men imbued with the Christian spirit believed in being kind and merciful to individual women but not in allowing women to be self-assertive or

independent *collectively*. "The head of the woman is the man," said
St. Paul, and in this principle most people concurred. How limited
were the opportunities of nuns to succeed as musicians!

5.

But as time went on the women's monasteries acquired such
wealth and power, such a tradition of skill and learning, that in a few
rich and favored houses, from the ninth century on, women began
to assert considerable artistic independence. In the ninth century,
the Byzantine nun Kassía composed a canon and a sticheron that
were incorporated with the liturgy of the Greek Orthodox Church
for Holy Week. In the tenth century the nun Hrosthwitha displayed
remarkable talent in writing poetry and drama. Into her various
works she inserted dissertations on mathematics and music, demonstrating her familiarity with these subjects.

Hrosthwitha got the materials for her dramas and legends in the
well-stocked library of Gandersheim, which included every kind of
classical and medieval literature, copied and decorated by generations of nun-scribes. It is thought that the reading of one of her legends, retold in her fresh and novel way, was a regular feature that
preceded the convent meal in the refectory and that the reading
closed with a grace of eight lines, probably intoned. This shows the
great stimulus that regular institutional support can give the artist
and musician. Hrosthwitha had a regular incentive, a participating
audience, a critical and sensitive group who wanted her work and
whom she tried to serve.

The women in great rich monasteries such as Gandersheim, Barking, or Origny St. Benoîte often had not much in common with an
ascetic, detached life and the dark garb of the traditional nun. This
is shown by the recurring efforts to get them to dress more soberly.
The greatest work of art produced in the women's houses—Herrad's
Garden of Delight—shows women in gowns of different colors, with
brilliantly colored red and purple veils. Herrad was a scholar, artist,
and poetess whose large and varied talents blossomed at Hohenburg,
a monastery on top of a high spur of the Vosges mountain, overlooking the Rhine. In the words she wrote for the nuns to celebrate their
espousal to Christ there is something of the spirit of the old epithalamium or wedding song of Greece. It is a very different spirit indeed

from the sickening sexiness of some masculine treatments of this idea
of the sacred marriage.

Hail, cohort of Hohenburg virgins,
White as the lily and loving the Song of God,
Herrad, your most devoted, your most faithful,
Mother and handmaiden sings you this song.
She greets you times countless and daily she prays
That in glad victory you may triumph over things that pass . . . .

Delights await you, riches are destined for you,
The court of Heaven proffers you countless joys.
Put around you noble circlets, and make your faces to shine
Fair, freed from mental strife.
Christ hates spot or stain, he abhors time-worn lines . . . .

With a dove-like faith call upon your Bridegroom,
That your beauty may become an unbroken glory . . .
Mary's Son's heavenly castle with its beauteous halls
Be your home when the term of life is past . . .
The shining Star of the Sea, the one virgin Mother
Will join you to her Son in bond eternal . . .
May you not leave the way before you have attained. Amen.[12]

Beside the great work associated with her name, Herrad wrote an
encyclopedia and much verse. The fragment of a two-part song and
two lines of a liturgical play remain to prove that the Abbess of Hohenburg cultivated music.

Another nun of great attainments was Mechthild of the literary
convent of Helfta, in Germany. Mechthild's visionary poems and
writings are thought to have been one of the inspirations of Dante's
Divine Comedy and to have been acknowledged by him in the
lovely episode where he meets Matilda in the earthly paradise. As
cantrix for thirty years in the Cistercian Convent at Helfta, Mechthild existed in music and for music. Whether she was in the work-
room or in the chapel, she poured out song from the bottom of her
heart. One large group of her compositions consisted of the so-called
"spiritual love song"—the love song to Christ. This whole category
had developed directly out of the prohibitions issued by Charlemagne and other authorities against women singing "winileodi"
(love or sex poems) as they worked at their daily domestic tasks.
Not being allowed to express love for a man, or even for the spring-

tide, the nuns transformed the words into passion for Christ. Lamprecht von Regensburg in 1218 recognized that women had invented the spiritual love song: "This art has originated with the women of our day in Brabant and in Bavaria. Good God, what kind of an art is it, that an old woman knows better than a witty man?" [13] Mechthild made many "winileodi," but her best work was centered in her musical settings for conventional ritual texts. When she was about to die, she asked the attending nuns to sing her own requiem.

One of the most typical of these nuns of the Middle Ages, in her association with music, her encyclopedic knowledge, her fresh approach to much that the male intellect was fumbling with, and her inevitable limitations, was the Abbess Hildegarde of Bingen on the Rhine. Her *Play of the Virtues* (*Ordo Virtutem*) is unique in the history of medieval music. There is no other liturgical drama of her era, or before, that treats spiritual material an as allegory. Its whole conception is original. In its thought and text, it contains the principles developed by Cavalieri four hundred years later in the well-known *Rappresentazione di Anime di Corpo.* The play, however, was only one of seventy musical compositions—antiphons, responsoriums, sequences, and hymns—that Hildegarde composed for the nuns and novices in her monastery at Bingen on the Rhine. The great abbess' favorite hymn, "*O virga diadema,*" is still sung in the village church at Bingen and in other convents. An edition of some of her works was made in 1895 by Dom Pothier of Solèsmes Abbey.

Hildegarde was also steeped in the life of the spirit. When very young, she had visions and made prophecies that brought her public recognition. In maturity she was credited with superhuman intelligence. Kings and bishops not only sought her advice but abode by her decisions. According to the way of all sibyls, she claimed that she had received her knowledge of musical modulation and harmony direct from God and called herself the zither (or harp) of the Holy Spirit, the strings of which were plucked by the spirit of the Lord. The abbess was equally famed for her practical contacts with the poor and sick of her community. She had an intimate knowledge of the medical lore of her day and a reputation for almost miraculous healing. Her book *Materia Medica* is still consulted for information about medieval medicine. As saint, prophetess, abbess, healer, musician, this remarkable woman seems like a primitive priestess, combining in one person all the ancient magics. She would have been a power in her time even if she had never composed a note of music.

6.

The histories and the musical achievements of these extraordinary nuns are significant for the relation of women to music in two ways. First, the fact that they composed music deemed important by their contemporaries goes far to explode the theory that women are inherently incapable of thinking in terms of music. Second, in the case of each of them, their place in history depends primarily on matters having nothing to do with music. The musical reputations of Kassía, Mechthild, and Hildegarde were by-products of their achievements in activities other than music. Kassía was the beloved of an emperor who pursued her until their affair became notorious. In the thirteenth century the popularity of mysticism brought several women into prominence, and nun-musicians became known because they were also mystics. Mechtilde, who lived in the Cistercian convent at Helfta with the celebrated St. Gertrude, was one of these visionaries. Having secured the attention of their contemporaries, whether intentionally or not, these nuns became recognized also as musicians and found a place in later histories of music and musicians. May there not have been scores of other nuns who were equally good composers, conducting their choirs, arranging and adapting the chant to suit the particular needs of their groups? Certainly in the early days this must have been the custom, since before the eleventh century and in some centers long after, music was not notated but was transmitted orally from teacher to teacher, from leader to choir. Such a practice naturally gave opportunity for local variations in the chants. For centuries, therefore, all nun-musicians worked in an environment that encouraged originality on the part of the choral conductor—provided, of course, the women were allowed to function freely. Even a Hildegarde could not rise out of a vacuum. Like Sappho, she had behind her and all around her other musically talented nuns. If they had been monks or clerics they would have been in the class from which the composition of music was demanded. On account of the stigma of inferiority cast upon women *collectively,* only those few nuns who were outstanding in some other way won a recognition that was accorded to many men of no greater ability. (See Plate 55.)

CHAPTER XIII

THE LADY

1.

THE abbess Hildegarde was the sibyl, the mystical oracle of a movement in Europe that was to have great consequences for the relation of women to music. In the late Middle Ages some abbesses enjoyed considerable intellectual companionship with churchmen, in a position of something like personal equality. Between high-minded and gifted men and women, these relations might be frank and quietly devoted, in a way not really possible in the case of men and women in any other walk of life. Such was Hildegarde's relation in her ripe middle years to a simple, earnest, rather narrow-minded monk named Bernard of Clairveaux.

Bernard deplored the selfish fighting amidst the princes of Europe. In conversations with Hildegarde and others, he developed the idea that all these warlike princes and knights could be made to live like brothers and their energies turned to a noble purpose if they could be inspired with a single social aim requiring the pooling of all their resources. Some knights and lords from northern France had already discovered such an aim—they had gone on a crusade to rescue the Holy Land from the Saracens. Bernard thought this idea of a crusade should be preached to all the people. He started on a preaching tour that soon had all Europe seething with excitement.

Meanwhile Hildegarde had a series of visions, of which she wrote in vague and burning words and which Bernard was convinced came straight from God. He presented these to the pope, saying that God had provided the world in this crisis with a prophet. The pope and the high councils of the Church, perceiving the great inspirational value of Hildegarde's writings at this moment, put the seal of the highest authority on them and granted that she was indeed inspired and ordained by God to guide them all in the great enterprise of recovering the Holy Land.

Thereafter kings and nobles who thought of taking the sign of the cross, and churchmen of all ranks, wrote to Hildegarde for advice or came to see her. Her writings, earnest, beautiful, though vague, were everywhere circulated among the few people who could read, and passages from them were repeated, intoned, trumpeted abroad.

Bernard entreated her not to slacken in her efforts to inspire the Crusade. "They tell us that you understand the secrets of heaven and grasp that which is above human ken, through the help of the Holy Spirit," wrote Bernard. "Therefore we beg and entreat you to remember us before God and also those who are joined to us in holy union. For the spirit in you joining itself unto God we believe that you can, in great measure, help and sustain us." [1]

Since Hildegarde was widely recognized as a musician, it is interesting to speculate how much of her music was included in the inspiration, the exhortations, and the prophecies she poured forth as the divinely appointed and officially recognized prophetess of the Crusades.

In any case, between her prophecies and Bernard's preaching, all Europe was seething. From every side bands of knights, trailing yeomen, peasants, and runaway serfs, were converging on the routes that led to Mediterranean ports, beating footpaths into roads with the ceaseless tramp of their feet and the clatter of their hoofs. Though there had been no congregational singing in churches, the great assemblages sang, fervently and religiously, finding their own tunes and words. "Fairest Lord Jesus, Ruler of All Nations" is one of the hymns of the Crusades we still sing in our churches.

Women and men, high and low, everybody wanted to join the Crusades. At all the gathering places and along the main routes, tradespeople set up shop. Entertainers staged shows with acrobatic stunts, tricks of magic, acting, and singing. Many of the entertainers were women—gypsy-like creatures traveling with their men and telling fortunes. The crusaders were often accompanied by their wives, who rode along beside them and joined boldly in all public services. Some highborn ladies even went without their husbands, volunteering to nurse or to set up hostels for pilgrims. The wife of the knight Hausten von der Niederburg bei Uelmer traveled eastward to find her lost husband. After a long search she discovered him bound to a plow, slaving for a harsh unbeliever. By means of her harp and her lovely voice, she charmed the owner of the fields to free the knight.[2]

Thus all the wild, free spirits of Europe were brought together and their disturbing energies turned on the infidel. And never again was Europe to be the same. In this great movement all bonds were strained or broken. The serf ceased to be tied to the land. He could run away, set up a shop on one of the crusaders' routes, and get rich. The knight ceased to be tied to his lord. He could carve out a piece of land for himself with his sword in one of the wildernesses of eastern Europe and became a lord himself. The people ceased to be tied to the Church. Great outdoor masses of people, even when they feel religious, cannot be bound and shackled to liturgy and doctrine. The moving masses of the Crusades were full of heresy, conscious and unconscious. And so in all this stir both women and music began to be released.

The Crusades, thus started, continued at intervals for three hundred years and were associated with profound changes in European life. The feudal system gradually disintegrated, and since feudalism was the mainstay of clerical dominance, the fortunes of the Church followed the fortunes of feudalism. Both were being undermined by an aggressive individualism and by a revolt from asceticism. There was, consequently, the beginning of a new development in the social aspects of music, a development that had its roots in changed ideas about women and in a changed utility for music. It is true that, throughout the Middle Ages, no lady could escape the ideal for her conduct set by the Church. Monasticism, far from declining in popularity, flared up with renewed vigor in the thirteenth century. Many new orders were established, some of them for women of the lower classes. In Russia, until the time of Peter the Great, it was the fashion for noblewomen in their castles to pray and fast at regular intervals exactly like nuns. Even those with no religious inclinations lived under the influence of the ecclesiastical interpretation of life. A European girl received her tutelage in books from a monk brought to the castle, or in a convent school where she was taught as if she were going to become a nun. But there was, at the same time, a partial return to the value of natural living. The "progressive nun" of those times threw off the veil of her dedication to chastity and appeared boldly as her natural self. Instead of becoming the bride of Christ in retreat, St. Elizabeth of Hungary remained true to her earthly lord and traveled over the countryside on errands of mercy. Although she identified herself with the real world, the Church recognized her as a saint and so sanctified the new ideal of at least a suggestion of conformity to the natural way.

2.

Up to this time the Church had been more or less successful in limiting the composition and performance of music. If the way of the autocratic theologians had been consistently followed, only a few Christian men and women to this day would have had the opportunity to compose or perform music. Since dancing was forbidden altogether, one of the greatest incentives for the creation of music fell into disuse. Instrumental playing was at first frowned upon by the Church for men and forbidden entirely to women. Singing was strictly limited to liturgical uses. Even at home, Christians were expected to set music only to psalms or religious canticles. Such restricted use would have changed the social aspects of music in our own culture completely.

The Church's all-inclusive ideal for music was challenged, however, from the beginning. Many people were reluctant to give up an art that had for ages past provided pleasure, spiritual recreation, and also a magic weapon. There was never a wholehearted, complete acceptance of the restrictive rulings. If there had been, the continuous repetition of prohibitions would not have been necessary. If there had been, the ritual music and art song of the former pagan epoch—rites and music that we now call folklore and folk song— would have disappeared; whereas the fact is that many of the ancient rites are still being practiced and are often accompanied by music that itself shows traces of an ancient origin.

Throughout the period known as the Dark Ages and throughout the Middle Ages, the majority of people continued to sing and dance and play upon instruments of music with the intention of influencing their environment. Peasants, townspeople, and nobles all believed that music had a supernatural power. The people of fourteenth-century France believed that music could influence the passions when they allowed a girl from Armentières in 1380 to be fined and arrested for making charms over a young man upon whom she had matrimonial designs. Artists even depicted a girl surrounded by a veil, a spiral, a heart, drops of blood, flowers, and birds practicing magic to attract her lover. Today, in Oberpfalz (Germany), an incantation for the same purpose is sung during the time of the waning moon:

"God thee greet, dear star of Eve, whom now and ever I love to view;
  May the moon shine in the nook where my dear love now lies in bed;
  Give him no rest, leave him no peace, until to me he needs must come." (See Plate 56.)

As late as 1517, Francesco Gonzago of Mantua ordered a *frottola*, composed by one Marchel de Cara, for soprano, violin, viola, and cello, to be played for the express purpose of curing his syphilis. The Duchess of Orleans employed musicians to play instrumental music for her at every confinement. She believed in the power of music to alleviate her suffering during childbirth. King Henry of Navarre implored his beloved daughter, Jeanne d'Albret, to bow before an image of the Virgin Mary at the foot of a certain bridge and sing:

"Help me, Mother divine,
  Deliver me safely of a son!" [3]

This conception of the magic properties of music prevailed among both people and priests throughout the whole of Christendom. The challenge to the Church's authority came, therefore, not from a disagreement about the nature of music, but from a dispute as to who should wield its power.

The rebellion of Christian women against these restrictions upon their musical activities was strengthened by contact with new pagan blood. As the Church spread out through Europe, it converted Celts, Teutons, Slavs, and other northern races to Christianity. In contrast to the effete Orientals and the luxurious Romans, the barbarians were strong, sturdy, and freedom-loving. Women had their own deities, priestesses, rites, and music. Morrigu, one of the famous Irish queens, led men to war and taught them stirring battle hymns. Bridget, goddess and priestess in Ireland, played her harp even as a Christian saint. Slavic women were endowed with magic powers of intuition, especially with the power of making music. Wild and untutored these northerners were, compared to the sophisticated Greeks and Romans. Lascivious and obscene they certainly were not.

Against the might of their nobility and against the wealth of their musical expression the Church struggled in vain, and was eventually forced to compromise.

About the thirteenth century, one compromise was the introduction of congregational singing into the Roman Catholic Church. Religious words and familiar tunes that had never been silenced out-of-doors became formalized into hymns sung at the high festivals of Christmas and Easter. These had come from outbursts of religious emotion among the singing multitudes on the Crusades. Another compromise was to dedicate a pagan festival to a Christian saint. Upon such occasions, women and girls continued to sing and dance in the traditional manner. In the little village at Vigo, Spain, the girls even now dance up the church aisle. In the Vosges Mountains today, during Whitsuntide, girls march in little groups to the abbey. They wear wreaths of flowers and sing certain songs called *kyrioles,* associated in that district with the girls' flower festival.

*Kyriole*s are popular religious songs that had their origin as far back as the ninth century, in the response of Kyrie eleison (Lord, have mercy), given over and over again in church by the people to the priest. Those of the Vosges Mountain girls are only a sample of a very large number. In Russia, especially, there is a whole category of women's songs known as "spirituals." The Church's early sanction of the singing of religious canticles in the home bore fruit in many lands—the one opportunity open to women was, like the talent of the faithful servant, increased tenfold.

There is no doubt that Christian priests have been the implacable foes of women and women's music. Even today, women's musical activities are much greater in regions where the whole population remained pagan until a comparatively recent date. Europe became converted to Christianity only gradually. Germany and Scandinavia came into the fold during the eighth and ninth centuries, Russia even later—at the beginning of the eleventh century. Lithuania, Latvia, and Estonia were the last strongholds of paganism. In their deep forests, the *pagani,* or backwoodsmen, of these remote regions held aloof until about 1400. Russia, Estonia, and Lithuania are the very places where, until the great world wars, peasants had the richest folklore, dance, and music. They are the countries in which the creative peasant-woman-musician had the highest standing.

How many Christians of the aristocratic class conformed to the ascetic musical ideals of the Church is not definitely known. Many undoubtedly did, just as some people today still object to dancing and just as Quakers, until very recently, denied themselves music in any form. Customs varied in time and place. But the very condition of women's life in the medieval castle made it difficult to enforce restrictions against music upon them. Medieval noblewomen lived in feudal households and spent a large part of their time with one another, separated from the men. They attended to childbirth themselves, occupied their time in sewing tapestries, and whiled away their long hours of leisure by singing. In Russia, especially, the ladies were segregated in the *térem,* that section of the medieval castle set apart for women. There they indulged in gaiety, in dances, games, and songs upon occasions of birthdays, baptisms, weddings, or at Christmastime. There the women held feasts separately from the men and sang special toasts to one another, songs for good health, called *zazdrávnizi.* They hung up swings and sang old songs to the rhythm of the swing. Many of these songs were brought into the medieval castle by the laundresses, the peasant nurses, and especially by the embroideresses—the "hall girls," as they were called, because they slept in the castle hallways.

At weddings, especially, enthusiasm for song and dance ran high. According to legend, Queen Guinevere and the Knights of Round Table (*c.* 500 A.D.) rejoiced when two of their company were married.

> The women sang . . .
> The men shouted. . . .[4]

Guinevere herself composed the songs. And according to history, it was during the seventh century in Rome, in Greece, in Byzantium, that many respectable upper-class Christians engaged formal choirs of girls to sing during the wedding feast.

In Scotland about 1050 Queen Margaret was famous for the ballads she composed and sang with her ladies in waiting. The French queens and duchesses, with their maids of honor, sang long historical romances. One, looking up from her needlepoint, would give the verse, and the others would answer with the refrain:

> "The Queen sings softly,
> Her voice blends with the harp;
> Her hands are lovely, her songs good,
> Sweet the voice and gentle the tones."[5]

Her theme often dealt with the equality of love between man and woman—an unrealized ideal for those days but one always popular with women.

3.

The forces that were making for a new secular music and poetry in defiance of the Church were all represented by Eleanor of Aquitaine, who was married to Louis VII of France, divorced by him, it is said, because she bore him only daughters, and then married to Henry II of England. Eleanor was a brilliant, strong-willed, high-spirited woman, who accompanied Louis VII on the Second Crusade and left a trail of legend in the Holy Land. Upon her divorce from him— a divorce she seems to have desired—she married the heir to the English throne, who was much younger than herself. She then carried to England the arts and stories she had picked up in the East and the arts of her homeland. Meanwhile she also discovered the charm of the Celtic singers, the "Breton minstrels," as they were called, and made the court a center for them.

The indications of what must have been, under Eleanor's direction and encouragement, a very considerable enterprise in collecting, adapting, and making socially available the folk music and folklore of Europe are to be found in the lays of Marie de France. These are generally recognized as the most finished storytelling in any European vernacular up to that time. The lays purport to tell stories picked up from minstrels and folk singers. "Folk tell it to the harp, and to the rote and the music of it is sweet to hear," [6] wrote Marie. "The lays usually please the ladies. They hear them joyfully and eagerly, for they are much to their liking," [7] wrote Denis Pyramus.

Whether Marie adapted folk tunes as she adapted folk tales is not known, but literature and music were at that time so much a single artistic impulse and a single art that it is quite likely. Since Eleanor's own son John, when he later signed the Magna Carta, used a seal because he could not write his name, we cannot assume any habit of reading at his mother's court. The lays must have been made known by being sung or rendered in a sort of recitative to the twanging of a harp. The melody of the recitative was the music of singers whose song Marie purports to translate. The purported taking of the music from somewhere may, however, be only an artistic device. Marie may have formed the melody of the recitative out of strains she had heard as neatly and artistically as she formed her stories.

These stories are written in clear, clean, musical, octosyllabic verse. With sure and graceful literary art, Marie frees the folk stories and legends from the monstrous accumulations and contortions of medieval invention and tells a clear, intelligent tale with quiet beauty and good sense. Out of Oriental tales, European folk tales, and King Arthur stories, which were just beginning to be retold and circulated in a literary form by court entertainers, she forms a kind of manual of the manners and ethics of courtesy from the point of view of a civilized woman. The civilized and almost modern tone of these works, admittedly inspired by women and representing their point of view on men's doings and women's personal lives, is sharply contrasted with the style of some *chansons de geste* composed at that time by men. Who Marie de France was is not definitely known. She is thought by some to have been Mary, Abbess of Shaftsbury, natural sister of Eleanor's husband Henry II and daughter of Geoffrey Plantagenet, Count of Anjou. She appears to have been a sort of mistress of court entertainment, at least in the women's circles. As such she may have directed or worked with a number of minstrels, encouraging the development of songs in a civilized and polished form of the vernacular, with music of an equally civilized quality.

4.

Provençe, the sunny southeastern corner of France, whose principal city, Marseilles, had originally been a Greek colony, had been overrun in the tenth century by Saracens. Saracen women, as courtesans and entertainers of men, were creative musicians, fashioning both words and melody in a sort of social and artistic ritual to the glory of love between men and women. It was a kind of love that had nothing to do with marriage and mating. It was a celebration of the free spirit and its defiant right to love according to its own laws. Ultimately the Provençals expelled the Arabs. But they did not restore the control of the Church over their hearts and music. Instead, they organized a heresy, a kind of religion of the "gentle heart," as they called it, in which a knight, as troubadour, worshiped a high and noble lady in song. Thus began the art of the troubadour, a kind of musical wooing of the lady of the castles. This lady, married without her consent to a husband she did not love, might, with proper musical incantations, be brought to love the troubadour.

At the turn of the twelfth century the aristocratic music makers grew bolder in defying the Church's rules concerning the use of music. They dared to set their spring songs and love songs to the rhythmic patterns and melodic lines of the liturgical plain chant. Considering the Church's point of view about the sinfulness of sex, the adaptation of religious chant to frankly sensuous poems was a radical move in the direction of musical freedom. It began, indeed, the new school of secular music, which was eventually to broaden into the operatic and symphonic art of our time.

Thus began four great social changes that were to direct the whole orientation of women to music. One was a kind of woman worship, artificial, without roots in any real function or value of women and without much effect at the time on their actual status. The second was the establishment of wooing as a complicated art, to be humbly performed by men, with the women in a passive position on a pedestal. The third was the limitation of the woman to the position of being the object of men's music, instead of the creator of music of her own. The fourth was the exaltation of the woman as the inspirer and sponsor of men's music.

But it is pleasant to record that the Provençal ladies, despite long discipline by the Church, by severely patriarchal husbands, and by the almost Oriental seclusion of their lives, still had spirit enough to make a little poetry and music of their own. Thirteen of the Provençal ladies have left songs. Others are reported to have composed songs of which no record remains. A typical lady was Beatriz de Dia, who has left five songs, one with music. A dark-eyed, olive-skinned young woman, in a society that prized golden hair and blue eyes, Beatriz found her whole soul and body lighted with beauty when she knew that she was loved. "On gladness and young-heartedness I feast," she sang. "May they ever be my meat. For my friend is the gayest of all. And so I, too, am gay and attractive." [8]

When she tried to hold off the advances of her lover, she cried desolately, "Now I see that I am abandoned because I have not given all my love." But the day came when she sang in exultation, "My heart have I made his, and my love, my every sense, my eyes, and my life." In the end her lover forsook her and she sang, "I now must sing of that I fain would not. So dark and sad my friend had made my lot." [9]

These few simple words, spoken out of the real heart of a real woman, illumine the psychological reality behind this new outburst of song—the radiance, the release of the young woman, married without love, when she is loved by her troubadour, and the inevitable heartbreak for a real woman in such an artificial situation. The wonder is not that troubadour lady artists were not as numerous as the lords, in a formal and rather learned pattern of verse and music set by men. The wonder is that, withal, these caged birds could still sing.

CHAPTER XIV

PRIESTESS OF BEAUTY

1.

FROM the fourteenth century on, there was a wonderful revival of the old Mediterranean culture, and with it a new value for women's voices. This Renaissance, as it was called, centered in Italy, where many cities had grown rich on the business of outfitting and transporting the crusaders and keeping them supplied. A flourishing trade between East and West had developed. From the lands opened to trade by the crusaders came rich rugs to cover the stone floors of castles, rich hangings to decorate the bare walls, silk brought from far-off China, and strains of different kinds of music. The old pagan world revived. People began to read Plato instead of the Church Fathers. Venus was rediscovered as a great goddess and representations of her appeared everywhere, with Venus shown in all her glowing nudity. The Mother and Child, a strong, natural deep-bosomed mother, a lusty and not always angelic child, appeared in a thousand reincarnations in church and chapel. They called her Mary and the child Jesus. But she was the natural mother coming to life and taking her place even in the holy of holies. In the relations of upper-class men and women there was a new and exciting freedom. Women began to take a natural part in the conversation of men, to sing and dance when men were present. (See Plate 57.)

The most wonderful release was the release of the woman's natural voice. Up to 1400 the Church had persistently refused to countenance anything but the high, clear singing of the Gregorian chants by the nuns. The rich, natural voice of the mature woman was considered to be outside the pale of decency. The peasant women were constantly forbidden to sing their myth-laden popular songs. But by 1400 the natural woman was beginning to come into her own, despite the priests. The Church was forced to yield to the popular will and tacitly condone the performance of pagan music under Christian titles, in the form of popular hymns and carols, even by women singing in the warm, rich tones of mothers not ashamed of their sex. This change of policy re-established freedom for music in the home—the focus of woman's activity. It would be difficult to overestimate the importance to women of permission to sing what they wished and in a natural voice. Everywhere the people were singing new folk songs, popular ditties, Christmas carols, and spirituals—many of them composed by women and girls. The names of these women composers have been remembered by later generations and have also been inscribed in old editions of songbooks.

> The one who had composed this
> and has prepared it anew,
> is a delicate maiden,
> she will make us many more of them
> in honor of a youth
> whom she knows well. [1592] [1]

Christmas carols as well as love songs often had their origin in rites that women and girls had long regarded as their own. One of the prerogatives of the ancient priestesses everywhere was the right to bless the home. All through the Middle Ages the "sorceresses" or "witches" whom the Church relentlessly persecuted had carried on the old practices of the priestesses. With charms and fortunetelling they had traveled around the country, knocking at the doors of those whom they might bless. By 1400 even these determined survivors of the pagan hierarchy were drawn into the movement that allowed the old charms and chants if they were duly Christianized. The familiar carol:

> God bless the master of this house,
> And bless the mistress too,
> And all the little children
> That round the table go. . . . [2]

was customarily sung in Yorkshire during the Christmas season by an old woman who came begging to the doors of the villagers' houses. She carried a box with dolls impersonating the Virgin and the Holy

Child, which she held out as a blessing while she sang her ditty. She was the spiritual descendant of those priestesses of the good goddess Hat-hor in Egypt who went to the people's houses shaking their emblems to bring prosperity.

In the general release of women and song, music began to be liberated from the restrictions that bound it to a single melodic line accompanying the liturgy. Experiments in polyphony were at first forbidden by the popes. Eventually, however, the authorities admitted that the new harmonic arrangements enriched plain chant. Creative musical imagination was thereby stimulated to proceed along the modern line of harmony and counterpoint—an apparently limitless field for artistic development.

2.

The change toward a sensuous enjoyment of music initiated in the rather grim castles of the troubadours was carried to a climax in the open, gaily frescoed, gorgeously decorated palaces of the princes of Italy whose families the Crusades had made very rich. Thence it was carried throughout the civilized world in aristocratic homes, first of the nobility, then of the rising bourgeoisie. Not the priestess, as in former times, not the nun, not the mother in her peasant home setting, but the queens of small courts in small states established new ideals and new customs involving a new relation of women to music.

A typical example of such a court was that of Ferrara. At the height of its glory, when two of the greatest ladies of the Renaissance, Beatrice and Isabella d'Este, grew up there, there were only a hundred thousand people living in Ferrara, but its ruling family was allied by marriage to ruling families of other states in Italy.

Among them they controlled a great deal of the money the crusaders had left in Italy. This money they poured into their daily living. Goldsmiths and silversmiths were busy all day long making chalices, goblets, and dishes. Tapestry weavers were weaving all ancient history, Greek history, Bible history, Roman history into hangings for walls. Fresco painters were painting the history of the family on other walls. Jewelers, sculptors, engineers converged on these ducal towns, bringing their finest work or most ambitious plans. And meanwhile there was a whole corps of musicians, poets, and entertainers to devise masques, dances, processions. In such a milieu, under the sunny smile of the reigning princess and often with the direct co-operation of her well-trained singing voice, music began to be elaborated into the art forms we know today.

For the most important asset of these rich families was frequently the baby princess. By bringing her up carefully and trading her off in marriage shrewdly, a family could do much to consolidate and expand its power. A girl was carefully educated to this end under the immediate direction of her mother, with the intention of making her a walking compendium of everything she ought to know by the time she reached the marriageable age of twelve. All day long the masters and mistresses were busy with her. One hears of girls who learned Greek, Latin, Hebrew, philosophy, theology, and medicine; girls who read the works of Plato through in the original by the time they were fifteen. They learned Greek mythology and Bible history and were equally acquainted with goddesses, nymphs, and the more interesting saints. They learned to make tapestry and to play the harp. Above all, they learned to make verse and to sing and compose in the new contrapuntal style.

The little princess was usually married between the ages of twelve and fourteen. Artistic talent and money combined to make her marriage a great day in Italian history. Family vied with family. She was received by her new relatives with celebrations that would make what her own family could do for her shrink to nothing. When King Alfonso of Aragon was married, fountains ran with wine and tables for thirty thousand were set up beside the sea at Naples. When the Duke of Urbino returned with his bride, the ladies and children of the city were ranged on the hillsides, carrying branches. Just as the people caught their first sight of the young couple, they all burst into a song composed especially for the event. The Goddess of Mirth descended to welcome them. Nymphs in Grecian robes and singers on horseback surrounded the Duchess and triumphantly escorted her in. At Milan, Leonardo da Vinci devised for the young wife of Giovanni Galeazzo a sort of firmament with planets circling and singing her praises. Sometimes the solemn and sedate little bride was carried by throngs of singing attendants bearing torches to her bridal chamber. There she was divested of layers of stiff brocade and her jewels and gilded headdress and put to bed behind the crimson curtains of the great carved nuptial couch with her husband, while all night the sound of singing and merriment rocked the palace.

So Beatrice d'Este went from Ferrara at fourteen to her young

From *J. Quasten*, Musik und Gesang, etc.

51. A bas-relief from the Villa Albani shows Roman women of the early Christian age shaking incense, beating a drum, and playing the double flute at a domestic altar. (See page 146.)

Musée de Louvre

52. Carved on a sarcophagus of the early Christian age are two Roman girls, typical of those young musicians condemned by St. Jerome as corrupters of men's morals. (See page 146.)

53. In an old Roman painting, the bridegroom watched women prepare the bride for marriage. Priestess-musicians burned incense and played the lyre at the home altar. (See page 146.)

54. Carved in stone, a Roman lady of early Christian times lies on her death-bed. Two women mourners and a woman flutist officiate. (See page 146.)

55. An illuminated initial in a religious book shows nuns singing in antiphonal chorus. (See pages 185 and 201.)

56. A fifteenth-century girl practicing magic to attract her lover. (See page 205.)

57. The return of women to a natural participation in music came by way of social diversion. Men and women are depicted on a miniature of early Renaissance times, playing and singing together. (See page 213.)

58. Francesco di Cossa, sixteenth century, painted a group of young women musicians such as might have performed at any Italian court. (See page 221.)

husband, the Duke of Milan; she was his ambassador to the court of Venice at sixteen. And when she died in childbirth at twenty-two, she was already known as a great patroness of music and art, and is so remembered to this day. For during her brief youth as a lovely young wife, much of the talent of Italy—poets, artists, and musicians —had converged on her court and had been encouraged by her eager interest in them.

So her sister Isabella went to her husband, the Duke of Mantua. But Isabella lived to the ripe age of sixty-five. She devoted herself so earnestly to the encouragement of every kind of art and beauty that she is usually considered the perfect type of these ladies of the Renaissance. In her status as mistress, she had the opportunity to patronize artists and musicians. Besides being a skilled performer herself, she was a critic. Since she had the authority to command her employee—the professional musician—and since she also usually possessed an intimate knowledge of good music, the lady as patroness was able to exert a real influence over new trends in artistic endeavor. As more literary and musical manuscripts from the period are being discovered, it becomes apparent that many great ladies played a part in directing the development of secular song away from popular vulgarity. From their consistent choice of aristocratic poems to be set to music, a definite change in musical taste resulted. As it was still the custom to enhance the emotional content of the text by means of music, the quality of secular song was heightened and refined.

At her best, in the courts of the Italian Renaissance, the lady was earnest, high-minded, and well trained. When the young bride took her place in one of these courts, which were lavishly competitive with each other in music and art, it was as if she had entered a university for the rest of her life, for she was henceforth in daily association with scholars, artists, and musicians of the highest caliber, and called on to exercise her judgment with respect to what they did. So, in time, some of these ladies, such as Vittoria Colonna, became very wise persons in their own right.

The solemnity with which these women regarded their functions is shown in a letter of Vittoria Colonna to Margaret of France.

In our day, the long and difficult journey of life compels us to have a guide; it seems to me that everyone may find in her own sex the most appropriate models. . . . I turned towards the illustrious ladies of Italy to find examples for imitation, and though I saw many virtuous among them . . . yet one woman alone, and she not in Italy, seemed to me to unite the perfections of the will with those of the intellect; but she was so high placed and so far away that my heart was filled with the gloom and fear of the Hebrews when they perceived the fire and glory of God on the mountain-top, and durst not draw near because of their imperfection.[3]

So, in Italy, and in all other courts where the new influence prevailed, as in those of England and France, the lady of the castle flowered into the priestess of beauty. As the patroness of social music and the object of song, she established a social and artistic norm for the literary and musical language of the emerging modern world. She fixed the code of social manners that prevails to this day and whose pattern determines the social functions of music. Through her mind and talk the revived culture of the classical age, in combination with a portion of the Christian culture of the Middle Ages, was filtered and passed on to us today.

3.

The education of the princess and the ladies attendant on her included all the essentials of music, because much of their waking hours would be spent on entertainments involving music. Historians and biographers of the Renaissance have written in glowing terms of the hundreds of musically talented ladies who spent a great part of their time singing and playing—"abandoning themselves in ecstasy to the composition of poetry and music." [4] They were encouraged to play the viol, lute, flute, and harpsichord, and especially to sing. A girl's training consisted in learning to read at sight, to harmonize melodies, and to express herself in the language of both poetry and music. It was the custom for composers to render their own music; and even when they wrote down notes for others to play and sing, they left a great deal to the musical imagination and discretion of the performer. A person would not have been worthy of the title "musician" without ability to embellish a melody with newly invented phrases or to improvise an accompaniment on lute or harpsichord. The two branches of musical art—performance and composition— went together as they had since time immemorial. Women appeared as performer or composer and frequently as composer-performer.

One of the highborn women musicians was Lucrezia Tuornabuoni, mother of Lorenzo the Magnificent. She composed Christmas carols and sang them with her children. Margaret of Austria (wife of Philip of Savoy) was another; she made beautiful love songs. Anne Boleyn was a third; she learned her music in Paris, where she had gone with Queen Mary, wife of Louis XII. Her accomplishments were many; she could dance and sing, she could play the lute and other instruments. One of her sad songs—"Death; O rocke me on slepe"—has been preserved. Still another song maker was Louise of Savoy. A skilled instrumental player herself, she often played for hours and presided over her women companions with their harps, flutes, and organs.

The lavish scale of social entertainments involving music demanded large numbers of trained voices. Most of the courts maintained *castrati*, whose soprano voices had been preserved by an operation performed before puberty. The *castrati* had been introduced into western Europe by the ecclesiastical authorities to sing soprano and alto parts in the church service. Having banished women from the liturgical choirs, they had to have a substitute for them, which they obtained by mutilating men. These strange creatures, spoiled, bedizened, spuriously feminine in appearance and personality, often had voices of unsurpassed strength, endurance, and brilliance.

After the fourteenth century, many kings, queens, and nobles had private chapels attached to their courts. They employed a choir, orchestra, and conductor to make music for both chapel and court. Queen Elizabeth, for instance, maintained four sets of singing boys. One set, called Children of the Revels, performed theatrical shows for the diversion of the courtiers and ladies in waiting. The Duke of Bavaria kept a group of about fifty men, boys, and castrati to sing in his chapel and also to perform at banquets and other secular occasions where music was desired. At one time his court musician was the famous Orlando di Lasso.

Since women were trained in music and since polyphony required many voices, there developed a need for the participation of women in addition to the castrati. But, despite the many references to the singing by women of *frottoli*, madrigals, and part songs, it is impossible to specify which of the songs were written for women. For when the polyphonic music was written down, the composer inscribed the music in any clef he preferred with no intention of indicating the pitch to be taken. *Cantus* meant the top part, *bassus* the lowest, no matter what the pitch. Any music of that period may, therefore, have been performed by women.

4.

In any case, the taste for women's singing at the courts soon developed to the point where it could not be satisfied by amateurs alone, no matter how well trained they were. There began to be a demand at the courts for professional women singers. During the year 1553 Donna Giovanna d'Arragona gave a musicale at her palace in Naples. Two castrati and two women singers performed. The women received the congratulations of the discerning guests for their perfect singing. About 1600 Vittoria Archilei and Francesca Caccini sang so beautifully that they turned the tide of the castrati's popularity in favor of the women singers.

As early as 1378 the professional woman singer had appeared. She traveled around from court to court seeking employment. Chantresses were paid by Philip at Cambrai. As the taste for women's singing developed, the courts began to compete for the finest talent and voices. At the court of Mantua, where Isabella d'Este had gone as a bride, one woman after another won fame as a singer, among them the famous "La Ariana." To display the singer's voice, musicians inserted more and more difficult coloratura passages into the madrigals. More and more attention was paid to a sensuous quality of voice. More and more interest was taken in showmanship. The most famous of these court singers were the trio at the Este court at Ferrara, Tarquinia Molza, Laura Peperara, and Lucrezia Benedidi. They performed with the many talented amateurs of the court in "concerts," which were not performances for an invited audience, but regular features of the social life at the palace. Under the leadership of Tarquinia Molza, Laura Peperara, and Lucrezia Benedidi, "the concerts of these ladies were for some time the greatest marvel of the Este court. . . . His Highness required the ladies to practice together every day, so that in those days in Italy and perhaps out of Italy, were no concerts of ladies better than these. Every day in summer they sang from 7 to 8. The organist sat at the harpsichord. Signor Firono, master of the chapel, played on the big lute. Signora Livia played the viola, Signora Guarina played the lute, and Signora Laura the harp." [5]

An orchestra of ladies, led by the brilliant Tarquinia Molza under the patronage of the Duchess Margarita, was a feature at Ferrara. An account in Otto Kindeldy's book on Italian music gives a vivid description of the women in action.

The orchestra consisted of ladies. On the days of the concerts they prepared in the hall a long table, at one end of which a large clavicembalo stood. The instrumentalists (women) stepped silently in one after another, took their places with their instruments at the table and waited in silence. Then the directress stepped out and sat herself at the other end of the table opposite the cembalo. She took a long flexible polished stick which lay ready for her and threw her glance over the orchestra, gave the signal and the orchestra played with a wonderful ensemble.[6]

When the Duke and Duchess of Ferrara visited other courts, they took the three ladies with them along with their men musicians and their most musical ladies in waiting. There was one particularly famous performance before Rudolph of Austria, whom Duke Alfonso had gone to meet at Brescello in 1571. In this concert sixty ladies and gentlemen took part. "And they make one of the concerts of about sixty voices and instruments: and behind a clavichord played by Luzzascho Luzzaschi sang the Signora Lucrezia and the Signora Isabelle Bendido, both together so well that I never heard better." [7]

Of the famous trio Tarquinia Molza stands out with a brilliance that makes one regret that the record of her so far discovered is so incomplete. One would like to have copies of the music she composed for lute, viol, and harp, as well as for the voice. It was performed by the ladies of the court orchestra conducted by her. It was also sung. (See Plate 58.) The extravagant praise of her concerts was apparently for the music as well as its performance. But none of it remains. Her brilliant career was cut short when Duchess Margarita dismissed her from the court as the result of her unhappy love affair with Jacques de Wert. She retired to her mother's country estate, and in her disgrace her music was perhaps banished with her. Since she had no longer an opportunity to present her works, her talent was stifled—at least so far as the known record goes. Such was the penalty for the woman who incurred the displeasure of the reigning priestess of beauty.

Tarquinia Molza was typical of the versatility of the woman musician. When she sang with Laura Peperara and Lucrezia Benedidi, composers from all over Europe flocked to hear the marvelous trio.

Luzzaschi, the concertmaster at the court of the Duke and Duchess of Ferrara, wrote a series of madrigals especially for these ladies. Few singers today could perform them. But she was almost equally admired as a conductor, and she was a composer.

So it was with most of the professional women musicians at the courts. Their unique assets were their singing voices. But they were all-around creative musicians. Many of the brilliant singers at the courts and *accademie* brought their own songs. Laura Peperara had her own style of reciting verses to the harp. Barbara Strozzi always performed at her father's musicales and often wrote her own songs. She published a set of madrigals for four voices. Laura Bovia, calling herself player and composer for the court of Mantua, published a volume of five-part madrigals. Francesca Caccini, one of the best of the sixteenth-century women composers, wrote madrigals, *ballate*, and dramatic works that were extremely popular wherever she took them. In France, Clementine de Bourges excelled in the composition of music. Women also composed in the new form of opera, received everywhere with enthusiasm. On the wedding day of Duke William of Bavaria, for instance, Orlando di Lasso arranged the performance of an opera by Mme Madeleine Casulana and of another opera by Caterina, niece of Adrian Willaert.

5.

Advantageous marriages could not always be found for daughters of the nobility. For the highborn girl who could not become a patroness of music and art and be a mistress of beauty at some court worthy of her birth, the convent was the alternative. And in the monastery, women were subject to the Church's age-old repression of their sex. An example of the definite regulations ordered by the ecclesiastical authorities can be seen in an edict given out in Rome on May 4, 1686:

Music is most detrimental to the modesty befitting the female sex, as it distracts from more proper actions and occupations; and on account of the dangers to those connected with it, instructors as well as listeners, no young girl, married woman, or widow, though for educational purposes, or else in convents or music schools under any other pretext, although studying music to the end of performing it in these convents, shall be permitted to take lessons in singing or any kind of instrument from men teachers.[8]

The rich convents were full of the sisters of the reigning ladies. They had had in youth the same education as their royal sisters. They carried to the convents the same aptitude, training, and taste for music. And the general trend away from the exaggerated repressions placed upon women by the Church was extending into monastic life. In Cologne, during the year 1550, an edict was given out by the bishop that the nuns might act the part of the Three Marys in the Easter plays. In Italy, many convents produced *sacre rappresentazioni*. Serafino Razzi wrote music for some young nuns in Florence to sing in their leisure time. Little dramas composed especially for nuns and novices began to appear. Marc Antonio Charpentier, for instance, presented the young women at Port-Royal a Christmas cantata that any group of schoolgirls today would enjoy. A story about the nuns of Bologna illustrates the new freedom in the monasteries. It appears that at the convents of St. Agnes and St. Christina there was great rivalry in the performance of liturgical song. During the year 1703 a prohibition was issued forbidding them to sing at all! At St. Christina this ruling was observed for one week, but at a ceremony of the taking of the veil, the choir was unable to suffer restraint. They broke into such sweet singing that crowds of people were attracted, bringing large sums of alms to the convent. Fortified by public approval, they continued to sing and inspired all the other convents to follow their daring example.

French and Italian nuns, like their laywomen contemporaries, profited from the musical renaissance which was taking place all over Europe. By the sixteenth century, women were attracting the musical public to the monastery chapels. At the Chiesa dello Spirito Sancto in Rome, the nuns sang vespers on Easter Monday with such perfection that the critic Pietro della Valle said he had never in his life heard such beautiful music. In the seventeenth and eighteenth centuries, French and Italian nuns received unstinted praise for their wonderful singing and playing. At the convent of San Vitale, Florence, Catabene de Catabeni and Cassandra Pigno were good *tenors*, Alfonsa Trotti a *basso*, singular and stupendous; Claudia Manfredi and Bartholomea Sorianati were sopranos (*soprani delicatissimi*). Rafaella de Magnifici and another Catabene were players of the

cornet—playing also every other sort of instrument. Olimpia Leon
(1621) played a viola and sang contralto with great feeling and a
beautiful voice. The famous walk to Longchamps (Paris) origi
nated in the eighteenth century as a pilgrimage of enthusiasts who
went to hear the nuns sing the Tenebrae on Good Friday.

It was for singers such as these that Palestrina, Lasso, Vittoria,
Monteverdi, Couperin, Lotti, and other famous church composers
wrote motets to be performed at special services.

In the convents of Italy there were several extremely good
women composers. Suor Beatrice del Sera was felt by music lovers to
be remarkably original. At the monastery of Santa Margherita in
Milan, Maria Caterina Calegari was famous as a singer and organ
player, attracting crowds of music lovers from far and near to hear
her play and sing her own compositions. Many others received recognition for their motets and organ compositions.

6.

What the Italian ladies did at their courts was done with greater
or less success at other European courts down to the nineteenth
century. In the latter part of the sixteenth century the courts of England and France were also centers of musical activity. Queen Elizabeth herself was a musician, and English girls of the aristocracy studied music like the Italian girls. Lady Mildmay, a sixteenth-century
English girl, in describing her pastimes to a friend, wrote: "Every day
I practice my voice and set songs of five parts to my lute." [9] There
was the royal pageantry in England and France involving special
musical compositions and performances. On one of Queen Elizabeth's "progresses," she was greeted by a party of girls dressed to
imitate the Greek graces and hours. They sang what is described as
"a sweete song in six parts." When King Henry II of France traveled
to Rouen, he too was entertained by a pageant. The chronicle of the
festival describes a show chariot on which ladies representing Vesta,
Royal Dignity, Triumphant Virtue, Respect, and Awe rode while
they sang a song of praise to the King. The very words and music
that they sang are still in existence—a four-part motet for three soprano voices and one alto by H. Lecouteux. (See Plate 59.)

Praise and glory, thanks for the favours!
Eviva the King, eviva." [10]

In the poorer and ruder land of Germany the courts were at first slow to take up the new fashion. In 1550, when the English ambassador reported to King Henry VIII his opinion of Anne of Cleves as a prospective queen, he said: "Nor yet she canne not synge nor pleye enye instrument, for they take it heere in Germanye for a rebuke and an occasion of lightnesse that great ladyes should be lernyd or have enye knowledge of musicke." [11]

But in the seventeenth and eighteenth centuries the German courts became centers for the patronage of music, supported by a widespread knowledge of composition, singing, and instrumental playing among the ladies of the nobility.

The Electress of Saxony—Maria Antonia Walpurgis—was extravagantly praised by Dr. Charles Burney. On his travels around Europe, he visited her court and described her talents: "This Princess is celebrated all over Europe for her talents and the progress she has made in the arts. . . . Her Highness is a poetess, a paintress, and so able a musician that she plays, sings, and composes in a manner which dilettanti seldom arrive at. She has, among other things, written in Italian two operas which she has herself set to music. . . . She sang a whole scene from her own opera Talestri in a truly fine style." [12]

In the late eighteenth century music flourished in Vienna under the Empress Maria Theresa. Caldara, for example, composed a four-part madrigal called "The Game of Cards" for the four archduchesses. Hasse wrote a charming litany for the Empress Maria Theresa and her eight daughters to sing in their private chapel. The Empress, who had a fine alto voice, took the principal solo part. The girls joined in the choral sections and the future Emperor Josef played the organ.

No women musicians in Europe or England could vie, however, with those of Italian blood and background. From Italy the spirit of the Renaissance flowed out, carried often by the melodious tones of a woman's voice. Sometime around 1700 a Venetian noblewoman, Antonia Bembo, went to Paris and attracted the attention of the great Louis XIV by her beautiful singing. Since she was performing her own compositions, the King believed her competent to be his court musician. While in the royal household and expected to produce a constant supply of new music, she composed freely. One of her most successful works was a Te Deum for mixed voices and instruments. This Te Deum contains a very fine trio for women's voices; the song extols the beautiful eyes of Princess Adelaide of Savoy. It was written by the order of the King to give thanks for the safe delivery of her baby boy. If it had been associated with the name of some great man composer, it would have been a celebrated piece.

Bembo was one of a very small group of talented women who attained the rank of musical leader at court. Only three are known to have been in the position held by countless men—Louise Couperin, a Frenchwoman who worked professionally for Louis XIII, Tarquinia Molza, and Antonia Bembo. Each of them, when under a stimulus somewhat comparable to that enjoyed by men, created the type of music demanded by their employers and demonstrated the ability of women to think and work in terms of contrapuntal music.

7.

So through the centuries, from the time the troubadours began singing to the lady in the castle, there was a series of momentous changes involving the relation of women to music and hence to the whole pattern of social life. By the fourteenth century the taboo against women playing instruments was removed. By the fifteenth century ballroom dancing, even with the kiss before the partners separated, was considered proper. By the sixteenth century disapprobation of women's natural voices changed to approval, and women became normal participants in the singing of madrigals and part songs. Old, young, and even servants were in demand where polyphonic music in the home required several performers. By the seventeenth century the ladies were acting on the castle stages. Castiglione, who described ideal courtly life, thought that music and singing were "pastimes most fitting when ladies were present." He set the standard for a great lady—"She must occupy herself with literature, music, painting, dancing and entertaining." [13] Music and women were no longer incompatible companions in Christian doctrine. A good Christian lady could improve herself with a little music. In this respect, times had changed.

With the freedom to make music, there was a limited opportunity at some courts for professional women musicians to work as conductors and composers. But such brilliant women tended to be unlucky and a little tragic. Society was not organized to sustain them or to further their genius. Where they emerged as composers they were social accidents. For the most part, the function of women at the courts was simply to provide inspiration to men musicians. And this function they fulfilled wherever a sufficiency of wealth and power was represented in some lady, carefully trained in music for her high position as fosterer of the genius of men.

In influencing and often initiating social changes and inspiring men to produce new music for new occasions, the priestess of beauty had a mission. She was the indispensable social background for the creation of secular music in the sixteenth, seventeenth, and eighteenth centuries. Through her, music came to be regarded as a direct extension of the functions of a lady. The aristocracy set the standard for the rising bourgeoisie, and even after the glory of the courts had faded many rich ladies of the nineteenth century retained the musical customs of the castle at their town houses or country estates. These dilettanti—those who delight in music—and amatores—those who love music—were quietly creating and maintaining that cultivated taste without which no men musicians, however great, can thrive.

This priestess of beauty was by no means the one whose coming had been crudely foreshadowed by the priestesses of the pagan religion. She was not a natural being, in the fullness of a free development, standing on the inalienable dignity of her own relation to life as mother and woman. Despite the earnestness of some of these ladies and the intelligent and hard work they gave to their social task, the priestess of beauty was an artificial creation, representing the subordination of the woman to an ideal of aristocratic family pride and power. But even so, the modern world owes much to her. In her, woman found again a real though limited place in the hierarchy of talent and power. The priestess of beauty symbolized for womanhood what Lodovico di Canossa attributed to music: "Music is the charm of life, its light, its sunny grace; no art responds thus to the needs of our nature, none brings us such various and vivid emotions. It calms and penetrates us and raises us to Heaven with the quick beating of its wings." [14]

It had been discovered that life cannot be fully lived without that charm.

CHAPTER XV

THE PRIMA DONNA

1.

*T*HE cultural pattern in which women as musicians function today was set at the beginning of the seventeenth century. At that time modern society, with new and revolutionary uses for music, began to take form.

The change began with the slow crumbling of Church and castle as the guides of the people's spirit and arbiters of their earthly fate. The Protestant rebels against the Catholic Church established their dominance in the northern European nations, which now assumed leadership. Though the Protestants frequently repressed women and limited the use of music, the religious and ethical monopoly of the Church as a whole was broken. Feudalism decayed or was violently destroyed. With its passing the power of the lady of the castle and the palace slowly declined.

Instead of looking to the Church to explain and control the vast powers of the universe, men gained increasing assurance, and increasing practical rewards, from exploring and controlling these powers through science. Instead of looking to princes and lords for material well-being, they began to find ever increasing means of getting well-being for themselves through trade and commerce and manufacturing.

All these new tendencies were best represented in America. Starting at the beginning of the new era with no real traditions based in medieval church and castle, it was free to make the most spectacular and universal application of trade, money-making, science, and invention. Modern America is now the supreme example of the change that had come over music and woman's relation to music.

Quite apart from the extension of music into new fields, during the seventeenth century there came a fundamental change in the idea of the utility of music—a change that amounted to a revolution in the social aspects of the art. The modern state and the modern educational system began to assume responsibility for leadership in thought and in the formation of ideals. As the new institutions gained in authority, music became an activity within the sphere of each, and musical expression from the talented individual found many new outlets. Instead of being inseparable from ritual, dance, and poetry, used primarily for the purpose of enhancing the emotional value of these expressions, music now began to be used as an end in itself. The stage, rather than the place of ritual or locale of work, became the setting for music. "Concert," which had meant music made concertedly by several people for their own edification or diversion, now came to mean a performance by skilled professionals in which the audience took no part. The focus of interest changed from what music could do to people to what people could do to music.

One thing that did not change, however, was the association of music with the most highly valued activities. Music had always been a magic means of inducing a spiritual state. The religious exercises that were believed to bring this about once occupied the most important place in the social life of the times. When religion lost some of its former dominance and other values developed, the nature of musical enterprise adapted itself to the changing environment. Trade, commerce, business, and money-making became the most highly valued activities. In the minds and lives of a great many people, business organizations and activity superseded the Church. And from the seventeenth century on until the present day, music entered a creative career as the handmaid of commerce. Thus the public performance for a price superseded the old religious practices.

The significance of this new relation of music to money is profound. Music lost the power that had been attributed to it from the beginning—the power to have some practical effect on the forces governing life. Music was no longer regarded as magic, but by many people merely as a means of making money, and by others as an amusement or diversion. But the more people were able to deal scientifically with physical and practical ills, the more they were left with a need for some other magic. So music became a means of spiritual escape from care and worry, even from the details of money-making. Other means had to be found to bend the powers of the universe to the will of the individual. But individuals still had no peace, no fullness of joy or reserve of vitality unless they harmonized themselves to the mighty rhythm of the universe. And the supreme means of doing this for modern people is music.

2.

Out of the quest for money and the need for spiritual escape developed the public concert, and with it a new popular goddess, the prima donna.

The popular concert gives to the people what formerly was the monopoly of court and castle and church. One does not have to ask the church or the lady of the castle for leave to enjoy skilled performances of music. One simply pays a price so small that any thrifty worker can afford it. This is an immense release to the spirit of man, and especially of woman. A woman buys her ticket equally with a man and attends what she pleases. The box office knows no sex.

The popular concert takes the ideal of the lady as priestess of beauty and gives her to the people as prima donna, the lady of their own worship. The lady of the castle and of the Renaissance palace had been a remarkable social institution. In her, aristocratic society had achieved a synthesis of the function of mother and wife and of the presiding spirit of music and social entertainment. In ancient society and in polished societies outside the West to this day, the mother and wife are one person, the hostess, musician, and entertainer quite another—a courtesan, a geisha, a singsong girl, often beloved and admired and highly cultivated, but deprived of the status of her who bears the burden of the race. In the lady of the castle and palace, the honorable wife and mother took over some of the arts, the charms, the social freedom, and the privilege of the courtesan. She could sing and dance in mixed company. She could be the object of the praises and admiration of men and musicians.

When the public concert developed, the people appropriated this lady and made her their own. A woman's charm and talent became legitimate public property. She could display it to any public audience, yet remain in person and in private reputation inviolate. The lady's voice was also appropriated. The Church could and did make rules against women's singing. But the people paid no heed. What they sought was a spiritual escape. There was no musical instrument that gave wings to the average person's spirit on which he or she could more easily soar away than the voice of a woman.

So out of the extension of the functions of the priestess of beauty to include all who could make a small votive offering at the box office, and out of the people's response to the woman's voice, there gradually evolved the prima donna. She thus became the modern goddess of music at whose altars a worshiping public burns incense of praise, on whom are showered all the gifts of the world, and whose managers profit by the devotion of her followers very much as pagan priests may have profited from the worship of old-time goddesses. And since women's voices early proved to be among the supreme attractions of the public concert, a way was opened for women to make large sums by the exercise of their own talents and to wield the power that money gives.

3.

The drift toward public performances featuring women's voices had begun in some of the palaces and castles whose owners made their own buildings and grounds serve, on occasion, the functions of community centers by opening them to the public. This was what happened when the Duke of Mantua allowed his master of music, Claudio Monteverdi (1567–1643), to develop the idea of drama set to music, which had already been tried out in Florence and elsewhere, into a stupendous performance for an invited audience of five thousand people. This drama or opera, the *Ballo dello Ingrata*, opened with an elaborate scene showing the Inferno, with the souls of the damned coming through its flames, two by two, singing of their sins and their eternal torment. The voices of women who took some of the singing parts thrilled the Duke's court.

Slowly the woman singer began to emerge from the safe seclusion of castle or court into some public places without losing caste. One intermediate step was the appearance of women singers of noble birth at the *accademie,* which were men's social clubs. Diana Paleotti, one of the famous seventeenth-century singers, was extravagantly admired by a certain Roman nobleman, Marc Antonio by name, and was followed by him from house to house where the *accademie* met, and where she sang and played. Yet when she appeared at some public entertainments, he exclaimed in surprise that a noblewoman would dare to sing before so many people.

Another intermediate step was the appearance of a composer's wife as a singer in an opera composed by her husband. Several of the writers of the new musical drama were married to skilled singers. When the Teatro San Cassiano, the first public opera house, was opened in Venice in 1637, the first opera to be produced was *Andromeda*. The composer, F. Manelli, sang the role of Neptune himself, and his wife, Maddalena, impersonated Andromeda, but the roles of the goddesses Juno, Venus, and Astrea were taken by castrati.

So great a revolution as the appearance of honorable women upon a public stage could not come to pass without stirring the opposition of the Church. Naturally, the authorities took steps to prevent girls from adopting musical careers. A series of decrees was issued. The first one appeared in 1588 and affected only the Roman theater, but in 1676 Pope Innocent XI extended the prohibition to cover the whole of Christendom.

When women did perform in a public place, an apology seemed to be in order. The prologue to the second part of the opera *The Siege of Rhodes,* one of the first English operas, is spoken by a woman who says: "Hope for our women less, whose bashful fear wondered to see me dare to enter here." When in Russia, at exactly the same period, orchestras were being organized and theaters opened by Peter the Great, even this notable reformer could not break down the tradition of the monastic ideal in which Russian women had been nurtured for centuries. He was obliged to import actresses from Germany for the first Russian operas. Russian women themselves shrank from the public gaze.

But as the seventeenth century progressed and the musical world went mad over opera, women solo singers were in great demand. The impressarios fully realized the sales value of a beautiful female voice. Unlike the Greeks, Europeans could not dispense with the actress, so they made her attractive offers in the forms of educational opportunities and financial rewards for singing in public.

With the rise of the middle classes in the eighteenth century, the career of the woman singer began to be soundly established along with the custom of public concerts and stage performances. Concerts of vocal and instrumental music, operas with ballet, and oratorios were performed in the public theater for the benefit of all who could pay admission. The fact that noblewomen were so accustomed to playing, singing, dancing, and acting in the castles undoubtedly in-

59. During the Renaissance period, women musicians participated in pageants and are so depicted upon a decorated chest. (See page 224.)

60. In a French lithograph from about 1830, a modern women's chorus can be seen in the making. The man, instead of waiting, is now in the center of the scene. Compare the men in Plates 13, 17, 19, 30, 32, 53. (See page 255.)

61. The seventeenth-century artist Florigerio has symbolized the relation of Western European women to music by painting an entertainer as the companion of men. A nun retreats from the group and the natural woman is missing. (See page 282.)

62. In this photograph of Martha Graham's "Primitive Mysteries," the grouping of the women and the position of their hands is similar to that in Plate 9. But while the Sherbro women *live* their rituals, these dancers merely *act* them on the stage. (See page 241.)

63. A Gray Lady with an auto-harp invokes the healing power of music for the rehabilitation of wounded veterans. (See page 290.)

64. Photographed in action, Vereda Pearson conducts a Neighborhood Home Festival. (See page 293.)

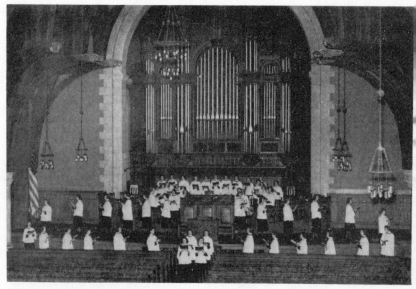

65. Vassar girls in vestments officiate at their chapel services. (See page 293.)

66. In a crayon drawing, the artist has expressed her appreciation of the spiritual sustenance she derives from singing in a women's chorus. (See page 293.)

fluenced public opinion in the matter of accepting women and girls of the middle classes as actresses and singers on the public stage. Even the continued opposition of the Church and the competition of the castrati could not turn the tide against the popular determination to make the public woman singer a trained musician with an honorable social status, whose highly lucrative career should be open to any girl of talent.

The alternative to women's singing was the singing of women's parts by castrati. Throughout the seventeenth and eighteenth centuries, sometimes women, sometimes castrati sang. The toleration of these curious substitutes for women was part of a general lack of verisimilitude in early Italian opera. No one seemed to be artistically offended if Hercules had a high soprano voice or if a maiden nymph was impersonated by Vittoria Tesi, a popular singer with an alto voice as deep as a man's. All interest was centered in vocal technique, in the ability of the singer to trill, shake, make "divisions," and reach incredible heights or depths of tone. Through the eighteenth century, wherever the Italian operas went, the castrati went with them. Upper-class groups and court circles pampered them. Clad in silk, velvet, and lace, with diamonds glittering on their soft, white, plump hands, they continued to warble and posture and to assume incredible airs, even in dealing with kings and potentates. In the portrait Seneseno had painted of himself, he represented himself as a Roman emperor, with ladies kneeling and kissing the hem of his coat of mail. Caffarelli complained to Louis XV that he did not receive the royal privileges accorded ambassadors. "All the ambassadors in the world could not make one Caffarelli," he said.[1]

While these creatures remained the darlings of some upper-class audiences, the genuine popular taste would have none of them. As the people with their increasing prosperity asserted themselves and the greatest opportunity for the singer came to be the concert stage, the castrati disappeared and the prima donnas took their places. Finally Napoleonic law made it a crime to castrate a boy. Apropos of the subject of incentives and stimuli to productive musical imagination, it is an important fact that, throughout their long history, castrati (or eunuchs) are never spoken of as composers and are not associated in any way with creative work.

The prima donna, who had already proved her worth in competition with the castrati, rose to greater heights of fame in the nineteenth century. The romantic movement sounded the death knell of artificiality. It was now the thing to capitalize human feelings. Love, longing, hate, despair, and other emotional states became the subject matter of music. The more a composer's music was capable of manifesting a mood, the greater its appeal. Audiences demanded men with bass voices and women with deep, rich, stirring voices to sing the new romantic songs and operas. The more passionately the women performers sang or played, the more fuel was added to the fire of enthusiasm for their musical service. The very qualities that had formerly made women unacceptable in vocal music now became their best assets.

While few singers could reach the heights of the great operatic prima donnas or concert singers, the way was opened for many skilled musicians to take the lesser parts. In the nineteenth century the limitless funds of the Americans and the ready enthusiasm of our great audiences made concert singing a most lucrative profession for the European women musicians. An American tour could make their fortunes for life.

4.

At her best the prima donna entirely transcended sex appeal and theatrical glamour and became a great representative figure, for women no less than for men. One of the most beautiful descriptions of Jenny Lind was that of Clara Schumann, who saw her with the eyes of a great woman and great artist.

"The Lind" has a genius for song which might come to pass only once in many years. Her appearance is arresting at first glance, and her face, although not exactly beautiful, appears so because of the expression in her wonderful eyes. Her singing comes from her inmost heart; it is no striving for effect, no passion which takes hold of the hearer, but a certain wistfulness, a melancholy, which reaches deeply into the heart, whether one will or no. At the first moment she might appear to some as cold, but this is not so at all; the impression is caused by the purity and simplicity which underlies her singing. There is no forcing, no sobbing, no tremolo in her voice; not one bad habit. Every tone she produces is sheer beauty. Her coloratura is the most consummate I have ever heard. Her voice is not large in itself, but would certainly fill any room, for it is all soul.[2]

Music like Jenny Lind's was made possible because it was wanted. The people had called forth in her powers such as had been dormant in other women for centuries. She could transcend the narrow and silly patterns of femininity still prevalent in the middle of the nineteenth century in a serene assurance of her power over so many hearts and minds everywhere. Wealth and praise were showered on her in her spectacular American tour, but she did not sing only for wealth or adulation. The lavishness with which Americans were ready to pour these at the feet of a prima donna rather overwhelmed her. In the midst of splendor she remembered her simple childhood and said wistfully, "Herrings and potatoes—a clean wooden chair and a wooden spoon to eat milk soup with—that would make me skip as a child." [3] The greatest prima donnas could always say in the words of Edith Wynne Mathison, "Nobody pays me for my art. That I give to the best of my ability. What I am paid for is what I must put up with in trying to give the world my art." [4]

At the present time, the popularity of the virtuosa—be she vocalist or instrumentalist—is undimmed. Newcomers on the stage are the wonderful Negro singers. When Marian Anderson was invited to sing one Easter afternoon on the steps of the Lincoln Memorial, the people of Washington thronged to hear her until the open spaces were filled with a vast surging crowd. This musician belongs to a race that, until only yesterday, had been barred from the professional musical life of European and American culture. Once the taboo was removed, once prejudice against the Negroes subsided sufficiently to give them liberty of action, several great singers rose to well-deserved fame. No better illustrations could be found of the way force of custom and taboo operate against the free use of human energy.

5.

While the prima donna was beginning to win her extraordinary place in modern music, the solo singers of the eighteenth century opened the way for the professional choral singer and her professional training. Before the eighteenth century there were no choruses in the modern sense. One or two performers to a part were regarded as sufficient to reproduce the composer's intention. Among the many new developments in musical customs was the rendition of music by large groups of trained people. Gluck's innovation in opera created a demand for the chorus. By introducing choral sections in addition to the solo parts, he required the participation of many more singers. As choirboys and castrati were far from plentiful enough to make up a large chorus, girls were pressed into service. The romantic movement increased the demand for them. No one would have been satisfied if beautiful young girls with trained voices had not sung the parts of the Polovetzian maidens in *Prince Igor,* or the priestesses in *Boris Godunov,* or the three Rhine naiads in *Das Rheingold.* The new interest in dramatic verity made women indispensable and opened up a wide avenue for musical activity.

The problem was to provide enough trained girls to take the feminine parts. Even as late as 1825, Spontini had to dress up choirboys in the robes of vestal virgins for his opera *Les Vestales.*

The demand for trained singers to take part in operas and oratorios prompted musicians to found special schools for the instruction of music. Hence, one of the new movements of the seventeenth and eighteenth centuries was the institution of schools for girls. Previously, girls had received their education at home from private tutors, or they had attended the monastic schools where they were educated as if they were to become nuns. One of the first schools for the professional woman performer was founded in France by Lully. He persuaded Louis XIV to allow girls to dance in the ballets of the operas he was composing. This was the origin of the Académie Française. Several princes in Germany founded singing schools for girls. In Hamburg a municipal theater was established—a unique institution in the history of German opera. A description of the activities there stated that "the female personnel is made up of daughters of destitute merchants and artesans." In 1711 seven girls are named in the records, their good social position being expressly specified, as if the authorities wished to make the profession respectable. Later, almost every city in Europe, England, and the Americas had several conservatories of music and, probably without exception, expected the attendance of girls, whose tuition fees were needed by the teachers to make their business profitable.

6.

The prima donna also broke ground for instrumental players as artist performers, though instrumentalists lacked an undeniable advantage or disadvantage in tone production. Women had here the competition of men, especially of those who started the fashion of playing on the new and improved pianos with a touch loud and heavy enough to break the strings. Nevertheless, many women have excelled in playing both the old-fashioned harpsichord and the new piano in public performances.

Supreme among all women pianists was Clara Schumann. All that makes the drama, the glory, and the tragedy of a woman artist's life was hers in full measure. Trained by her father as a child wonder and taken on concert tours by him, she was treated with the utmost harshness by him when she married the impecunious musician and composer Robert Schumann. Her father took her savings from her earnings and would let her have nothing to begin married life. Though her husband loved her dearly, admired her art, and constantly spoke of the inspiration she gave him, they both took it as a matter of course that she would make a daily routine that would be convenient to him. In her diary Clara wrote: "My playing is getting all behindhand, as is always the case when Robert is composing. I cannot find one little hour in the day for myself." [5]

Seven children and a husband who spent his later days in an asylum drove her to resume her concert career. A woman of thirty-five, she took up the task of making Beethoven's work, then considered baffling and abstruse, known through her exquisite playing. She was the inspiration and critic of Brahms, who was fourteen years younger than she and who adored her. She devoted herself to making his music known, by her beautiful playing, along with that of Beethoven and her husband. In city after city of Europe the lovely lady, "almost a widow," her slight figure very slender in its tight bodice above her full skirts, sat at the piano. Steadily, tirelessly, with a standard of execution that was the wonder of all the musicians who heard her, she kept up her tours, playing to bring her husband back to health, playing to support her children, playing to make known new and beautiful music the world had not learned to appreciate. These were her incantations.

For those talented girls who could not attain the success of a Clara Schumann, a Mme Carreño, or many others, the piano proved to be a practical means of providing a satisfactory career in professional performance and especially in teaching others to perform. In modern times, no other instrument has surpassed it in popularity and in practicability for the woman musician.

Next to the professional piano players, violinists presented themselves to the public. Maddelina Lombardini, a particularly brilliant musician of the eighteenth century, rivaled Tartini in her playing. Like the ladies of the courts, she often played her own compositions.

In the nineteenth century numerous others performed before admiring audiences. Soloists of either sex performing on wind instruments in public were extremely rare until the most recent times.

7.

But the genius of individual performers could not break down entirely the old taboos against women in music. What was yielded to an individual woman of genius or charm was not yielded to women collectively and as a right. In no field do the curious anomalies that have been inherited in our culture from a dark past show more clearly than in the barriers women encounter as players in orchestras.

Among men, professional instrumental players of lesser skill found many opportunities for a musical career in the opera and symphony orchestras, which were increasing by leaps and bounds throughout the nineteenth century. But here women were, and still are, at a grave disadvantage. Players and conductors in the newly forming orchestras at first consisted entirely of men who used music as a means of making a living and who resented the competition of women. For some unknown reason, harpists proved to be an exception to the general taboo against women appearing in an orchestra. A single woman playing the harp graced almost every concert. Since the First World War, competent instrumental players have been pouring out of the conservatories, seeking employment in the large orchestras, in various types of chamber orchestras, or in jazz bands. But still controversy rages over the question of the participation of professional women instrumental players in orchestra associations supported by the public. The women have their supporters and their antagonists announcing diametrically opposed opinions as to the worth of women musicians.

On the one hand, these instrumental players have many supporters, especially in localities where women themselves are accustomed to independence. At Long Beach, California, for instance, an all-women orchestra is maintained by municipal tax. A short time ago Leopold Stokowski said: "I find that women are equally as talented as men." And in the New York *Times* of September 29, 1940, appeared a statement by Izler Solomon, conductor of the first all-women symphonic orchestra to appear regularly on the air: "It is perfect nonsense to say that women are inferior to men in the world

of music. . . . In many instances, they are better than men. . . .
Women are more sensitive and are apt to have a finer perceptive
reaction to phrasing." Hans Kindler, in 1946, represents the most
liberal attitude toward women players: "Their ability and enthusiasm constitute an added stimulant for the male performers . . .
they were a veritable godsend to most conductors during the war
years. The National Symphony has re-engaged its fifteen women
players." [6]

On the other hand, José Iturbi goes so far as to agree with some of
the nineteenth-century conductors in believing that women can
never be "great musicians." On that account, he refused to accept
girl graduates from the Eastman School of Music as players in the
Rochester Symphony Orchestra. In a recently published article, Sir
Thomas Beecham boldly announced that "Women Ruin Music." He
explained his meaning by adding: "If the ladies are ill-favored the
men do not want to play next to them, and if they are well-favored,
they can't." [7] In this remark he makes himself out a cad, or, as his
countrymen say, a "bounder." But he also places himself in the category of the early Church Fathers, who wished to make the life of the
spirit, including music, a man's business with no thought of women's
emotional needs.

Even today, in most parts of Europe, England, North and South
America, however, women have an uphill fight to secure a desk in a
professional orchestra. Many irrelevant reasons are advanced for
their exclusion. Women, it is said, cannot attend rehearsals on account of their home duties, women cannot travel, women interfere
with men's liberty to swear and spit, girls might flirt with the patrons. . . . These difficulties are overcome by managers of theatrical and ballet troupes because girls are essential to the success of
their business. Orchestral music can be performed without women.
Hence, excuses are made to exclude them.

As a result of excluding women from the regular civic orchestras,
women have organized instrumental groups of their own. Musically, these groups are without justification, since in instrumental
playing the sex of the player should make no difference, unless, of
course, feminine sex charm is advertised as box-office appeal. What
the serious woman musician hoped was that skill, when demonstrated, would enable her to be employed in a regular orchestra on
terms of merit. But when the women's organizations first appeared,
they were met by the critics with a conspiracy of silence. In 1896,

for instance, the concerts of the Women's String Orchestra of New York were never reviewed by the press. Later, sarcasm was employed. Patronizing remarks about women's orchestras are still the rule rather than the exception. It is the reporter's favorite joke to compare women players to sirens or angels. The old idea of the Jewish rabbis and the Christian Church Fathers, that a woman musician must be either a seducer of good men or a sexless spirit, dies hard. Most critics, indeed, treat with levity the legitimate attempts of women to earn their living by means of instrumental music: "Eight hundred feminine members of the American Federation of Musicians campaigned for the right to toot the trombone and blow the bassoon—for pay. They charged that the eighteen thousand masculine members of the union so dominate the field of professional music in New York that a woman can obtain jobs only by playing the harp, piano, or organ." [8]

Unless a girl attains the rank of a successful virtuosa, she has far less chance for a profitable and interesting career as an instrumentalist than if she were a man of equal native talent and proficiency.

8.

Despite the cultural backwardness of some men musicians in positions of authority, the prima donna was a constant inspiration to the woman musician. As she soared to her great glory in the nineteenth century, women engaged in a determined but uphill battle to assert leadership in other kinds of endeavor associated with music. Within the last two or three decades this is beginning to show some real results, especially in America. As conductors, as critics and musicologists, as composers, as teachers, and as dancers, women have been able to do more or less original work—not nearly as much as they might do, but an increasing amount with increasing freedom and effectiveness. A few individuals have been able to compete successfully with men on men's own ground. For a representative of leadership in every modern department of the modern musical world, there is Nadia Boulanger. As performer, conductor, composer, and teacher, she attracted men and women from the four corners of the earth to her institute at Fontainebleau, and has become a distinguished leader in the advancement and dissemination of intellectualized music.

Nowhere has women's initiative in enterprises associated with music been more original than in creating new forms of the dance. Since the dance as a religious expression was forbidden by organized religion, ballets in operas developed in the most artificial and barren manner. But by the end of the nineteenth century the public became ravenous for new sensations. At the same time women were beginning to be sufficiently emancipated to act as free lances. From Isadora Duncan on, a steady supply of women artists has been revitalizing the old primitive dance forms that expressed subconscious desires and strivings. Like her primitive ancestress, the dancer of today usually combines the functions of creator, performer, and leader. (See Plate 62.)

In conducting music, however, the same barriers that keep women players out of orchestras were, and still are, effective. Men were already intrenched in musical leadership, and exclusion from classes in conducting added to the handicaps confronting a woman leader. When Antonia Brico, now a successful orchestral conductor, worked her way to Berlin and persuaded Karl Muck to accept her in his class, he was at first reluctant. Even in 1920, a woman leader seemed to be an anomalous creature. When a woman did succeed as a conductor, she had to overcome the general prejudice against women as leaders of public enterprises. The majority of people (including women) questioned a woman's ability to understand or demonstrate the music. Although she might have proved her authority, still they condemned her. Emma Steiner, a brilliant musician in New York City, successfully led the Anton Seidl Orchestra of eighty players. One of her admirers, Heinrich Conrad, said that he would like to promote her to be a conductor of the Metropolitan Opera Association, but that he did not dare to brave public animosity against a woman. Although prejudice against women leaders has abated sufficiently for several to have achieved marked success, still, except occasionally as guests, women are not asked to conduct the most important symphony orchestras.

On the other hand, a forecast of better times brings hope to young women musicians. Many of them are benefiting from a change not only in the attitude of teachers toward them but also in the new liberality of public opinion toward women leaders. Girls who enter the Westminister Choir School at Princeton, New Jersey, suffer from no suspicion of incapacity. This school is affiliated with the low-church Protestant groups that have taken the lead in breaking down barriers against the participation of women in the religious ceremony. The girls are trained not only to be choral singers, but also to be choir directors and organists. Young women graduates are as much in demand as their men companions. For missionary outposts and rural communities, married couples are at a premium. As a result of the general change in attitude toward the natural women, the number of competent women conductors is annually increasing.

9.

It is especially in the art of teaching that women have been able to break new ground by emphasizing social values of music that tend to be neglected by men musicians. The exclusion of women from musical activities where men have strong vested interests has forced women to initiative and enterprise, which, in time, if women prove to have a sounder sense of social responsibility, may prove to be a boomerang to men.

Many farsighted women have worked hard to establish music teaching in public and private schools and to develop methods of their own. As far back as 1850, an Englishwoman, Sarah Ann Glover, invented a sol-fa system for reading music. By virtue of it, hundreds of new choral societies sprang up in England. Opportunity for more individuals to participate in choruses and choirs was tremendously increased. From her day, almost a hundred years ago, to this, there has been a steady stream of women leaders intent upon breaking down the pre-emption of musical authority by the few and upon helping more people to experience music firsthand. A contemporary leader among women musicians is Olga Samaroff, the distinguished pianist. Realizing the lack of an adequate technique in so many adults for hearing music, she planned a course of study to give a person who has never been musically educated the elementary training for listening. The "Layman's Music Course" has been widely circulated to the enrichment of thousands previously incapable of enjoying music.

Though women, in general, have lacked adequate institutional support, this also is granted to gifted individuals on occasion. An outstanding example of this is the permission granted by the Catholic Church to a nun, Mother Georgia Stevens, to train the teachers, both men and women, who were needed to carry out an important reform in the musical usage of the Church. It is now ordained that the members of Roman Catholic congregations shall be taught to give their responses to the priest in Gregorian plain chant, according to a very ancient custom. Hence children in the parish schools are now given systematic instruction in singing.

For this a nun, Mother Georgia Stevens, who sums up in herself the long tradition of music in women's convents, organized and directed classes and trained teachers, many of them women. She wrote a graded series of six music textbooks to teach sight reading and the elements of composition—entitled the *Tone and Rhythm* series—which are a beautiful example of the application of intelligence, imagination, tact, and charm to teaching music. This teaching she designs not for the purpose of making skilled performers, but to restore to music its rightful place as a universal language for the deepest human emotions.

In her work as a teacher up to her death in 1946, and in the books she has left behind her, Mother Stevens has brought into the life of children and young people in the United States something of the leadership and power of the great nuns of the Middle Ages. Any child trained in her methods will henceforth possess music as a natural language and a spiritual resource. As regards participation in congregational singing, Catholic women and girls will eventually be in a position vastly superior to that of their Protestant sisters. Unfortunately, as yet the number of teachers trained in Mother Stevens' methods is insufficient to reach more than a few parishes. Like so many of the new musical customs in which women are having the chance to participate in a natural manner, only a beginning has been made, and only a very few women are profiting from changing attitudes.

10.

Mother Stevens' work was a long step in the right direction. But elsewhere in the great educational system that had been developing throughout western European and American civilization, the cleft between different types of musicians was widened. There were patrons, producers, impressarios, publishers, conductors, performers, and composers. Each group required intensive training and often cultivated quite different capabilities. All together, they served as a hierarchy of men and as purveyors of men's musical ideas to an expectant public. Women were no more in this hierarchy than they had been in the priesthood, except in the capacity of performers of men's music. Here the prima donna shone. But she shone alone. The expression of collective womanhood through music was lacking.

Under some circumstances the brilliant achievement of the prima donna might have provided a more vital stimulus and braver musical leadership for women. But she reached her height in connection with a general social tendency to overrate virtuosity as an end in itself and to underrate creative self-expression through composition. It is true that some prima donnas were composers. When the excellent professional singer Josephine Köstlin-Lang was a young girl of fifteen, Mendelssohn spoke with enthusiasm of her talent: "She has such a gift for composing and singing songs as I have never heard. She gives me the greatest joy musically I have ever experienced." [9] In later life, Josephine sang at her own recitals and also published many songs that were received with admiration. She was only one of many women performers who both composed and sang or played her own music. Clara Schumann composed for the piano and for the voice. The brilliant pianist, Mme Carreño, composed a stirring song that became the national anthem of her country.

But as the demands of virtuosity compelled performers to devote themselves completely to their task of acquiring a more and more brilliant technique, the urge to create was stifled. Men, too, became specialized into either performers, conductors, or composers. Anton Rubenstein is a good example of a musically talented boy who neglected his creative impulse in favor of virtuosity on the piano. Pianists and violinists even gave up composing their own cadenzas in concertos. Not the slightest stigma of spiritual or intellectual deficiency was attached to these artists—men or women. It was simply that custom had changed. Women, therefore, followed the fashion and lost the one springboard they had had for creative work.

The glorification of performing artists out of all proportion to their real service to society leads us to a secondhand and vicarious participation in music. Love, joy, grief, symbolic union with the rhythm of life find musical expression through witnessing performance on the stage rather than through actual participation by people themselves. A "festival" too often means a public performance by professionals rather than public participation by the people who are affected by the spirit of such a festival. We are satisfied to celebrate a victory by listening to a symphony. We have accustomed ourselves to hearing requiems away from the presence of the dead, and to watching dancers on the stage step through the paces of a primitive puberty rite, as in the beautiful conception of Martha Graham.

Such vicarious participation in music tends to deceive youth into thinking that men and women can dispense with the work of making every detail of living right and vital and that they are to look for beauty and art only in museums and on the stage. Thousands of girls and boys who should be learning the rudiments of music, who should be regarded as precious raw material from which genius is refined, are diverted from a straightforward, natural attitude toward music. Merely average ability to sing or play becomes mistaken for marked talent. Girls and boys glorify actors, actresses, movie stars, opera singers, and attempt to emulate them rather than aiming at the ideal of incorporating music into their own daily lives.

Overemphasis on virtuosity is now reaping its just reward. Our young composers—men and women—are at a distinct disadvantage when compared with those of former times. Societies have to be organized to "encourage" creative work. Prizes are offered to "stimulate" expression in terms of music. The public is not interested in new works, but places a far higher value on some popular singer or conductor who is able to exert a temporary magical charm over spiritually starved listeners. By following too intensely the ideal of *showmanship,* we narrow the groove for musical expression rather then opening wide the gates to limitless realms of imagination.

So the prima donna has been the representative of two great tendencies in modern music. On the one hand, her refulgent glory has helped gifted individual women to function as musicians. The light shed by her has been a sort of sunshine insensibly melting the frozen and sterile attitudes of the Church toward the natural woman musician. On the other hand, she has become the representative of a deplorable tendency to substitute highly finished performance of others' music for original musical creation, and to listen to music instead of participating in it. In glorifying the one spectacular woman who reaches heights of virtuosity, the influence of the prima donna and her spiritual descendant, the motion-picture star, has not been wholesome. As a popular goddess of music and charm, she is a dangerous deity whose presence in our midst needs now to be challenged if we are to revitalize the spirit of our young men and women by means of music.

CHAPTER XVI

THE CAMILLAE

1.

WHEN the priests and priestesses of ancient Rome approached the altars, they were attended not only by boy acolytes, but also by girl acolytes. These girls were called camillae.

So the modern priestess of beauty, the prima donna, has her attendants in the many amateurs who have been inspired by music. These are her camillae.

These amateurs have two functions. One is to act as patronesses or sponsors of performing artists. The other is to perform music themselves, in co-operation with or under the leadership of professionals.

For recognition and support, musical talent depends upon intelligent music lovers. As organizers of musical enterprise in all its forms, women continue to play an important role. The ranks of the few aristocratic ladies who patronized musicians in palatial residences have now been increased by thousands of prosperous ticket buyers for public concerts. In almost every city, women are associated for the purpose of assisting local artists and of helping to support the large orchestras and choruses. While there are still those who agree with Cosima Liszt that women were put into the world to serve great *men,* an increasing number are making a point of supporting women artists. Many a women's club now engages women musicians to sing or play at the meetings. And this tendency found a broader expression in 1939, when the General Federation of Women's Clubs, meeting in New York, stated that it would henceforth encourage those orchestras that employed women as well as men players.

Although women are so active and so beneficial an influence in the essential task of advertising and planning music, and although more women than men attend concerts, still the directing boards of the large orchestras and opera companies are made up primarily of men. The reason for this is that since the performance of music must be a profitable business, members of the board must have business, rather than musical, experience. To register her disapproval, the patroness may boycott an individual or an organization, but rarely from the inner circles does she make ultimate decisions about new trends in music. Her control is more negative than positive, more conciliatory than self-assertive. She herself determines this attitude and deliberately chooses to curb her power. In the musical world women actually have more power than they are exercising at the present time, but they allow their relation to music to be governed by their relation to men and to the type of culture in which they live.

Just as our modern art of music depends on amateurs as patrons, so it also depends on amateurs as performers in private and for their own pleasure. On the desire of amateurs to perform music themselves, a vast musical enterprise flourishes—including teachers and music publishers. Without these acolytes many professional musicians could not find means to live. As amateur performers of all kinds, women are now as numerous, as enthusiastic, and as powerful as men.

2.

But there is one field that requires a special discussion, and some historical background, for here amateurs participate to the virtual exclusion of professionals. This is the field of choral music. In this department of our musical civilization, amateurs are essential. Without their voluntary and temporary service on the stage, the great choral groups of modern times would be a financial impossibility. For women who love and crave music but who do not wish to be professionals, this custom has enormous benefit—for it enables them to participate in the greatest music with a professional conductor, accompanied by a professional orchestra and soloists, without interfering with their home life.

The rise of the middle classes to prosperity enabled many more people to pay admission to concerts. In the seventeenth century these new public audiences clamored not only for operas but also for other types of choral music. The men and boys trained in church choirs could not entirely satisfy the demand. Students' choral societies from the men's universities often gave both private and public concerts. Older men, too, who had singing societies and glee clubs for their own diversion, invited guests to hear them sing the popular part songs and madrigals. But such men as these and the trained church choirs were hardly fitted to present great oratorios and other forms of sacred music to the public. Then it was that volunteer choirs of men and women offered their services and immediately became indispensable. As early as 1680, mixed choruses appeared in France. By 1780 they were found in practically every city of Europe, England, and the United States.

Oratorios were first written about 1600, at the same time as the first operas. An oratorio differs from an opera in that it deals with a religious subject. The name "oratorio" was used because the oratory of churches was generally the place of practice and performance. It is said that the first oratorios were action songs, just like the operas. And it seems certain that women participated. But the presence of women in concerts of a sacred character, especially when they were performed in church, was objected to by many church officials and by the pious conservatives. In the first mixed choruses organized for singing oratorios, women sang only the soprano parts. Often, in public performances, they merely reinforced the choirboys' voices. In 1784 at the Handel commemoration in Westminster Abbey, for instance, *eight* ladies were permitted to assist the boys. Forty-eight men sang the alto parts, and indeed, until very recently, in many English churches and concerts men continued to sing alto. In one of the early American choruses, women seemed to be admitted out of a feeling of tolerance for their eagerness to sing. The Stoughton Musical Society, organized in 1774, gave women the treble but not the alto parts. Men sang the alto line and women merely imitated the tenors an octave higher in the treble range. Only gradually did the women take a natural place among the singers. When Mendelssohn and Spohr organized groups, they insisted upon giving women the alto parts to sing. After about 1840, women supplanted choirboys and even the male altos, and thus established beyond recall the modern mixed chorus.

The latest development of the mixed chorus has come about through the colleges for women and co-educational colleges. The establishment of institutions where women could gather for study and training made centers where women could function collectively as amateur chorus singers. They immediately established their high value for music. Men's colleges now send formal invitations to the girls to join with them in producing the great choral works.

Some of these mixed choirs are famous, appearing on the stage in special hierarchal costume. The St. Olaf Choir is clothed in purple velvet and the Westminster Choir in red with white satin surplices. So as far as the performance of vocal music is concerned, the mantle of the nun-priestess musician of former times has fallen on the shoulders of the modern college girl.

This has made a great many changes in choral music. Not only has the personnel of the chorus changed, but the sound of the music has changed. The B Minor Mass, Handel's oratorios, the Missa Solemnis, and other choral works that were written with the sound of falsetti, or boys, in mind are now associated with the sound of women's voices.

Another change has been the change in the character of the music. Modern audiences respond to music that expresses human emotions. For the purpose of enhancing the emotional effect, they prefer the joint performance of men and women. Brahms composed his German Requiem for adult men and adult women to sing together. Without the quality of maturity and experience with life, this appealing work could not be affectively interpreted. And ever since Brahms' time, this lead has been followed by composers of great choral music.

At the same time that women and girls were edging their way into the mixed choruses and were being trained as professional performers of music, some leaders in the musical world agitated for their inclusion in regular church choirs.

By the middle of the nineteenth century, women had been singing in enough choruses to have changed public opinion about the value of their joining regular church choirs. A contributory factor to liberality in the matter was the change that had taken place in the kind of music thought to be suitable for church use. Churchgoers became interested in giving to music that accompanied the religious ceremony the quality of a concert. Organists were expected to be virtuosi; solo singers were employed on a professional basis; women were included in choirs in order to facilitate the performance of elaborate anthems. Presbyterians in America, especially, followed the trend of concertizing all music and sanctioned the solo quartet—two men and two women singers who rehearsed and performed as if at a musicale.

Today, however, a distinction is still drawn between liturgical singing and other religious choruses. Where church music is regarded as a kind of sacred concert—a performance by trained singers for an audience that listens—women are admitted to choirs. But where music is a liturgy and the members of the liturgical choir are thought of as attendants of the priest at the altar, women are excluded. Women may entertain an audience, even in church, and attract people into the service by their voices, but they may not be official representatives of worship. This prohibition applies wherever there is liturgy, in its ancient and traditional sense, in the church service—whether the church be Catholic, Greek Orthodox, Jewish, or Protestant.

Protestant church singing is founded not on liturgical singing but on congregational singing. The formal choir, even in vestments, is composed of trained singers whose function is theoretically to lead the congregation in singing. To such choirs many Protestant churches admit women, and so greatly enhance their music and the interest it has for the public. In Flint, Michigan, working men and women have thus made their city famous by their reverent musicianship. At St. Paul's on the Hill, an Episcopal church in Minneapolis, men and women chant Georgorian plain song antiphonally. Dom Anselm Hughes, the well-known English music scholar, spoke of this choir in 1940 as being the most remarkable he had heard in America. There is clearly no musical reason why women should not sing in church, and the custom preventing them from taking an equal responsibility with men in the religious ceremony is a survival of a taboo on women that is now repudiated by public opinion. The exclusion of women from the liturgical choir constitutes the last barrier to the complete participation of women in the vocal music of our civilization.

3.

The mixed chorus with orchestra is the high point of our musical life. But there are also the separate men's choruses and women's choruses, both of which are sound musical ventures and sound social institutions with a longer history than any other musical group. At the present time, the social need for either has been transcended by the far greater need for choruses of men and women together. But as long as there are men and women, there will be times when men prefer to sing in their own groups and when women, or girls, find satisfaction in singing with each other without men. If a men's chorus is socially justified, then a women's chorus is equally justified.

There is, however, a striking difference between the two groups, and this difference is the cause of public respect for men's choruses and of lack of interest in women's choruses. Modern men's choruses are similar to the men's groups in primitive societies. They are, indeed, a continuation of very ancient secret societies. In primitive tribes today, men perform their own rites and invoke their own spirit at initiation, in preparation for war or hunting, and at many other times. The modern men's chorus is an offshoot of the synagogue or church choir in which men's religion (their relation to God) is expressed. Whether the men in a men's club today have ever sung in a synagogue or church choir or not, whether they believe in the Jewish-Christian God or not, they believe wholeheartedly in the power of men collectively. They sing with vitality, self-confidence, and in the assurance that they are right. In the glee club or college chorus, men celebrate their own moods, be they grave or gay. They sing music composed by one of their own members or by a professional man musician. They have their own leader. The secular chorus is merely one more institution organized by men themselves for the affirmation of their manhood.

As men sing now, so women once sang to their own deities, inspired with a proud, collective sense of their importance as women. And so they still sing among many primitive and peasant groups. But at the moment, the talent of peasant women in many countries has been forced into a channel that is still flowing swiftly and deeply like a mighty underground river, fertilizing the soil above it but only here and there surging up to the surface. In these groups women themselves are often conscious of their repressed power. Even a hundred years ago, strong personalities like the Gaelic Máire Ni Dhiubh burst out regretfully: "Where are the dark women of the glens, who would keen and clap their hands. . . ." [1]

And in our civilization women are so far devitalized by the long suppression of their real inner life and its voice in music that they do not even know why they are still not in the right relation to music. When women gather to sing now they have no background. Owing to the negative attitude of organized religion as a whole toward women and girls, the women's chorus of modern times has never been a religious expression, as the primitive and peasant women's choruses are. Even the Protestants missed the opportunity, which had presented itself so forcibly in the Reformation, to dignify their daughters and to crystallize the trend away from the debasement of women. They planned nothing for their girls in the way of official participation in religious music, and to this day accept the negation of womanhood. This principle, supported also by women themselves, has conditioned the whole development of the women's chorus and even the music composed for it by men.

When our civilization developed, only the nuns in the convents had music, and some wonderful music was composed for nuns by men. Even today this constitutes the best music for women's choruses—that is, the most nearly equal in quality to music for mixed choruses.

So far as early secular singing by women in groups is concerned, there is no record of the music sung by women together in the castles. We know of no music composed for them by men until the sixteenth century. Then some madrigals were written for especially skillful singers. Later in private chapels a few pieces were composed by men for women to sing. Much of the music now regarded as classics for women's choruses was composed for and sung by boys.

The women's chorus, as we know it, began in the music school or in the girls' boarding school—both products of the seventeenth century. At that time, singing teachers in France were gathering their pupils together to give them practice in "ensemble." And Mme de Maintenon was persuading Louis XIV to endow a boarding school for girls of the French aristocracy. In this school at St. Cyr, the Ursuline canonesses in charge of the girls taught them to sing beautifully in their private chapel. So charming were the girls' voices that Racine was inspired to write the operas *Esther* and *Athalie* for the girls to perform. His friend J. B. Moreau composed the music. Both operas were given several times before the king and royal guests with such success that the attention of the church was attracted. Objections were made to the nuns' and their pupils' spending so much time on secular music, and development along these lines stopped short.

In Protestant England, the girls' schools were often centers for the performance of new music. Purcell's lovely opera *Dido and Aeneas* came to life at Mr. Priest's school for girls in Chelsea. One of the pupils, Lady Dorothy Burke, took the leading part, and her companions sang and danced in the choruses. Like Mr. Priest, other schoolmasters were often skilled in music and advertised the teaching of song and dance as a particular advantage of school life. They frequently composed masques and operettas for their pupils. Susanna Perwich is an example of a young woman musician who had the incentive of leadership to develop her creative musical imagination. She and her mother directed a school for girls. As music teacher, she conducted a chorus, a ballet, and an orchestra. She herself invented the dances and wrote the orchestral compositions for the pupils. In America the Moravians in Bethlehem, Pennsylvania, were unique, apparently, in making adequate provision for their girls to be choristers. Division of the congregation into "choirs" according to sex and age brought each group into prominence as singers and made antiphonal singing a feature of the service. In the famous Moravian School for Young Ladies, founded by the Countess von Zinzendorf in 1742, the girls were taught to regard singing as a serious contribution to community life, and from their ranks came a number of hymn writers.

Russian "institutes," or boarding schools for aristocratic girls, were founded by various empresses. The first one in St. Petersburg was called "The Society of Genteel Maidens" and became known later as the Smolny Institute. Music played a great part in the lives of the girls who attended these schools. Choirs were organized as a matter of course. The girls often gave performances for guests or in celebration of some national event, and in that way had opportunity to participate in operatic music. In 1773, for instance, the pupils at the Smolny Institute performed Pergolesi's *La Serva Pardona,* and in 1775 they commemorated the treaty of peace just signed with the Turks. Dressed in the attire of vestals, four hundred girls took part while forty of them guarded a sacred flame upon an altar erected for the purpose.

During the nineteenth century, high-ranking musicians such as Glazounoff and Liadoff composed special cantatas for the girls to sing in welcoming church dignitaries and members of the imperial family. Most of these schools had private chapels in which the girls performed religious music with wonderful sincerity and skill. At the services held every Saturday evening and every Sunday morning, the choir was customarily led by one of the older girls and assisted by soloists drawn from the student body. The most wonderful singing was achieved during Lent and especially at the midnight service on Easter Eve. At the Vladimir Girls' School, where women teachers were trained for the parochial schools, the choir was particularly famous. It was the custom for legends and facts about the choirs, their leaders, and the soloists to be passed down from class to class, building up an unwritten tradition of effort and excellence.

During the seventeenth and eighteenth centuries, the famous Venetian conservatories for orphan girls gave tremendous impetus to the participation of girls in singing and playing instruments. In music-loving Venice, when prosperity enabled influential citizens to spend money for the arts, it was only natural that public institutions should also benefit from the prevailing interest in music. The directors of the four orphan asylums hit upon the happy plan of training the girls to contribute to their own support by means of concerts. Musical directors of high standing—among them such great masters as Hasse, Porpora, Gasparini, and Vivaldi—were engaged to compose vocal and orchestral music for the girls. The result was that soloists, the girl choirs, and girls' orchestras became famous all over Europe. Visitors flocked to the conservatory of the Incurabli to hear the choir, to the Pietà to hear the orchestra, to all four conservatories in order to hear the enchanting solo voices. Especially during Lent, when the theaters were closed, the fashionable world crowded into the churches attached to the institutions to enjoy the concerts given by these girls and their nun teachers.

Strangely enough, the Church, although it required a promise from the girls that they would not go on the stage after leaving the asylums, did not object to these concerts. Even when frankly secular music was performed, the ecclesiastical authorities shut their eyes to the activity. The decline of the conservatories did not come from suppression by the Church. It followed the Napoleonic invasion, with its consequent disruption of social life. In the history of women and music, the Venetian conservatories stand out as a milestone. A choral literature for women's voices arose; prejudice against a women's choir was somewhat overcome; the foundation was laid for later developments in other schools and centers where girls congregated; and precedents for the participation of women in music were established. These have not since been reversed.

In the latter part of the eighteenth century and in the early years of the nineteenth century, J. A. Hiller in Leipzig deliberately undertook to train amateurs for oratorio singing and orchestral playing. Hiller organized classes for different classifications of singers, giving the beginners only simple music and graduating them into groups capable of singing polyphonic motets and oratorios. His idea was to increase the supply of singers for oratorios and especially for church choirs. The Swiss Nägeli, too, had amateurs grouped together according to their proficiency. In 1824 he incorporated the several choruses and published the rules for membership. Respectability was one of the first requirements. The early nineteenth century still regarded group enterprises on the part of women as open to criticism. Nägeli gave a great impetus to the movement by his genuine faith in the ability of girls to sing religious music competently. He announced publicly *that the voices of young girls between the ages of twelve to sixteen compared favorably to those of boys and proved to be more supple and educable.* In a newspaper entitled *Morgenblatt für die gebildeten Stände* for November 8, 1808, an article appeared that praised extravagantly Nägeli's work and also the wonderful singing of his young girl pupils. What the public had long expected to hear sung only by boys trained in Protestant choir schools was now performed much better, so the critic said, by these girls with their higher, clearer, and more flexible voices. Nägeli's own conviction, too, that the most beautiful effects in religious music could be obtained by capitalizing the natural contrast of male and female voice lent authority to his efforts in behalf of the natural girl and woman. As time went on, nearly every music school had a chorus, formed by the girl students as an integral part of its social life. (See Plate 60.)

The Hamburger Frauenchor, for which Brahms composed practically all of his literature for women's voices, is well known to all choral singers. In 1859, when Brahms lived in Hamburg, one of his piano pupils, Friedchen Wagner, used to entertain him at her house. She asked him to arrange folk songs for her and her two sisters to sing. Brahms was pleased with the opportunity to exercise his skill, and suggested that the group be enlarged, promising to bring new music for each meeting. A concert was once given in St. Peter's Church. Upon another occasion the original group joined with the pupils of Grädener's Conservatory and gave a private concert. The Frauenchor has become famous because Brahms became famous, just as Nanette Fröhlich's pupils are mentioned in *Grove's Dictionary* because Schubert composed music for them. Hundreds of other groups functioned in the same way. The leader, associated with a conservatory, was the prime mover, and his (or occasionally her) interest lay chiefly in the musical experience to be derived from conducting and composing.

After about 1870 women began to organize their own music clubs, but these, too, generally depended upon a professional leader drawn from the conservatory or university group. This movement toward independence had no place in Russia, Italy, Spain, or, indeed, in any of the countries dominated by the Greek Orthodox or the Roman Catholic Church. It belonged to the Protestant and to the democratic nations. In Germany, especially, the choral singing of women was woven into the warp and woof of the aristocratic and upper-middle-class woman's life. Meeting in the drawing rooms of the large houses, some women joined several groups and went from one to the other, often singing four or five hours a day. And while in the nineteenth century no one group developed into an institution to promote the choral singing of women, the great number of isolated units in many parts of the Christian world brought about the revival of the women's chorus.

But women's choruses did not perform on the public stage. The appearance of more than one woman at a time implied collective independence and strength—a state for womanhood in which people took little interest. Even in the United States, where women had so much personal liberty, a public concert by a woman's chorus in 1888 received sarcastic comment. A well-known music critic wrote that were the choir composed of angels and led by St. Cecilia, it would still be musically unsatisfactory.

The conventional attitude toward a suppressed and reticent womanhood was reflected in the music produced by men for adult women to sing. Nineteenth-century composers who knew the love and companionship of individual women had not yet been sufficiently leavened by the romantic movement to regard *collective* womanhood as of the same caliber. The music these men composed for women is, as a rule, sentimental, sometimes mawkish, and generally inadequate to bring out the strength inherent in the female voice. The contrast between the bridesmaids' song in Glinka's opera *A Life for the Czar* and the Russian peasant mothers' wedding cycle illustrates with remarkable clarity the gulf between the artificial and the natural. Glinka has made a song for wavering, timid twittering of repressed young misses. One can imagine that he subconsciously desired the listeners to experience a sense of unfulfillment—a sense of longing for the bass voices of men to support the treble. How different is the musical effect produced by the deep, rich, emotionally satisfactory voices of the peasant mothers!

The composers often chose texts depicting women as sirens, witches, Loreleis, fantastic creatures without the creative power of the spirits of antiquity. Legends about the "errant," or wandering, moon lady became converted into sentimental poems about an "erring" girl mourning the loss of her chastity! Or the words of songs are inconsequential, placing women in the class of devitalized dolls, angels, even morons. Still more depersonalized for a women's chorus are the words of a man's love song—like Brahms' *"Minnelied,"* Op. 44, No. 1. In this choral literature, the real flesh-and-blood women, as well as the expression of strong, human attitudes, are conspicuous only by their absence.

In 1905, when Gustav Holst first went as director of music to St. Paul's Girls' School in London, he wrote his daughter: "I find the question of getting music for the girls' schools perfectly hopeless. I get reams of twaddle sent me periodically, and that is all the publishers seem to think is suitable for girls." [2] Even in the twentieth century, England's most intelligent girls were being treated like musical children.

After the First World War there was a great acceleration in the development of women's choruses, owing to the vastly increased attendance of girls in schools and colleges and the institution of women's clubs. As women became more independent in their daily lives, their choruses sprang up like mushrooms after a fertilizing rain. Many more women are joining choruses; more have organized the societies themselves; more choruses have women conductors. The newer the group, the more likely it is to be independent. The military girls, Wacs, Waves, Spars, and their British equivalents, invariably had bands and choruses with their own leaders.

Many of the Catholic church schools have wonderfully trained girl choirs. The most renowned of these is the group at Manhattanville, trained by Mother Stevens. These girls sing from the gallery at the Sunday services of the Church of the Annunciation, attracting visitors from near and far to hear their beautiful voices and polished performances. In at least some of the secular women's colleges, choral singing by the girls now forms an integral part of college life. Vassar girls, trained to keep on pitch for a whole evening's performance, enrich their chapel services with beautiful and appropriate singing. Mt. Holyoke girls have made their college famous by their sympathetic rendering of Christmas carols. The singing of Bryn Mawr girls has been metamorphosed and electrified by the arrival of a young woman conductor, Lorna Cooke Devaron.

Through the organization of clubs, women have been establishing new customs for their participation in music. The chamber-orchestra or chorus constitutes one activity in the larger life of the group. At annual meetings, these amateur musicians give a concert. No effort on their part to attract an audience is required, since the club members and their invited guests expect to be so entertained. In adopting this method, women have shown initiative in creating ways and means *convenient to them* for the gratification of their musical aspirations.

One significant result of such independence has been a change for the better in the quantity and quality of music composed for French, English, and American women's voices. In Germany, on the other hand, the decline in output is marked. In Italy, modern music composed for women's voices is practically nonexistent, since the amateurs' movement of the nineteenth century never materialized there. But where the women's clubs and college choruses evince an attitude of independence on the part of women, several composers and conductors are beginning to appreciate the enormous musical possibilities of women's choruses. They are featuring rich and moving alto parts, making interesting experiments with the low range of women's voices, testing a dynamic balance of soprano and alto, and introducing varied instrumental accompaniments. Most modern composers are setting their music for women's voices to appropriate texts, which treat women's interests and reactions with dignity.

Women's choruses are now a recognized social institution and their public appearance on a stage is no longer a cause for facetious comment. This change has occurred only since 1912. In that year Margarete Dessoff was asked to bring her women's chorus from Frankfort, Germany, to participate in a great German Brahms festival. She conducted it in singing Brahms' choral works for women, on a par with other performing groups. This was a landmark in the history of women's choruses. For the first time in history, a women's chorus made a public appearance on an equality with other musical groups in a serious musical enterprise. Since 1912 the development of women's choruses has been greatly furthered by the women's colleges and the women's part of co-educational colleges. Here women are gathered in strength under conditions that make for study and training and collective authority. Having developed music for and within its own group, the college women's chorus is in a position to appear on the public stage with prestige.

In recent years two great women's choruses conducted by women have set very high standards for performance. One was the Adesdi Choir of fifty women conducted for ten years, from 1925 to 1935, in New York City, by Margarete Dessoff. She made this chorus unique in that it sang only music composed originally for women's voices, and of the highest quality. The standard she set was maintained and even surpassed by the chorus of girls trained by Mother Stevens. At a concert given by her pupils in Philadelphia in 1940 three thousand people came to hear her and praise a girls' religious choir, trained by women and conducted by a woman. Before the war, these two remarkable American women's choruses were matched by others, also directed by women, in England, France, Germany, and South America. A significant fact, entirely unrecorded by critics or historians, is that the outstanding women's choruses of modern times have been under the leadership of women.

On the whole, the women's chorus has made phenomenal gains since its inception in the schools of the seventeenth century, but from the psychological point of view, the choral singing of women is still in a state of repression. People are still saying that women's voices alone are beneath the serious attention of a composer and that a chorus of women is uninspiring to a musical audience. Yet people do not complain that the low voices of men alone are inadequate to satisfy either the composer or the audience. At least ten times as much music has been written for men's voices alone as for women's. At least a hundred times more concerts have been given by men's groups than by women's. Curiously enough, there is still some indefinable barrier that keeps a women's chorus from being a complete success. The reason for this is not, however, far to seek. It is a social, not a musical, reason.

All musicians know well that a men's chorus is an inferior musical instrument to a women's chorus. Women's voices have more brilliance, clarity, and flexibility than men's. The missing sonority can be readily supplied by organ or by other instruments, whereas no instrument can adequately supply the mass of high tones lacking in men's voices. Finally, women's voices lend themselves more easily than men's to a greater variety of musical climaxes. There is no valid *musical* reason for the slur cast on the women's chorus.

But a women's chorus is not like the primitive and peasant groups —the ritual and musical expression of women collectively. The modern women's chorus is not an offshoot of church choirs. Jewish and Christian women have been excluded from religious choirs for many centuries. And nuns never sang to *affirm womanhood*. A few modern groups of women singers have been successfully conducted by women, but even they do not win public recognition as an expression of women's moods, thoughts, and desires. Without a new point of view, indeed, they cannot, since the ideal for Jewish and Christian women is a negation of the principle that women have anything to express.

Like the nuns' choirs, the modern women's chorus has been adapted by men (with the consent of women) to conform to the creed that men only are creative in body and spirit. Jewish and Christian women have been in this relation to men for so long that their ability, and even their desire, to assert themselves by means of group music is dormant. People think that what is missing in a women's chorus is the sound of men's voices. Rather it is the vitality with which men endow the sounds that is lacking. Women's choruses will never be as socially or as musically acceptable as those of men until women and girls feel inwardly—as primitives and peasants do—that their singing is merely one manifestation of their power and natural authority as women.

Because of the present-day emphasis on virtuosity, women find it impossible to regain this sense of power. Singing in a women's chorus should be one of the means by which women can revitalize their own depleted psyches. But to achieve this, such a chorus must fulfill several conditions that are generally neglected. It must be led by a woman, not by a man. The woman leader must have a full rich sense of the spiritual power of music and the latent spiritual power of women, and the ability to communicate this inspiration. Women must first meet to sing with no idea of training for a concert. They must be seeking *first* what music can do for them, not for an audience. A concert should be the by-product of success in achieving spiritual entity, not the end and aim of musical participation. Especially valuable in group singing is the companionship with others in orchestras and chorus—the thrill of hearing one's own part in strength, the discipline of giving way in turn, in order to perfect the sound of the whole. The chorus then becomes a tremendously important musical experience. The participants are stimulated to learn our great heritage of musical art by actually playing and singing it themselves. The necessary foundation is laid for spiritual enrichment and for collective self-expression.

4.

The *principle* of a dynamic participation in music applies equally to choruses of boys and girls in schools and colleges—which are now the best places for education in music. But unfortunately the over-development of the concert, and of the ideal of virtuosity, has cast a shadow over the rich experience. School authorities, influenced by current ideals, run a grave risk of overemphasizing the value of public performance.

In this they apply to music a standard they would not tolerate in connection with literature and language. Students are taught English, or any other language, with the primary object of mastering the use of the language terms and of becoming intimately familiar with the masterpieces of its prose and poetry. The acting of a play or the reading aloud of a novel in public is never made the goal of a season's work, but merely the occasional offshoot of activities that are broader in scope. In music, the giving of a concert is too often the end toward which all the efforts of the chorus or orchestra are directed. If practically all the available hours are spent preparing for the display of one composition, then there are not enough hours left for becoming familiar with other great compositions. No literature class would be satisfied with knowing only *one* of Shakespeare's plays; at least a speaking acquaintance with them all is required of an educated person. How few people know, much less have sung, half a dozen of Bach's two hundred cantatas, or Brahms' choral music other than his Requiem!

School and college years are the golden time for acquiring musical literacy. A similar opportunity rarely occurs again. Too many students leave their schools or colleges without the proper foundation for using music as a normal activity in postgraduate life. The prevailing attitude toward the value of virtuosity definitely deters the average girl and boy from taking a direct, natural approach to music as a language.

Women as camillae, or acolytes at the altar of music, are suffering from the juxtaposition, in our culture, of two sterile influences, one applying to them as women, and the other a general characteristic of our Western civilization. They have been spiritually starved as women by the long tradition of the Church, and by the requirement that, in matters of the spirit, they accept men's formulations and men's music. And they share with men the overdepartmentalization of music that limits music lovers to passive listening to virtuosi or to vain attempts to become virtuosi themselves. As audiences, as students of voice or instrument, as singers in mixed choruses or in women's choruses, the camillae may be serious and hard-working, but the deity they serve is not capable of giving them a tithe of the spiritual sustenance they obviously crave.

CHAPTER XVII

ST. CECILIA

1.

SINCE the sixteenth century, the virgin Cecilia has been the patron saint of music and the misleading symbol of woman's participation in music during the period of its great modern development. Her picture, with eyes upcast to heaven and cherubs showering roses on her as she plays, hung over the piano in thousands of nineteenth-century homes. Here was inspiration to guide the fingers of generations of little girls through the daily chore of piano practice.

Piano playing and, if a girl had a "voice," a little parlor singing were something a lady acquired by diligent and even painful effort, along with a waist laced in to be three inches smaller than nature made it, a foot that would fit a slipper half an inch shorter than itself, and a soft, flattering recognition that man is the woman's natural god. "He for God only. She for God in him." [1]

So St. Cecilia beamed and languished, as "divine woman," inspiration, and patroness of masculine genius. Over the centuries from 1550 till today, music was developed into a great and complex art by a series of great men—and not a woman composer of first-class stature among them. As representing opportunity for a participation by women in the creation of music expressing their own hearts and lives and their unique function as the mothers of the race, St. Cecilia is an utter fraud. The very word "patroness" has something spurious about it. It is made by the lacy addition of "ess" to the word "patron," whose root means father. An honest word for an honest woman saint of music would be founded on a word whose root meant mother, as the word "matron" does.

Why Cecilia was chosen for her anomalous position is one of those perplexities in men's scholarship and writing of history that baffles a sincere woman's mind. St. Cecilia did not compose music. She created no ritual such as the primitive women had created. She helped no woman to approach the divine altar, to understand the rhythm of her own being, and to demonstrate its implication for the life of the spirit. St. Cecilia was a Roman girl of noble family who in the second century was martyred for her faith. Her connection with music consists in the fact that her father arranged to have an organ played at her wedding to a young man named Valerian. But she refused to be married "and sang in her heart to God alone." [2] In no remote sense did she reflect the activities of Christian women in religious music, as the old musician goddesses had reflected the musical activities of the women of earliest times.

When St. Cecilia was established in 1550 as the presiding spirit of music, women had not had, for many centuries, sufficient free participation in music to warrant any woman's being made a saint of music. As a symbol of something to come, St. Cecilia held out a false hope. At best she represented a sentimental sanctification of the Renaissance conception of the priestess of beauty.

Yet, in a sense, St. Cecilia is a true representative of the pattern within which women as musicians have been confined during the whole of the modern period.

In that period the great structure of wonderful music has been reared by men, pleasantly encouraged by women as purveyors of beauty and charm. Compared with the early woman musicians in the crude dignity of their ritualistic approach to the divine life, the priestess of beauty was no priestess at all when she first began to reign in the courts of the Renaissance. She seemed to have a greater degree of honor and liberty than the forcibly silenced and suppressed woman of the ruder Middle Ages, but she had this only within the limits that had been set in the fourth century. The pattern itself had not changed, and it has not changed to this day. It has merely been obscured in some flowers of sentiment. The woman, as priestess of beauty, from the early Renaissance till now, when as queen of beauty she appears in hundreds of public celebrations, serves the male human being only, in his vanity and his power. She officiates at no genuine altar, and such altars as there are she is not allowed to approach save as she kneels at the foot of a male priest.

This is why there are no woman composers of the highest stature. Certainly, women do compose, and some women composers com-

pare favorably with second- and third-rate men. Some compositions
of the women composers are better than some of the published material of even the greatest composers. But when one considers what
music is, and how it must be composed, it is a wonder that one can
say even that.

Music, of all the arts, has its origins in the deepest levels of the
subconscious. It is, of all the arts, the most profoundly religious. It is
indeed the voice in which the human being speaks to the life that is
over and above this human life. Even in modern times, since 1550,
the really great music has had its focus in religious feeling. The musical idiom developed primarily for religious worship has merely been
transferred to secular music. It would actually be enough explanation of the lack of first-class music by women to say that they could
not compose because they were barred from authoritative positions
as church musicians. One could say, with reason, that there is no
feminine Bach because no woman had a position like his—which was
that of church organist with the duty of composing music for the
religious service.

2.

But there is something much more serious to say about what the
lack of women composers of the first stature reveals. There is a
wrong and a poison at the heart of our society, and an essential fal-
sity in the whole modern tradition of secular learning and religious
teaching.

Consider what a woman faces, even today, in free and enlight-
ened America, from the day she begins to have any formal training.
She goes to school and begins her struggle to think logically in the
words she has already learned from her mother's lips. And then there
begins the difficulty with the English pronouns, in some sentence
like "If anyone looks at this object closely, *he* will see." Why should
"anyone" be a he? Why not a she? Is she not to look at this object
closely, too? The teacher explains patiently. When we mean a person of either sex, we always say "he"! But the little girl looks at the
little boy near her, who is no brighter than she, and she thinks, But
why should he stand for girls and boys too? *I* am *she*. No one tells
her that the language in which she must speak for the rest of her life
is so distorted because the modern vernacular was formed when
men still completely dominated learning, and that the first grammars

were written by men. There ought to be a pronoun to represent both men and women. But there is not.

As the girl goes on learning, she faces this problem again and again. There is the word "man." It stands for all humankind. The life of "man" is the life of everybody. But why should a man stand for everybody? She goes further and begins to learn Latin. "Virile," "virtue" come from the word *vir*, meaning man. They are grand words. They mean strength and courage. "Feminine" comes from *femina*, meaning woman. But what does feminine mean? Something soft and mildly attractive. If the girl has a good mother—and according to the testimony of men, good mothers appear to be very numerous—the girl knows that this word "feminine," with its soft, silly connotations, by no means represents what mother is—strong, patient, able to keep the family secure and happy. Is there no word for women's *strength,* in a world where women must have so much strength, if not of muscle, certainly of nerve and will and soul?

Meanwhile the girl goes to Sunday school and church. If she is a Catholic the truth may dawn on her only slowly, for in the Catholic Church there are Mary and many women saints, and an atmosphere of family love in the innumerable pictures and images of Mother and Child. The girl may innocently suppose that these figures of angels, singing, kneeling, adoring the new baby, are daughters. They look like girls with their long curled hair and long dresses. But if she has a mind and begins to use it as the time for confirmation approaches, the truth may dawn upon her. God is a man only. He has a son but no daughter. He has priests but no priestesses. Mary is only a handmaid, not an equal partner. Mothers are not fit to serve God at the altar. Women may not even sing in the choir, saying their prayers to music. They can only listen to men singing their prayers.

And why is this? Because a woman is of different sex from a man. And what is this difference? A man starts the baby in what may be only a moment of careless and often irresponsible pleasure. But a woman takes up the burden and carries it alone, through months of unique experience to a great life and death struggle. This is what distinguishes her as a woman. This is her sex. And for no other reason, God, who is male, will not have a mother stand and speak at the altar. The door of the holy of holies, with its symbols of regeneration derived from her own function as life bringer, is closed to her, who brings the child into the world.

3.

In the formation of this dogma, Catholic and Protestant theologians have been equally guilty. Women did not sing in the liturgical choir from the fourth century on, and they do not do so to this day, either in Catholic churches or in Protestant churches *that have real liturgical singers, who are properly speaking the attendants of the priest and priestess.* This is to say that where music is regarded as worship, and so used in the church service, women may not sing in the choir, and the music requiring high voices must be sung by immature boys. The only exception to this was from early times the singing of nuns in their own chapels. But here a special voice was cultivated, clear, high, sexless. Women did not sing in their natural voices.

The Protestant Church based its music not on the liturgy but on Luther's noble principle of congregational singing. For this selected strains of folk music were converted into hymns. These are the basis of Bach's chorales. To ensure a high quality of church music, the Lutherans established schools for boys, like St. Thomas' in Leipzig, where Bach served. No schools trained girls to be official singers, organists, or composers for the church.

In the Calvinist churches in Switzerland and France there may have been trained women's choirs. Goudimel, in 1565, set eight psalms for four high voices. In the preface to his collection he says that he composed the music for both home and church use. But in England the authorities spared no pains to prevent the participation of women and girls in choirs. Henry VIII issued warrants permitting boys with good voices to be impressed for service in the cathedral choirs. In Queen Elizabeth's time boys were taken from their parents without compensation to serve as Children of the Chapel. At the time of the Restoration, 1660, there were no trained choirboys available at all, owing to the fact that the choirs of the Anglican Church had been disbanded during the Commonwealth. The soprano part was played on what was called a cornet. Men, who habitually took the alto parts and still do in many places in England, at that time often sang the soprano in falsetto, rather than allow a woman to use her natural voice in religious song.

In America the early settlers were torn with dissension over the question whether a woman should be allowed to sing to God. One

of the questions to be decided by the Massachusetts Bay Colony
was: "Whether the people join in singing the Psalms, or the Minister
alone?" It was agreed that the congregation should join, and then the
age-old question came up for decision—"Whether women sing with
men, or men alone?" [3] Even the bravery and fortitude of women
bearing the dangers and toil of a pioneer life could not do away with
the long prejudice that classed them as inferior in matters ecclesiastical and juridical. The intrepid Anne Hutchinson succeeded in persuading John Cotton, minister of the Boston Congregational Church
in 1637, to allow women to sing in his church. Before the other colonial settlements took the liberal point of view, however, Mrs. Hutchinson was expelled from her community for her theological and
political dissent. The matter of the church singing was one of the
grievances cherished against her by the Puritan authorities.

In most Protestant churches, women's participation in congregational singing became accepted as a matter of course. But for the
participants, hymn singing in church has a far greater social than
musical value. Inspiring though congregational music is, it has never
been developed by any religious group in our culture beyond the
elementary stage of unison singing accompanied by all-pervasive
organ playing. The trained choir, however, demands a special skill,
and the exclusion of women and girls from it had a direct bearing
upon their relation to music.

This exclusion has continued in part down to the present day, despite many efforts on the part of liberals to do away with it. When
William Tuckey came from England in 1752 to be choirmaster at
Trinity Church, New York, he first organized a choir of boys and
girls from a near-by charity school, but, as *Grove's Dictionary* expresses it, he soon "succeeded in eliminating the female element" and
established choir singing in the proper English manner. Although
some Episcopalians favored liberality in the matter, the revival of
medievalism by the Oxford Movement in England in the nineteenth
century tended to restore the taboos of the Dark Ages, and checked
any move to sanction girl choristers. When about 1850 the Reverend
Dr. Haweis, a Church of England minister, put surplices on women
choristers, he was vehemently attacked by one faction of his parishioners. The Roman Catholic Church made a few compromises, even
permitting a Catholic newspaper to publish a favorable comment on
Brahms' beautiful religious motets for four women's voices. "No
offense could be taken by even the most pious on the *setting* of the

liturgical texts," the critics conceded. But instead of following the modern trend, the Catholics reacted against the participation of women in the formal church choir, and explained why in the *Motu Proprio* of Pope Pius X (1903). After stating that women may not be admitted to the priesthood, the edict says: "On the same principle it follows that singers in Church have a real liturgical office, and that therefore *women, being incapable of exercising such office, cannot be admitted to form part of the choir.* Whenever, then, it is desired to employ the acute voices of sopranos and contraltos, these parts must be taken by boys, according to the most ancient usage of the Church."

To this day, women do not sing in every church as a matter of course, nor are they regarded as having an inalienable right to be there. In conservative groups the opposition against women is strong. G. S. Stubbs, organist of St. Agnes' Episcopal Chapel, Trinity Parish, New York City, represents a considerable body of opinion as he writes about women choristers in vestments: "While it is not certain that these choirs will increase to an alarming extent, steps may have to be taken to check their growth." [4] A long correspondence on the subject of mixed choirs was recently carried on between various dignitaries of the Catholic Church. It was finally decreed that men and women could sing with propriety in a religious choir—but not in a strictly liturgical choir—provided they sat in galleries at the back of the church as far as possible from the altar, and provided the sexes were separated by some physical barrier, such as an organ or a railing.[5]

In spite of the new policy of the Catholics toward congregational singing—which includes the participation of women even in a cathedral—the ecclesiastical authorities still object to *choruses* of women within the most sacred precincts. During the year 1938, Mme Lila Pereira, professor of singing at the Conservatory of Santiago in Chile, organized a choir of sixteen women with the intention of singing at certain special services in the cathedral. The choir's repertoire was limited chiefly to religious motets by Palestrina, Victoria, and other great composers of church music. Although Mme Pereira was respected in her city as an individual and as a musician, she had to appeal every three months for permission to take her choir into the cathedral. The women were not allowed to sit in the choir stalls, but had to sing from seats placed in the nave. Eventually, the *vicario* notified Mme Pereira that the pope had forbidden the women to take any part in the religious ceremony. This order effectively prevented the choir from functioning and caused it to disband.

Even the Protestant National Cathedral Chapter, in Washington, D. C., excludes women from its formal choir. A new custom could readily have been established here, since a girls' school and a boys' school are both situated on the cathedral grounds. Both schools are supported by the cathedral chapter. The girls receive musical instruction adequate to qualify them as choristers, but they take no part in the formal musical activities of the cathedral. Conducting their commencement exercises in the crypt is the extent of their participation.

The National Cathedral is sponsored by men and women of all denominations in the United States. It purports to be a national shrine for all people of our country, a center for the dissemination of American democracy and Christian ideals. Yet the authorities allowed Dorothy Maynor to sing from the chancel, while they will not allow mothers and daughters who regularly attend the services to join the choir. Spiritual pastors and masters prefer to exalt the prima donna rather than the women who are the bulwark of our civilization. They cannot yield on the fundamental principle on which all the vested interests of religious hierarchy are based, that the human being who creates half the child and nourishes it from her own body in love and duty is, *by reason of this,* unfit to sing to the Source of all being.

This principle is supported by the cathedrals of all Jewish and Christian sects, whose function it is to set standards for the maintenance of tradition and for correct usage. The Orthodox Catholic Church, the Church of England, the Episcopalian and Lutheran Churches will not tolerate women in cathedral choirs.

People are prone to rationalize about women in church choirs by claiming that a boys' choir is musically "better" than one that includes women and girls; or they say that they prefer the "purity" of boys' voices. But the pure, sexless quality can be produced quite as well by young girls of high-school age. Unless the singers are seen, no musical inferiority, indeed, no difference in boys' and girls' voices can be detected. It is the guilelessness of youth, not the sex of the singers, that recalls the heavenly choir. But even if the boy choir were musically better, that would be no excuse for excluding girls or women. The church is not a place of entertainment, nor is it the primary function of the church to give performances of music. The question is: Who should sing in a representative capacity to the divine force? Is this the privilege only of the male—mature and immature? As for the boys, their young voices are lovely. But behind their present use in cathedral choirs lies a tradition that seems morbid to the modern mind. There is the refined homosexuality of Greece when young boys were substituted for girls as the romantic objects of a mature man's love. There is the long, revolting history of the castrati and their use in ecclesiastical services. The boys' voices should never sound sweet in any decent person's ears till they sing side by side with their sisters. The equally beloved daughters should sing together with the sons to the glory of life's mighty rhythm. The mature voices of mothers, of equal value with fathers, should sustain and support the fourfold human song.

In this attitude of the churches to woman's song much more is involved than the participation of any special group of singers in a special activity. For from the purely musical point of view, even if women and girls were still excluded from the choir of every church, it would today make little difference to them as far as participation in the performance of music is concerned. They are now able to take part in music through many other institutions and in affairs that are musically more important than any sponsored by the churches. But the point is that women and girls who have proved their competence in singing reverently the most sacred motets and masses at a concert, even in a church concert, are not allowed to sing the same music when it accompanies the ritual.

The churches are supposed to represent the organized feeling of the whole community about the relation of human beings to the realities and the mysteries of life. The word "religious" means the relation of individuals to a higher power and the expression of the relation in conduct. These organized religious groups—and the most powerful denominations agree in this matter—are perpetuating the disgraceful fallacy that women are of less value in the scheme of life than men. No primitive taboo upon the free use of human energy was ever more damaging than this dogma. Its result is to deprive women of a reverence for their own way in life and of the confidence that comes only from genuine self-respect. As long as women are denied public recognition of the fact that they are spiritually of *equal value* with men, *equally* able to advance civilization to a higher level, as long as women are not expected to find in worship their most appropriate outlet for musical expression, just so long will they fail to take their rightful place in society and in the art of music. Just so long will our whole communal consciousness be vitiated by this morbid fallacy at its heart.

4.

Though both music and modern learning appear to be secular in origin and tone, the patterns set by Greek classical thinking and by the Church influence professional men to this day. A careless, slighting attitude to women has come down through the ages in clerical and scholarly circles. In the sixteenth century the monk Acidalius announced that women were not human beings, and were therefore incapable of thinking in terms of the spirit. Rousseau reflected current eighteenth-century ideals in his famous saying: "Once it is demonstrated that men and women are not and ought not to be constituted alike in character and temperament, it follows that they ought not to have the same education. Let girls be trained definitely for wifehood and motherhood. *The whole education of women should be relative to men.*" [6] A hundred years later Schopenhauer was saying that women remained big children all their lives. In this opinion he was supported by a group of German scientists who, in the Breslau Conference of 1884, produced what they considered proof of woman's closer resemblance to animals and her resultant deficiency in the higher human faculties.

As recently as 1940, Catholic Church dignitaries, meeting in Kansas City at an educational conference, discussed the familiar affair of Adam and Eve and the apple. Adam was held responsible for the act of disobedience; Eve was pronounced blameless. Because she was a woman, she was incapable of knowing right from wrong. In the thousand and a half of another thousand years, woman has progressed—if one wishes to call it "progress"—from an aggressively evil power to a negative quantity, innocent only because *powerless.*

Many people regard the Catholic Church as too conservative to be representative of the modern spirit toward women. But the same attitude of denial of woman's power can be found in the latest editions of dictionaries. Under the word "woman," for example, the editors of Webster's Unabridged Dictionary quote a passage from Shakespeare—"Women are soft, mild, pitiful, and flexible"—in order to explain the way the word is used. So also in the new language of Esperanto, the word for "mother" has been formed as *patrino,* a derivative of *patro,* father. If generally adopted, this new language term would forever divest "mother" of its connection with independent activity and authority. What theologians formerly did to the goddess symbols, university professors are now trying to do to language symbols.

Even the psychologists, who should be saving woman from the outward mandates of theologians, emphasize the early Christian's negation of womanhood. Only yesterday, in 1944, a group of doctors meeting at Atlantic City concluded that women lack creative imagination. What new name they expected to coin when referring to the many tangible forms of that faculty as demonstrated by many women was not announced. Their conviction that they were right—which significantly enough was not shared by the women doctors present—is evinced by their general use of the words "masculine" and "feminine." All activity is called masculine. Passivity is feminine. A woman is told that any activity she undertakes is a development of the "masculine" part of her nature. In this terminology, the strength—even the existence—of feminine urges and desires is given no recognition.

From the psychologists, too, comes the devastating condemnation of mothers as a beneficent influence over their sons. Not content with a *negation* of woman's power, they give it a *positive,* evil aspect. Because young soldiers and sailors far from home called, in loneliness and fear, for their mothers, doctors pronounced this love a damaging thing. Like the early Church Fathers, they dogmatize reverence for "Mom" as "silly and devoid of reason."

It follows from the peculiar wisdom that the males of our culture have revealed to males that musical art is exclusively masculine. A French critic said of Augusta Holmes, one of the foremost of the women composers of her time: "Why do these women try to make people forget that they are women?" He was only one of many to insist upon the disqualification of women for creative work in music. George Upton claimed that women lacked "objectivity," the power of projecting themselves outwardly and expressing themselves in terms of symbols. Anton Rubinstein, on the other hand, thought that women were lacking in "subjectivity" and initiative, wanting, indeed, courage and conviction. Rubinstein, who like his brother Nicholas managed one of the large Russian conservatories, extended his distrust of women into the field of performance. In this opinion he was supported by Carl Reinecke, who said openly that he believed there was a point where women stopped developing. Even as a performer, he claimed, a woman was prevented by her timidity and indecision from satisfactory demonstration of the composer's intention. Did they not all fail to realize that the timidity and indecision they noticed resulted directly and inevitably from the very denial of the value of women's independent ego?

There is no end to the careless gratuitous insult that these wiseacres heap on the function of giving birth. In 1945 the harp player Salzedo told his girl pupils at his summer school in Maine that only men compose music. "Women," he said, "are born to compose babies." [7] That women are born to compose babies is true enough. The difficulty lies in the silly and illogical deduction that men make from this obvious biological fact. Why, because one lives through— or is physiologically prepared to live through—the most vivid experience life can offer, should one be incapacitated from using the strength and wisdom gained through that experience in other fields? "When old and familiar things are made new in experience—there is art," [8] says John Dewey, and many women have proved and are proving today that this is so. To teach a girl the contrary is, indeed, as death-dealing to her spirit as any doctrine of the early Church Fathers.

5.

Against this the woman struggles, suppressed and reticent. But even so, it might have been possible for her to do something more in music if anything like fair opportunity had been open to her to acquire the training and experience necessary for the production of modern music. In early Greece, women were just beginning to develop real music out of their personal experience, with a steady accretion of knowledge and a refinement of art. But modern music is another creation altogether. It has developed in circumstances that prevented women from sharing the experience that men were accumulating or from obtaining any institutional support for the development of their inspiration. For when the complex forms of modern music were in the making, professional musicians received their training and much of their experience through contacts with the Church. They often combined religious and secular musical posts. Practically all of the great composers of the Renaissance period were primarily composers of church music. Their madrigals and other forms of secular music were merely by-products, written in the same idiom. A favorite device was to clothe a religious text, such as Salve Regina, in a distinctly gay, unecclesiastical setting, and to present the incongruous whole at a social gathering. The organization for Christian music was self-sufficient and, as we have seen, made only special demands upon the natural woman musician.

The obvious result of this new development of polyphonic music was to render the composition of music infinitely more difficult and complicated than in the days when the troubadours sang their melodies to the simple strumming accompaniment of the lute. No one could now attempt serious musical composition without long training and experience. Many rules evolved or were invented—some natural, some arbitrary—that had to be learned, observed, and incorporated into a musical production that would be both correct and pleasing.

Even after the power formerly wielded by the Church began to pass to the university system, every such institution adapted the organization of the Church to further its scholarly, social, or political aims. Women had no corresponding institutions. Even many of their monasteries had been dissolved and their revenues diverted to the universities. Not till late in the nineteenth century did it occur to anyone to found colleges for the higher education of women.

The reason women took to performing men's music rather than creating their own was, of course, not because the intricacies of contrapuntal writing were beyond their powers, but because they were excluded from the Church, and later from the schools, where the knowledge could be obtained and the art practiced.

In one field only has woman's opportunity and recognized function in music been equal to that of men—in the solo performance of the prima donna. But the modern institution of the public concert or stage production for a price has widened the cleft between performer and composer. The teaching of expert performers became the principal justification of the institutions where girls were taught. Virtuosity was the end and aim of the student's interest. Every girl approached music as if she expected to become a concert performer. Since leadership was regarded as being out of their sphere, girls were discouraged from entering classes for conducting. As a general rule, they were excluded from classes in theory and composition—independent thinking being regarded as the prerogative of men. Until late in the century, women could not compete for prizes or receive diplomas at European conservatories.

Although Elizabeth Stirling's orchestral setting for psalm 130 passed every musical requirement for earning the degree of Musical Bachelor at Oxford University (England), in 1856 her application for it was rejected. No authority existed in the university for conferring the honor upon a woman. For the same reason, years later, in 1918, Lili Boulanger was disqualified from receiving the Prix de Rome, which she won at the age of eighteen in an anonymous competition. The donors of the prize had limited the applicants to the class of unmarried men under thirty—this class being the one in their experience most likely to produce a great composer. Far from advising girls to concentrate on music as an intellectual discipline, even serious men musicians treated aspiring pupils with levity. Sibelius once resorted to a trick to rid himself of two girl composition students. When, at his suggestion that they go for a walk outdoors, they had left the room, he turned to the young men and said: "It would be a pity if the young ladies' cheeks were to lose their beautiful country color!" [9] With a characteristic roguish smile, he began to instruct his men students in the theory of music. Such attitudes were effectual in stifling germinating talent. For the composition of major works, a knowledge of counterpoint and orchestration was essential, as well as the faith that intellectual discipline could be borne. Many girls acquired an inferiority complex about their musical imagination, allowing the easy habit of listening and the ideal of virtuosity to dominate their musical lives. Thinking in terms of even the simplest forms of music long ago fell into the discard. Even in eighteenth-century Venice, where the rich ladies in their salons were composing songs and instrumental music and where some of the convents allowed the nuns to spend most of their time at music, the talented girls of the conservatories received but little encouragement to be creative. Pupil and nun-teacher often substituted for the professional director of music, it is true, and pupils were taught to resolve a figured bass at sight. Their authority, however, stopped short of the point where incentives for composition began. The musical directors were always professional men musicians who happened to be in Venice at the time as organists of the large churches. These conductors promised to produce a new suite, motet, cantata, or oratorio at regular intervals. Theirs was the opportunity and incentive for creative work. Women had no such incentive because they had no similar outlet for an achievement.

It was the same story in the newly founded colleges for women, where musical activity was generally limited to a glee club conducted by a man. Young girls neglected to seek training in musical thinking, and young college women apparently made no concerted effort to establish forums for musical experimentation. Their symbol of music was not Artemis with her lyre.

Throughout the nineteenth century the stage, educational system, church, and even home all restricted the musician in some manner. And although singing in a chorus, dancing in a ballet, playing in an orchestra, even teaching and conducting music do not necessarily lead to the development of outstanding musical imagination, yet any restriction upon participation is a barrier to composition. Participation in music is a condition precedent to creative work in music, as it is in any other language. No one would expect to write a book in a strange language, but would first learn the words, construction, and idioms. Any artificial limitation to acquiring familiarity with a language and ease in its use automatically lowers the number of competent craftsmen ready to use it. Women achieved their outstanding measure of success in composing piano pieces and songs—the two types of music with which the greatest number had the most familiar and the most satisfactory experience.

Nor can there be any dispute that leadership in music definitely increases the chances for a musician to find occasions for the exercise of creative imagination. The great body of religious music—hymns, anthems, motets, compositions for organ alone—came from the organist, who was also the choir director, and not from musicians outside the circle. Choral literature for women's voices in the nineteenth century can be traced in almost every instance to the conductors of the choruses—to the men who carried the responsibility of finding music for the group to perform. When women had the responsibility, they too had the practical urge to compose appropriate music, and often did. Luise Reichardt, in the early part of the century, and Mabel Daniels, in the latter part, are examples of conductors who composed music for their own women's choruses to sing. It was while she was the conductor of an orchestra that Emma Steiner seized the opportunity to present a program of her own works. Alma Grayce Miller is a present-day example of a composer whose talents have been stimulated by a definite task. Organist and choir director of St. Agnes' Church, Arlington, Virginia, she has written three Christmas masses and also other music for the use of her choir. As she herself expresses it, whenever she cannot find appropriate music, she composes it. Even the most casual glance at contemporary publishers' catalogues reveals at least ten times as much music composed by women in various positions of responsibility as there was twenty or twenty-five years ago. To the extent, then, that women are excluded from positions of leadership, they are automatically limited in adding a substantial number of women to the ranks from which a possible genius might emerge. Superlative achievement comes only from an already high plateau of experience. And as long as women are regarded as a class apart from men, they will have to build their own plateau.

Persons of discernment never fail to realize that the women composers of the eighteenth, nineteenth, and twentieth centuries possess talent, sometimes to a marked degree. Critics of the women's compositions often concur and, in their judgments, add to information that the composers lacked adequate training and experience in working with contemporary musical idiom. Not being in the class or group from which music was expected, the women of our era had neither the emotional nor the intellectual foundation to enable them to assert freely their own conception of music. What they achieve in creative work is in spite of, not because of, the way of their world. Granting the suppression and the deliberate shaming of woman in connection with her unique mission of motherhood, granting her exclusion from spiritual authority and equality by the institutions of our civilization, granting the persistent discrimination against her by those who held the keys to knowledge and gave the permission to participate in music; granting all this, many people maintain that genius cannot be downed. If a feminine Mozart had been born, they say, she would have been immediately recognized. But these same people ignore the fact that genius in a man is not always recognized, if there is no demand at the time for his particular type of genius. A great general, for instance, does not appear in time of peace; he rises to power only when there is a demand for military efficiency. Even Napoleon could not have manufactured a war if his people had not been in the mood to follow his lead.

Musical talent, too, has often been blocked in men by barriers inherent in the way of life of a particular group. For example, though the Quakers of the seventeenth century at first sang fervent hymns at their meetings, they shortly abandoned the use of music altogether. In neither the religious ceremony nor in community life did they allow music. It is only within the last few years that Quakers in

America have introduced music into some of their schools and colleges. Is it a matter for surprise that, despite their deep spirituality and their high intellectual attainments, neither Quaker men nor Quaker women have been creative musicians?

Again, the America of the eighteenth and nineteenth centuries was clearly not the place for a sophisticated musician. Americans, intent upon developing a new country, had but little time for the arts. They gave their highest rewards and recognition to those who were successful in theological pursuits, or landed or business enterprise. In fact, they definitely discouraged and looked down upon artists and musicians. Consequently, no important musicians of native American stock appeared. At a later period, when the pioneer stage was over, people began to feel the need of music and turned to Europe for their musicians. Only Europeans were expected to be musicians. Even those seriously engaged in the profession of music were forced to adopt foreign names, speech, and manners. As late as fifty years ago, American performers and composers attained only grudging recognition. In the face of these barriers, American men— many of them of German stock—were helpless as musicians. Their native musical talent lay latent. They had to wait until the general background had changed, until the pioneer period was over, until Puritan asceticism had died, until people had time, energy, and money to develop genius along artistic and musical lines.

In Europe composers of the highest stature appeared and disappeared in response to environments that fostered or failed to foster them. Eighteenth- and nineteenth-century western European civilization provided, on the whole, the inspiration and incentives for men to create and to produce music. But despite the general background of a favorable environment, conditions varied locally.

In Germany, environment and racial temperament converged fortuitously to bring out native talent. Hence the Germans were able to carry musical art to its highest expression. Italian and English names, so conspicuous in former centuries, largely disappeared from the lists of great composers. The fact is that barriers against any kind of musical activity by men are always effective in preventing men from performing that activity. Moslem mosques, for example, make no use of music. No Mohammedan Bach has risen to compose great choral and orchestral works.

Wide misunderstanding, indeed, exists as to what constitutes the so-called "musical talent." Different musical capabilities may be inherited—an instinct for rhythm, the melodic impulse, a sense of harmony and of counterpoint. Nonmusical qualities also essential to a great composer—persistence, infinite capacity for taking pains, a sense of artistic proportions—may also be inherited. One might call those gifts of the fates. An individual, however, may possess all these gifts and yet never produce any music of importance. In addition to the possession of native talent, a potential musician must be brought up in an environment that demands music as an integral part of life, must be also one of a class that is expected to create music so that he or she may normally obtain the intensive training essential for serious musical composition.

Many unthinking people whose musical experience is limited to listening assume that a divinely inspired musical genius can pour out a song with the naïveté of a bird. The nightingale, however, has absolutely no talent for musical composition. No note of his unchanging melodic phrase is composed by him, but was unconsciously evolved for him by countless generations of ancestors. While these same people recognize vaguely the mysteries of counterpoint and of orchestration, they assume that to learn to compose a simple song requires little more training than to learn to run an automobile. As a matter of fact, the training in musical composition required for a simple song of importance would more nearly approach that required to build an automobile, or to invent one, if none existed. The compositions by Brahms with which he expressed himself as most satisfied were simple-sounding piano accompaniments to forty-nine folk songs. To the student, these piano parts are marvels of artistic construction and proportion, their simplicity achieved only by the elimination of every superfluous note. Written near the end of Brahms' life, but at the height of his powers, they were the result of long years of artistic musical experience. None but a master could possibly have produced them, yet to the uninitiated they seem as easy as the sleight of hand of a magician's trick.

The more elaborate the composition—and modern compositions become increasingly so—the more complex is its conception and production. Hence longer and more intensive training is required. The difficulties in connection with music are much greater than in literature, where the potential poet or novelist becomes familiar from earliest youth with the use of words. With us, thinking in terms of music and the use of musical symbols by children is unusual. A musical genius, of course, is able to absorb the necessary knowledge and training and so to obtain the techniques infinitely faster than the person of average talent. However, it will be found that all great composers went through a rigorous grind of practice, experiment, and absorption of the musical past before they produced their masterpieces. Mozart, always held up as an example of spontaneous musical generation, was in fact intensively trained by his father as a musician from the cradle. His entire childhood was occupied with thinking, playing, and writing music under encouragement. Had he been born and brought up by unmusical parents on a farm in Kansas in 1880, would his genius ever have flowered?

Even if a girl has been born and brought up in a musical atmosphere, even if she has evinced creative talent, the chances are that she has not been expected by her parents and friends to become a composer, but that she has been directed into performance and taught accordingly. The general public attitude toward woman, and particularly toward woman and her music, effectively discourages confidence in her individual self as a composer and in her women contemporaries collectively as potential creators of music. It also precludes public demand for her to compose—a condition essential for production. Finally, it prevents a naturally endowed girl from procuring easily, and her parents from seeking for her, that early and intensive training necessary for the composition of important music. When combined, these three conditions result in an environment in which the creative musical imagination of only a few women can flower. Until it is changed, the sleeping beauty that is music in the feminine soul will not awaken.

When one sees how effective social barriers are in preventing men from composing music and realizes how many have been the barriers to composition by women, the comparative silence of women musicians during the last three hundred years can easily be understood.

Withal, the real core of the matter is not woman's failure to have created great music. It is what that failure, when analyzed, reveals of the constitution of our society and the deep denial of life on which it rests. Even if women participated equally in every current musical activity, our cultural pattern would still be against their creating music as a spiritual expression of their inner life. This inner life is half the spiritual life of humanity. In so far as it differs from that of men, it differs in the possession by women of a unique experience that touches the heights and depths of emotion and sensation, and calls on a deep and intuitive wisdom, a kind of at-oneness with all the processes of growth and decay, birth and rebirth, in the universe. Primitive woman had begun to put this experience into ritual and music, and had proceeded far enough to give us some hint of the direction woman's genius might have taken.

But just as her attempt to evolve her own religion and music from her own experience began to approach the forms of civilized art, woman received a death blow from man's schematic religions. The bases of her own dynamic relation to life were knocked from under her. The need for her music was not institutionalized. Mary, as a goddess, was a tentative and uncompleted conception. From the Protestants, woman received no symbols.

Nothing now remains of the woman's rites to make her proud and positive. At puberty she begins to go to social dances. And there she dances the dance of life only if a boy asks her. At marriage she is "given away" by her father to her husband. At death she kneels desolate, her old proud power to invoke the rebirth gone, while some man intones. What does he intone? Why should a woman care?

And still St. Cecilia hangs over the piano—insincere, ineffectual. How long now until women learn not to go near these altars from which they were cast down, and take courage to make their own religion and their own music anew, and beat out with faith the measure to which their daughters and their daughters' daughters may dance? (See Plate 61.)

CHAPTER XVIII

ARTEMIS STIRRING

1.

*E*VERY cultural pattern has its strength as well as its weakness, its place in time, its time for passing. The hour has now come when many different currents of thought and many new conditions are converging to bring about changes in our culture. As far as women are concerned, some of these new influences are tending to nullify the force of the old ideas that regarded women as of inferior value to men in an advancing civilization. If taboos compatible only with a primitive attitude and the equally childish superstitious dogma of the Church Fathers still live, they are threatened, like King Canute, by the swiftly rising tide of an articulate womanhood. It seems today that woman is about to assume a natural relation to life, that Artemis is about to be reborn.

The biological theories of Aristotle, who maintained that men alone possess the creative spark, are now disproved by science. Modern research has demonstrated that to the soul of the newborn child, to that particular bundle of inherited aptitudes and characteristics which will make her or him a distinct individual, mother and father have contributed equally. Science restores to woman her biological dignity and with it her sense of power, as a being creative in her own right.

Science tends also to give validity to women's groping explanation of the mystery of the universe. On the whole, the kind of thinking implicit in the early rites of the life cycle—thinking that was plastic, intuitive, and that sought its expression in the rhythm of birth and rebirth—is consonant with modern science and with our ever widening knowledge of the forces of the universe.

There is today a profound change in the thinking about the sym-

283

bolic relation of human beings to the invisible, yet perceived, higher powers. The rigid theological propositions of yesterday are losing their appeal. More and more we are returning to the primeval sense that all life is one and indivisible, different manifestations of the same life force. Scientists are daily offering new evidence of the intimate relation of plants, animals, and human beings. Now, too, there is again a tendency to believe that the path toward the spiritual is by way of reverence for all processes of life, in the world around and in both the physical and psychic life of human beings.

Belief in the unity of all life is itself a rebirth for women. The basis of their imagery was destroyed with the introduction of the idea that the spirit can develop only by denying the flesh. In primitive times women were always combining the imaginative with the real, always symbolizing personal experiences, always endowing natural states and normal human urges with spiritual significance. So women may now take up the *principle* behind their old rituals, knowing that the world's thinking will henceforth be with them and not against them.

2.

This changed relation of women to religion is not entirely new. It has been steadily developing for several centuries and coincides, significantly, with a change in men's and women's attitude toward musical activity, an attitude that has also taken some time to become general.

When Christian culture first dominated western Europe, a very small group of men fixed the rules for the use of music. Music was to be controlled by the hierarchy of the Church for the purposes of the Church and for no other purpose. After a thousand years of revolt against these rules, the people finally succeeded in establishing new customs for music. But under the patronage of the nobles, music was confined to the castle or the baronial hall. After 1700 the new hierarchy of professional musicians, which rose to power with the middle classes, carried music into public halls and into secular educational institutions where many more people could hear it and participate in it. The latest development in the social aspects of music is the reaction of amateur musicians against assumption by the professionals of an undue authority over the education and performance of music. Amateurs are again beginning to strive for a knowledge of the language of music for their personal use, for a more direct and intimate contact with it than can be derived from mere listening to the performance of professionals.

Slowly but surely education in music is being incorporated into the school system. It is the type of education that trains ear, eye, and mind for the acquisition of experience in the language of music. Instead of training every child as a possible virtuoso, educators are making sane attempts to train every child to be musically literate. Whereas people formerly supposed that to sing, one must be born with a "good voice," they now begin to realize that all voices are good enough to be trained for the satisfaction of one's self and for intelligent participation in group singing. Scores of girls and boys are demonstrating the feasibility of acquiring enough skill on a musical instrument to join a school or college orchestra. Above all, in the forward-looking schools, musical education is including practice in creative work, with the result that more players and singers are able to make music available socially. This does not mean ability to play or sing "art music" as soloists for an audience, but to be capable of transposing, adapting, and improvising—in other words, to be musically articulate.

It is nothing new, of course, for non-professional musicians to play and sing skillfully for their own satisfaction. The innovation in modern musical custom is to give community encouragement and support to amateur musical activity. This is a return to the Greek idea that "music" belonged to the "Muses," or to the arts and culture in general, and that it should be an integral part of a liberal education. But the foundation upon which the intricate art of our music rests was formerly given to children spasmodically and accidentally only in homes in which the parents happened to be "musical." Now the elements of the language of music are taught to children, and even to adults, in institutions such as schools or summer camps, some being organized especially for the purpose of musical culture.

It is not only educators who are establishing new customs for musical activity. Amateurs already skilled in the performance of music are here and there beginning to give organized effect to their urge for participation in group music.

The adverse conditions of wartime England could not deter thirty of forty men and women from meeting during their summer vacation for the purpose of playing together in an orchestra. Living in tents or lodging in neighbors' houses, they played morning, noon, and night for the sheer delight of it, for the refreshment of their spirits.[1] The experiment of organizing groups larger than a quartet is followed by a New England "musical house party" that is held annually for a ten-day session. Both groups place emphasis upon the fact that the orchestra is organized for the benefit of the players rather than the players existing for the prestige of the orchestra. In England the conductor is an amateur; in America he is a professional, but in the employ of the amateurs and temporarily devoted to their interest.

Meeting in a private house in Merion, Pennsylvania, for the purpose of performing choral music *but with no intention of preparing for a concert,* a hundred and more skilled singers and instrumentalists form the "Accademia dei Dilettanti di Musica." This group is conducted by an amateur—the host—whose only demand upon these expert sight readers is that they love music and that they have had the training to enable them to understand and execute, without previous drilling, such compositions as Bach's cantatas and Brahms' Requiem. The Accademia has been meeting for twenty years, eight or nine times a season. The total number of men and women who have attended these "singing parties" now reaches nearly two thousand. Professionals come as amateurs. No one requires an audience, but each is impelled to come solely by the privilege of participating in great music.[2]

These societies of amateurs are probably as yet unique. Their success has depended upon the strong personalities who originated them and now carry them on. They are pioneer ventures, not yet institutionalized. But a precedent for forming permanent societies to encourage amateurs and choral music can be seen in both England and America. Various organizations serve the purpose of introducing musicians to each other, but of leaving them free to function in any way they wish. As a rule, the benefiting members pay dues, but patrons and patronesses in the community supplement the dues with contributions, thus giving the sanction of society at large to nonprofessional activity in music.

In many ways the musical renaissance of today is a repetition of the rebirth of music in the thirteenth and fourteenth centuries. Then people were overthrowing the restrictive regulations of the Church. Now people are finding the framework for musical activity erected by professional musicians too narrow—again, they are opening new paths for music lovers. When the nobles in their castles instituted new customs in music, they did not interfere with the older customs of the Church but created a demand for more trained musicians. In the same way today, amateurs are not curtailing the need for the virtuosi and other professionals but are adding to the occasions when music can be enjoyed.

The results of these changing musical customs cannot yet be foretold. One trend, however, is already determined—the trend to emphasize the primitive use of music as an affective power for a specific occasion and purpose. In certain uses, music today retains its former application. Music in churches still has this affective purpose—it is supposed to influence the higher powers and also to bring the people into harmony with each other. And who has not felt the power of waltz or rumba rhythm—far more potent an invitation to the dance than the spoken word—or the irresistible command of fife and drum to march behind the flag? Now music is reattaining its primeval value, which in no way interferes with the value of concert giving and virtuosity. Music, which produces an inner harmony, is being introduced into homes, schools, colleges, moving pictures, and theaters, and especially into hospitals for its direct power over emotionally disturbed people.

The need for musical therapy received impetus in the great wars of our times with their aftermath of wounded men and women. The important point made by the experts in this field is that the music used should be of the type that reduces emotional strain. In an age when people are already overtaxed with disruptive forces, they require tones and rhythms that will give them a feeling of security and a sense of harmony with their surroundings. Equally important is the type of person employed as a musical therapist. Virtuosi, or amateurs trained in the spirit of virtuosity, cannot do this work. Many gifted musicians are unsuited to perform music in the sympathetic, adaptable way essential for success in favorably influencing a patient. Different musical qualities from those developed by most musicians are therefore demanded; another set of musical talents is now given community support. How provocative to the imagination it is to learn that scientists have recently discovered the magic in the "sonorous fluid" that primitive men and women have known for countless years! Music has been scientifically proven to be capable of influencing people to think, feel, and act. Music actually can give access to depths in the unconscious where nature and spirit are one. So now a new type of music has the possibility of developing upon the principle behind the great musical art of primitive societies.

3.

Increasing recognition of women's human capabilities, converging with public insistence upon variety in musical enterprise, has radically altered the relation of women to music. Women and girls are at last on the way to approaching music in a free and natural attitude, untrammeled by taboos and superstitions.

It is one thing, however, to make the categorical statement that barriers between women and music no longer exist; it is rather like the boast of a Chinese visitor to this country that his government has forbidden illiteracy. He made the claim as a *fait accompli!* But everyone knows that long years of planning and of hard work on the part of Chinese leaders and teachers combined with the co-operation of the people will be necessary before China can become a nation of literate men and women. So it is now with women and the creative aspects of music. The falling of the barriers is only the beginning of the reform. An attitude of affirmation toward women as potentially creative musicians, accompanied by community backing and intensive training for all who desire it, must lay the foundation, build the plateau from which the creative woman musician can eventually take her natural place in the musical life of her society.

The next step for the friends of women musicians to take is the planning of practices for the future benefit of talented women and the opening up of opportunities for women already trained in leadership and in the composition of music. Obviously, men are firmly intrenched in most of the established musical enterprises of today. For the proving of their capability women will therefore do better to find new fields and untrodden paths. Happily, several opportunities already await further leadership and initiative on the part of women.

The home is the oldest institution we have and the one most closely associated with woman's authority and her creative music. In the home women's songs were sung. Much of our wonderful heritage of folk literature originated in connection with daily work, love, and death. Today these associations have largely ceased to exist. Modern life has robbed this center of many of its former activities. So has the modern utility of music changed. Song is now rarely used as a direct, affective agent. Even the lullaby has been condemned by child specialists. The relation of women to music in the home is now entirely different and comparatively without meaning.

Since the days of the melancholic Robert Burton, fathers have been complaining that the money they spent on their daughters' musical education was largely wasted. Once a girl was married, she neglected her music and appeared content to do without it. This complaint remains true for the twentieth century. Far too often girls "give up" their music. But is it not because custom decrees that it shall lead nowhere except to concertizing? All playing and singing become a concert in miniature, instead of being indispensable to woman's principal business of bringing and fostering life.

But now the idea that music benefits oneself or one's child has captured the imagination of at least some parents. An annually increasing number of young people with a practical musical equipment are becoming parents, and upon the young mother falls the full impact of the demand to make music an integral part of the child's preschool education. Here, in the home, or in the nursery school and kindergarten, is the opportunity for creative work—arranging, adapting, and inventing appropriate rhythms and melodies to be used in giving little children an inner harmony of spirit.

In the larger life of the community, outside of school and home, women have their music clubs. Choral literature for modern women is sadly in need of replenishment and invigoration. What better medium could there be for the woman musician than in the supplying of this demand, bringing fresh musical ideas to her companions, to be sung and played upon convenient occasions, according to women's own interpretation of their spiritual needs?

Some communities have already provided a new outlet for the woman musician in the practice of therapeutic music. Eva Viscelius and Agnes Saville contributed invaluable work toward building morale in the sick and wounded by means of music. Then came Harriet Ayer Seymour, a prime mover in the movement to give music a practical, affective use. During the First World War she had charge of music in army hospitals, and afterward was the chairman of the Hospital Music Committee, where she gave courses for the training of "musical doctors." The last few years of war have greatly increased the demand for women qualified to play and sing "healing" music in hospitals. In the Philadelphia area an experiment was undertaken under the auspices of the Southeastern Pennsylvania Chapter of the American Red Cross to supply instrumentalists and singers.

Selected from the association of Gray Ladies, about twenty women qualified as competent to go about the wards of several hospitals. Working separately or together, each one modifies beautiful, simple melodies into music of therapeutic value adapted to the emotional state of the different patients.[3] (See Plate 63.)

The institutionalization of affective music, already underway in education and in the moving-picture industry, is now taking place in the field of therapy. After the First World War, the National Foundation of Musical Therapy was founded by Mrs. Seymour, and through it scores of devoted musicians have since been working in hospitals and other institutions. At the present time, therefore, both professionals and amateurs are drawn into a common musical cause, the importance of whose social consequences no one can predict. Together they are blazing a path for a new class of official women musicians. The intimate knowledge these pioneers are gaining through experience of the action of music upon the subconscious mind, purifying it of evil influences and revitalizing it, may well be the foundation upon which some gifted woman will create new and wonderful music.

Among our rural people an opportunity for creative work awaits a woman of talent and initiative. By turning her eyes to the Grange and to the now popular festivals celebrating the principal agricultural crop of a country area—such as the Apple Blossom Festival in Virginia and the Potato Blossom Festival in Aroostook County, Maine—a country music teacher may make her position the steppingstone to original composition.

The Grange is one of the most remarkable institutions of American folk life. In it the culture of our country districts centers. Because of the secrecy of its rituals, few outsiders are aware of its importance. Founded in America in 1867 by a group of Masons, the Grange draws on old agricultural rituals that have come down from antiquity through the Masonic orders. Here can be found the old idea of birth and rebirth, reformulated by our American farm population for itself with a Christian coloring but with the use of the old symbols. Nothing is more American than the Grange; yet nothing in our modern life has deeper roots in the earth and in that early religion of nature of which woman was once the priestess and musician.

The opportunity offered by the Grange to the woman composer arises chiefly from the fact that, in this organization, women have a status equal to that of men. While they are still in grammar school,

girls and boys are taught the lore of the Grange and learn its traditional motions with songs from the *Grange Song Book*. Girls and boys
walk in couples in the processions, and grow up with a full recognition of the honored place of each in the great scheme of life. Women
and men also attend the ceremonies in complete equality—"matron" and "patron" of husbandry. The "chaplain" is often a woman.
The post of "lecturer" is also often filled by a woman. From the
point of view of music, the "lecturer" is the more important of the
two, for upon her falls the responsibility of providing entertainment,
which must be of educational value and uplifting to the group. So
eager are the people of the Grange for anything that enriches their
simple ceremonies that a talented woman would undoubtedly find
reward for creating appropriate music, perhaps a new and mighty
song of rebirth springing from the heart of our fertile land and from
the religious spirit of our American farmers.

Community ritual and music has been developed in an entirely
new way by Dr. Rachel Davis Dubois, formerly professor of inter-
cultural education at New York University. In co-operation with
Dvora Lapson, a musician and mime-dancer, she has made experiments in the cure of socially sick groups and now offers training in
the techniques involved at the New School for Social Research in
New York.

Rachel Dubois' services as an expert in analyzing social industrial
discords are called for where there is trouble in crowded industrial
or urban areas, race riots or other disorders beyond the control of
regular social agencies. Sometimes she works under the public
school system. Sometimes she is called in by a group of churches—
usually Protestant, Jewish, and Catholic churches in combination.
Sometimes she is sponsored by the Quakers, being herself a Quaker.
Sometimes she works in connection with a social agency.

Her mainstay, and the original element in her experienced and
competent handling of social disorder, is a new kind of social gathering that she calls a "neighborhood-home festival." With the help of
her co-operators in the district, about thirty assorted individuals representing all the types and cultures that cannot or will not mix socially are persuaded to gather at some convenient center. The chosen
place is always dressed up for the occasion with the flowers or fruits
or evergreens of the season, and with informal seating arrangements.
At such a gathering held just before Christmas at the Friends' Meet-
inghouse in New York City, the vestibule was transformed by ever-

green trees and candlelight, the cushions dragged out of the pews inside and placed in a circle on the floor. Flowers, fruits, candlelight, and firelight are the beginning of the magic.

After the people have come and have been charmed into relaxing and waiting to see what will happen next, Dr. Dubois starts a conversation with an observation on something connected with the weather or the seasons. She has discovered a sure social solvent—reminiscence of early childhood connected with seasonal activities. On an autumn day Dr. Dubois gets the group to talking about preparation for Thanksgiving or for Jewish or national harvest festivals, always pushing the reminiscence back to earliest childhood, centered in home and mother. Then Rachel Dubois introduces the critical questions: "Did your mother sing while she was doing this? What did she sing?" And out of the group she begins to draw the old songs they heard or learned in childhood, songs going back to many lands, in many parts of the world. The smooth varnish of Americanism is rubbed off. These people begin to meet on aboriginal levels of folk memory and folk song.

It is amazing to see that any thirty Americans, gathered at random, in our racially mixed city areas, will have among them three or four people who can sing the whole of some unique song. It is a great moment in such a gathering when some unadjusted old woman of foreign birth lifts up her voice and sings. She often breaks down in joyful tears when neighbors upon whom she had looked with distrust draw around her, admiring and obviously moved.

Within an hour after she starts to talk to an apparently dull and uninterested group, Dr. Dubois and her trained musician assistant have the people circling with clasped hands, walking in processionals with lighted candles, singing folk songs and hymns of all faiths, even reverently repeating prayers together. Nine hundred of these "festivals" were given in New York City one season mainly in the least "privileged" part of the city. A visitor to many of them says that each one was entirely different from the others and that every one had some moments of startling and poignant beauty. An artist observer said, "If one could get the secret of this, one would have a new art that would cure almost everything that ails us." [4]

In Rachel Dubois can be seen an educated woman of modern times not only creating a new art, in which music is integrated, but doing so in order to provide rites practical and effective enough to solve a social problem brought about by modern conditions. This is precisely the way her remote ancestors made rituals thousands of years ago when women were creative musicians. Dr. Dubois' remarkable initiative in developing this technique by reviving old rites and music, buried in the memories of people indiscriminately chosen, and by improvising an affective integration of motions and melodies capable of smoothing out the souls of skeptical participants, is significant to the modern woman musician. Not only does it demonstrate that woman's inherent ability to use music creatively is as potent as it ever was; it also suggests that, while women still find it difficult to compete with men in the conventional practice of music, there is now opening to them the opportunity to create healing, beneficent music of immense social value. (See Plate 64.)

But in spite of the giant strides taken by women toward a fuller participation in the musical life of our times, an outworn attitude still holds them back from the full realization of their new opportunities. Women, unfortunately, have long regarded their women's activities as *unimportant* and as *unworthy* of artistic effort. Musicians have a predilection to strive for recognition in men's arenas by writing symphonies and operas—forms invented and used by men for centuries in their own organizations. But if women would sing first for themselves, sincerely and enthusiastically, ignoring critics with preconceived notions about either women or music, their song would eventually burst out of the bounds of home, sickroom, or club and would flow into that stream of rhythm, melody, harmony which is forming the music of tomorrow. (See Plates 65 and 66.)

4.

The woman musician of today is at the crossroads Her relation to music depends upon her relation to the society in which she lives and to the religious expression of that society. This relation transcends any specific barriers that may have been erected in the past between given groups of women and their participation in music. And since all civilization is now in the throes of rebirth, woman's place in the musical life of the new world is dependent upon what new religious ideas will be formulated, what new customs will be made.

Woman's apparent sterility in musical creation, in comparison with man's of our times, is not at all due to any inherent deficiency in her ability to think symbolically. Given the proper environments, where her culture demands music and where her contemporaries confidently expect her to produce it, where she receives from early childhood the training necessary to make her a creative musician, woman has already been at least the equal of her man in composing the type of music required by that culture. And this flowering of woman's natural musical talent has been by no means confined to aborigines of early cultural levels. The Tuareg poetess-musicians, Sappho and her colleagues, the Arabians, Hildegarde and other nuns, many ladies of the Renaissance, as well as the Russian and Lithuanian peasants are witnesses proclaiming woman's power to express herself in the language of music.

Scientists agree that the innate capacity of the human brain for creative, artistic, and intellectual accomplishment has not materially changed during the past sixty thousand years. Neither can the *relative* capacity for men and women for such activity have changed. When we find, therefore, that at many times and in many places, women have equaled their men in music making, we may be sure that the comparative silence of modern women in musical expression is not the result of inherent incapacity or of spiritual inferiority to men.

Nor is woman's comparative silence in music due to the fact that our music has become overintellectualized. Scores of modern women have demonstrated intellectual capacity of the highest order. The intelligence quotient of the average girl is fully equal to that of her brother. Both are equally educable, as has been recently discovered, in the abstractions of mathematics. No chimpanzee could be taught to multiply three by four or to resolve a dominant seventh chord. The existence of many women of high intellectual capacity, of superior artistic imagination, and of ability to express themselves in the modern idiom of music conclusively disproves the possibility that the female sex is disbarred from the sacred circle of creative musicians.

As we have seen, woman's silence in musical expression is, on the contrary, due to historical causes that have brought about a nonpermissive environment for the woman musician. The music of our culture was originally bound indissolubly to organized religion and limited to church use. Women were disbarred from official participation in the religious ceremony and so became automatically cut off from opportunity to create music. Nuns, who had a specified place in the hierarchy, composed only liturgical and extraliturgical music, and within the limits of their opportunities. When men and women freed themselves from the heavy restrictions placed upon the free use of music by the churchmen and began to use music apart from ritual and liturgy, women were *theoretically* able to function again as musicians. But the leaders in music were still those connected with, or employed by, religious officials, and according to the established custom of over a thousand years, were all men. Effective musical education and training was still in the church. Since the supply of men musicians was sufficient, women were not in demand but were expected rather to patronize and to perform men's music. Furthermore, even though ecclesiastical authority waned, authority in church, state, educational system, and home remained largely in the hands of men. And it was an authority reinforced by the religion that women were spiritually and intellectually inferior to men.

The Fathers of the early Church said: "Every woman should be ashamed of the thought that she is a woman."

This is the pernicious doctrine that has determined the relation of women to the body politic and to religious expression, and that has stifled woman's collective imagination. Its poison has survived even in the most up to date of men's teaching. The terms "masculine" and "feminine," when used in association with "activity" and "passivity," tend to give women the same sense of powerlessness and so carry over into modern education the idea that feminine attributes cannot be active and beneficent; that, in order to develop creative imagination, a woman must ignore her sex and build upon attributes and qualities now associated with men. This is as negative and as emotionally conflicting a creed as that taught by the early Christian Church.

How different is the faith in a spirit-bearing womanhood expressed by a great woman of the nineteenth century, Rahel Varnhagen: "I am at one with myself and consider myself a good, beautiful gift." [5]

Here is the clarion call to women—the holy dogma for the affirmation of collective womanhood. In it is implicit all that women need to give them that spiritual independence and self-assertion essential for any kind of creative work. Most of all for the rearing of good and beautiful children.

By regarding herself as a good, beautiful gift, any woman can be sure that she is endowed with every attribute of brain power and spirituality now possible for human beings. She need have no more misgivings about the inherent power of women to evince imagination.

In the words "I am at one with myself" lies the assurance that childbearing, even the female equipment for bringing life, provides one of the most driving incentives to develop imagination that the world has ever seen. Believing this, a mother knows that evidence of creative imagination, or a desire to develop it, does not make her less of a woman and an ineffective imitation of man. She knows that she can accept her natural role without emotional conflict and with the assurance that womanhood is a creative role in the scheme of life.

New ideas are always slow in gaining momentum. Throughout history, they can be traced back far beyond the time they became a force, running parallel to older conceptions of what is right until they either disappear or become the core of another religion. The idea that women are a creative and beneficent power is actually one of the oldest in the world and appears today in the great majority of primitive societies. It reached its most beautiful expression in the oldest known civilizations of antiquity. Wherever the creative power of women is a factor in the making of religious and social institutions, women have authority in such institutions, in the magic arts of healing body and spirit, and in music. From their rites, their music, and from their own leaders (both real and symbolic), women draw the inspiration to revitalize, at fixed intervals, their own powers.

Running parallel to the religion that regards woman as creative and beneficent is the diametrically opposed belief that she is evil, or, in some cases, merely powerless. Even in a few of the most primitive tribes, there are evidences of a movement to degrade the value of the female and to challenge her humanity. This movement reached its climax around the years 400 to 800 A.D., and has had a dominating influence upon the schematic religions founded by men from about 800 B.C. to 600 A.D. Such religions include Brahmanism, Buddhism (although to a lesser extent), Confucianism, Orthodox Judaism, ecclesiastical Christianity, Mohammedanism, and Nazism. It has been the religion of modern civilization. Wherever and whenever the value of womanhood is degraded, women neglect to emphasize the life-bringing value of their natural ways and allow men to pre-empt the creative arts of healing body and spirit, and of music. Although today, in our society, these arts have become separate departments and specialized, they are still endowed with a quality of mystery and magic. Religion, medicine, and music are still the three fields from which men would like to exclude women and in which they most resent women's influence.

It is only very lately that women have taken organized steps to replace themselves in a creative, beneficent relation to life and to reassert their own values. But hardly yet do many face boldly and honestly the crux of the woman problem: religious ideas, symbols, ceremonies, and economic customs that place women in the position of receiving bounties, even the gift of life, from men can never bring women into the right relation to life and free the subconscious for creative thinking.

For women to attain the state of collective spiritual independence, to be reborn as adult human beings, their inner lives must be given the spiritual sustenance so long withheld, and given it more intensively on account of their long starvation.

Instead of those symbols and religious ceremonies that allow a woman only a vicarious relation to the life force, others, giving her a realization of her own potentiality for activity, must be substituted. In ritual, the great truth should be reiterated that woman is a beneficent manifestation of the rhythm of all life. As girl, mate, mother, worker at life's tasks, and finally as one ripe with experience, she should be told and told again that each stage of her life span has its own peculiar wisdom that is needed in the community; that, without her, the torch of life would flicker and die.

So are women now needed to assert their leadership over women, and over men who would work with them, in those departments of life in which women have experiences denied by natural laws to men. Men have great areas in life where their leadership can be properly exercised. But in all matters pertaining to women's female function and to her inner emotional life, the assumption by men of exclusive authority does the feminine psyche grave harm and stifles its free expression. Today it is scientists, doctors, and psychiatrists who possess the modern magic. The exclusion, or the discouragement, of women in these fields is as damaging to women as the exclusion of women from the priesthood was in early Christian times. Healing, religion, and music are the three fields in which woman is pre-eminently fitted by nature and by experience to express herself and to serve her fellows. Unless women are trained in modern methods and equipped with the learning of the ages to be doctors and psychiatrists, able to advise girls in adolescence, in the period of sex relations, in childbirth, and at the threshold to middle age, women will never have the foundation for formulating the new faith, for developing the new rituals and customs that will give spiritual integrity—the foundation of creative expression in music.

Once leadership by women trained in scientific thinking has been established and recognized, women can then make a concerted effort to release their imagination from the age-long repression. They must find their own symbols to remind themselves of their own peculiar power for good. They must find rituals and music to reinforce their own spirits in the crises of womanhood. And they must have representation in the larger life of the community for the authority of the natural woman; then can the Daughters of the Moon proceed boldly and confidently to the task of objectifying their experiences in whatever way they find opportunity and incentive.

Even now, the crescent moon is rising in the sky. One day it will grow again to its full splendor. And Artemis is reaching for her lyre, courageously striking the opening chords of woman's ageless song:

Here, Queen Goddess, light-bringer, divine Moon,
Who move in a path of night, wandering in the darkness.
Torch-bearer of the mysteries, Moon-maiden, rich in stars,
You who gave and diminish, who are both female and male,
All-seeing, enlightener, fruit-bearer, Mother of Time,
Splendor of amber, soulful, illuminator, you who are Birth.
Lover of all-night wakefulness, fountain of beautiful stars!
Whose joy is the tranquil silence of the blissful spirit of night,
The lustrous one, giver of charms, votive statue of night,
You who bring fruit to perfection, visions and sacred rites!
Queen of stars, in flowing veils, who move on a curving path,
All-wise maiden, blessed one, keeper of the treasury of stars,
May you come in beautiful gladness, shining in all your brilliance;
And saving the youthful suppliants who turn to you, Maiden Moon! [6]

NOTES

The very large number of books and articles necessary as a background for the story of women, religion, and music is naturally too great for inclusion here. Only those from which direct references have been taken are listed in this volume. In several instances, I have omitted original sources and have given instead the name of a book in which the source material is used. Such books themselves throw light on the relation of women to music and broaden the base of my approach to this provocative subject.

CHAP. I

1. J. G. Frazer, *The Magic Art* (New York: The Macmillan Co., 1935), I, 125.
2. C. Troyer, *Traditional Songs of the Zuñis*, Wa-Wan Series of American Compositions (Newton Center, Mass.: Wa-Wan Press, 1904), Vol. III, second series.
3. K. Bücher, *Arbeit und Rhythmus* (Leipzig: B. G. Teubner, 1909), p. 401.
4. Personal letters from J. G. Giorgiades, Athens, Greece.
5. Katherine Swan, *The Participation of Russian Women in Music* (MS. at Smith College and at University of Pennsylvania), p. 40.
6. *Records Nos. 12B and 13B Jemima Gibson (Cayuga)* (Six Nations Reserve, Canada, Jan. 23, 1941). Fenton Collection I in Library of Congress from an unpublished MS. of Dr. W. N. Fenton, Bureau of American Ethnology.
7. J. R. Swanton, *Social Organization and Social Usages of the Indians of the Creek Confederacy* (Bureau of American Ethnology, 1924), XLII, 324.
8. Fenton, *op. cit.*
9. F. H. Cushing, *Outlines of Zuñi Creation Myths* (Bureau of American Ethnology, 13th Annual Report, 1891-92), p. 446.
10. Swan, *op. cit.*, p. 10.
11. Alice Fletcher and F. LaFlesche, *The Omaha Tribe* (Bureau of American Ethnology, 1905-06), XXVII, 426.
12. D. A. Talbot, *Women's Mysteries of a Primitive People: The Ibibios of Southern Nigeria* (London: Cassell & Co., Ltd., 1915), p. 205.

299

13. M. Walters, *Le Peuple Letton* (Riga, 1926), p. 112.

14. F. R. Boas, *The Social Organization and the Secret Societies of the Kwakuitl Indians* (Report of the U. S. National Museum, 1895), p. 584.

ADDITIONAL REFERENCES

Böckel, O. *Psychologie der Volksdichtung.* Leipzig, 1913.

Brinton, D. G. *Nagualism: A Study in Native American Folklore and History.* Philadelphia, 1894.

Frazer, J. G. *The Golden Bough.* New York: The Macmillan Co., 1935.

Katzenelenbogan. *The Daina: An Anthology of Lithuanian and Latvian Folksongs.* Chicago: Lithuanian News Publishing Co., 1935.

Lumholtz. *Through Central Borneo.* New York: Charles Scribner's Sons, 1920. Pp. 310, 350.

Routledge, W. S. & K. *With a Prehistoric People.* London: Edward Arnold & Co., 1910. Pl. CXVI.

CHAP. II

1. T. Michelson, *Autobiography of a Fox Indian Woman* (Bureau of American Ethnology, 1918-19), XL, 319.

2. Personal communication from Marion Szekely Freschl.

3. J. C. Lawson, *Modern Greek Folk Lore and Ancient Greek Religion* (Cambridge: Cambridge University Press, 1910), p. 547.

4. L. von Schröder, *Die Hochzeitsbräuche der Esten* (Berlin: 1888), p. 186.

5. G. H. Dalman, *Palästinischer Diwan als Beitrag zur Volkskunde Palästinas Gesammelt und mit Ubersetzung und Melodien* (Leipzig: 1901), p. 312.

6. E. Martinengo-Cesaresco, *Essays in the Study of Folksongs* (London: 1886), p. 385.

7. B. I. F. Laubscher, *Sex, Custom, and Psychopathology* (London: G. Routledge & Sons, Ltd., 1937), p. 147 & Pl. XI.

8. H. Trilles, *Les pygmées de la fôret equatoriale* (Paris: Bloud et Gay, 1932), p. 412. English translation of the poem by Katherine Garrison Chapin.

9. Swan, *op. cit.,* p. 28.

10. J. T. Bent, *The Cyclades* (London: 1885), p. 183.

11. A. Hauffen, *Die deutsche Sprachinsel Gottschee* (Graz, 1905), Example 105.

12. M. T. de Lens, "*Sur le chant des moueddin et sur les chants chez femmes a Meknès,*" *Revue de Musicologie,* Nov. 1924, pp. 152-63.

13. M. C. Fauriel, *Songs of Greece,* tr. by C. B. Sheridan (London: 1825), p. 230.

14. D. Corkery, *The Hidden Ireland* (Dublin: M. H. Gill & Son, 1925), p. 39.

15. J. G. von Hahn, *Albanesische Studien* (Vienna: 1853), II, 135.

16. *Ibid.*, p. 136.

17. Poem translated by Frances Herskovits, *New Republic*, Sept. 4, 1935.

18. P. H. Buck, *Vikings of the Sunrise* (New York: Frederick A. Stokes Co., 1938), p. 205.

19. Marjorie Kennedy-Fraser, *Songs of the Hebrides* (London: Boosey & Co., 1917), I, 115.

20. M. J. Herskovits, *Dahomey: An Ancient West African Kingdom* (New York: J. J. Augustin, 1938), II, 320.

ADDITIONAL REFERENCES

Buschan, G. *Illustrierte Völkerkunde*. Stuttgart: Strecker und Schröder, 1926.

Coomaraswamy, R. K. *Catalogue of the Indian Collection at the Boston Museum of Fine Arts*. Boston: Harvard Press, 1926. Part VI, Pl. IV, pp. 14, 657.

Hall, Mr. & Mrs. S. C. *Ireland, Its Scenery Characteristics*. London: 1841.

Herzog, G. *Jabo Proverbs from Liberia*. London: Oxford University Press, 1936.

McConnel, Ursula. "Mourning Ritual on the Gulf of Carpenteria," *Oceania*, 1936-37. Vol. 7.

Ortoli, J. B. F. "*Les voceri de l'ile de Corse*," *Collection de chansons et de contes populaires*, 1887, Vol. 10.

Rathery, E. J. B. "*Les chants populaires de l'italie*," *Revue des Deux Mondes*, 1862, Vol. 38.

Warmelo, N. J. von. *Contributions toward Venda History, Religion and Tribal Ritual*. Union of South Africa, Dept. of Native Affairs, Ethnological Publicators, Vol. III.

CHAP. III

1. Kennedy-Fraser, *op. cit.*, II, 110.

2. J. Combarieu, *La Musique et la magie: étude sur les origines populaires de l'art musical: son influence et sa fonction dans les sociétés* (Paris: Picard, 1909), p. 123.

3. C. Velten, *Gebräuche der Suaheli* (Göttingen, 1903), p. 17. Poem translated by Henry S. Drinker.

4. Wm. Thalbitzer and H. Thuren, *On the Eskimo Music in Greenland* (Copenhagen: 1914-23), p. 155.

5. F. La Flesche, *The Osage Tribe* (Bureau of American Ethnology, 1927-28), XL, 687.

6. Swan, *op. cit.*, p. 18.

7. Talbot, *op. cit.*, p. 77.

8. G. W. Stellers, *Beschreibung von dem Lande Kamschatka* (Leipzig, 1774), p. 332.

9. M. Friedlaender, *Brahms' Lieder,* tr. by C. L. Leese (London: Oxford University Press, 1928), p. 248.

ADDITIONAL REFERENCES

Earthy, Dora. *Valenge Women.* London: Oxford University Press, 1933.

Hála, Ján. *Pod Tatrami.* Mikuláši: Vydal "Tranoscius" v Liptovskom Sv., 1942.

Kheiri, M. A. *Indische Miniaturen der Islamischen zeit.* Berlin: Ernest Wasmuth. Pl. 42.

Sachs, C. *Die Musikinstrumente Indiens und Indonesians.* Berlin: G. Reimer, 1915.

CHAP. IV

1. H. A. Junod, *The Life of a South African Tribe* (London & Neuchatel: David Nutt, 1912).

ADDITIONAL REFERENCES

Evans, I. H. N. "Notes on the Religious Beliefs, Superstitions, Ceremonies, and Tabus of the Dusuns of the Tuaran and Tempassuk Districts of British North Borneo," *Journal of the Royal Anthropological Institute,* Vol. XLII, 1912.

Jochelson, W. *The Koryaks of Siberia.* New York: Publication of the Jesup North Pacific Expedition, 1908. Vol. 6, Pl. III and IV.

"*Lieder u. Sangesweisen u. Geschichten der Wanyamwezi,*" *Berlin Universitat Ausland Hochschule Mitteilungen.* Berlin and Stuttgart, 1901.

Nioradze, G. *Der Schamanismus bei dem siberischen Völkern.* Stuttgart: Strecker und Schröder, 1925.

Underhill, Ruth. "The Autobiography of a Papago Woman," *Memoirs of the American Anthropological Association,* No. 46, 1936 (supplement to *American Anthrop.,* Vol. 38, No. 3, Pt. 2).

CHAP. V

1. S. N. Kramer, *Sumerian Mythology: A Study of Spiritual and Literary Achievement in the 3rd Millennium, B.C.* (Philadelphia: American Philosophical Society, 1944), Chap. II, section 3.

ADDITIONAL REFERENCES

Frobenius, L. *Mdsimu Dsangara.* Berlin: Atlantis-Verlag, 1931. Pl. 36 and 51.

Gusinde, M. *Die Feuerland Indianer* (Ona tribe). Vienna: Anthropos-Bibliothek Expeditions, Series 1-2, 1931-32.

Hentze, C. *Mythes et symboles lunaires: Chine ancienne, civilisations anciennes de l'Asie, peuples limitrophes du Pacifique.* Edition "de Sikkel," 1932.

Obermaier, H. *Fossil Man in Spain.* New Haven: Yale University Press, 1925. Pl. IX.

Stow, G. M., and Bleek, Dorothea. *Rock Paintings in South Africa.* London: Methuen & Co., Ltd., 1930. Pl. 71.

Tongue, M. Helen. *Bushman Paintings.* Oxford: Clarendon Press, 1909. Pl. XXVIII.

CHAP. VI

1. G. M. Haardt and L. Audouin-Dubreuil, *Across the Sahara by Motor Car* (London: T. Fisher Unwin, Ltd., 1924), p. 229.

2. Denham and Clapperton, *Narrative of Travels and Discoveries in North and Central Africa* (London: 1826), p. xiii.

3. Haardt and Dubreuil, *op. cit.,* pp. 212, 231.

4. R. Briffault, *The Mothers: A Study of the Origins of Sentiments and Institutions* (New York: The Macmillan Co., 1927), I, 385.

5. *Ibid.,* I, 385.

6. Janet R. Buttles, *The Queens of Egypt* (London: A. Constable & Co., 1908), p. 168.

7. A. Erman, *The Literature of the Ancient Egyptians,* tr. by A. M. Blackman (London: Methuen & Co., Ltd., 1927), p. 279.

8. *Ibid.,* p. 12.

9. A. Erman, *Zaubersprüche für Mutter und Kind: aus dem paprus 3027 des Berliner Museums* (Berlin: 1901).

10. A. Erman, *Life in Ancient Egypt,* tr. by H. M. Tirard (London: The Macmillan Co., 1894), pp. 320, 387, 389.

11. S. Langdon, *Tammuz and Ishtar* (Oxford: Clarendon Press, 1914), p. 11.

12. *Lyra Graeca* (London: Loeb Classical Library, 1922-27), I, 265.

ADDITIONAL REFERENCES

Bull, L., and Scott, Nora. *The Tomb of Rekh-mɪ-rē.* New York: The Metropolitan Museum of Art, 1943. Vol. II, Pl. LXVI.

Davies, Nina de G., and Gardiner, A. H. *The Tomb of Amenemhet.* Egypt Exploration Fund, 1915. Pl. XIX.

Evans, A. *The Palace of Minos.* The Macmillan Co., 1931-35. Vol. I, Fig. 167; Vol. II, p. 2, Sup. Pl. XXV; Vol. III, Pl. XVIII, Figs. 38, 39.

Fyzee-Rahamin, A. B. *The Music of India.* London: Luzac & Co., 1925.

Galpin, F. W. *The Music of the Sumerians and Their Immediate Successors, the Babylonians and Assyrians.* Cambridge: Cambridge University Press, 1937.

Gombosi, O. *Music in the Old Aegean World.* American Musicological Society, March, 1940.

Sachs, C. *"Musik der Antike,"* *Handbuch der Musikwissenschaft.* Wildpark-Potsdam: 1931. Pl. 7.

CHAP. VII

1. Briffault, *op. cit.*, I, 358.
2. Briffault, *op. cit.*, I, 346.
3. Clarisse Bader, *Women in Ancient India* (London: K. Paul, Trench, Trubner & Co., 1925), p. 9.
4. H. H. Wilson, *Rig Veda,* Vol. V, Hymn 28.
5. Briffault, *op. cit.*, I, 346.
6. Jane E. Harrison, *Themis: A Study of the Social Origins of Greek Religion* (London: Cambridge University Press, 2nd ed., 1927), p. 205.
7. G. Murray, *The Bacchae of Euripides* (New York: Longmans, Green & Co., 1919), p. 14.
8. *Ibid.*, p. 12.
9. *Loc. cit.*
10. *Ibid.*, p. 10.
11. *Ibid.*, p. 42.
12. Nilla Cook, unpublished translation of an Orphic hymn.
13. H. T. Wharton, *Sappho* (New York: Brentano, 1920), p. 102.
14. *Ibid.*, p. 111.
15. *Ibid.*, p. 110.
16. D. M. Robinson, *Sappho and Her Influence* (Boston: Marshall, Jones Co., 1924), p. 89.
17. Athenaeus, *The Deipnosophistae,* tr. by C. B. Gulick (London: Wm. Heinemann Ltd., Loeb Classical Library, 1927-41), VI, 331.
18. Clarisse Bader, *La Femme Grecque* (Paris: 1872), p. 45.
19. F. Poulsen, *Delphi,* tr. by G. C. Richards (London: Gyldendal, 1920), p. 264.
20. *Lyra Graeca,* I, 73.
21. *Lyra Graeca,* III, 13.
22. J. A. Platt, "Sappho," *Encyclopaedia Brittanica,* 1926.
23. C. R. Haines, *Sappho: The Poems and Fragments* (New York: E. P. Dutton & Co., 1926), p. 77 and Pl. XII.
24. J. F. Rowbotham, *A History of Music* (London: K. Paul, Trench, Trubner & Co., 1885), II, 91.
25. A. E. P. B. Weigall, *Sappho of Lesbos: Her Life and Times* (New York: Frederick A. Stokes Co., 1932), p. 220.
26. Haines, *op. cit.*, p. 138.

ADDITIONAL REFERENCES

Encyclopédie Photographique de l'art. Paris: Musée de Louvre, Editions TEL. II, 172.

Furtwängler, A. *La Collection Sabouroff.* Berlin: 1883. Vol. I, Pl. LI.
———. *Griechische Vasenmalerei.* Munich: 1932. Vol. III, Pls. 125 and 171.

Kinsky, G. *Geschichte der Musik in Bildern.* Leipzig: Breitkopf und Härtel, 1929.

Poestion, J. C. *Griechische Dichterinnen.* Wien: 1876.
———. *Griechische Philosophinnen.* Bremen: 1882.

Thomson, G. *Aeschylus and Athens: A Study in the Social Origins of Drama.* London: Lawrence & Wishart Ltd., 1941.

Weniger, L. *Über das Collegium der Thyiaden, Delphi: über das Collegium der sechszehn Frauen und der Dionysos in Elis.* Weimar: 1883.

CHAP. VIII

1. R. T. H. Griffith, *The Hymns of the Reg-Veda* (Benares: 1897, 2nd ed.), II, 596.

2. Hanna Rydh, "Symbolism in Mortuary Ceramics," *Bulletin of the Museums of Far Eastern Antiquities* (Stockholm: 1929-30).

3. J. Langdon-Davies, *A Short History of Women* (New York: Literary Guild of America, 1927), p. 148.

4. *Ibid.,* p. 59.

5. Jane E. Harrison, *Mythology and Monuments of Ancient Athens* (London: The Macmillan Co., 1890), p. lxxxv.

6. *Ibid.*

7. Weigall, *op. cit.,* p. 82.

8. This phrase is used by Hélène Deutsch in *Psychology of Women.*

ADDITIONAL REFERENCES

Endzelins, J., and Klaustini, R. *Latvjutautas Dainas.* Riga: Izdevusi "Literatura," 1928. Vol. XI, Frontispiece.

Gerhard, E. *Auserlesene Griechische Vasenbilder.* Berlin: 1840. Vol. III, Pl. XXIX.

Lenormant, C. *Elites des monuments ceramographiques.* Paris: 1844. Vol. II, Pl. 7.

Perrot, G., and Chipiez, C. *Histoire de l'art dans l'antiquité.* Paris: Librairie Hachette & Co., 1911. Vol. III, Pl. VII; Vol. VIII, Fig. 24.

CHAP. IX

1. M. Granet, *Chinese Civilization* (New York: Alfred Knopf, 1930), p. 146.

2. M. Granet, *Festivals and Songs of Ancient China* (New York: E. P. Dutton & Co., 1932), p. 41.

3. A. C. Burnell, *The Ordinances of Manu* (London: Trubner & Co., 1884), pp. 130, 131.

4. *Ibid.*, p. 247.

5. Judges 5:3.

6. Judges 5:12, 27.

7. Exodus 15:20.

8. Exodus 15:21.

9. Judith 15:12, 13; 16:1, 2.

10. Ecclesiastes 2:8.

11. Ezekiel 26:13.

12. A. Z. Idelsohn, *Jewish Music: in its historical development* (New York: Henry Holt & Co., 1929), p. 97.

13. Euripides, *The Bacchae,* phrase translated by Henry S. Drinker.

14. G. Murray, *The Bacchae of Euripides* (New York: Longmans, Green & Co., 1919), p. 62.

15. *Ibid.*, p. 53.

16. Aeschylus, *The Eumenides.*

17. S. N. Kramer, "A Sumerian 'Paradise Myth,' " *Crozer Quarterly,* July 1945, XXII, 3.

Chap. X

1. Matthew 22:37; Mark 12:30.

2. John 15:5.

3. W. O. Clough, *Introduction and Notes to Gesta Pilati: The Reports, Letters and Acts of Pontius Pilate* (Indianapolis: 1885), p. 155.

4. E. A. T. W. Budge, *History of the Blessed Virgin Mary* (London: Luzac & Co., 1899), p. 99.

5. F. Legge, *Forerunners and Rivals of Christianity: Being Studies in Religious History from 330 B.C. to 330 A.D.* (London: Cambridge University Press, 1915), p. 300.

6. G. R. S. Mead, *Fragments of a Faith Forgotten* (London and Benares: Theosophical Society, 1906), p. 419.

7. T. Gérold, *Les pères de l'église et la musique* (Paris: Librairie Felix Alcan, 1931), p. 196.

8. G. R. S. Mead, "Ceremonial Game Playing and Dancing in Mediaeval Churches," *The Quest,* Vol. IV, Oct. 1912.

9. W. Bright, *Age of the Fathers* (London: Longmans, Green & Co., 1903), II, 275.

10. J. S. Black and K. Lake, "Mary," *Encyclopaedia Brittanica,* 1926.

11. L. Fendt, *Gnostische Mysterien: Ein Beitrag zur Geschichte des Christlichen Gottesdienstes* (Munich: 1922), p. 51.

12. J. Donaldson, *Woman, Her Position and Influence in Greece, Rome and Early Christianity* (London: Longmans, Green & Co., 1907), p. 166.

13. R. Lanciani, *Pagan and Christian Rome* (Boston: Houghton Mifflin Co., 1893), p. 357.

14. J. Quasten, *Musik und Gesang in den Kulten der heidnischen Antike und Christlichen Frühzeit* (Munster in Westfalia, 1930), p. 181 and Pl. 9.

15. Gérold, *op. cit.*, p. 156.

16. Langdon-Davies, *op. cit.*, p. 182.

17. *Pseudo-Matthew*, Chap. VI, Apochryphal Gospels, Ante-Nicene Christian Library, XVI.

18. Donaldson, *op. cit.*, p. 160.

19. Chrysostomus, *Exposito in psalmum XLI* in Migne. Patr. gr. LV, 157.

20. J. Julian, *Dictionary of Hymnology* (London: John Murray, 1925), p. 206.

21. Gérold, *op. cit.*, p. 109.

22. *Ibid.*, p. 34.

23. Clement of Alexandria, *Protrepticus.*

24. M. L. MacClure and C. L. Feltoe, *The Pilgrimage of Etheria* (London Society for Promoting Christian Knowledge, 1919), p. 45.

25. K. Meyer, *Der Chorische Gesang der Frauen* (Leipzig: Breitkoff und Härtel, 1917), p. 1, note 3.

26. Ephraemus Syrus, *Select metrical hymns and homilies,* ed. and tr. by H. Burgess (London: 1853), Hymn XVII.

ADDITIONAL REFERENCES

Abbott, N. "Pre-Islamic Arab Queens," *American Journal of Languages,* July, 1941.

Baumeister, K. A. *Denkmäler des klassichen Altertums zur Erleuterung des Lebens der Griechen und Römer in Religion, Kunst, und Sitte.* Munich: 1885. Vol. I, Fig. 218.

Eckenstein, Lina (revised by Celia Roscoe). *The Women of Early Christianity.* London: The Faith Press, Ltd., 1935.

Ramsay, W. M. *The Church in the Roman Empire before A.D. 170.* New York: G. P. Putnam's Sons, 1893.

Rush, A. C. *Death and Burial in Christian Antiquity.* Washington: Catholic University of America Press, 1941.

Sachs, C. *The History of Musical Instruments.* New York: W. W. Norton & Co., Inc., 1940. Pl. VIII.

Vucasovic, V. V. "Funeral Customs and Rites among the Southern Slavs in Ancient and Modern Times," *The International Folk-Lore Congress of the World's Columbian Exposition.* Chicago: Sergel Co., 1898. Vol. I.

CHAP. XI

1. Luke 23:28, 31.
2. Tertullian, *Decultu feminarium* in Migne, Series Prima, Vol. II, col. 1305.
3. Clement of Alexandria, *Paedagogus*, LL, 2.
4. Luke 1:38.
5. Bright, *op. cit.*, I, 523.
6. G. Reese, *Music in the Middle Ages* (New York: W. W. Norton & Co., 1940), p. 65.
7. S. Glennie, "Traditions of the Archaic White Races," *Transactions of the Royal Historical Society, 1889.* Quoted from von Bunsen, *Egypt's Place in Universal History*, IV, 396.
8. W. Christ and M. Paranikas, *Anthologic-Graeca Carminum Christian-orum* (Leipzig, 1871).
9. A. W. Chatfield, *Songs and Hymns of the Greek Christian Poets* (London: 1876).
10. W. Wright, *Apochryphal Acts of the Apostles* (London: Williams & Norgate, 1871), II, 155.
11. Meyer, *op. cit.*, p. 13.
12. L. M. O. Duchesne, *Early History of the Christian Church: From Its Foundation to the End of the Third Century* (New York: Longmans, Green & Co., 1909), p. 110.
13. Meyer, *op. cit.*, p. 10.
14. *Ibid.*, p. 10, note 2.
15. Bright, *op. cit.*, II, 33.
16. Quasten, *op. cit.*, p. 169.

CHAP. XII

1. Lina Eckenstein, *Women under Monasticism: Chapters on Saint Lore and Convent Life between A.D. 500 and A.D. 1500* (Cambridge: Cambridge University Press, 1896), p. 60.
2. *Ibid.*, p. 65.
3. Gregory of Nyssa, *The Life of St. Macrina*, tr. by W. K. L. Clarke (London: Society for Promoting Christian Knowledge, 1916), I, 34.
4. *Ibid.*, pp. 50-2.
5. *Ibid.*, p. 68.
6. *Ibid.*, p. 59.
7. Eckenstein, *op. cit.*, p. 390.
8. D. I. Lanslot, *Handbook of Canon Law* (Rome: Ratisbon, 1911), p. 277.
9. Eckenstein, *op. cit.*, p. 317.
10. *Ibid.*, p. 326.

11. Rush, *op. cit.*, pp. 182, 204.

12. Eckenstein, *op. cit.*, p. 253 and Appendix.

13. L. von Strauss und Torney, *Deutsches Frauenleben in der Zeit der Sachsenkaiser und Hohenstaufen* (Jena: Eugen Diedrichs, 1927), p. 80.

ADDITIONAL REFERENCES

Bobillier, Marie. *La Musique dans les convents de femmes depuis le moyen age jusqu'à nos jours.* Paris: Schola Cantorum, 1898.

Gmelch, J. *Die Kompositionen der heiligen Hildegard.* Düsseldorf: 1913.

Nisard, C. *"Des Poesies de Radegunde attribuées jusqu'ici à Fortunat,"* Revue Historique, 1888.

Ursprung, O. *"Katholische Kirchenmusik,"* Handbuch der Musikwissenschaft. Fig. 19.

CHAP. XIII

1. Eckenstein, *op. cit.*, p. 260.

2. Von Strauss und Torney, *op. cit.*, p. 68.

3. J. Combarieu, *op. cit.*, p. 52.

4. E. K. Chambers, *The Mediaeval Stage* (Oxford: Clarendon Press, 1903), III, 235.

5. Alice Kemp-Welch, *Of Six Mediaeval Women: to which is added a note on mediaeval gardens* (London: The Macmillan Co., 1913), p. 32.

6. Dorothy Gardiner, *English Girlhood at School: A Study of Women's Education through Twelve Centuries* (London: Humphrey Milford, 1929), p. 59.

7. *Ibid.*, p. 59.

8. Collection of Jean Beck.

9. J. H. Smith, *Troubadours at Home: Their Lives and Personalities, Their Songs and Their World* (New York: G. P. Putnam's Sons, 1899), pp. 102, 105.

ADDITIONAL REFERENCES

Farnell, Ida. *Lives of the Troubadours.* London: Nutt, 1896.

Ploss, H. H., and Bartels, M. and P. *Woman: An Historical, Gynaecological and Anthropological Compendium.* St. Louis: C. V. Mosby Co., 1936. Vol. II, Fig. 545.

Rokseth, Yvonne. *"Les femmes musiciens, du XII aux XIV siècle,"* Romania, Oct. 1935.

CHAP. XIV

1. O. Böckel, *Deutsche Volkslieder aus Oberhessen* (Marburg: 1885), p. 13.

2. E. Lovett, "The Vessel Cup," *Folklore*, March 1902, XIII, 1.
3. M. A. R. de Maulde la Clavière, *Women of the Renaissance: A Study of Feminism* (New York: G. P. Putnam's Sons, 1900), p. 450.
4. *Ibid.*, p. 274.
5. A. Solerti, *Ferrara e la Corte Estense* (Citta di Castello, 1899), p. 134.
6. O. Kinkeldy, *Orgel und Klavier in der Musik des 16 Jahrhundert: ein Beitrag zur Geschichte der instrumental Musik mit Notenbeilagen* (Leipzig: Breitkopf und Härtel, 1910).
7. Solerti, *op. cit.*, p. 134.
8. C. Ricci, *Vita Barocca* (Milano Cogliati, 1904), p. 59.
9. Gardiner, *op. cit.*, p. 182.
10. Meyer, *op. cit.*, p. 64.
11. L. C. Elson, *History of American Music* (New York: The Macmillan Co., 1925), p. 8.
12. C. Burney, *The Present State of Music in Germany, the Netherlands, and United Provinces* (London: 1773), p. 125.
13. De Maulde la Clavière, *op. cit.*, p. 261.
14. Nesta de Robeck, *Music of the Italian Renaissance* (London: The Medici Society, 1928), p. 91.

ADDITIONAL REFERENCES

Rokseth, Yvonne. "Antonia Bembo, Composer to Louis XIV," *Musical Quarterly*, April 1937.

Rubsamen, W. H. *Literary Sources of Secular Music in Italy*. University of California Publications in Music. Vol. I, No. 1, 1943.

Schubring, P. *Cassoni: Truhen und Truhenbilder der Italienischen Fruhrenaissance*. Leipzig: 1915.

Treverrow, Ruth C. *The Beginnings of Virtuosity in the Italian Madrigal of the 16th Century*. Smith College: May 1945.

CHAP. XV

1. W. H. Hadow, "The Viennese Period," *Oxford History of Music* (London: Oxford University Press, 1929), V, 25.
2. J. N. Burk, *Clara Schumann: A Romantic Biography* (New York: Random House, 1940), p. 243.
3. *Ibid.*, p. 244.
4. Personal communication to Marjorie Barstow Greenbie.
5. B. Litzmann, *Clara Schumann: An Artist's Life*, tr. by Grace E. Hadow (Leipzig: 1913), I, 313.
6. *New York Times*, Oct. 20, 1946.
7. *New York Times*, Oct. 20, 1946.
8. *Philadelphia Evening Bulletin*, May 19, 1938.
9. Friedlaender, *op. cit.*, p. 167.

Chap. XVI

1. Corkery, *op. cit.*, p. 170.
2. Imogen Holst, *Gustav Holst* (London: Oxford University Press, 1938), p. 217.

Additional references

Bennett, W. "The Celebrated Women Chorus Singers of Lancashire," *The Choir*, Feb. 1936, p. 27.

Krille, Anna Marie. *Beiträge zur Geschichte der Musikerziehung und Musik ubung der deutschen Frau (von 1750 bis 1820).* Berlin: 1938.

Locke, A. W. *Selected List of Choruses for Women's Voices.* Smith College Monographs, No. 2, 1927. New Edition, 1946, containing 514 compositions for women's chorus, 10 of which are by women.

Les Spectacles à travers les âges. Paris: Editions du Cygne, 1932. P. 122.

Chap. XVII

1. John Milton, *Paradise Lost,* ed. A. W. Verity (Cambridge: Cambridge University Press, 1921), Bk. IV, line 299.
2. S. Baring-Gould, *The Lives of the Saints* (Edinburgh: John Grant, 1897).
3. Elson, *op. cit.*, p. 8.
4. G. E. Stubbs, "America, the Music of the Episcopal Church." Gardner and Nicholson, *A Manual of English Church Music* (London: Society for Promoting Christian Knowledge, 1923).
5. L. Bonvin, "Women in Church Choirs," *The Caecilia,* Sept. 1934, Vol. 60, No. 8, p. 339.
6. W. Boyd, *History of Western Education* (London: A. & C. Black Ltd., 1921, 3rd ed. 1932).
7. *Time,* July 16, 1945.
8. J. Dewey, *Art as Experience* (New York: Minton, Balch & Co., 1934), p. 267.
9. K. Ekman, *Jean Sibelius* (New York: Alfred Knopf, 1938), p. 136.

Chap. XVIII

1. Bernard Robinson, Bothamstead, Berkshire, in 1927 started Music Camp.
2. Mr. and Mrs. Henry S. Drinker, Merion, Pennsylvania, in 1928 organized the Accademia dei Dilettanti di Musica.
3. Mary Padgett, "Gray Ladies Praised for Hospital Music." *Philadelphia Inquirer,* Jan. 16, 1944; *The Inquirer's Everybody's Weekly,* Feb. 20, 1944, with illus. taken at Valley Forge Army Hospital.

4. Rachel Dubois, *Get Together Americans* (New York: Harper & Bros., 1943).

   "Try a Neighborhood Festival," ed. by Marjorie Greenbie, *Parents' Magazine,* Sept. 1943.

5. Mary Hargrave, *Some German Women and Their Salons* (London: T. W. Laurie, 1912), p. 107.

6. Nilla Cook, unpublished translation of an Orphic hymn.

ADDITIONAL REFERENCES

Barnes, E. N. C. *American Women in Creative Music.* Washington, D.C.: Music Education Publication, 1936.

Ebel, O. *Women Composers: A Biographical Handbook of Woman's Work in Music.* Brooklyn: F. H. Chandler, 1902.

Elson, A., and Truette, E. E. *Woman's Work in Music: Being an account of her influence on the art, in ancient as well as modern times; a summary of her musical compositions, in the different countries of the civilized world; and an estimate of their rank in comparison with those of men.* Boston: L. C. Page & Co., 1931.

Hughes, R. *Contemporary American Composers.* Boston: L. C. Page & Co., 1900. Chap. V.

Sutro, Florence C. *Women in Music and Law.* New York: Author's Publishing Company, 1895.

SOME BOOKS AND ARTICLES DENYING THE CREATIVE POWER OF THE WOMAN MUSICIAN

Barbacci, R. *"La Inferioridad mental de la mujer y su reflejo en la actividad musical."* Lima: *Revista Musical Peruana,* Ano 1, no. 9, Sept. 1939, pp. 1-5.

Brower, Edith. "Is the Music Idea Masculine?" *Atlantic Monthly,* March, 1894.

Drewes, H. *Maria Antonia Walpurgis als Komponistin.* Leipzig: 1934.

Ladd, G. *Why Women Cannot Compose Music.* New Haven: Yale Publication Association, 1917.

Towers, J. "Woman in Music," *Musician,* April, May, and June 1897.

Upton, G. R. *Woman in Music.* Chicago: A. C. McClurg & Co., 1909.

INDEX